The Early Origins of the Social Sciences

The Early Origins of
the Social Sciences

LYNN McDONALD

McGill-Queen's University Press
Montreal & Kingston • London • Buffalo

Fondly Dedicated to my mother
Mollie McDonald

© McGill-Queen's University Press 1993
ISBN 0-7735-1124-5

Legal deposit fourth quarter 1993
Bibliothèque nationale du Québec

Printed in Canada on acid-free paper

This book has been published with the help of a grant from
the Social Science Federation of Canada, using funds
provided by the Social Sciences and Humanities Research
Council of Canada.

Canadian Cataloguing in Publication Data

McDonald, Lynn, 1940–
    The early origins of the social sciences
    Includes bibliographical references and index.
    ISBN 0-7735-1124-5
    1. Social sciences – History. I. Title.
    H85.M34 1994   300′.9   C93-090420-6

Typeset in Times 10/12 by
Caractéra production graphique inc., Quebec City.

Contents

Preface

The Early Origins of the Social Sciences was prompted by a sense that contemporary social scientists do not know the beginnings, history, or uses of the methodology of their own discipline. The literature is rife with attacks on the use of empirical methods in the social sciences, calling them narrow-minded, exclusive of all consideration of values, and oblivious to political and social context. The use of empirical methods is said to necessarily support existing power relations. To this radical critique of methodology has been added a feminist critique: that the use of objective methods and the search for laws, let alone any quantification, implies "malestream" methodology and is antithetical to the interests of women. Good feminists are told that they ought to do "qualitative" work instead, as if the two could be so conveniently separated. "Feminist methodology" and "postmodernism" began to appear as interchangeable terms. An emerging environmentalist critique would have scientific method necessarily result in the domination/exploitation of nature. The scientific method – as opposed to the greed and gluttony of us humans – is said to be responsible for environmental degradation and pollution.

I have been an empirical researcher throughout my academic life and have found empirical methods useful, even essential, in my political, feminist, and environmental causes as well as in my academic work. It grated to hear the very methods I needed in my struggles condemned in the name of those very causes. (I have been at various times in my life a Member of Parliament for the New Democratic Party, critic for the federal caucus on justice and the environment, president of the National Action Committee on the Status of Women, the largest feminist organization in Canada, and founding member of the board of Energy Probe. I am currently active with the Campaign for Nuclear Phaseout.)

I was at a loss to know precisely what methodologists were guilty of the offences so commonly charged. Certainly I knew of none and names were rarely cited. Nor were specific names or works forthcoming when I enquired of critics. Usually the response would simply repeat familiar secondary sources giving similar critiques, also without specific culprits. It seemed that a whole new generation of social scientists would enter the profession convinced that the charges were true, indeed so obviously true as not to need documentation. This approach is both poor scholarship and counter productive.

The Early Origins of the Social Sciences challenges the radical, feminist, and environmental critiques by examining the actual record. It differs from other treatments of the subject by going much further back in time, to the earliest emergence of the elements of the social sciences in classical Greece. It views the seventeenth- and eighteenth-century contributions as basic. It does not take the view of so many texts that sociology emerged suddenly in the mid-nineteenth century thanks to the work of three great men: Marx, Durkheim, and Weber. These three contributors are indeed central, and are dealt with accordingly, but they are treated as part of a long line of gradual evolution. My concerted efforts to find women contributors to the subject were successful. Thus women appear along with men, not only as collaborators and editors, but as contributors of key concepts and examples of social research. Contrary to what the feminist critique would lead one to expect, some of the staunchest advocates of women's rights also turned out to be keen proponents of empiricism, which they saw as a useful tool in making their case for equality. Similarly, some early links between environmental advocacy and empirical methods appeared.

The Early Origins of the Social Sciences does not attempt to be a comprehensive history. It cannot deal with the whole *oeuvre* of any author, some of whom published more than twenty books on an enormous range of issues. The focus is the *methodology* of the social sciences, including how we acquire knowledge: the roles of observation, experiment, hypothesis, probability, verification, theory, cause, and law. How each methodologist dealt with social and political theory is described, particularly from the perspective of the radical critique of empiricism. Attention is given to gender relations in social theory, especially to how the methodologist treated the female half of humankind. Relations between humankind and the natural environment, where the methodologist discussed these, are reported, so that we can examine the environmentalist critique of methodology. Some attention is also given to relations between the social sciences and history, literature, and the arts. *The Early Origins of the Social Sciences*, in short, deals with some central issues in methodology and society, but it does not do many things a conventional history would.

No methodology/school of thought emerges in isolation. For as long as anything identifiable as empiricism has existed there has also been an anti-empirical, idealist approach. The two have contended over the centuries so that many of today's critiques are merely variations on a theme from earlier times, as are the alternative solutions. The wise consumer looking for an alternative to empiricism should examine the competition, its history and uses. The present work does not pretend to be an impartial examiner of the opposition to empiricism, but it is careful to give both sides of the methodological debate and main sources for and against. This enables people concerned that empiricism is inherently conservative, sexist, or anti-environmental to see how well the alternatives fare on just those same points.

Many people assisted by reading earlier drafts of the manuscript or chapters: Thelma McCormack, Stephen Straker, Lorenne Clark, Neal Wood, Patricia Marchak, Tom Bottomore, Louis Greenspan, and Gregory Baum. None of them, obviously, is responsible for any errors or deficiencies remaining but all gave advice and suggested sources I found helpful. I benefited as well from comments made by colleagues in discussions on various parts of the work given in departmental colloquia and lectures. The Naegele Lecture at the University of British Columbia, the Snider Lecture at the University of Toronto, and the Sorokin Lecture at the University of Saskatchewan were three such opportunities. Departmental colloquia at the University of Waterloo and at Simon Fraser, Queen's, and Dalhousie universities all gave feedback at different stages of the manuscript's evolution. I owe a very profound thanks to Thelma McCormack, not only for reading the entire manuscript at several stages, but for general advice and encouragement over the many years of research and writing.

The research reported here was based overwhelmingly on printed sources, some of them in obscure, limited editions scarcely more available than unpublished manuscripts. The three chief libraries I used were the British Library, the Bibliothèque Nationale in Paris, and the Robarts Library of the University of Toronto. Manuscript collections used were the British Museum, the British Library of Political and Economic Science, and the Wellcome Institute for the History of Medicine in London, the Bibliothèque Royale in Brussels, and the Institut and the Bibliothèque Marguerite Durand in Paris. Librarians in all these places, and in a number of other university libraries, gave much appreciated assistance.

A further book, *The Women Founders of the Social Sciences*, will give more detailed attention to the substantial contribution of women, especially Catharine Macaulay, Germaine de Staël, Harriet Martineau, Florence Nightingale, and Beatrice Webb.

Lynn McDonald
University of Guelph

The Early Origins of the Social Sciences

1 Methodological Debate in the Social Sciences

The social sciences are far older and wiser than we give them credit for being. While histories commonly date them to the nineteenth century, with precursors in the eighteenth, the basic elements can be seen as far back as the fifth century B.C. Fragments from the sixth century B.C. show the germ of certain of those ideas in the notions of regularities, laws of nature, probability, and convention. Contrary to popular belief the social sciences are at least as old as the natural sciences. The two grew up side by side; the same people often pursued interests in both. The first recorded cross-disciplinary borrowing in fact is *from* the social sciences *to* the natural, in the fifth century B.C. no less. The very word for the ordering of the universe, *cosmos*, was adapted for scientific purposes from the ordinary terms for housekeeping and gardening. Yet the social sciences continue to be berated for imitating their supposedly older sibling. Nor were there barriers between mainstream empirical social science, with its focus on general explanation and interest in particular great events and people, the typical subject of "historians." Rather, from the time of Thucydides on there were social scientists integrating the two. Examination of the record crumbles another long standing complaint: the separation of the social sciences from the humanities, fine arts, and literature. Not only did the same people do both the natural and social sciences, they also wrote poems and plays.

As we approach the end of the twentieth century and the new millennium, social scientists are unsure of their discipline. Students wonder whether they should be doing research at all – doesn't it necessarily support the *status quo*? It is contended that social science can be no more than one person's story, with no greater credence than that of any other person. Feminists and environmentalists have joined the attack on conventional social science, raising new and compelling critiques.

Defences of ordinary empirical sociology exist but are rare. *In Praise of Sociology*, for example, gives ten illustrations of innovation in method and sophistication in theory.[1] *A Measure for Measures* similarly fights back, looking to the return of confidence in empirical sociology, including refined quantitative methods. Still, its author feels he has to warn against "unreconstituted positivism fuelled by political expediency."[2] Far more often methodological discussion means *only* condemnation and ridicule.

The methodological debate of the 1970s and 1980s left many victims but little resolution. The focus of attack then and now has typically been "positivism," usually undefined, but understood as entailing some use of quantitative methods such as social surveys. At the extreme any testing of hypotheses with data and any attempt to generalize from data is rejected. This disillusionment with the social sciences has been expressed differently in different countries but occurs wherever the social sciences are pursued on any scale. It has been greatest in Europe, where the social sciences began. In Germany in the late 1960s there was a shift from empirical work to methodological discussion. Journals that had been fat with research results came out less often, in slimmer numbers. In France empirical work has become a minority activity, engaged in, it has been said, by people unable to think theoretically. In Sweden by the early 1970s a whole generation of students was going through university with little acquaintance with empirical work – this in a country with a strong empirical tradition.

In Britain, the United States, Canada, and Australia empirical research is still plentiful, but researchers now seem to suffer more doubts. Some lose the faith entirely, while potential replacements wonder if it is ethical to do research at all. Many universities have eliminated requirements in basic theory and research. They have become optional parts of sociology to be studied only if one is so inclined. Course titles were changed from "political science" to "political studies" to show that no false claims to scientific accuracy would be made. Modesty is undoubtedly a virtue, but is the aim of true knowledge/correct information/accurate prediction to be abandoned? Just who *studies* politics without criteria? Who decides, on what basis, whether a particular theory or explanation is substantiated?

Beginning with the 1970s empirical work came under attack from a new quarter, feminism. Scientific method was denounced as "male-stream methodology."[3] Feminist analysis defined objectivity as a lack of concern with human values. Precision implied lack of concern with context. Interest in trends or variables implied forgetting about real human beings. Causal relations became abstract so that no one (men) could be blamed for what was wrong. The academic literature, feminists pointed out, is rife with examples of bad work thanks to sexist prejudice. Studies done exclusively with male university students are then generalized to the whole human species, often called "man." Male characteristics are taken as normal; female become the deviant, to be explained. Thus wives do who not vote as their husbands do are a subject of investigation, not husbands who do not vote as their wives. Established male academics have used "objectivity" as a weapon to exclude upstart feminists. In practice it has meant that poor work by men is immune to feminist criticism, for men set the "universalistic" standards of the profession. One can understand why feminists denounce objectivity and universalism as standards, but the alternative need not be a post-modernist rejection of the social science model itself.

The fact that women have taken part in the development of the social sciences from the beginning is simply not known. Undervaluing women's scholarly work has meant that important people and ideas have been ignored. Histories of the social sciences by men typically include *no* women among the "founding fathers." Yet in the chapters to follow it will be clear that there were women in *every* age making their contribution. Some were feminists, advocates of sexual equality as well as of empiricist methodology, which they found useful for the cause. Long before the term "feminism" came into use Mary Astell, Mary Wollstonecraft, Mary Hays, and Catharine Macaulay used the best evidence possible to argue for women's equality. Prominent in the nineteenth century were Harriet Taylor Mill, Harriet Martineau, Flora Tristan, and Jane Addams. Beatrice Webb was a latecomer on women's rights but eventually served that cause too, along with social reform, socialism, and modern methodology. As for *political science*'s being a "male methodology," one of its earliest proponents was a woman, Germaine de Staël.

Even Stephen Turner's excellent *Search for a Methodology of Social Science* (1986) includes no women contributors. De Staël, Jane Addams, and Beatrice Webb are simply absent. So is Florence Nightingale, although her collaborator, Dr Farr, is included. Harriet Martineau appears only as Comte's translator, while J.S. Mill apparently worked alone.

Moving through the 1980s into the 1990s, there has been no lessening of the attack on empiricism. Mazlish, in *A New Science* (1989), castigates empiricists for modelling their subject on the natural sciences, amd curtly dismisses statisticians like Quetelet. He finds literary sources more worthy. Still, after some twenty years of the contemporary women's movement and women's studies, no women are included among his founders of sociology.

Environmentalists have recently joined feminists in the attack on empiricist methodology. No less than the depletion of the earth's resources has been blamed on positivism.[4] In *The Re-enchantment of the World* (1981) Berman argued against *all* the basic tenets of scientific methodology in the name of ecology, including causality, objectivity, and the distinctions between observer and observed, fact and value. Cartesian dualism and the science erected on its false principles was "the most unecological and self-destructive culture and personality type that the world has ever seen."[5] Schumacher in *Small is Beautiful* (1973) gave a superb analysis of the problems of the environment and social organization apparently bent on destroying it. Yet this great friend of the earth was content to follow the herd in the attack on positivism as "interested solely in know-how," denying "the possibility of objective knowledge about meaning and purpose of any kind."[6]

The Early Origins of the Social Sciences was written in response to these attacks from radicals, feminists, environmentalists, and generally disillusioned social scientists. In it I trace the basic elements of empirical methodology over the centuries, beginning in classical Greece and ending with the modern methodology of the early twentieth century. I consider the contributors of original methodological ideas and practical methods of each period. What were their motives? Whose side were they on, and how did they help that side? While this book is not a history of political and social thought *per se*, I do briefly discuss it in the context of various methodologies. Links, especially any borrowing, between the social and natural sciences are noted. Relations with other scholarly interests, literature, and the "humanities", are considered. With the environmentalist critique in mind, I look for implications for the natural world and its survival. With the feminist critique in mind, I look for the involvement of women scholars and the positions taken by men and women methodologists alike on equality issues. At the end of each chapter I revisit the charges against empiricism in the light of what actual methodologists of the period did and said.

The bare facts of this intellectual development – who said what, when, to what purpose, and with what effect – are still little known. A major purpose of this book, then, is simply narrative, telling a story to current social scientists – teachers, students, researchers, theorists, and practitioners of various sorts – interested in the origin and development of their subject. The astonishing accomplishments and near misses in the earliest development of the social sciences are the subject of chapter 2. There we see the emergence of the ideas of convention, probability, and hypothesis with the sophists, Hippocratics, Democritus, and the sceptics. The recovery of ancient materialism and nominalism after the fall of Rome begins in chapter 3. The sixteenth century saw the last great recovery of scepticism, the *sine qua non* of any social science. By the seventeenth century the more familiar figures of Bacon, Descartes, and Locke emerged. The French Enlightenment, especially Voltaire, Diderot, Condorcet, and de Staël, is the subject of chapter 4. British developments of the eighteenth century, especially Adam Smith, Hume, the Scottish moral philosophers, and the Utilitarians, are covered in chapter 5. Chapter 6 explores the nineteenth century and the theorists commonly treated as the founders of the social sciences: Saint-Simon, Quetelet, Mill, Marx, Durkheim, and Weber. Women contributors are included where they appear, and they do appear, both as major figures in their own name, like Martineau and Beatrice Webb, and as translators, editors, and collaborators. A short chapter 7 sketches developments in methodology in the post-Weber period and then revisits the critiques of empiricism with which the book began.

While the focus throughout is the development of the methodology of the empirical social sciences in each period, I also examine the idealist competition. Thus in the ancient period Socrates, Plato, Aristotle, Augustine, and the neo-Platonists are considered. As modern methodology emerges, I discuss Descartes, Malebranche, Leibniz, Spinoza, Berkeley, and Kant. The tensions between the two dominant traditions and attempts at reconciliation between them are a major theme in the analysis.

My focus is the development and defence of the empirical social sciences, but this cannot be done in a vacuum. From the fifth century B.C. on, competing approaches in epistemology were available, so that scholars interested in methodological questions had choices to make, models to emulate or refute. An empiricist/idealist opposition is germane for most of this history. There are exceptions to be sure, attempts at reconciliation, and people who were inconsistent or who changed their minds. Nevertheless the dichotomy serves over this long stretch of time at least as a heuristic tool. Most methodologists subscribed to one or other of these basic approaches/ traditions/principles as it was developed at the time in question. Many identified themselves explicitly, affirming allegiances to earlier contributors of their own choice and distancing themselves from or denigrating the founders of the rejected approach. Exceptions are noted. Descriptions of the defining characteristics for these two competing approaches appear later in this chapter.

WHAT'S WRONG WITH THE SOCIAL SCIENCES?

There is seldom smoke without fire, and the case against the social sciences, at least as in recent practice, is impressive. Much of what passes for sociology is intellectually light weight, nor can it be justified as a first step to something better. The level of problems tackled in most empirical studies has long been a bad joke. Few sociologists ever actually test a theory or even a loose set of hypotheses. Empirical work usually means only that some data have been collected somehow. Often the results are a foregone conclusion; the data serve to illustrate a point the researcher wants to make. Statistics may add a quasi-scientific veneer to a pet theory, but properly speaking are no better than anecdotal evidence.

The usefulness of much, if not most, research can be found in its public relations function: legitimizing the *status quo*. Prisoners are shown to be seriously deviant, and so needing to be locked up. Inner-city children are shown routinely to do badly at school, and so little should be expected of them. Some people may be actually harmed by social science investigations; certainly few have benefitted. Companies selling products we don't need or want (and which may injure us) benefit from research on consumer habits, the military learns how to recruit more efficiently, and governments decide on programs for their immediate vote-getting potential, not long-term usefulness.

I accept all the standard criticisms of contemporary social science. Research seminars are too often opportunities to score points, not to pursue knowledge. Textbooks on research methods often give over-simplified accounts. Statistics can be misused. Researchers confound a research instrument, such as a questionnaire, with the whole complicated reality it is supposed to tap. Actual frauds are probably rare; it is not so much that answers are faked as that inadequate questions are asked. Empiricism requires that nature/society be given a chance to say "no." Yet this seldom happens.

The attack on empiricism, however, goes far beyond this sort of criticism. The culprit is not the abuse of social science but its most basic elements. The critics themselves include prominent theorists eminent in the discipline and related fields. Alvin Gouldner's attack is lengthy, but typical: "Positivism always in effect affirms the reality and rationality of 'what is,' of the *status quo*; its impulse is to sidestep issues and problems by avoiding conflicts over values, goals or ends."[7] Randall Collins has given much practical advice to improve research methods, but still follows the standard line on the wickedness of positivism: "Positivism is basically a program for replacing politics and morality with technicians, in effect a value choice for marginal reform within the shell of any particular status quo." He claimed that the "dominant schools of American sociology have been positivist," meaning the "emulation of physical science in methods and conceptions" and ignorance of "questions of value conflict."[8] Jeffrey Alexander did not argue that social science should be considered a non-science, but still blamed the "positivist persuasion in contemporary sociology" for having "an impoverishing effect on the sociological imagination, in both its empirical and theoretical modes."[9]

George Grant's condemnation was more graphic. Positivists do not deal with "the most serious questions," which become "dim in the positivist night."[10] Social scientists are "required" to interpret their science as "value free," asserting their account of reality to be objective, in contrast with previous accounts (118). Even the distinguished Alain Touraine stated that sociology has represented a "conservative tendency,"[11] although its task was to "denude" oppressive social processes and institutions (18). For Georges Gurvitch "positivism" was the glorification of "given and observed facts," as if they were pebbles scattered on a road asking to be picked up.[12] In *The*

Political Context of Sociology (1961), Bramson denounced "the rusty pad-lock of dogmatic positivism" as no longer representing "a useful method-ological approach for sociologists, if it ever did."[13] Other authors put their disdain right in the title of their book: in *Systematic Empiricism: Critique of a Pseudoscience* the culprit was no less than a "methodological villain."[14]

Critical theorist Jürgen Habermas considers the focus on general expla-nation (nomological science) an extension from the natural sciences to economics, sociology, and political science. Sociology is accused of being "indifferent to history. It processes its data without regard to any specific context."[15] Admittedly some sociologists do process data without consid-ering the context, but that hardly establishes that they *must*, that such is inherent in the subject. For Habermas "the positivistic self-understanding" of the nomological sciences suppresses action. Efficiency and technology are the result, incapable of orienting action or meaningful change. "Soci-ology, which believes itself to be completely detached from its historical context, falls victim to the immanence of what exists" (20). Yet, not only is sociology not separated from its historical context, there are, as we will see, close links from the earliest origins of the social sciences and work to the mature formulation of its sociological methodology in the nineteenth century.

Making Knowledge Count (1991) offers much earnest advice on how social scientists can do research on the most crucial policy issues of the day, including survival against environmental destruction and the prospect of nuclear annihilation. Metta Spencer points out how global social problems are held in place by prevailing unexamined myths, such as that keeping the peace requires expensive weaponry and that military expenditures are good for the economy. She urges social scientists to do research to dispel these myths.[16] Harries-Jones is undoubtedly correct in observing that "the canons of method in social science have a chilling effect on social intervention" (15). Yet along with these sane observations the authors find it necessary to denounce objectivity, or the "myth of objectivity," make truth relative and plural, and describe science as a "conversation." That the social sciences were born and had their greatest growth in times of crisis seems to have been completely ignored. Yet we will see that major founders of the social sciences were highly involved in the global issues of their day. The demar-cation of a separate sphere of "policy research" or advocacy is a compar-atively recent innovation.

Feminist post-modernist Jane Flax opposes the "privileged place" accorded science and philosophy as forms of knowledge. She holds that reason, knowledge, science, freedom, and human happiness are not con-nected, as Enlightenment thinkers supposed, but rather were and are antag-onistic.[17] Flax uses "Enlightenment" pejoratively (41). "In many ways," she says, "women never 'had' an Enlightenment. Enlightenment discourse was not meant to include women, and its coherence depends partially on our continuing exclusion" (230). Yet we will see in the chapters to come that women took an active part in the struggles of the Enlightenment and used its values to promote equality for themselves and other oppressed groups.

While I share the deep dissatisfaction of many critics of empiricism, the merits of their remedies escape me. Half of Mazlish's *A New Science* (1989) deals with novelists. The very development of sociology is said to have depended on the evolution of the novel.[18] Mazlish proposed as the one "truly great British sociologist" Herbert Spencer, a prolific writer of what might better be called social philosophy, who never sullied his hands with empirical research (143). The main alternative for most critics of empiricism is an escape into subjectivism. From a conservative ethnomethodology to radical critical theory and anarchistic post-modernism, they reject external, objective criteria for judging theories. Because it is impossible ever to be completely objective, they maintain, we should not try. Because values shape our choice of questions, we need not seek objectivity in answering them. The result, characterized at its worst, is a despairing anti-intellectualism. What the critics of empiricism seem not to have realized is that when they abandon objective criteria the alternative is an appeal to authority. *Which* authority is taken on faith. George Grant was very revealing when he indicated his preferred alternative: "The centre of true scholarship is the careful reading of what the wisest men have written about the most important questions."[19] In the meantime, official sociology goes on. Studies showing that delinquent children "need" certain treatment go unchallenged. Surveys show that people want nuclear power. Moralistic objections to government programs are raised to no effect. The social sciences, or rather the selective use of quantitative data, increasingly become weapons of the authorities. Radical criticism, without a scientific foundation, becomes increasingly irrelevant.

THE ELEMENTS OF EMPIRICISM

My thesis here is that we need to return to the social sciences to search for explanations, for causes and effects in a real, social world. Here the answers are not subsumed in the question, and the results may be profoundly critical of existing social arrangements. The principles of empirical social science are basically sound even if their practice has been found wanting. Although it is not always well articulated, a set of methodological principles is understood in the profession. There is a respectable textbook literature expounding the foundations, and they are reflected in some excellent empirical work.[20] Whether mainstream, Marxist, Weberian, or even structuralist sociology, the purpose of the social sciences is *explanation*: why certain events happen and others do not. Prediction is a related objective, in that correct predictions are a sign, although no guarantee, of correct theory. One can be right for the wrong reason. Universality in theory is a goal – the more explained the better – but the criteria for determining how generally a theory applies are empirical tests against an external, objective world. There is no *assumption* of universality for any proposition. Long series of predictions, or correct predictions across widely ranging phenomena, are indicators of broad generality. Again there can be no assurance. In the case of social matters there is a further constraint in the capacity of humans to reflect back on the laws they have discovered and to use this knowledge to change the world around them.

A real, external world is assumed; the scientist's task is to go into it to study it. There is an underlying order in the social world, as in the physical, so that the social scientist's task is difficult but not futile. Knowledge in empiricism is typically viewed as highly elusive. There have been some confident empiricists, but most have believed the laws they sought to be well hidden. The social scientist's strategy, accordingly, must be to approach this external world humbly and diligently, waiting on it and asking it to reveal itself as much as it will. The assumption is not that objectivity can be achieved but rather that it should be the social scientist's goal. Subjective views guide the choice of problems, and any source of inspiration is legitimate for the formulation of hypotheses or theories. In order to test propositions for assertions about *validity*, however, concerted efforts to insure objective procedures must be made.

The choice of actual research methods depends on the nature of the phenomena to be studied. Social scientists are greatly limited in the experiments they may perform, which are largely confined to indirect experimentation or comparative analysis. The elucidation of great single events is a type of enquiry within the rubric of the social sciences. The same assumptions of underlying order are made in the study of single and multiple events; the difference is one of focus. For general explanation there are, as in the natural world, regularities to be observed and theories to be described to account for those regularities. Great events are interpreted in the light of these general laws. Empiricist methodology implies nominalism, the notion that definitions are of intrinsic value not in themselves but as a convenience, acceptable in so far as they serve a useful purpose. Thus there is no such thing as "knowledge" of a concept, and a concept cannot be right or wrong.

The assumption of underlying order includes no suggestion that it will be discovered. Nature is believed to answer questions properly put to it, but there is always the possibility that the question was not properly formulated, or the answer improperly understood. More fundamentally, because knowledge is grounded in what can be observed, it will always fall short of total reality. There is always considerable scope for error, and the proper social scientist will be accordingly tentative in all conclusions. Not a defining characteristic, but a part of empiricism for many social scientists, is the application of knowledge for social good. The precise goals have varied, but for centuries empiricists have believed that understanding the causes of problems can help in their solution.

The portrayal of empiricists as somehow uncouth and uninterested in ideas does not bear scrutiny. Ideas, and certainly ideals, goals, and values are elements in the world empiricists study. Those in this study were intensely interested in ideas. Many were deeply religious. The difference between empiricism and idealism as methodological approaches lies not in interest in ideas as such but rather in how they are studied. For empiricists there can be no short cut through intuition or introspection just because the object of the study is an idea rather than a concrete object. The extent to which people are motivated by any idea/goal/value/article of faith is itself an empirical question. To reject idealism *as a methodology* is not to reject ideals or beliefs in one's own life, political struggles, or concept of good in society.

The debate over "value-free" social science largely reflects misunderstanding of where and why empiricists wish to limit reference to values, a subject to be returned to particularly in the discussion on Weber. The social sciences cannot be "value-free," for values will always shape the choice of what is studied and how. In the process of testing hypotheses or otherwise analyzing data, however, every effort must be made to put aside our prejudices/biases/values for the sake of objectivity. That this is difficult to do, and will never be done perfectly, does not mean that we should not try. Commitment to objectivity in processing data simply means fairness. Values may, even must, shape the choice of research questions because they shape one's sense of what is important. Yet we are not entitled to distort results so as to make them suit our own values, however laudable those values may be. The end does not justify the means. Etzioni has helpfully explained that objectivity simply means suspending one's personal values while making judgments about data, not having no values.[21]

The separation of facts and values has become a fundamental tenet of empiricism. It was not always so, and some methodologists over the ages considered it possible to make deductions from the "is" to the "ought." This belief remains a precept for many advocates of idealism, so much so that empiricists are pilloried for their lack of ethical concerns. Ethical questions for both methodological traditions, of course, have been primordial. The motivation for most empiricist methodologists has been a better world, somehow conceived, and including both material and non-material components. Knowledge has been a means to better food, shelter, and health care as well as for education, culture, and the more intangible aspects of the decent life. Idealist methodologists have been no less lofty in their intentions, and there has been diversity in both camps as to what constitutes the good life. Yet I share Weber's view that the Sermon on the Mount cannot be refuted or substantiated scientifically.[22] Ethical questions will be a part of this study in so far as they influence questions of methodology, usually as they guide the motivations of methodologists. They will not be a subject in their own right. Writers like Alasdair MacIntyre in *After Virtue* lament the abandonment of this search for answers and disagree with my point. Yet where is the evidence that the study of ethics ever led to better conduct by individuals or nations? Who, thanks to a belief that the "ought" can be derived from the "is," becomes a better person from research thereby? Are such people any more likely to do what they ought to do, and not do what they ought not? Is there more health in them than in us poor, miserable empiricists?

Empiricist methodology in no way implies a disdain for the processes of thought or reflection. Empiricists over the centuries have pointed to the need for careful consideration of all sense data collected. With rare exception empiricists have not treated the processes of observation and inference as simple or automatic. The difference with idealist methodology is not one of *whether or not* to take recourse to intellectual processes, but *what role* such processes can play. Empiricists have insisted that intellection, speculation, intuition, introspection, rational thought, cogitation, or whatever thought is called cannot be relied on for *valid knowledge*. Errors in reasoning occur, as do errors in perception. Errors in observation may be corrected through reasoning – but they may not be. Empiricists, further, have tended to consider thought processes prone to error and generally less reliable and more subject to personal bias than sense perception. It is not that thought has no role to play – it has an important role – but that no amount of recourse to the processes of reasoning can guarantee accurate knowledge.

Different schools can be identified within the empiricist tradition in terms of what their proponents consider important to study (normalcy or change, a revolution or a mental hospital) and what substantively they look to for explanation (economic variables, religious belief, the structure of language). But these differing schools share these *methodological* principles, which together can be distinguished from subjectivist, intuitionist methodologies. I will not attempt to separate a more historical or interpretive sociology from the mainstream focus on general explanation. Rather, I will examine each when it appears, showing how integrated the two approaches have been. From Thucydides through Ibn Khaldun, to Bacon, Hume, Macaulay, Voltaire, and on to Weber we will see methodologists subscribing both to a methodology of general explanation and to a delight in the particular.

Rationalism is a term to be avoided for its ambiguity. It has been used synonymously with idealism, but many empiricists like to consider their choice of methodology reasonable, hence rational. Durkheim, for example, in the preface to the first edition of his *Rules of Sociological Method*, said that positivism was a *consequence* of rationalism.[23]

IDEALISM AS A METHODOLOGICAL TRADITION

The chief defining characteristic of idealism is confidence in the capacity of *mind*. It is not that empiricists are necessarily confident in the capacity of the senses (many have been highly sceptical), but empiricists have had the same, or greater, doubt about purely mental processes. Idealists have not shared these doubts, and many have gone so far as to affirm the capacity of mind to acquire error-free, absolute truth. Idealists have tended to be less interested in ordinary cause-and-effect theories; some consider them to have a useful, if modest, role, others considering them to have no role whatsoever in the acquisition of knowledge. Idealists have often sought a more profound level of knowledge, not "mechanical" explanation, *how* something happens, but an explanation in terms of ultimate purpose. They have typically been greatly interested in definition, some considering the "right" definition, that which captures the thing's true essence, as knowledge.

The debate between idealism and empiricism is a major theme of this book. It has been fought on somewhat different grounds in different centuries, but it is remarkable that the same arguments appear and reappear in only slightly altered form. Attempts at reconciliation of the two sides are chronic; the proposals of one side are never convincing to the other. There was a time, however, in pre-Socratic Greece, when the ideal/material distinction did not hold. Explanations of phenomena embraced both material elements and non-material entities or forces. Most important there was no good/evil distinction paralleling the ideal/material. The gods, and people's souls, were material – fine, ethereal substances. The term "materialist" for these early theorists is not their own. The rigid distinction between ideal and material as between good and evil came with Socrates, Parmenides, and Plato and was reinforced by Aristotle. The motivation seems to have been religious. It is with Plato that matter became repugnant, contaminating, pulling down our higher natures into the mud, as it were. Also for religious reasons, idealists made a sharp distinction between the social and material (i.e., non-human) worlds. People and animals were seen as belonging to radically different spheres of life, whereas to empiricists the differences have been rather as on a continuum.

One of the most important differences between idealism and empiricism has been the level of knowledge each seeks. The most important idealists have held that certain knowledge, "the truth," is attainable in at least some matters (thus Parmenides, Aristotle, Plotinus, Augustine, Aquinas,

Descartes, Leibniz, Spinoza, Malebranche, Kant, Althusser, Horkheimer, Marcuse, Adorno). The tendency has been to see error as the result of sense perception, sometimes correctible by mind, which has its sources independent of sense perception. It follows that error can be avoided by not relying on the senses. Mathematics, logically, has been the model science for idealists. (To empiricists, mathematics is not a science, in the sense of not entailing knowledge of the real world, but an abstract system built on definitions and axioms.) Idealists in fact have tended to be better mathematicians (notably Descartes and Leibniz) than empiricists, an odd fact now, when mathematical proficiency is associated with empiricism. Some of the great founders of empiricism were actually notorious for their lack of mathematical skill: Epicurus, Bacon, Gassendi, Locke, Hume, Saint-Simon, Marx, Weber, and Durkheim.

The criteria for evaluating theory in idealism devolve on internal, mental processes. Consistency or agreement with propositions otherwise accepted is important. Many idealists have frankly relied on intuitive judgment, instantaneous perception of the truthfulness of propositions. Although facts about a real, external world have no place, sense data may be useful for making suggestions to the mind, for providing opinions. Yet it is the mind that must sift truth from error.

A NOTE ON TERMS

Since "positivism" has become a pejorative term I have tended to avoid it for "empirical" and "empiricism," while being fully aware of their common meaning. The terms were used interchangeably during most of the history covered with no connotation of rigidity or narrowness. "Positive" simply referred to something in the real, as opposed to the theoretical, world. A positive law was one passed by a legislature or decreed by a king, as opposed to divine or natural laws affirmed to exist by believers. Positive facts meant the results of observation, in contrast with, as Saint-Simon put it, "the supposed facts of conjecture." The positive sciences were those based on empirical observation, as Marx put it "without any mystification and speculation."[24] "Empeiria" is simply the Greek work for experience, hence empirical observation. Saint-Simon, Marx, Mill, Durkheim, and Weber all used "empirical" and "positive" in the same way and with no pejorative baggage. Weber's last lectures were entitled "Positive Criticism of the Materialist Interpretation of History," meaning an examination of the theory against historical data. No apology will be made here for the terms "social science" or "social sciences," understood as aiming at tentative, hypothetical, and probable knowledge as opposed to certain truth. The expression emerged in the French Revolution in the search for a new social order, a social science needed to ground the social art.[25] Condorcet, a French speaker, used the term originally in the singular, "science sociale." The English translator put it into the plural, "the social sciences," which use is followed here.

THE METHODOLOGISTS

Since methodologies, with ideas, are formulated by people, this history is organized around people. The investigation began with the simple, Who said what when? Ideas were traced to their sources as much as possible, in effect to the first people whose work has survived. Some biographical material is included to place the methodologists by period, school, and, very briefly, their personal circumstances. That intellectual creation is a cumulative process becomes clear in relating the evolution of ideas. The person thought of as the originator of a theory sometimes turns out to be simply the best writer on it of the day. Often several people are saying much the same thing. At times much earlier exponents are still ignored because their ideas were not taken up at the time. Frequently originality lies in the *adaptation* of an idea from another sphere, for example from religion to science. Where possible, the series of steps will be shown, with the connections and the false starts. As a result this study includes people normally omitted in histories of the social sciences or empiricism. The acknowledged major founders are still accorded a prominent place, but their lesser-known predecessors are also included when they made a key contribution. Some people are included for their timely examples of empirical work, even if they made little or no theoretical contribution.

The methodologists include individuals, such as John Locke and David Hume, known primarily for their work in philosophy, especially epistemology. Others, such as Adam Smith and Saint-Simon, are known more for their substantive contribution or the development of key concepts. Still others devoted most of their professional lives to other pursuits, making some signal contribution to the development of social science methodology along the way. Thus there are priests, lawyers, journalists, doctors, teachers, politicians, diplomats, bureaucrats, natural scientists, and social workers as well as the more conventional professors of philosophy. *The criteria for inclusion were the originality and importance of the methodological contribution, regardless of the person's professional status, academic connections, or other activities.* That there should be such a diversity of backgrounds and occupations simply attests to the diversity of people interested in the subject who made a notable contribution to it.

A piece of research necessarily reflects the concerns of the period in which it is done. This book is fundamentally a response to the contemporary and recent attacks on empirical work in the social sciences. It is directed to social scientists rather than academic philosophers and specialists in epistemology. It includes the classical period because that is when the first elements of the social sciences appeared. Classicists, as academic philosophers, should be warned that the focus is the development of the methodology of the social sciences; their heroes are treated, for better or worse, from that perspective. *The Early Origins of the Social Sciences* is not a conventional history of any period, but the central developments in methodology proper (assumptions and prescriptions) of each period are set out and major examples of actual empirical work given. I have described the social context in which methodological advances were made, notably the conditions that prompted the new development. The debate with the methodological alternative of the day is made clear.

This is not a history of the connections between the arts and social sciences, but I have addressed prevalent misconceptions. Contrary to received opinion, astonishing numbers of methodologists were involved in artistic expression, writing poetry, plays, and novels as well as methodology and substantive social science works. In some cases the methodologist first loved the arts, only turning to other work when unable to make a living as an artist. Some produced and published in both fields. There is simply no rigid division when the people are considered, although all of them carefully separated their methodological from their artistic work. They all knew which hat they were wearing at any time, but did find it necessary to change hats. It will become clear that the common portrayal of empiricists as limited, unimaginative people does not match the historical record.

One of the most unexpected discoveries of this study was the importance of religion, individual methodologists being influenced by their own religious beliefs and by authorities determined to support orthodoxy. Some influence had been expected, of course, but not so much and not in *every* period. Thus ancient idealism emerged as an extension of a certain doctrine of the soul, and later versions would depend on divine guarantees of knowledge, illumination or a "vision-in-God." Epicurean materialism was, in part, an alternative religion. Scientific explanation would allay people's greatest fears of death and of the gods that kept them under religion. Scepticism and materialism were rejected for centuries because of Catholic doctrine. The struggles of the eighteenth-century Encyclopedists were as much *against* the Catholic Church and His Christian Majesty as *for* empiricism. Weber did his first empirical work for a church group his mother got him to join. Beatrice Webb became a sociologist after searching for a craft *and* a creed. Nightingale's passionate statistics were grounded on a religious philosophy of life.

Religious considerations are perhaps even more important in the reception given methodological views. Ideas often appeared apparently "before their time," meaning that they were attacked and suppressed. If a particular idea seems a long time in coming it may not be that no one thought of it, but that whoever did got into a lot of trouble. Thus in the seventeenth century empiricism was developed both by French Catholics and English Protestants, but English Protestantism proved to be a much more favourable climate for it. For much of the history covered here authors had to obtain permission to publish. Further, books could be suppressed after the fact and authors and publishers punished. Censorship did, more often than one likes to think, have its intended effect. The history of methodology is strewn with fragments of missing works, most of them out of favour with the religious authorities of their time.

Another unexpected finding was the dangerousness of the lives of methodologists. As a former criminologist I was hoping to leave behind that sordid world for philosophical gentility. Instead I found that methodologists changed addresses like bookies and crossed borders like dope smugglers. We all know about the sorry ends of Socrates and Galileo, but I was not prepared for prison doors clanging, blood spilling, and hasty escapes in *every* period of this history. Few methodologists went to the stake, a punishment seldom used on intellectuals, but a fair number lived in fear of it. Many spent time in prison; without a helpful tip-off and a fast get-away many more would have.

2 The Ancient Origins of the Social Sciences

It will be obvious that it is impossible to understand how in reality
each thing is.   Democritus[1]

The gods have not revealed to mortals all things from the beginning;
but mortals by long seeking discover what is better.   Xenophanes[2]

But if he who desires to have before his eyes a true picture of the
events which have happened, and of the like events which may be
expected to happen hereafter in the order of human things, shall pro-
nounce what I have written to be useful, then I shall be satisfied.
                                                              Thucydides[3]

The lack of scientific thought assails the doubting heart
No knowledge how the cosmos came to be and how 'twill end
... What wonder that mankind condemns itself
And leaves place in its thought
For mighty power and marvellous strength of god
To govern all things?   Lucretius[4]

Most of the history of the social sciences consists of variations on themes developed in the sixth and fifth centuries B.C. The sixth century B.C. has left only rough, fragmented hints, but they are enough to indicate that the basic notions of social convention, causal relations, and hypothetical knowledge had already been formulated. By the fifth century B.C. there was a fairly sophisticated understanding of many methodological issues.[5] The earliest surviving book of social science, *The Peloponnesian Wars*, dates from this time. The attack on materialism and scepticism resulted in what we can now see as the beginning of the idealist tradition.

The ancient Greeks not only laid the foundations of the natural and social sciences but they had a direct and important impact on modern formulations. The great methodologists of the seventeenth and eighteenth centuries (and some even of the nineteenth century) were educated in the classics. During those centuries idealists, after the long rule of Aristotle, turned primarily to Plato to become neo-Platonists. Materialists turned to a variety of ancient materialists, so that modern positions on methodology to some extent depend on the choice of Greek model. Francis Bacon was an admirer of Democritus above all, while Gassendi focused on Epicurus. Thomas Hobbes translated

Thucydides. John Locke's favourite author was Cicero, the best source on ancient scepticism. Adam Smith shows the influence of the Stoics and Empedocles. David Hume was another sceptic. Karl Marx, in the nineteenth century, found a model in Epicurus, by this time as an alternative to Hegelian idealism. Marx's doctoral dissertation was on the differences between Epicurus and Democritus, and the "turning on its head" he found in Epicurus *vis-à-vis* Democritus is suggestive of his own relationship to Hegel. At the middle of the twentieth century Harold Innis urged, in *The Bias of Communication*, a return to the pre-Socratics. For him, the oral tradition was the attraction; in this book it is the early scepticism and understanding of convention.

Fewer women methodologists than men had the benefit of a classical education, but those who did were no less inspired or provoked. Mary Wortley Montagu while still a young woman translated the Stoic Epictetus. Catharine Macaulay's liberalism was fed by her reading on the Roman republic. Mme Roland found comfort in Tacitus while waiting for her execution. Florence Nightingale was a Plato expert. The feminist socialist Frances Wright translated a fellow radical, Epicurus.

The writing of this early history is complicated by the different survival rates of empiricism and idealism. Most of Plato's and Aristotle's works are available, while for the ancient materialists and sophists there are only fragments. Luckily, we have Thucydides' *Peloponnesian Wars* and some Hippocratic essays. There is bias also in the secondary literature, for most of the commentary on empiricists at the time was by idealists. Some recent scholars have charged deliberate misrepresentation of empiricist views. Thus sources pose more of a problem for this early time than any other period. The contemporary researcher, however, is better off than any since the Roman Empire – extensive work has been done on the available fragments, and much is now available in modern translations.

THE CONCEPT OF CONVENTION

The first step toward a crucial element of the social sciences, the concept of social institution or convention, was taken during Solon's great reforms in the sixth century B.C. Poor farmers had been forced into debt, those unable to pay into slavery. The poor cried out for redistribution of land, the rich for law and order as usual. Solon's reforms were the solution, his analysis of what was wrong the earliest surviving example in western culture. The very fact of creating new laws showed that laws were a matter of convention, not of mystical origin. Solon's constitution, apart from freeing many people from slavery, yielded a crucial understanding in the social sciences.

Solon (c. 630–c. 560 B.C.),[6] "the law-giver," figures on every list of the wise minds of antiquity. He has been called the "most germinal mind" of early Greek thought, the father of sophistic thought, and the grand-father of all political science. He came from a noble family, was well travelled, and may have been a merchant. His great contribution began with recognition of the plight of the poor farmers. He recited poetry in the market place to bring their situation to public attention and warned of the dire consequences if some remedy were not found. The extraordinary result was that Solon was elected archon, or chief ruler, of Athens and given the power to bring in new laws. He drastically revised Draco's legal code (from which came the term "draconian"). The compromise Solon worked out satisfied neither party, but was accepted and worked.

Only fragments remain of Solon's poems, but these are enough to show his deep concern for the victims and pride in his achievement:[7]

Such are the ills that are rife within our state; while of the poor great numbers are journeying to foreign lands, sold into slavery, and bound with shameful fetters.[8]

Many men I restored to Athens, their native city divinely-founded, men who justly or unjustly had been sold abroad, and others who through pressure of need had gone into exile, and who through wanderings far and wide no longer spoke the Attic tongue. Those here at home who were reduced to shameful slavery, and trembled at the caprices of their masters, I made free. (215)

Solon was certain that the cause of the difficulties was the greed of the wealthy:

It is the people themselves who in their folly seek to destroy our great city, prompted by desire for wealth; and their leaders, unjust of heart, for whom awaits the suffering of many woes, the fruit of their great arrogance, since they know not how to check their greed ... They have wealth through their following of unjust works and ways ... Neither the sacred treasure nor that of the state do they spare in any wise, but they steal, each in his own corner, like men pillaging. (207)

The causes were human, and so were Solon's remedies. Lawlessness brought ills but obedience to the law brought order and harmony, shackled the unjust, and checked greed. Social processes were like natural ones. The state's coming to ruin was like violent snow and hail coming from clouds, and thunder from lightning – "so from men of rank comes ruin to the state, and the people through their ignorance fall into the servitude of rule by one man" (209). Solon's actual reforms were moderate. He refused the demand of the poor for redistribution of land, but cancelled existing debts. Slavery was not abolished but slaves who had been citizens were freed. New laws forbade the securing of loans by personal bond, so that debtors could no longer lose their freedom for nonpayment. Solon also instituted a number of provisions to improve the economy. He brought in a new system of weights and measures to facilitate trade. He required fathers to teach their trades to their sons. He started a census on income. "To the people I have given just as much power as suffices, neither taking away from their due, nor offering more; while for those who had power and were honoured for wealth I have taken thought likewise, that they should suffer nothing unseemly. I stand with the strong shield flung around both parties, and have allowed neither to win an unjust victory" (208).

These modest changes mark the first steps to democracy in the Greek city-state. Top government posts continued to be reserved for the rich, but lower positions were opened. A system of popular juries was instituted. For the first time all (male) citizens could attend the assembly. For our purposes *how* these new laws were made is important. So clearly of human origin, they belie the notion that law was divine or immutable. Soon other social institutions would also be seen to be conventional. Solon's work, in short, made possible the early Greek political theory and sociology of Democritus, Thucydides, and Protagoras.

ANCIENT MATERIALISM

The first known natural science theories date from the same period as Solon, but even fewer surviving fragments remain to tell about them. The theories addressed change – how something could appear one way one day and the next quite differently – while logic taught that something and its opposite could not both be true. Out of this came the concept of underlying, constant, matter. The first known debate in natural science concerned what constituted this primeval matter.[9] The earliest theories of sensation followed, and from them came the whole methodological debate.

The first person known to have formulated a theory about ultimate matter was *Thales of Miletus (c. 625–c. 545 B.C.)*, whose primary substance was water. *Anaximander (c. 600–after 567 B.C.)*,[10] the first theorist known to have written and the first to have used prose, called the original matter the Boundless or Unlimited. Nature was a cosmos, a harmonious realm within which elemental powers waxed and waned. He conducted "ideal experiments," considering the possible consequences of a cosmic explosion. The materials for his imagination were technological (the hot blasts of bellows in a forge), his speculation was grounded on observation. Anaximander has been credited with the discovery of the principle of sufficient reason in the course of reaching his unbounded concept. Since there was no reason for the primal substance to stop anywhere, thought Anaximander, it must be boundless. Or, "*until a definite reason to the contrary can be assigned, we have to suppose a symmetrical distribution of things or possibilities.*"[11] Although Anaximander reached the wrong conclusion, the process of thought he used marks "one of the most momentous breaks in the career of humanity ... as much an innovation in the way of thinking that came before as the whole of science has been since" (36). It was risky, too, undermining the usual assumption of a specific pattern ordained by Providence. Yet not only was Anaximander not stoned, a statue was raised in his honour in the town square!

Winspear and Silverberg called Anaximander "the greatest and most mature" of the Ionian physicists for quite different reasons. They too credited him with great powers of conjecture, but stressed the *source* of his speculations in the social world. A surviving fragment refers to *justice* and the settling of conflicts. The elements of the physical world "make reparation and satisfaction to one another for their injustice as is appointed according to the ordered process of time."[12] Justice and the conflict of opposites within the state as developed by Solon are now transferred to the natural world. For us, accustomed to the physical world as the model for the social, this is an extraordinary reversal. *Yet this fragment from Anaximander is the oldest prose fragment preserved in our culture.* Winspear and Silverberg unambiguously concluded that physical speculation arose out of interest in the meaning of justice. For de Santillano, *both* Anaximander and Solon thought in terms of the city because it was the only self-regulating system they knew.[13]

Anaximander is also one of the first people to have used the term "cosmos" in a natural science context to denote the ordering of the universe. In Homer and other early usage both the noun and its corresponding verb refer to social and practical matters, as in good housekeeping, a well-tended garden, or a disciplined army.[14] "From the beginning, cosmos was applied to the world of nature by conscious analogy with the good order of society" (223). Again, contrary to the conventional wisdom, the borrowing is *from* the social *to* the natural world.

The next person known to have entered the cosmological debate was another Milesian, *Anaximenes (c. 586–before 494 B.C.)*, whose primal matter was air. To him, all things sprang from air through the processes of rarefaction and condensation. His term for condensation was taken from the term for felt making, another example of the importance of technology for the early development of science.[15] *Anaxagoras (c. 500–c. 430 B.C.)*[16] was the first thinker to introduce a non-material entity, cosmic Mind, into a cosmology. He was also the first thinker to work exclusively in natural science and the first natural scientist to live in Athens. Little is known about his methodology except that it included observation, experiment, and analysis. Observation alone was not enough, data had to be fitted into a logical framework. Sensation was an adequate source of data as far as it went; the problem was that one could never gain sufficient information. Anaxagoras was a great lover of general theory. He believed that the same kinds of matter existed in all parts of the universe and that the same physical laws therefore applied everywhere.

Archelaus of Miletus (fifth century B.C.), Anaxagoras' pupil, took materialism back to its pure state after his teacher's dalliance with Mind. A Milesian by birth, Archelaus lived many years in Athens, where he probably taught Socrates. His primitive matter was similar to air intermingled with a fine, material substance: mind. Archelaus taught that what is just and what depraved was so by convention, not nature. He is thus an example of the sophists' social science interests coinciding with the natural science of the materialists.

Heraclitus (c. 540–c. 480 B.C.), whose element was fire, was the last of the single-element materialists. He is also the first western theorist to locate reality not in the world we perceive but in a formula hidden in it. The meaning of the world was not to be found by looking outward but in probing one's own soul. Heraclitus is believed to have written one book, out of which 120 fragments survive. Little is known about his life except that he came from a royal/priestly family in Ephesus. He was vehemently anti-democratic but kept out of active politics. Concerned with political and ethical matters as well as natural science, he dealt with them all in one comprehensive theory.

Heraclitus has been called the philosopher who discovered *change*.[17] Earlier Greek philosophers were more influenced by oriental notions, viewing the world as a huge building. To understand it one had to know the materials from which it was built. With Heraclitus there was no building, no stable structure, but one colossal *process*. Totality was not a sum of things, but of events/changes/facts. In the course of reducing all things to flames, Heraclitus discovered what we now see as the makings of law. Having destroyed the cosmos as an edifice he re-introduced it as inexorable process. His concept differs from later scientific law by his belief that natural laws, with those of the state, are enforced by punishment. As did Solon, Heraclitus transposed a political notion, punishment, into a physical process. Might was now right; the Furies, the goddesses who punish, served Justice.

Perhaps the most famous saying of Heraclitus is that one cannot step twice into the same river. It follows that nothing can be known about particular objects, for they change even while being examined. The senses are the paths by which we receive impressions, and so are necessary in the search for wisdom, but cannot give more than fleeting impressions. The senses, Heraclitus maintained, were fundamentally untrustworthy. "Human nature has no power of understanding; but the divine nature has it."[18] Nature loves to hide, so that the closer we look into it the more it dissolves into motion. Sense information about particular objects, then, cannot constitute wisdom.

Heraclitus' political views reflect his contempt for sense information. Politics was a disgusting business because it was dominated by the many, with their false opinions. Most people lived only by the senses, hence were wrong. Human laws, however imperfect, drew their life from the one, divine Law. Heraclitus may have been a materialist, but his identification of actual, positive, laws with a higher, divine, law is much more characteristic of idealism.

Empedocles (c. 521–after 444 B.C.)[19] was a politician, physician, and religious reformer as well as the author of an extraordinary cosmology and methodology. He is still honoured as a democrat for having declined the offer of a crown, but his attempt to become recognized as a god failed. More of his writing has been preserved than any other pre-Socratic writer's, eighteen pages of two books, both in verse. *On Nature* describes his methodology in the context of a whole, atomistic cosmology. Perception occurs through the physical meeting of particles, objects throwing off effluvia, which land on the sense organs of the perceiver. Sight and hearing effluvia are lighter than touch, but all make their way up the fine passages of the body to the sense organ in question.

Sensation yields only a doubtful truth. That is, the senses convey reliable evidence if we but know how to use it. We should not rely on any one sense exclusively, or any one sense more than the others. Thought is necessary for the proper assessment of sense evidence, to keep it within proper bounds. Sense data remain essential, however, as the first step toward true knowledge. Some higher knowledge is also possible, through intuition or revelation. Forming a consistent picture involved rejecting much information and moulding together the remaining pieces. It required long preparation, brooding over the problem, and work with sense data. Experience increased understanding. Knowledge was always contingent on what one happened to come across. It could not convey a true picture of the ultimate realities of life and death nor any but a dim understanding of the total cosmic process. Empedocles also promised mastery over nature – to stop the rains and find drugs to cure all illnesses, even old age. The surviving fragment of his *On Nature* suggests that he believed that by understanding nature we could control it.[20]

By the end of the fifth century B.C. theories of matter ran from a single substance (water, air, or fire) to an infinite number of infinitesimal seeds. This was the time for synthesis, which was provided by another Milesian, *Leucippus (active 430 B.C.)* Leucippus devised no system but saw his role as a reconciler of ideas. The result was the basic principles of atomism later elaborated by Democritus. The single, primary substance posited was atoms divided into an infinite number of particles. These atoms, so small as to be invisible, were compact and eternal; between them was void. Only matter was real, for only matter could be touched. Diversity in matter occurs through differences in the *shapes* of the atoms: smooth atoms for sweetness, jagged atoms for bitterness. Soul atoms were said to be distributed throughout the body, giving it life and sensation. Certainly there is no suggestion of passivity. Nor was there "matter over mind" for mind (or soul) had the same capacity to act on matter as the body had on the mind. Both were composed of the same ultimate matter: atoms.

Leucippus took over Empedocles' concept of sensation as entailing physical contact between object and sense organ. Thought was understood as the reproduction of visual sensations – one must imagine a host of miniature movie screens in the mind. This was, apparently, a thoroughly acceptable formulation to the Greeks, and one we shall see repeated in subsequent versions of atomic theory. The senses if properly used are reliable means to truth, as far as they go. But they cannot alone acquire full and complete knowledge. It is not that the senses make mistakes but that a good part of reality is not accessible to the observer. There is also a fragment giving Leucippus's position on determinism: "Nothing happens at random; everything happens out of reason and by necessity" (91).

Democritus (c. 493–403 B.C.)[21] is most known as the formulator of the mature version of atomic theory, but he is as important for our purposes for his sociology and political theory. He studied at some time with Leucippus and travelled widely, to Egypt, Ethiopia, Persia, Babylon, and possibly even to India. Some 300 fragments of his writings survive, enough to suggest a superb mind and broad knowledge. One of the most quoted of these fragments shows his commitment to science: "[I would] rather discover one cause than gain the kingdom of Persia."[22] And Democritus knew whereof he spoke. He is one of the first thinkers to have developed a notion of social institutions as conventions arrived at by consensus. His accomplishments are impressive also in natural science, and he evidently had no difficulty going back and forth between the two spheres. He is the source also of practical political advice on how to make democratic institutions work. Democritus, in short, is one of the key figures in the early history of methodology.

Democritus' version of atomic theory began, from Leucippus, with atoms and the void. The creation of the world was a wholly natural process, even inevitable. Compounds were created through the collision of an infinite number of atoms in infinite space. Some atoms would bounce off the atoms they struck, but others, depending on their shape, would hook together. He was probably not responsible for the idea that atoms fell only in straight lines. (He had them vibrating, like particles of dust in a sunbeam, or swirling in a great, cosmic whirlpool.) Thus, Epicurus' "correction" of Democritus, of which Marx made so much in his doctoral dissertation, seems to have been based on a misunderstanding.[23]

Democritus' conceptualization of necessity effectively became the standard approach of empiricism in the seventeenth century. Everything has a cause, although we might not always be able to ascertain it. Chance implies unexplained causes, not suggesting any external forces, but simply the limits of human intelligibility. Democritus' theory of knowledge was more complex than his predecessor's. Now the human soul had two sections, a "reasonable" part of finely packed soul atoms in the breast, and an "unreasonable" or sensible part of atoms distributed throughout the body. Because of its greater density of soul atoms the mind was able to pick up perceptions the body missed. The processes of sensation and thought were the same, each requiring physical contact between effluence and atom. There is no *subject* of consciousness, but the atoms themselves do the perceiving.[24] Thought is simply the "peculiar sensation" resulting from the disturbance of atoms in the mind.

Democritus' views on the validity of sense data and the possibility of attaining certain knowledge have been variously interpreted. At the extreme, he has been taken to be a thorough sceptic convinced of the unreliability of sense data. He refers to "bastard" or obscure knowledge (sense data), and "genuine" knowledge (thought). The components and process of thought are so similar, however, that this denounces thought as well. "We know nothing about anything really, but Opinion is for all individuals an inflowing (of the Atoms)."[25] Other commentators have balked at such a sceptical interpretation as inconsistent with Democritus' scholarship. How could he have devoted so many years to research if all is but illusion? One plausible solution is the distinction between primary and secondary qualities. Objectively correct knowledge is possible on the primary qualities of atoms, their shape and size. For secondary qualities, such as colour and taste, subjective factors intervene, for different observers have different impressions. This allows for relativity of sense impressions without denying the objective existence of the material world. Another interpretation involves a distinction between experience and inference. One could not gain "genuine" knowledge from the senses but could infer it from them. The mind needs premises for its conclusions, which are provided by the senses.

Unlike Parmenides and idealists generally, Democritus did not believe the rift between the senses and thought to be unbridgeable. Certainly he stressed the numerous possibilities for error in sensation, describing the process and pitfalls of sensation for each sense. Touch was the most important sense, as it was the least liable to error. Concern about error in sensation, however, has never necessarily implied a total scepticism. Indeed we shall see a long line of methodologists filling books about the unreliability of the senses, but nevertheless committed to empirical study.

A small, but valiant, band of scholars has suggested that Democritus' writings might include a comprehensive, original anthropology.[26] The evidence for this is sparse, but there is enough to suggest this may have been the case. The fragments include several pages of causal explanations of the origins of civil society. The account is remarkably consistent with his atomism, more complex units building up from simpler. Certainly the process described is naturalistic, with no sharp break between explanations of human and other phenomena. The first task for humans was protection against attack by wild animals. Accordingly the first legal right to be recognized in civil society was the right to kill other animals. Agreement on what was right and wrong in this respect then became the basis for other legal rights. Forces for collectivity and competition constantly contended with each other. For human beings the task was to promote those supporting the collective solution of problems. Democritus was a strong believer in mutual aid: "When the powerful prevail upon themselves to lend to the indigent, and help them, and benefit them, herein at last is pity, and an end to isolation, and friendship, and mutual aid, and harmony among the citizens; and other blessings such as no one could enumerate."[27]

Democritus edvidently considered compassion a kind of human energy that could have long-lasting, structural, effects. Interestingly he related the revelation of technology to compassion as in the Prometheus myth. A number of fragments reveal an attempt to justify democratic measures while still allowing for experts to occupy high positions. Democritus' keenness for democracy and dislike of oligarchy cannot be mistaken: he would prefer poverty under democracy to prosperity under oligarchy, as freedom to slavery.

Democritus' political writings imply a social contract but, unlike Hobbes, it was between the people and their government, not among the people to a sovereign. "Custom law" or "*nomos*" in Democritus is not something contrary to nature. Rather there is an understanding of customs developing with usage, in response to nature, and then superimposed on nature. There is no inherent conflict between the two spheres. Nor is there any notion of permanent solutions. Democritus probed for answers but was content to leave much unresolved. There are no claims to have identified "justice" or "the good."

Whether or not Democritus was the source for the Hippocratics, Thucydides, and the sophists will likely never be known. His supporters have made a plausible case from the similarities – convention over divinely ordained arrangements, the concept of the precariousness of early human life as contrasted to the idealist idyllic past. For so many writers to have come to the same conclusion, they argue, suggests not only a common source but a highly respected one. Who more likely than Democritus? To explain how his ideas were lost, these authors suggest changing interests in philosophy and skullduggery. Socrates shifted the focus away from naturalistic explanations. Plato then took over certain *details* of Democritus' anthropology but not his perspective. There is regress instead of progress

and, where technological progress occurs, moral decline, adding an authoritarian twist to Democritus' naturalistic family. Interestingly, his name is
not mentioned in any of Plato's known writings. There is the story that Plato
as a young man had the urge to buy up all of Democritus' books and burn
them.[28] Aristotle continued the anti-Democritus propaganda and evolved his
own teleological approach. The flowering of Greek social science was brief
indeed.

Whatever Democritus may have suffered from his enemies he was not
well served by his friends. Epicurus took over many of his ideas, sometimes
distorting them. More to the point, Epicurus' interests were ethical rather
than scientific, and he adjusted theory accordingly. As well, tastes changed
so that ethics and politics became the chief concern of philosophy in the
next century after Democritus.

Epicurus (341–271 B.C.),[29] author of the final ancient formulation of
atomism, was "the most powerful and most radical opponent of idealism."[30]
As well, although the evidence is fragmentary, it seems that he made
noteworthy innovations in political theory. Society existed by convention,
not nature, and slavery offended the Epicureans' democratic sensibilities.
The Ionian interest in natural science was revived. Epicureanism was a
missionary philosophy, its namesake revered as the founder of a religion.
Adherents wore badges with Epicurus' image, put up statues of him in town
squares, and held communion-like meals in his honour. The sect itself was
remarkably successful as a minority movement. It lasted some seven centuries, spreading to Alexandria, Rome, and throughout the Roman Empire.
The philosophy was deliberately kept simple so that it could be widely
understood and practised.

Epicurus established his school in Athens in a garden near the Academy.
He wrote some 300 works, including systematic critiques of previous philosophers. He apparently did not lecture but held discussions with students
and gave advice. The school was open to slaves, including his own slave,
whom Epicurus freed in his will. Both respectable women and courtesans
could attend, which also displeased many people. Cicero faulted the school
because a woman philosopher, Leontion, had the effrontery to criticize a
male philosopher, Theophrastus.[31] Little of Epicurus' writing survived past
the third century A.D., but three major letters have, which include a summary of his philosophy of science. Lucretius' poem also provides a faithful
account of Epicurean philosophy.

It seems that life at the school was frugal. Bread and water, or wine
mixed with water, was the standard diet. Much has been made of Epicurus'
request to a friend to bring him some preserved cheese – so that he could
have a feast.[32] Epicurus indeed asserted pleasure to be the end of life, yet
not "the pleasures of profligates and those that consist in sensuality," but
"freedom from pain in the body and from trouble in the mind" (89). He

advocated the simple pleasures, believing that luxuries cause ever-increasing desire. Given that satisfaction can be attained either by greater supply or lesser demand, Epicurus favoured the latter. Epicureanism was never the philosophy of "eat, drink, and be merry."

Epicurus took on most of the elements of atomic theory of Leucippus and Democritus, although without acknowledging either. He used the theory differently, however, as a basis for ethics. Philosophy for him was a means to free human beings from their two greatest fears: death and the gods. Philosophy must provide explanations of human life and the wider world that would take away the terrors of both. Epicurus' philosophy sought to do just that and, if one can accept its central thesis, it succeeds admirably. Atomic theory provided the physical explanations needed. Human beings had material bodies and souls, both mortal. There was no place to go after death and no physical pain to fear, for death itself meant the end of sensation, painful or otherwise. Epicurus' gods were quite irrelevant to human life. They had nothing to do with creation and even lived apart in a sort of middle world. They, too, were material entities, composed of finer atoms than humans.

Epicurus' version differs from earlier atomic theory by rejecting the notion of necessity. Philosophy must provide a model for free, independent human action. Necessity was a constraint as objectionable as the fear of gods. It was perhaps even worse, for gods at least could be placated. His philosophy had to remove the barrier to the full enjoyment of life, and it had to do so right in its physics. Epicurus was nothing if not consistent in pursuing the logical consequences of his moral precepts. The individual atom symbolized the human individual and so must be endowed with the capacity for self-movement. It could not be merely the object of natural forces. He accordingly specified a new kind of motion, "declination," or deviation from straight-line fall. This side-ways movement of atoms resulted in collisions and the creation of compounds. The implications of this innovation are staggering: free, undetermined action becomes a necessary condition for the creation of the world. The principle also means a fundamental deviation from science. To what extent Epicurus was aware of what he was doing we cannot know. Certainly he raised one of the great problems of philosophy, and his solution to it, that freedom must involve violation of natural law, has long since remained. It was largely for this repudiation of necessity that the young doctoral student, Karl Heinrich Marx, found Epicurus attractive.

On the question of validity of knowledge, Epicurus' philosophy again respects his moral objectives. Philosophy must be a practical activity, open to the ordinary individual. Criteria for determining truth must accordingly be within the means of ordinary people, and here Epicurus was unswerving: *the* criterion for determining truth was sensation. Epicurus was thus the first person to make explicit the egalitarian potential of empiricism. The validity of sense data, moreover, could not be questioned, for what else was there against which sense perceptions could be checked?

If sensation was not the origin of knowledge it was the criterion for the confirmation, or not, of propositions. Epicurean sensation was the usual bombardment of particles. When not too close or too far away, a "clear image" of the object was produced, which was the proper object of scientific inquiry. One must *look*, and not merely *see*, for a clear image to be formed, suspending judgment until a clear image is achieved. Isolated sensations are meaningless, both for purposes of scientific study and practical life. The image must be compared with a "general concept," so that what it is can be determined, doubts raised, and the inquiry continued or not. Sensation was neither a simple nor a passive process.

Epicurus' treatment of cognition is intriguing. The act of perception stirs up neighbouring soul particles, setting up a chain reaction that eventually reaches the mind, which Epicurus located in the breast. The mind sponta- neously compares the new image with previous general concepts. This process is similar to that of the senses actively observing an object. Both sensation and thought imply active participation. A general concept is itself formed over time as series of images are processed. Dissimilarities disap- pear, leaving what is common to all as the "general concept."

Epicurus' differences with Plato and Aristotle were as great, and delib- erate, on political theory as they were on methodology. He was well aware of the disastrous effects of Plato's attempts at political advice-giving in Syracuse and Aristotle's in Assos. He found the noble-lie approach to political theory to be deeply offensive in actual practice: Athenian resettle- ments of cities was an early version of "pacification" in Vietnam. The price of the city-state – injustice – was too high. Epicurus saw no hope of political reform from above but instead chose to work to change people's attitudes and behaviour. People, if only they knew it, needed little to live on and peace of mind was available freely to all. Epicurus followed the sophists, Hippocratics, and Democritus on the origin of society and the gradual building up of social institutions. His notion of social contract was benign in the extreme, stressing voluntary relations and not law. Consequently he took the view that the least government was the best government, and here he may have influenced Locke.

Throughout most of western history Epicureanism has been the only philosophic school considered worse than scepticism. Epicurean revivals have been infrequent, half hearted, and short lived. The current one may be, too, but kinder things have been said about the Epicureans in recent decades than at any time since the school closed. At the extreme is the suggestion that Epicureanism served as a forerunner to Christianity. The parallels between the early church and the Epicurean groups are striking: egalitarian values, inclusion of women and slaves, attraction to the lower and middle classes, meeting in homes, and common meals. Paul's epistle, according to this interpretation, was directed to Epicureans, arguing that the Christian faith was a better answer to the human terror of death: Death, where is thy sting? Grave where is thy victory?[33]

Lucretius (c. 99–c. 55 B.C.)[34] is typically treated as a faithful, if unoriginal, preserver of Epicurean philosophy, to whom we must be grateful because of the loss of most of Epicurus' own work. The very excellence of Lucretius' poem *De Rerum Natura* worked against him; anyone who wrote that well, in verse no less, could hardly be a serious methodologist! More recent critics, however, have credited him with going beyond the ancients on evolution, biological and social. Certainly he was an accurate recorder of Epicurean physics and methodology. His style as well conveys a passion for science:

> To help you see the heart of hidden, murky things
> And so this darkened terror of the Mind must be dispelled.
> Not by the rays of sun or gleaming shafts of day.
> But Nature's laws, by looking in her face.[35]

Epicurus had "longed to be the first to crack the cramping bonds of nature." The voyages for discovery were:

> Like conqueror crowned in victory, the news of Nature's laws
> Of what could come to be and what could not
> The code that binds each thing, its deep-set boundary stone
> And so religion in its turn is trampled under foot and trodden down. (6)

On the differences between the materialist and idealist theories of knowledge:

> So mind can never be without the brain,
> No consciousness apart from blood and cells. (194)

Concerning early human life Lucretius followed the line of Democritus and the Hippocratics, adding grim detail. Primitive people lacked such fears as that the sun would not return – actually they were afraid of being eaten by other animals. "Ground by their teeth and gulped down ravenously," the piteous cries went unheard: "while living flesh was buried in a living tomb" (229). But Lucretius also noted the barbarousness of his own times, of war and murder. He recorded much progress in civilization and was aware also of reverses, including the vices of his own Rome. He described the early development of private property and legislation. He gave considerable space to the mastery of technological skills. As for civil society itself, it was only gradually that:

The human race learned gentler ways
Neighbour to neighbour pledged word.

People were eager to form friendships and refrain from mutual harm. Pity evolved; people learned to spare the weak. Concord was a lesson hard to learn but:

Most of mankind was loyal to its pledge
Else would the human race in earliest times have failed
Nor wealth of progeny sufficed destruction to avert. (230)

Lucretius' treatment of both gods and people was naturalistic. The gods were composed of atoms too fine for sensation and had no role in creation or judgment. People lived in nature without any rights over other creatures. To think that the will of a god or gods brought forth the glorious universe for the sake of human beings was "foolishness, my friend" (194–5).

Lucretius suffered the usual fate of dissidents: his reputation was smeared and his work ignored by respectable intellectuals. Cicero obviously knew *De Rerum Natura*, for he discussed it in correspondence, but he never mentioned Lucretius in a publication.[36] Almost nothing is known about Lucretius' life. He is supposed to have come to the bad end of atheists: he went mad at age forty-four and committed suicide.

De Rerum Natura was consigned to oblivion for over a thousand years. Since manuscript copies existed in medieval monasteries, the work was apparently ignored rather than lost. It was not until the fifteenth century that scholars took any interest in the poem. Lucretius was then revived as a poet rather than a methodologist. Montaigne used him. Bruno quoted him on the boundlessness of the universe, an idea that made sense again with the discoveries of the new world. As Rome had apparently had no bounds in the first century B.C., with global exploration the universe again seemed boundless. Hobbes drew on Lucretius for his modern atomism. The naturalist John Ray translated him.

MIND OVER MATTER TO EARLY IDEALISM

The word "philosophy," meaning "love of wisdom," may have been coined by *Pythagoras*, who probably also had something to do with the Pythagorean theorem. So little is known about his life and work that scholars often refer to "the Pythagoreans" rather than try to distinguish who in the school taught what.

Pythagorean religious doctrines are important for methodology, for the first time a mind/body distinction appears. The mind is still material but body takes a lower place.[37] The Pythagoreans did not reject materialism but now gave idealism a foot in the door. Now also for the first time idealist methodology was connected with conservative politics.[38]

Linguistic evidence also suggests the earlier origin of materialism. The very words for thought and soul have physical origins, soul from breath, and thought from sap or juice.[39] In Homer, deep reflection is conversation with oneself, and thinking is speaking. Perception implied a breathing in, and the organ of breath, the lungs, was identified with the organ of thought.

The Pythagoreans were more interested in religion and ethics than science. The school was, in effect, a religious sect with an elaborate hierarchy, strict secrecy rules, and initiation rites for disciples as they were admitted to ever more esoteric "knowledge." The soul now was divided into a higher, more spiritual, and a lower, more material, part. For the first time in western intellectual history the body became in some way inferior. In the Orphic religion the aim had been release from the body, not because it was evil but because life was a vale of tears. The soul yearned for freedom without necessarily opposing matter. Although women's status was declining, they were not yet identified with the body, men with mind. Women apparently could join the sect on the same basis as men, and a number did. Pythagoras' wife is known to have taught at the school.

The Pythagoreans' mathematical conceptualization of the world had the universe as a kind of musical scale with all parts in harmony. This was a notion that inspired scholars as far apart as Plato and Kepler. Numbers were real quantities in the Pythagorean system, although with mystical connotations. Pythagorean number theory complemented its politics. As all parts were in the cosmic harmony so was there order on earth – by the subordination of the inferior to the superior. Interaction in either case implied no balancing of forces, but acquiescence of the inferior. Justice consisted of giving each its due (the notion elaborated by Aristotle as distributive justice). Simple arithmetic equality was irrelevant.

Parmenides (c. 515–at least 450 B.C.) and the Eleatics took the Pythagorean promotion of the soul and demotion of the body – the mind/body dichotomy – a step further by adding for the first time in the West a parallel division between thought and the senses. The senses became identified with deception, thought with truth through revelation. Pythagorean religion was the source, but the formulation was now philosophical. Parmenides is also the source in the West for the identification of being and thinking. Parmenides gave his theory of knowledge a suitably dramatic introduction in an epic poem titled "Truth," which was supposed to be no less than the relevation of the Goddess of Truth herself. She distinguished between opinion, by the senses, and truth, by the mind. She forbade Parmenides to take the way of the undiscerning eye and echoing ear, but to learn from Reason. Truth was a revelation from Mind with no connection at all to sense data.

That something cannot be because the mind cannot conceive it was simply asserted: what intellect can think, exists; what it cannot think, does not exist. The mind cannot conceive Not-Being; therefore Not-Being does not exist. "It is the same thing to think and to be."[40] The world becomes an undifferentiated and never changing sphere. With nothing outside the world, the thinker and the object of thought are together within and, with no diversity within, are the same. Thus Parmenides has to his credit not only the creation of a dichotomy (between sense and thought) but a demolition (between the object of thought and the thinker).

Parmenides' conclusions have been attacked on ordinary empirical grounds: we do, in fact, see beginnings, changes, diversity, and endings. Failures in logic have also been argued. Then, if there is no differentiation within the sphere what can be wrong with sense perception? Surely the perceiver and the perceived must be one with the thinker and the object of thought. Nevertheless, Parmenides still has a respectable following. He has been lauded as the "founder of western rationalism."[41] He was the first philosopher to deal with such general concepts of being, knowing, unity, and identification. He is the first person known to have set out propositions unrelated to the real world as a basis for deriving further propositions. The "majority school" considers Parmenides the "deepest and sharpest" thinker of the pre-Platonic period. For the minority the Eleatics were "the beginning of an evil that has been spreading ever since ... and is today still menacing all genuine philosophy with suffocation."[42] Whether or not divine assistance aided Parmenides in writing his poem, it seems to have watched over the work's preservation – 161 lines, one of the best survival rates of antiquity.

Parmenides' work was carried on by his reputedly unoriginal, but zealous, pupil, *Zeno of Elea (c. 490 B.C.–?)*. Zeno wrote a book defending his teacher's theory mainly by attacking the opposition. The method was to take a hypothesis from an opponent and show its conclusions to be self-contradictory. This method of "antinomies" won him Aristotle's recognition as the "founder of dialectics." Thus Zeno "proved" an arrow apparently moving through space was not really moving, for an object cannot be in more than one place at a time, and any object in one place cannot be in another. Zeno was reputedly proficient in politics and, like the Pythagoreans and later idealists, in maintaining the favour of the landed aristocracy. He came to a terrible death in a plot to overthrow the democratic, or non-aristocratic, government. He was tortured to death for refusing to name his fellow conspirators.

MEDICINE AND THE SOCIAL SCIENCES

The Greeks were the first western people to try to ascertain the causes of disease in wholly naturalistic terms. They early began to observe and record the course of the patient's condition as treatments were applied. In so doing they developed notions of cause and effect that were to become the common understanding of empiricism. Some scientific work in medicine is evident from the sixth century B.C., in Alcmaeon and the Pythagoreans. By the next century there were rival schools of medicine, of which the Hippocratic is the most important for the development of methodology in the social sciences.

With *Alcmaeon (c. 540 B.C.–?)*[43] we see the close connection between empirical medicine – he has been called the first medical scientist – and scientific method. Alcmaeon is believed to have written the first book on natural science; its surviving fragments reveal interesting observations and suggestions. He probably did the first research on sense perception, including the first excision of the eye. He correctly identified the brain as the "seat of sensation" and the "governing faculty," a point lost on many later writers. He described the paths to the brain of the various senses. All animals had the faculty of perception, but only humans could relate sensations to each other and form a whole. Objective knowledge, however, was beyond our capacity; only conjecture was possible. Alcmaeon recognized strict limits to human capabilities, then, but always insisted that what knowledge we did acquire came through the senses. In these fundamental points he gave direction to the whole materialist movement and the empiricism that drew from it.

Alcmaeon was the most distinguished member of the earliest medical school, in Croton, south Italy, about half a century before Hippocrates. He described a theory of opposites in some respects like the Pythagorean, but applied to the human organism. There were bitter-sweet, wet-dry, hot-cold, and so forth. Health was the "equality of rights" of these functions, and disease the "single rule" (monarchy) of one half of any pair. Here again is the borrowing of terms *from* the political/social *to* the medical/natural science. Good health required a proper balance between the two opposites. Sickness indicated imbalance, which it was the physician's function to rectify. This interest in opposites, or contradictions, recurs throughout the ancient period. It is certainly a theme in idealist philosophy, but Alcmaeon shows that it had practical uses as well. He also admitted environmental factors and injury as causes of illness.

Little is known about *Hippocrates (c. 460–? B.C.)* and it is not clear which Hippocratic writings are his and which were written by his colleagues or pupils. Hippocrates founded one of the first medical schools, on Cos, an island off the north coast of Greece. He practised for many years in Abdera, probably knew Democritus, and may have been his student. A naturalistic understanding of causation is probably the Hippocratics' greatest contribution to methodology. The notion of cause was slow to develop in Greek thought – the word itself originally meant responsibility or blame. With the

Hippocratics a naturalistic connotation gradually emerged. Their paper on public health, for example, declared that "each disease has a natural cause, and nothing happens without a natural cause."[44] The cause of diseases lies in certain substances, which when present always produce the same result. Similarly, every cure has its cause, although it might be difficult to ascertain exactly what that is. The majority of plants and preparations contain substances with remedial properties, so that cures after use should not be credited to chance. What seems to be chance is the operation of some not yet understood substance (84).

The Hippocratics' understanding of the influence of climate on temperament was explained in "Airs, Waters and Places." A variable climate produces a "fierce, hot-headed and discordant" temperament, while "quietness and calm" dull the wits (109). As a rule the constitution and habits of a people follow the nature of the land where they live: weather, terrain, and water supply. The Hippocratics' causal relations more often went from the physical to the social and psychological, at least in surviving works, but the process could go either way. Europeans were not subjected to monarchy as Asians were, while people ruled by princes were the most cowardly: "Those who govern themselves will willingly take risks because they do it for themselves. They are eager and willing to face even the worst of fates when theirs are the rewards of victory. It is clear, then, that the tradition of rule has no small influence on the courage of a people" (109). Natural and social causes were mixed together. (Hippocrates is considered to have been the source for Thucydides' similar treatment of cause.) Confidence in natural causes extended even to epilepsy, for which there was then no cure and little understanding. Each disease had its own nature and power, and none was irremediable. Most were curable by the same means which had produced them.

"Ancient Medicine" (or "Tradition in Medicine") includes one of the first clear statements of empirical methodology. Observation is stressed, with confidence that systematic knowledge can be drawn from it. The laws of human physiology are special forms of universal laws.[45] To know how humans function one must know the nature of the world. Nevertheless, medicine can and should proceed without waiting for the riddle of the whole universe to be solved. There was no expectation of certain knowledge. "Medicine has for long possessed the qualities necessary to make a science. These are original observations and a known method according to which many valuable discoveries have been made over a long period of time. By such a method, too, the rest of the science will be discovered if anyone who is clever enough is versed in the observations of the past, and makes these the starting point of his researches."[46]

After asserting the impossibility of making discoveries any other way, the book's tone again becomes more humble. This appears in a discussion on diet, a prime concern of Hippocratic medicine: "One aims at some criterion as to what constitutes a correct diet, but there is no standard by reference to which accuracy may be achieved; physical sensation is the only guide. Thus exactness is difficult to achieve and small errors are bound to occur. I warmly commend the physician who makes small mistakes; infallibility is rarely to be seen" (17). The science of medicine was not to be rejected because of mistakes. Even if not accurate in every respect, medicine should command respect; it was approaching infallibility where before there had been great ignorance. "Good and true investigation" was responsible for the discoveries that had been made, and not "chance happenings" (19). Practical limitations were noted. A science could not perform what was outside its province, or nature accomplish "unnatural things" (85). Consequently, the physician should not attempt impossible cures.

The Hippocratic view of human life was evolutionary and optimistic. Life in earlier times had been tougher; there was no Platonic golden past. Rather sickness, pain, and violent death were the common lot of primitive people. Thanks to the development of scientific medicine and other social institutions, improvements had been made. At the same time there was an underlying assumption of constancy. Human nature was relatively stable and uniform, changing in response to external stimuli. This made prediction in the social sciences possible – if the same conditions held, the same results would appear. This is precisely the approach taken up by Thucydides and the sophists, and the Hippocratics were a main source for them.

A trend to theory and isolation from practice was apparently already a problem when "Tradition in Medicine" was written, for it deplores philosophical intrusions. The denigration of manual work of a slave society meant that physicians did not know anatomy; they learned from books and did not dirty themselves with dissections.

THE SOPHISTS

The sophists have suffered so many centuries of derision that it is even now difficult to approach them without bias. The word "sophist" comes from the root for wisdom, but "sophistry" has come to imply deception or specious argument. So little sophist writing has survived that they are known largely through hostile secondary sources. Plato, using Socrates as his speaker, led the attack, making the sophists out to be mistaken in their methodology and dishonest. More courteous and moderate, Aristotle nonetheless continued this negative portrayal. More favourable opinions began to appear only in the nineteenth century.[47] The trend continued, and by the 1930s the sophists were being praised as champions of progress and enlightenment.[48] Popper ranked them with the "Great Generation" that made a "turning point in the history of mankind."[49] Compare this with Plato's slurs:

"consciously insincere ... mere opinions ... illusionism ... verbally portentous."[50]

There was never a sophist school as such and teachings ranged widely in subject and opinion. The sophists all taught for a fee, normally rhetoric plus some other specialty such as natural science, mathematics, poetry, or music. All but Gorgias also claimed to teach political "excellence," the subject at dispute between the sophists and the idealists. The idealists maintained that the necessary skills and attitudes for government could not be taught – at least not in the normal way – to average citizens. The implication was that the prerequisites of governing could only be had by birth. Note that Plato's education for the guardian class in *The Republic* featured a rigid segregation of potential rulers, and ultimately eugenic selection. The sophists sided with greater participation. Their pupils were the sons of the rising mercantile class, keen to take part in Assembly debates and hoping to become political leaders. The sophist/idealist conflict was thus at the same time a democratic/oligarchic split. (Democracy excluded women and slaves, but for some time in Athens all free men had significant political rights.)

The sophists taught phenomenalism – that the world is what it appears to be. There is no underlying reality. Here they went beyond Democritus and Anaxagoras, who accepted some kind of real structure under appearances. Concepts such as justice and beauty the sophists held to have no existence outside the human mind. Protagoras' famous statement that we humans are "the measure of all things" is a declaration that the world is no more and no less than what we perceive it to be. For idealists, the trouble was that this led to rampant relativism and scepticism. Knowledge was reduced to mere opinion differing according to perception. Moral relativism was worse, yet there could be no ethical absolutes for there were no absolutes of any kind. In both respects the sophists were continuing trends begun by Ionian scientists. Democritus' methodology was already strongly sceptical and the Ionians already had a reputation for atheism and agnosticism. The leading sophist, Protagoras, openly proclaimed his agnosticism and another major figure, Prodicus, was a known atheist.

Sophist teaching encouraged scepticism. Rhetoric was an important subject, with training in arguing both sides of an issue. Protagoras and Gorgias have been called sceptical to the point of being unhelpful to science. It does not seem, though, that the sophists were anti-science in any deliberate way. A number of them studied natural philosophy, and some taught it. Gorgias, for example, was a pupil of Empedocles, and Protagoras is thought to have studied with Democritus. None of the sophists made any scientific discoveries, although one is credited with a mathematical discovery. Their scientific writings were apparently no more than handbooks, compilations of available knowledge. They used naturalistic explanations for social phenomena, evidently seeing no abrupt break between the formation of the natural world and the human. Continuities between humans and animals were stressed as they had been by earlier materialists and would be by later empiricists. The sophists were believers in evolution, in the sense of favourable progress, again in line with the materialists and in contrast with the idealists. I would note, however, that similarities between the natural and social worlds should not be taken to mean necessarily an influence of natural on social science, and that earlier periods saw instances of the reverse and reciprocal influences.

The great dichotomy for the sophists was not between the physical world (or natural science) and human world (or social science) but between *nature* and *convention* (*physis* and *nomos*). The sophists were consistent believers in social institutions, including statute law, as arrangements *chosen* by people at a particular point in time. This brought them into conflict with the idealists, who viewed basic social institutions, especially law, as belonging to a higher, eternal order. Thus for the sophists there was nothing immoral in arguing against any particular law, for it was only a convention that suited at some time, but which could be changed. A social compact approach to law was at least implicit – if laws do not come from nature or the gods where else? "The edicts of the laws are arrived at by consent, not by natural growth, whereas those of nature are not a matter of consent."[51] As Solon called slavery unjust but legal, so could the sophists criticize existing laws as unjust or not in the best interests of the citizenry. Ultimately no law could be held to be universally binding, for every individual was the judge of right and wrong. Again sophism led to moral relativism.

This conceptualization of law made radical criticism of existing laws possible, although it seems this rarely happened. The few liberal statements are worth noting, however, for it was to be a long time before we see them again. It was the sophists who developed a notion of community across the whole human race, high and low born, Greek and barbarian:

Alcidamus (a pupil of Gorgias): God has sent forth all men as free, nature has not made any man a slave.
Philemon: By nature no one was ever born a slave.
Antiphon: By nature we are all alike, Greeks and barbarians, for we all breathe the same air.[52]

Idealists of the same time, and later, justified slavery as being grounded in nature. Yet there was no necessary liberalism in sophism. It could be used, and was, to argue for repression.

Protagoras (c. 481–c. 411 B.C.), the only sophist Plato treated with respect, was by reputation an honourable person, a competent scholar and teacher. One of the few methodologists of working-class origins, he is known to have worked as a porter. Protagoras was born in Abdera, Thrace, where he probably studied with Democritus. For some forty years he taught "political excellence," charging high fees and making a small fortune, although pupils did not have to pay if they are not satisfied. He visited Athens for extended periods but was refused citizenship. A good friend of Pericles, Protagoras was probably a major source for the principles of Athenian democracy. He is known to have written a number of books; fragments remain from three. At least one of his books was publicly burned.

Protagoras is most known for his unqualified relativism/subjectivism: "Of all things the measure is human, of the things that are, that they are, and of the things that are not, that they are not."[53] His agnosticism appears in one surviving fragment: "About the gods, I am not able to know whether they exist or do not exist, nor what they are like in form; for the factors preventing knowledge are many: the obscurity of the subject, and the shortness of human life" (126). Authorities differ as to how this should be taken. Protagoras presumably at least meant that everyone was the judge of his or her own sensations. If he meant that there was no such thing as a falsehood, then there could be no universal truths. Science could only be opinion and knowledge only sensation. There would be no way of choosing between opinions for all sensations would be equally true. Alternatively, Protagoras could have meant that perceptions are inherent in matter and differences in perception result from seizing on different aspects. This would mean that there was no reality *behind* appearances.

Protagoras' teaching apparently featured arguing both sides of a case. Yet, while there were no absolute truths in sophism, some sensations were better than others. One could argue for a certain course of action, not because it was true, but because it would likely lead to better results. As a doctor would urge a patient to follow a certain treatment, so a sophist could urge a city to adopt a certain policy. Protagoras' only claim as a teacher was that he could help others to do a little better. Everyone taught political virtue: parents, nurse, teacher, and the state. Some did so better than others.

Plato's dialogue, *Protagoras*, contains a quintessentially sophist explanation of the origins of political virtue. Protagoras was made to give his account in the form of a myth, not because he believed such things, but because it made a good story. Human beings were said to have missed out accidentally on all the protective devices given nonrational creatures: fangs, claws, hooves, and so forth. When this was realized they were given technical skills and fire as substitutes. This enabled them to make houses, clothes, and shoes, but not to run a city.

Thus equipped, men lived at the beginning in scattered units, and there were no cities; so they began to be destroyed by the wild beasts, since they were altogether weaker. Their practical crafts were sufficient to provide food, but insufficient for fighting against the beasts – for they did not yet possess the art of running a city, of which the art of warfare is part – and so they sought to come together and save themselves by founding cities. Now when they came together, they treated each other with injustice, not possessing the art of running a city, so they scattered and began to be destroyed once again. So Zeus, fearing that our race would be wholly wiped out, sent Hermes bringing conscience and justice to mankind, to be the principles of organization of cities and the bonds of friendship.[54]

Asked if those gifts should be distributed unequally, as specialized skills, Zeus said no: "Let all share in them; for cities could not come into being, if only a few shared in them as in the other crafts" (15). Athenians will listen only to carpenters on carpentry but for running a city will accept advice from anyone, "for all must share in that sort of excellence, or else there can be no city at all" (15). Note the parallels with Democritus' sociology – protection against wild animals was the first motive for organizing a community, and the skills of political organization were only slowly and painfully learned.

"HISTORIANS" AND SOCIAL SCIENCE

Herodotus (c. 490/484–429/425 B.C.),[55] a contemporary of Protagoras who was acquainted with Ionian science, begins our account of single-event social science. Life on the margins between East and West, it seems, prompted him to ask questions not posed before. The subject matter was the Persian Wars, his methodology the first attempt to account for an important event in terms of general explanations. Earlier compilations of chronicles are known but Herodotus was the first to have gone beyond the preservation of records to active data collection and interpretation.[56] The demarcation of this early social science from still earlier myths, poems, epics, and prophecies is always a difficult matter, but by Herodotus, and even more so with Thucydides, there is ordinary human consciousness. (Note that the demarcation between history and myth is not identical with that between poetry and prose. Chadwick in *Poetry and Prophecy* has persuasively shown how much objective, scientific content there can be in verse, which we have already seen with Lucretius.)

The influence of Homer on Herodotus and the other early historians was strong. Like the epics, Herodotus' histories were composed to be recited and were only later written down. Echoing Homer, Herodotus used hypothetical speeches to convey motives. To him, the individual was the driving force of history, private motives stronger than public ones. Facts on the wars were hard to come by, but Herodotus was assiduous in pursuing those he could. Tradition has it that he crossed the eastern Mediterranean to check a single point. Working roughly a generation after the war, he used what few written documents there were but relied far more on interviews, of eye witnesses where possible. Herodotus was fair in his reporting, mentioning desirable traits and customs of the Persians as well as of the Greeks. The work was well organized, in nine parts each with its own theme. Book Two, for example, sets out the geographic background and make up of both Greece and Persia. As did the Hippocratics, Herodotus considered that climate, soil, and diet influenced customs and laws.

Thucydides (c. 460–c. 400 B.C.)[57] attempted to apply Hippocrates' healing methods to the study of social life. He had the faith of a scientist, it was said, because he was inspired by contact with positive science. He has also been called a sociologist. From a wealthy family, well educated and travelled, Thucydides was about thirty when the Peloponnesian Wars began. He was given the command of a fleet in Thrace but failed to prevent the capture of the town Amphipolis. Exiled in disgrace, he spent the rest of the war as an observer and recorder. The history was never completed.

The Peloponnesian Wars is an exciting book to read even now. While Herodotus' histories seem antiquarian, *The Peloponnesian Wars* does not. Thucydides continued to use hypothetical speeches, forty in all, to provide motives. Yet there is much straight, factual, description. His dispassionate account of the plague is still praised for its careful attention to detail (Thucydides contracted the disease). The Hippocratic influence is obvious in his descriptions. Like Hippocrates, Thucydides moved easily between natural and social science material. Explanations were naturalistic throughout, not exceeding available information. Written/recited in the third person, Thucydides began with his own motives: "Thucydides, an Athenian, wrote the history of the war in which the Peloponnesians and the Athenians fought against one another. He began to write when they first took up arms, believing that it would be great and memorable above any previous war."[58] Both sides were at the full height of their military power, and the rest of the Greeks took sides with one or other side. No movement ever stirred Hellas more deeply, nor was shared by so many of the barbarians, and the war might be said to have affected the world at large. Thucydides cautioned against accepting other accounts, for people took little trouble in the search after truth, accepting what first came to hand (1:14). One must not rely, he maintained, on the exaggerated fancies of the poets or the tales of the chroniclers who sought to please the ear rather than to speak the truth, as it was impossible to test their accounts.

Thucydides' aim was thorough and objective knowledge. He did not venture to speak from "any chance information, nor according to any notions of my own; I have described nothing but what I either saw myself, or learned from others of whom I made the most careful and particular enquiry. The task was a laborious one, because eye-witnesses of the same occurrences gave different accounts of them, as they remembered or were interested in the actions of one side or the other." Thucydides was proud of his achievement. "My history is an everlasting possession, not a prize composition which is heard and forgotten" (1:15). He consulted written documents when they were available but relied largely on the observations of participants. His research standards were high, differing from present standards only in a failure to note sources in the text itself. Here, remember, the work was composed for recitation.

Thucydides gave reasons for his use of hypothetical speeches. It was hard for him to recollect exactly what had been said, some of which he only heard second hand. He therefore put into the mouth of each speaker the sentiments proper to the occasion, expressed as the person would likely have expressed them (1:14). At the least Thucydides tried to give the general purport of what had actually been said. The most famous example is Pericles' funeral speech, one of the greatest of all defences of free institutions. Before praising the dead Pericles would point out the institutions and manner of life that had made Athens great. Athenian practices were not copied from their neighbours but were an example to them. It was true that Athens was called a democracy, "for the administration is in the hands of the many and not of the few. But while the law secures equal justice to all alike in their private disputes, the claim of excellence is also recognised" (1:117). Distinguished citizens were rewarded for their merits and given preference in the public service. Poverty was not a bar to public life. There were games and sacrifices for relaxation. Athenians enjoyed the goods of other countries through trade; the city was open to foreigners. "We rely not upon management or trickery, but upon our own hearts and hands. And in the matter of education, whereas they from early youth are always undergoing laborious exercises which are to make them brave, we live at ease, and yet are equally ready to face the perils they face" (1:118). Thucydides/ Pericles thus made a virtue of the easy life of Athens compared with the rigours of Sparta: "If we prefer to meet danger with a light heart but without laborious training, and with a courage gained by habit and not enforced by law, are we not the gainers?" (1:119). This was not idle rhetoric, Thucydides believed that it was *because* of her free institutions that Athens had been able to beat a militarily stronger state.

Thucydides' causal analysis was based on the same understanding of nature as the analyses of the Hippocratics and sophists. Human nature was relatively stable and uniform, responding predictably to outside influences. For Athens the outside influence was the shock of the Persian Wars, which gave impulse to imperial expansion. Explanations were offered suggestively, not dogmatically. Where the gods appear they do not replace human motives. Oracles have their effect through people, and chance is cited only for what lies beyond our capacity for knowledge. The crucial causal agents lie in social institutions, unwise policies, and natural conditions like climate, soil, and plague. Causal analysis required going below the surface to underlying conditions, not just to the precipitating factors. When Thucydides was not sure he knew the cause, for example, of an eclipse, he was content to describe the facts. Although he could not account for the cause of the plague, he could describe its clinical and psychological effects. Thucydides' originality lies in his bringing all human action within the realm of natural causes. Both social and physical factors are included, each with its own mode of functioning.

Thucydides described the social institutions that shaped the attitudes of Athenians and Peloponnesians. The Peloponnesians cultivated their own soil and had no public or private wealth. But "wars are supported out of accumulated wealth, and not out of forced contributions" (1:90). People with property at stake are more ready to serve. In a single pitched battle, the Peloponnesians would be a match for all Hellas, but they were not able to maintain war against a power quite different from their own. Factors leading to the defection of Sparta's allies are described, as are those contributing to the success of Athens.

Explanations, Thucydides believed, could be at the level of individual motive or collective trend. Society was no organism, but the individual was the unit, and the relation of the individual to society was problematic. This is especially clear in another speech on another enduring theme, punishment and deterrence, in which the speaker pointed out the futility of severe punishment, specifically the failure of the death penalty to deter. He argued that punishments had become increasingly severe in the hope of achieving security from evil doers. In earlier times punishments had been milder. Now they were seldom short of death: "And still there are transgressors. Some greater terror then has yet to be discovered; certainly death deters nobody" (1:198). Poverty inspired people to daring while wealth engendered avarice. Mistaken reliance on the death penalty would drive the rebellious to despair; milder treatment would cause them to capitulate when they saw the weakness of their revolt.

Finally, Thucydides linked the past to the future. Knowledge of the past would help predict the future. He would be satisfied if his writing aided those who sought a "true picture" of events that had happened and might in the order of human things be expected to happen in the future (1:15). Thucydides, sadly, was not to be satisfied. Important as his contribution to methodology is now recognized to be, it was not acknowledged by the generations that succeeded him. Plato rejected naturalistic explanations for *a priori* conceptions. In place of interviews with observers there would be abstract essences. Even Aristotle, who wrote on the constitution of Athens, did not once refer to Thucydides. It was to be centuries before anyone of the same calibre appeared.

That person, *Polybius (c. 200–118 B.C.)*, was the first writer known to have attempted a history of the entire known world. His subject was Rome, specifically how it had gained supremacy over the entire "civilized" world, making it into "one regular and consistent body."[59] Critics have noted that a universal history could not have been written before the Roman Empire, for the world was simply not enough of an entity for the project to have occurred to anyone. Polybius himself was apparently acutely conscious of being a pioneer.[60] He is also the first person to have used the term "history" in a specialized sense, not just "an inquiry."[61]

Polybius' view of the human condition was essentially pessimistic. Thus, while a great admirer of Rome, he did not consider that it would be eternal. His *General History*, published after his death, is largely contemporary history, covering the period 220–144 B.C., including events in which Polybius himself participated. Five of his forty books survive, about one third of the total work. Critics tend to thank him for aiming at the right goals even if his expression was not inspired. Polybius followed Thucydides in considering direct experience to be the best teacher. Contemporary history was thus the only true history; at the very least one had to be close enough to the events to consult actual participants. All knowledge derived from hearing and sight, with sight being the "more conformable" to the truth. For military history, it followed, the best writers would be experienced generals, for they had the most direct knowledge of the events.[62] Travel was indispensable for history writing; one had to see for oneself. Accurate geographical knowledge was also essential. In all these respects Polybius took the same position as Thucydides. As was his predecessor, he was impressed by the success of the sciences of his day, which were enjoying their last spurt before the Middle Ages. He made conscious analogies with medicine. Like most natural scientists he used chance to explain the imponderable, irrational, and uncontrollable. At the same time he argued against attributing to fortune what was really human.

Polybius' concern throughout was telling the truth. Historians should give a bare relation of such facts and discourses as really happened. Historians, unlike writers of tragedy, were to report only what was actually said, no matter how commonplace. (Polybius was here presumably reproaching Thucydides for his hypothetical speeches). Minor errors were excusable, especially in an extensive work, but deliberate distortion was never acceptable. The importance of speaking the truth became clear at the stage of application, for Polybius, at least as much as Thucydides, believed that one could learn from the past. "History professes to give lessons of improvement even to future times" (1:163). Polybius' preference for universal history flows from this concern for the truth and the possibility of practical application. Because specialized studies failed to put things into adequate context and thus obscured real causes and effects, they were of antiquarian interest only. Polybius conceded, however, that if such studies truthfully related the facts, then they, too, deserved to be called history. The truth was the principal and essential part.

Causal knowledge for application was the historian's aim. One must first consider what happened, then the motives, the means, and whether or not the goals were fulfilled. Otherwise history is "mere amusement," not capable of yielding sound instruction or being of lasting service (1:213). "For unless we have made due reflection upon the conduct of men in former times, how shall we learn the arts of gaining allies and friends, when any danger threatens our country?" (1:212). Polybius, however, was a voice crying in the wilderness. Not for another 200 years, with Tacitus, would there be any identifiable social science writing. The next real improvements in methodology were not to come until the seventeenth century.

Tacitus (56/57–c. 118 A.D.)[63] wrote the usual Roman chronicles but two of his works stand out as recognizable social science. "Germany" and parts of *Agricola* treat the social institutions of different peoples in a comparative fashion. Tacitus was interested in *why* German and British institutions were different from Roman ones. He showed no interest in methodology as such, but at least knew good standards of research. Although he was unsystematic with sources, historians generally consider him better than his contemporaries.

As are so much modern sociology, anthropology, and history, "Germany" is a study of subject peoples by a member of the conquering state, written for citizens of the conquering power. It provides detailed information on German geography, everyday life, religion, marriage, the family, political and economic organization, and the military. Regional/tribal differences are noted. The book has been much quoted for its portrayal of women, for Tacitus was much impressed with the fierceness and high status of German women. Nowhere did he explain precisely how he collected his data, but the book ends with a methodological note. Tacitus had to dismiss some "fabulous" stories: "Reports of this kind, unsupported by proof, I shall leave to the pen of others."[64]

Agricola was largely a flattering account of his father-in-law's life and exploits, focusing on his rule of Britain. Tacitus provided background information on the strange people of the province, its geography, soil, mines, and climate – "unfavourable; always damp with rains, and overcast with clouds" (7:97). He described the system of government, military organization, and the ordinary life of the people, including women. He noted that women could accede to the throne and command armies, and that it was only by luck that the Romans had managed to reconquer Britain after Queen Boadicea's rebellion. Again Tacitus reveals nothing of his research methods, but he did distinguish his work from rhetoric: "Antecedent writers adorned conjecture with all the graces of language: what I have to offer will have nothing but the plain truth to recommend it" (7:92).

Tacitus has been much appreciated for his values. He believed that even the most ruthless tyrant could not suppress free speech. Events have causes, ultimately human, so that in the last resort people give history its shape.

His outlook on life, like Polybius', was gloomy. Yet Tacitus was never sceptical about the potential of the human spirit. He continued to believe that ordinary people, whoever their rulers, could be good. The claims he made for the beneficience of Roman rule were clearly exaggerated, and the eulogizing of his father-in-law is sometimes excessive. Nevertheless *Agricola* is far superior, in my opinion, to other social writings of the period and "Germany" is even more so. Indeed they both surpass any work of the Middle Ages and Renaissance until Machiavelli.

MATURE IDEALISM

Who was Socrates? A Christ-like martyr for knowledge, the brains behind the anti-democratic oligarchy in Athens, the founder of idealism, scepticism, induction, the scientific method, any or all of these? Admittedly, it is unusually difficult to assess *Socrates (c. 469–399 B.C.)*.[65] He left no written work and the main sources from his time are unreliable in major respects. If the claims of certain recent biographies that Socrates was a member of a secret politico-religious society are correct, the complications only become worse. To Crossman, the tragedy of Socrates' execution was that it was justified. Considering results rather than motives, Socrates' teachings were disastrous. They inspired no moral revival but a counter-revolution by a "ruthless and cynical gang of wealthy adventurers."[66] Crossman went on to surmise that Socrates must have realized his failure – and that is why he drank the hemlock rather than escaping. At the other extreme, Popper portrays Socrates as a friend of democracy, supporting it in the best way possible by criticizing it. To Popper, Socrates was perhaps the "greatest of the Great Generation," for his faith in human reason and wariness of dogmatism.[67]

Socrates earned his place in methodological history by forming a theory of knowledge out of the Pythagorean/Parmenidean concept of the soul. The Pythagoreans had promoted the soul from its earlier semi-existence to a position of independence and honour. But if they gave it a desire to be free, they left it entombed in the body. Socrates now brought it out into the light of day, if you will. The soul became the seat of normal, waking intelligence and moral character. In the "Phaedo" Socrates asked if the body was not a hindrance to the acquisition of knowledge. Have sight and hearing any truth in them? Are they not always inaccurate witnesses?

"Then when does the soul attain truth? – for in attempting to consider anything in company with the body she is obviously deceived."
    "True."
    "Then must not true existence be revealed to her in thought, if at all? And thought is best when the mind is gathered into herself and none of these things trouble her

– neither sounds nor sights nor pain nor any pleasure, – when she takes leave of the body, and has as little as possible to do with it, when she has no bodily sense or desire, but is aspiring after true being?"[68]

The questioner asked if there was absolute justice, beauty, or good. The answer was yes, but these are never reached by the senses. Isn't the nearest approach to knowledge made "by him who orders his intellectual vision as to have the most exact conception of the essence of each thing which he considers?" Some of us may have difficulty making our intellects comply with instructions, but Socrates apparently did not consider this a problem. "He attains to the purest knowledge of them who goes to each with the mind alone … he who has got rid, as far as he can, of eyes and ears and, so to speak, of the whole body, these being in his opinion distracting elements which when they infect the soul hinder her from acquiring truth and knowledge" (2:204–5). The body is a source of endless trouble, requiring food, liable to disease, and filling us with lust, fear, and foolishness. It takes away the power of thinking, causing turmoil and confusion, and preventing us from seeing the truth.

Since the soul cannot, while in the body, have pure knowledge, either knowledge is not to be had at all or can be had only on death. Clearly it is only after death that the soul is unencumbered by the body and thus able to learn. According to the "Meno," the immortal soul, having been born many times and having seen all things, knew and could remember them all. The soul could with effort elicit everything in a single recollection (2:40). Consistent with this, Socrates claimed only to be a mid-wife, assisting in the birth. (His mother was a mid-wife.) He made much use of the Pythagorean body-as-prison image. Until philosophy received the soul, he explained in the "Phaedo," "she could only view real existence through the bars of a prison, not in and through herself; she was wallowing in the mire of every sort of ignorance, and by reason of lust had become the principal accomplice in her own captivity" (2:226). The moral superiority of the intellectual life, which continues as a theme in Platonic writings informing the whole idealist tradition, was not to be challenged seriously until the Reformation.

The learning-is-recollection doctrine was demonstrated in an encounter with a slave boy. The boy had not been taught any mathematics, but Socrates nonetheless elicited a series of correct answers from him. Socrates concluded that the boy must have possessed mathematical knowledge in a previous existence since he could not have acquired it by normal experience.

Socrates' most original contribution to methodology was his teleology: a thing was explained by what it was meant to be. He knew the empiricist alternative through Anaxagoras, but found it unsatisfying. The teleological bent Socrates gave to idealism remained important until Descartes. Even then it did not disappear, but stayed on as a minority movement and re-emerged in evolution theory. Plato's dialogues show Socrates to have been interested mainly in such questions as "What is justice?" or "What is beauty or goodness?" His aim was to achieve some absolute definition of such concepts, which to him constituted knowledge. This task interests some methodologists as an early example of induction, for Socrates' method was to examine particular instances of justice, goodness, or whatever, compare examples, and arrive at the "true essence" of the thing. Socrates may not have been the first person to use induction but he was the first to recognize its importance.[69]

The method of argument was to advance an initial hypothesis, then to ask what must logically follow. In the typical dialogue Socrates had his opponent advance the hypothesis. He then posed the questions, forcing his opponent to admit contradictory statements. Since two contradictory statements could not be true, the initial hypothesis would have to be abandoned. To anyone not devoted to the Platonic tradition, the dialogues are full of non-sequiturs, shifting definitions, and clever semantic tricks. Admirers of Socrates insist that he never asserted that the hypothesis under examination was self-evident or true. But the dialogues do show him discussing hypotheses with great confidence. There is no notion of verification in the sense of testing propositions against physical reality. Nor could there be, given his suspicions about the usefulness of sense data.

The theory of ideas can be seen as a bold attempt to answer Heraclitus' dilemma: how can we know anything when everything is in flux? One cannot know sensible objects for they are incessantly changing, but one could know the eternal, changeless forms. It seems that Socrates did not try to explain how forms were related to sensible objects, but rather was concerned with the forms of abstract ideas like justice. Plato and Aristotle, however, did develop answers to this question, and it is to them we must turn for a mature statement of the theory of ideas.

Plato (427–347 B.C.)[70] looms in the history of methodology as a powerful, usually revered giant. The problem tends to be what about him was greatest: his genius, dramatic gifts, anticipations of modern science, or his pioneering efforts at social science. "To few men," said Taylor, "does the world owe a heavier debt than to Plato," who taught that philosophy, the "loving, single-minded devotion to truth" was "the great gift of God" and "rightful guide" of human life.[71] Or, according to Jowett, "He was the greatest metaphysical genius whom the world has seen; and in him, more than in any other ancient thinker, the germs of future knowledge are contained."[72] This is so much the standard view that alternatives, like Crossman's, that Plato was above all a failed politician, shock for their irreverence.

Even Plato's enemies have deferred to his accomplishments. Popper, who called him the originator of political propaganda, conceded he was one of the first social scientists, and described his sociology as "an ingenius blend of speculation with acute observation of facts."[73] His most severe critic, Winspear, who did not even think him a good observer, still praised his artistic and poetic gifts.[74] Harold Innis credited Plato with saving the remnants of the oral tradition in the dialogues.[75] His mixture of the oral and written traditions enabled him to dominate the history of the West. The account here, which draws heavily on Winspear, Popper, and Crossman, will be negative both on Plato's idealism and his substantive sociology.

The founding of the Academy, around 371 B.C., marks the turning point of Plato's career. After his own education, years of travel, and early writing Plato returned to Athens to devote the next twenty years of his life to running his school. He left it with a formidable reputation as an educational institution, administratively sound, and in good financial shape. It is not known if he lectured, except for one famous lecture on "the good," recorded by several students including Aristotle. The Academy seems to have been Plato's third attempt at his prime object in life, political influence. Having given up on a political career for himself at Socrates' death, and having failed to become the *éminence grise* to the tyrant of Syracuse, Plato turned to training young men for political office. (Women could be students at the Academy but could not attain office or vote.) The Academy was the first non-medical institution of higher learning in Greece. Mathematics featured in the curriculum as a subject suitable for training the mind. Natural science was not taught at all, or very little. The school survived about four centuries, for the most part as the main bastion of idealist philosophy. There were brief lapses into scepticism, however, and longer into Stoicism and various combinations of Platonism and Stoicism.

Plato's idealism was, as it would be for most of his successors, dualistic. There was an external, objective world known, so far as was possible, through the senses. The best that could be achieved was probable knowledge or belief. At worst, the senses were disparaged as sources of error, thoroughly unreliable indicators of the real world. "True knowledge" was possible only for the invisible world of ideas of "being," not "becoming." For Plato this ideal world was the only real world, for only it was permanent. What we call the real world is not, for it cannot be relied on to continue as it was. Objects only "participate in the ideas," while ideas have real being.[76] In the *Timaeus* the distinction was between "that which always is and has no becoming" and "that which is always becoming and never is."[77] What intelligence and reason apprehend, said Plato, is always in the same state, but "that which is conceived by opinion with the help of sensation and without reason, is always in a process of becoming and perishing and never really is" (3:716). One could quibble that sensation always excluded reason and surely people do change their minds.

The implications of this idealism are staggering. God is the only immortal being in Plato's system, hence the only "real" being and the only proper object of study. Theology is thus the only field completely worthy of study, the sciences serving only as means to an end. In the extreme Platonic system the natural world becomes a place to look for theological clues. Quite how one attains certain knowledge of the world of being was not spelled out, except that the senses are excluded. In the *Republic* Plato called the purely rational process "dialectic," although why is not at all clear – certainly there is no dialogue. Rather dialectic is achieved "when a person starts on the discovery of the absolute by the light of reason only, and without any assistance of sense, and perseveres until by pure intelligence he arrives at the perception of the absolute good."[78] How one knows one has arrived, of course, remains a problem. Nevertheless, dialectic alone went directly to first principles and did away with hypotheses (231). The ordinary sciences were only preparation for dialectic.

The famous cave scene in *The Republic* is both a powerful defence of idealism and a contemptuous dismissal of empiricism. We are asked to imagine people living in an underground den with an opening toward the light. The people have been chained from childhood so that they cannot move. All they can see is shadows on a wall cast by a fire behind them. The cave stands for what empiricists call the real world while the light and beautiful world outside is the idealists' real world. People released from the cave find the world outside painful. The shadows to which they have been accustomed seem truer to them than the objects they see outside. This difference between the two worlds next becomes a justification for the rule of philosophers. Those "best minds ... who have seen the truth" descend into the den, where they will be able to see 10,000 times better than its chained inhabitants. The state would be better run by such governors with no fights about what are "shadows only" (215). True philosophy would make one look down on political ambition.

There are methodological implications as well in Plato's curious views of the earth, which he correctly considered to be a round body (if in the centre of the heavens). According to the "Phaedo," only a small part was inhabited, the hollows about the sea. We were deceived into thinking we live on the surface of the earth, like a creature at the bottom of the sea who does not know how much nicer it is up top. Not the least of the problems of sense perception is that we are in the wrong place to conduct observations, we deep-water fish observing a murky bottom atypical of the larger reality.

Much as Plato disdained the world of becoming he produced some interesting theories about it. *The Republic* includes some remarkable sociology interspersed with political advice, ethics, and methodology. The goal was ambitious: to account for the early origins of human society and the stages of social organization that follow. *All* human societies were the subject for, as with other objects, actual societies were copies of a single, ideal model. All change should then happen in the same fashion. Plato began with the isolated individual and made individual insufficiency the cause of the first social organization. The need for food, clothing, and shelter created the first society; society has its basis in *nature*. Plato idealized this original society so that Athens, or any other contemporary city, could only compare badly. In it, people had all they needed materially. There were snug houses and plentiful, wholesome food: bread, grains, vegetables, and wine. Cooking had evolved sufficiently for an adequate diet short of *haute cuisine*. Pottery was produced for use but not exchange. There were no precious metals, money, or surplus. People lived in families. Altogether Plato paints a pretty picture, but hardly that of a primitive society. Weaving, house construction, brick making, and pottery require skills that probably took thousands of years to develop. Language and the nuclear family must have taken no less time. The problem is that in his methodology the original model is perfect; corruption occurs in the copies. Thus it was necessary to postulate some such perfection, however much it contradicted history and common sense. More plausible accounts *were* available, in Democritus, Thucydides, and the Hippocratics – all stressing the rigours of early human life. It was not for ignorance of alternatives that Plato made his choice, but methodological preference.

Having established a primeval paradise Plato next had to account for its fall, which he did in Book 8 with a long causal chain focusing on economic conditions: a surplus was created, then private property and slavery. For the first time in sociological theory there is a clear statement that social divisions are based on economic ones. Consistent with Plato's first-is-best philosophy, the original state is the most perfect – timocracy, literally the rule of the noble. Eventually the rule of the noble was succeeded by the rule of the rich oligarchy. There were envy, greed, and corruption. Divisions between rich and poor sharpened, making inevitable civil war and, eventually, the rule of the many in democracy.

In order to understand Plato's importance in the seventeenth century, we must turn to his views on natural science in the *Timaeus*. In its creation story, the soul of the world is created before the body. The earth was composed of the usual four elements, themselves derived from basic, formless matter. They were all reducible to triangles, varying in shape. The triangles resemble Democritus' atoms, but with a Pythagorean signification, for different shapes mean different numbers. The natural world, in other words, was ultimately reducible to numbers. Natural laws were essentially mathematical laws – and herein lies Plato's relevance to the revival of science in the seventeenth century. For Plato, the natural world was run by causal laws, in a sense, but there were two levels of cause. "Necessary" causes were only secondary, used by God as ministers in creation. The primary cause was divine. The *Timaeus* is also where Plato grouped women with animals, describing them as reincarnated from men who were cowardly or unrighteous (3:513).

Even such an opponent of idealism as Winspear credited Plato with understanding the complexity of phenomena under study.[79] While materialists of the same period tended to be simplistic in methodology, Plato was acutely aware that facts do not explain themselves. The researcher has to do more than merely collect them. Plato conceived levels of thought, but at the expense of tearing knowledge out of the world of things. The empiricist might complain that Plato separated the levels *too* much, not admitting any middle ground between abject ignorance of things and certain knowledge of ideas.

There is still debate as to what precisely Plato meant with his theory of forms and how committed he was to it. The first examples of forms were opposites like justice/injustice and good/evil. Plato had Socrates wonder if things with no opposites, like the earth, could be forms. By the time of the *Timaeus* the forms receive only honourific mention, and in Parmenides are described as a "juvenile theory of Socrates."[80] It seems that Plato viewed forms as having a real existence, that there is some place where absolute beauty and justice exist. Certainly there is a fundamental difference from empiricism, where abstract concepts like beauty and justice are derived from particular instances by a rounding off process. Forms proved to be an enduring feature of idealism, which then became *the* official theory of knowledge of Europe. Lovejoy contended that Plato was the main source of the position that objective knowledge of facts and values could be reached by reflection, independently of sense apprehension, hence the "otherworldliness" of western philosophy.[81]

After the extremism of Plato's theory the cautious, ever moderate approach of *Aristotle (384–322 B.C.)*[82] comes as welcome relief. Yet, for all his qualifications and empirical research Aristotle remained an idealist, and in many respects a Platonist, in methodology. He could criticize the theory of forms, but his own syllogistic logic assumes much the same superiority of mind over matter. Aristotle was a skilled and dedicated collector of data, an empiricist in practice if not in theory. It is unfair to blame Aristotle for the "ism" named after him, still less for scholasticism. However much he misrepresented his pro-empiricist forebears, he never claimed infallibility for himself. That scholarship consisted for centuries of commentaries on his texts was not his idea. That later scholars should hold to the syllogism and forget his own example of fieldwork is a great misfortune of methodological history.

Aristotle was not appointed to the directorship of the Academy on Plato's death, although he had studied and taught there for twenty years and was probably the best of the candidates. He travelled, did biological fieldwork, and taught in the Macedonian court, notably the future Alexander the Great. In 335 B.C. he returned to Athens in style, with books, maps, and specimens to create a new school, the Lyceum. He ran it for some twelve years, branching out into politics, history, and methodology as well as continuing in biology.

The Lyceum was, in effect, the world's first university, considering that the Academy excluded the natural sciences. There were roughly 2,000 students at the school's height, somewhat more than the Academy. The two competed for admissions, although students could take courses from both. The library was the most comprehensive in antiquity, marking the first concerted effort to collect books systematically on the various subjects of instruction. It included teachers' lecture notes, as well as vast archives of unpublished material, such as poems, maps, and lists of Olympic Game winners. Alexander the Great sent new material from his conquests. With minor set-backs, the school prospered for a good hundred years, its fortunes rising and falling with those of the Macedonian Empire. It apparently did not survive the collapse of the empire although the exact time of its demise is not known. When Cicero visited Athens in 79 B.C. there was no sign either of it or the Academy.

Aristotle's methodological goal was causal knowledge of things natural and social, organic and inorganic. As explained in the *Physics*, we think we know each thing when we know its first causes or principles.[83] Aristotle defined four distinct types of cause. The material cause referred to the matter from which a thing was made (the material cause of a bronze statue was bronze). The formal cause meant the laws by which the object developed, from the Platonic notion of form as an organizing principle. The efficient cause referred to the agent or starting point in the process. But the final cause dominated and gave Aristotelian methodology its distinctive teleological character. It was the completed result of the whole process. So the "nature" of a thing consisted in its end, when its growth was completed, whether for a person, horse, or family.[84]

Empiricists/positivists are usually blamed for the practice of modelling social theory on biological, but in fact Aristotle was the prime mover. This is understandable in that he came to political studies after years of biological research and early training in medicine. Thus he analyzed the state by component parts, as an organism. He identified normal functioning and set out remedies for malfunctioning. He stressed the naturalness of the state, especially its origin in biological needs. "If," said Aristotle, "we begin at the beginning, and consider things in the process of their growth, we shall best be able, as in other fields, to attain scientific conclusions" (3). The dominant theme throughout Aristotelian politics, as in biology, was development being guided by an object's end. In the case of a biological organism it was development into a mature being from the initial seed. In the case of the city-state it was development from earlier associations in the family and village. In both cases there is an unfolding from potentiality into actuality. Implicitly there is some kind of form guiding the process.

Aristotle's biology included both observation, considered plodding and overly empirical by some, and speculation, where everyone agrees Aristotle's errors were on the grand scale. The *Historia Animalium*, an example of the former, is a report of the observed differences between animals, preliminary to the construction of a taxonomy. Aristotle's speculative errors include limiting the role of the human mother in reproduction to supplying the *matter*, while the male supplied the *form*, which organized a foetus into a recognizable human being. Since the form came from the male the offspring should normally also be male (like father, like son). Females then have to be accounted for as aberrations, the result of a defect in development. The worse effects of this theory can be seen in the Middle Ages, when the form/matter hierarchy came to mean that women had inferior souls.

Aristotle's errors in physics were less original but still bizarre. On the composition of the world, he went back to the early four elements theory, insisting on qualitative differences between the elements in place of the atomists' quantitative ones. He described the materialists in some detail, often erroneously, so that his work became a biased source on them. His over-simplified account of the theory of primary matter was known when original sources were lost. Another of Aristotle's bolder errors concerned the sun's revolving around the earth. (Socrates and Plato, by contrast, held the Copernican view.) This affected far fewer people than the misogyny, but scholars were to suffer death, torture, and imprisonment for challenging it.

If the early materialist theories of perception were naïve with their images of moving screens behind the eye, Aristotle's was a colossal leap in the wrong direction. Like so many of his errors it followed from the form/matter dichotomy. In perception the soul took the form of the object to be perceived into itself, leaving out the matter. Sense perceptions were transmitted through the blood system to the heart, the chief organ of sensation. Recall that the function of the brain had been discovered at least by Alcmaeon, and was correctly taught in the fifth century B.C. by the Hippocratics and Plato. There were vestiges of Parmenides also here in the suggestion that knowledge, in a way, *was* the object of knowledge, and perception the object of perception.[85]

Like the earlier idealists Aristotle insisted on a rigid distinction between perception and thought. If thinking were like perceiving – horror of horrors – thought would be affected by its object. But thought was above mere objects, so must remain unaffected. Sense perception was dependent on the body, the intellect was not. And the intellect was always right (69). Aristotle paid more attention to the material world than did most idealists but his methodology was fundamentally idealist. Much as he protested his differences with Plato, he was as sceptical of the value of sense perception as his former teacher. His notions of knowledge and truth were similarly anti-empirical. Time and again he stressed the inadequacy of sense perception.

Sense observations yielded no more than "experience," which, however useful, was not science. Experience dealt with things severally, while science dealt with universals. People with experience could discern the fact *that*, but not the reason *why*. The senses "do not tell us why fire is hot, but only that it is hot."[86] Thus sense perception could never lead to scientific truth; it could not *explain* facts. Science, rather, consisted of *proved* knowledge, which involved knowledge of conclusions from premises. Proof was simply the pointing out of the connection between the truth we call the conclusion and other truths we call premises. Aristotle admitted a process of forming universals by abstraction by rounding off particulars. This did not produce science, however, for science required *demonstrated* truths, which sense observations never were.

The proper order for the development of science is to begin with the simplest principles, to reason to the more complex. In practice, though, one had to start with what is "more known and *clearer* to us," and work to "what is by its nature *clearer* and more known."[87] The assumption is that the most general laws of nature are the most hidden. Conversely, what can be observed is not very useful, and does not get us close to laws. There is a fundamental problem in that the simplest principles, by definition, cannot be inferred; demonstrated knowledge excludes first principles, which have to be accepted on the basis of sense observation or intuition. Aristotle was not consistent in saying which.

Aristotle's *Politics* has been one of the most influential books in the West in both the study and practice of politics. The work is a collection of essays on both the ideal and actual states: their composition and development, types of constitution, perversion, and change. There is practical advice on education and avoiding revolution and change. For Aristotle as for Plato, the state had to serve a high ideal for anyone to lead the good life. Most people, however, would have no opportunity to live the good life, for a large support staff of slaves was needed to serve the few.

One of the chief themes of the *Politics* was the *naturalness* of the state and the institutions on which it is based. Aristotle acknowledged the contrary conventional view of the sophists but paid it little heed. The state was a natural body, responding to biological needs. It was made up of pairings – male/female, parent/child, master/slave – that could not live without one another: "*The polis, or political association, is the crown: it completes and fulfills the nature of man; it is thus natural to him, and he is himself 'naturally a polis-animal.'*"[88] People were intended to live in society and could not reach their full potential unless they did. Aristotle held this for slaves, women, and children, as well as for those who benefitted more from the arrangements. The family or household was the first type of association, leading to the village or extended family, which had a king/patriarch type of ruler. (Like Plato, Aristotle had no notion of a mother-based family.) The city-state was the final form of political development. It was, in another sense, also *prior*, for the whole, or completed stage, is necessarily prior to the part, The state was similarly prior to the person (meaning the male citizen), as the "presupposition of his true and full life" (2).

Slavery was a natural institution and occurred for the same reason as did the state. Biology determined that some people (free men) were able to rule while others were capable only of following. This was effectively a mind/body distinction in the idealist tradition. Aristotle used the same naturalistic argument to deny political rights to women and to relegate them to a subservient role relative to their husbands. He nowhere adduced any evidence of the inferiority of women but simply announced that men were more fit to rule (13). Aristotle, no more than Plato, could imagine attaining a good life for anyone without sacrificing a large number of people to domestic servitude and slavery. Both men were quite prepared to do this and to argue that the results were for the good of the whole community.

The still current battle between theory and practice can be traced ultimately to Aristotle's distinction between theoretical and practical knowledge, although the lines of demarcation have changed. The theoretical sphere for Aristotle meant phenomena that "could not be otherwise" or truths independent of human will. The scientist's goal was general laws, the motivation for them curiosity. Aristotle believed curiosity to be innate; we all "naturally have an impulse to get knowledge."[89] Disinterested knowledge would be satisfying as such, without any utilitarian end. Mathematics and physics were the main subjects. The practical sphere involves phenomena susceptible to human intervention. The purpose now is application, rules to guide us to some end. Satisfaction occurs when some concrete end is realized. Thus an engineer's concern was not with the theory of bridge building, but actually building a bridge. Medicine, economics, and politics were all parts of practical philosophy. A more modest level of law had to be accepted, general rules which hold in the majority of cases, but liable to exception. In the case of theoretical knowledge the goal is universal truths, deducible with logical necessity from self-evident principles.

The high place apparently given practical knowledge in Aristotle's philosophy turns out to be deceptive. Politics was important eventually only to insure the stable society necessary for the noble employment of leisure. Practical knowledge was thus valuable only as a means to theoretical: art, music and, above all, the disinterested pursuit of knowledge. This is the reverse of the empiricist notion of using theory for practical goals. The still pervasive down-grading of work from ordinary manual labour to empirical research follows from a related Aristotelian doctrine. In the *Politics* Aristotle argued the need for leisure for political activity, which he saw as requiring lengthy discussion but no particular skills. Any work that would interfere with this leisure would thus disqualify a person for citizenship!

Training in the skilled trades would be enough, and the harder one worked and the more skills developed the less qualified one would be for citizenship. Aristotle's advice in this respect was followed for centuries, so that the only occupations considered worthy were the Church, the state, and the law.

Aristotle took great pride in being the founder of formal logic, a subject beyond the scope of this study. Both his *Prior Analytics* and his *Posterior Analytics* still have their *devoté(e)s*. His thesis was that the sciences were properly expounded in formal, axiomatized systems. What Euclid had done for geometry Aristotle wanted to do for every branch of knowledge. The body of truth each science defined was to be exhibited as a sequence of theorems inferred from a few basic postulates. What seems often to have been forgotten is that the results of this formalizing can be no better than the research on which they are based. How can one expect "marvels of certainty and exactitude" if the original data are uncertain and inexact?[90] Only by imputing to the mind the power to sift out error from truth can there be any solution. Aristotle indeed insisted, with no qualification, that the intellect was always right.[91] If one believes this, why bother with observation at all?

There are problems, too, in the selection of initial input. The observed facts should be set out. Then, after discussing the difficulties, one went on "to prove, if possible, the truth of all the common opinions" or, failing this, of the greater number and the most authoritative.[92] But what if authoritative opinion is wrong? Aristotle's methodology simply does not allow for this; indeed his errors were repeated century after century. Admittedly, one was not to do violence to phenomena, but how phenomena might be used to disprove an opinion was never specified. Rather the first task was to assemble the views held on the matter by all or most people, or any significant group or serious thinker. We are to profit from the sound suggestions of our predecessors and avoid their errors. But how to tell the sound suggestion from the error is precisely the point. Aristotle himself often could not and, worse, he often misrepresented his predecessors. Note also the conservatism of the approach; one begins with *authoritative* opinion.

A number of Aristotle's doctrines make him a poor candidate to become *the* philosopher of Catholic Europe, but that he became. There was no place for creation in his natural philosophy, but matter and motion had always existed and would always remain. God was the unmoved Mover, a single god but one who contemplated himself instead of caring for the world. The highest human activity was contemplation, not loving God or neighbour. Such difficulties provoked elaborate attempts at reconciliation. There were earnest attempts at Aristotle's salvation, for the "divine" philosopher could hardly have gone to hell with regular sinners. The whereabouts of Aristotle's soul was indeed a topic of heated debate of medieval scholasticism.

SCEPTICISM

At the same time that Aristotle was developing his methodology for certain knowledge of universals, a sceptical opposite was emerging to deny the possibility of certain knowledge at all and to stress more limited, practical goals.[93] Early hints of scepticism, of course, go back to the first glimmerings of social science with Solon. Popper paid *Xenophanes (c. 570–c. 480 B.C.)* the supreme compliment by crediting him with the invention of the methods of conjecture and criticism.[94] Xenophanes' scepticism is clear in his declaration that no one would ever know about the gods, for even if someone did have the truth "he himself is nevertheless unaware of it." "Opinion is fixed by fate upon all things." Another fragment similarly proposes that "these things be stated as conjectural only, similar to the reality."[95] He was conscious that his own teaching was conjecture. If he considered rational knowledge superior to sensual, it too was relative; opinion was the lot of humankind. Truth was not a revelation of the gods but the result of research. Instead of uttering dogmas, like Heraclitus, Xenophanes brought out his own ideas in debate with common opinion.

Xenophanes' teachings on religion were deviant. He advocated a single, great, motionless god governing all things by mind at a time when the Greeks had hordes of mindless, active gods who specialized in murder, incest, and promiscuity. There were many worlds in Xenophanes' cosmology, all of them perishable. The human race, too, would perish, but there would be another beginning. Xenophanes is also the source of the first preserved statement on progress. The gods did not reveal all things from the beginning but people in the course of time, through searching, found that which was better (22). Xenophanes himself saw things getting better – he lived to a ripe old age in a period of technological advance. His teaching then reflects *experience*.

Other foundations of scepticism can be seen in Heraclitus' argument of the impossibility of studying phenomena in flux. As well, the Hippocratics were scrupulously careful to treat medical theories as provisional, although one had to carry on even with incomplete understanding. Socrates said that the only thing he knew was that he knew nothing. The sophists were typically modest in their claims. Thucydides searched for the best sources available, recognizing that they might be incomplete, biased, or both. Democritus explained how perception was shaped by qualities in the perceiver as well as the object. It seems he was always aware that his theories were conjectural. He taught that there were severe limits to knowledge; one could study phenomena only, not ultimate causes. It was not until the fourth century B.C., however, that all these various notions were brought together and an identifiable school of scepticism emerged. The school is also known as the Pyrrhonist, after its founder, *Pyrrho of Elis (c. 360–c. 275 B.C.)*

The Pyrrhonist school was founded about five years after Aristotle's Lyceum, twenty years before Epicurus' Garden and Zeno's Stoa. Pyrrho apparently used the Socratic question-and-answer method, although he also lectured. The idea was to doubt the explanations of things that naturally came to mind. One was to think, investigate, and suspend judgment as to all ultimate truths. The method could have promoted science by exposing inadequacies in theory and finding internal contradictions or conflicting evidence. As theories and evidence accumulated, the sceptic, theoretically, would have to keep up. Certainly the object was to continue the search, and the word "sceptic" means "inquirer," not "doubter." But there is no evidence that the method *in fact* promoted scientific research. Some commentators have stressed the mystical, Indian, roots of Pyrrhonism.[96]

Conflicting theories or data served to make one suspend judgment for "quietude," or "unperturbedness." The method of doubt was to make decision impossible; one could not know which sense impressions to believe: "The Sceptic, having set out to philosophize with the object of passing judgement on the sense-impressions and ascertaining which of them are true and which false, so as to attain quietude thereby, found himself involved in contradictions of equal weight, and being unable to decide them suspended judgement; and as he was thus in suspense there followed, as it happened, the state of quietude in respect of matters of opinion."[97] Sceptics did not dispute obvious sense impressions – the stove is hot – but would not go beyond these to the "essential" nature of anything. A sceptic accepting a sense impression simply stated what appeared, undogmatically, without making any positive assertion regarding external realities. Thus, honey is sweet, but whether it has the "essence of sweetness" or simply tastes that way is not known. Pyrrho taught a similar relativism in social matters along the lines of the sophists. Nothing was good or evil by nature, but became so through law and custom. Scepticism did not exclude the possibility of certainty, for that would be to make an assertion. Properly speaking, a sceptic did not know whether certain knowledge was possible or not.

With no positive doctrines to guide them, sceptics still had to live in the world. Pyrrho never advocated withdrawal, and other sceptics were more worldly than he. They lived in accordance with the normal rules, laws, customs, and instincts of life. There were no abstract moral principles and no natural law. Sceptics might suspend judgment as to the legitimacy of a practice, but followed it nonetheless. Religions demanding conviction had reason to fear scepticism, civil authorities did not.

Pyrrho's school later moved to Alexandria where it was associated with the Empirical School of Medicine, renewing an old connection. Within Greece itself the next evolution of scepticism occurred – of all places – in Plato's Academy. It happened that a head of the Academy, *Arcesilaus (c. 315–c. 240 B.C.)*, came across sceptical teaching and found it a welcome improvement over the doctrinaire atmosphere of his own institution. Thus the most prestigious school in Greece was publicly proclaiming scepticism within a few years of Pyrrho's death. This constituted a triumph in one sense, but the takeover by the Academy also meant oblivion for the Pyrrhonist school.

Arcesilaus brought back the discussion method for teaching in the Academy. It had apparently become unnecessary to search for the truth, but Plato's teaching had become the criterion. Arcesilaus developed his theory of knowledge gradually, in response to attacks both by the Stoic, Zeno, and Pyrrho's successor, Timon. Against the Stoics he argued the impossibility of distinguishing true from false representations. Absolute knowledge was impossible, Arcesilaus argued, a dogmatic statement a pure Pyrrhonist would reject. He also rejected the Pyrrhonist practice of following custom in lieu of uncertain knowledge. Rather he proposed a kind of probable knowledge, that one should make decisions on ethical as well as scientific matters on the basis of what appeals to reason. Conceptually, this is an important advance, but it seems that there was no immediate benefit for science. Arcesilaus, unlike Pyrrho, used abstract arguments, not scientific data.

Carneades (214/3–129/8 B.C.), head of the Academy a century later, extended Arcesilaus' "reasonableness" approach to arrive at a notion of probability that is still familiar. He is responsible for the most systematic criticism of Stoicism, pointing out that there could be no criterion of truth in reason, for all material used by reason was acquired by sense perception. The "dialectic" could demonstrate only formal relations of thought, producing no real knowledge. So it could not be an arbiter of truth and falseness. Neither could the criterion be the wise person, for every wise person, at least at some time, was ignorant. Rejecting both the senses and reason as infallible guides, Carneades argued instead for distinctions to be based on "subjectively satisfying grounds." Although not certain, some sense impressions seemed better than others, and so should be preferred. Judgments could be ranked as to how persuasive, and hence probable, impressions were. Here Carneades specified four levels of judgments of reliability:

1. the apparently false (good grounds to believe false);
2. apparently true (no grounds to believe false);
3. probable and uncontradicted (some positive evidence for, none against);
4. probable, uncontradicted and closely tested (as above, but with more testing).[98]

Impressions that have been carefully scrutinized are more credible than those for which there is less evidence, while any amount of real world data is better than none. Carneades apparently stressed the importance of ideas in forming degrees of probability. It was not sense impressions themselves, but associations from past experience, that gave the basis to probable knowledge. This is even clearer in Carneades' teaching on causation.

Carneades evidently wanted to preserve some notion of causality without denying materialistic explanation, and managed to find an appealing solution. He rejected the Epicurean doctrine of declination as false, arguing instead that the action of atoms (and souls) could be from their own inner nature. He granted that there was no motion without a cause, but a cause did not have to be exterior and prior. The mind's own power served for its voluntary actions. It has been said that no one before Carneades analyzed causation so profoundly, nor indeed did anyone for centuries to come. As for Arcesilaus, knowledge, uncertain as it was, was to be used in practical life. Not custom but the course of action that seemed best, on the available evidence, was to be chosen. Cicero cited Carneades to the effect that it was not refusal to admit certainty that made life difficult, but refusal to admit probability. Thus the wise person would make use of whatever "apparently probable presentation" encountered, "if nothing presents itself that is contrary to that probability."[99]

Carneades' immediate successor diluted his theory of knowledge and later heads of the Academy moderated it even further. Enough evidently remained, however, for Cicero to include an excellent discussion of Academic scepticism in his book about the Academy. But the Academy gradually reverted to its Platonism, teaching it and an equally dogmatic Stoicism. A probabilistic theory of knowledge did not appeal to the Romans, but the Pyrrhonist school in Alexandria kept alive some version of the old Pyrrhonism. The next developments in scepticism took place there, with the Empirical School of Medicine. Alexandria became the chief medical centre of the western world under the Ptolemies. A number of schools flourished there, teaching competing theories of medicine, and conducting a great deal of empirical research.

The next known contributor to scepticism was an Alexandrian Greek, *Enesidemus (c. 100–40 B.C.)*. His book, *Pyrrhonist Discourses*, is known only in summary through Sextus Empiricus. Apparently it attacked both the Stoics and Academic sceptics. Enesidemus seems to have been a subtle, if negative, thinker. He raised many of the arguments on causation associated with Berkeley, Hume, and Mill. Causal knowledge was impossible. That one could not know an object in itself meant for him the end of knowledge. Enesidemus is also known as the compiler of the "ten *tropes*," or ways of producing doubt. These are effectively all the possible sources of error in the senses and reason, and still appear in arguments against empiricism. While they were not original to him, Enesidemus gathered them together into a systematic statement.

It is only through Roman secondary sources that we have any knowledge of ancient scepticism. *Marcus Tullius Cicero (106–43 B.C.)*[100] and Sextus

Empiricus are the chief sources, and even their works were effectively lost for over a thousand years. Both were important in the modern formulation of empiricism. Cicero wanted to write an encyclopedia on Greek philosophy to acquaint the Romans with the Greek classics. He completed eight books, including *Academica*, before his final return to politics. His *De Natura Deorum* also includes some discussion of methodology. Cicero claimed no originality. His method was to translate whole passages from major, relatively recent works. He often did not use original sources and accuracy suffers accordingly. Yet he is much appreciated as a stylist, raising philosophy back to the level of literature after it had become "crabbed technicality."[101]

In *Academica* Cicero defended the original principles of Academic scepticism, largely against Stoicism. He was firm that probability was *all* that was possible, that assertions ought to be correspondingly modest. The object was to "draw out and give shape to some result that may be either true or the nearest possible approximation to the truth." Cicero saw no difference between "ourselves and those who think that they have positive knowledge except that they have no doubt that their tenets are true, whereas we hold many doctrines as probable, which we can easily act upon but can scarcely advance as certain"[102]. The senses made mistakes and even the wise person was not a "statue carved out of stone," but had a body and a mind, a "mobile intellect and mobile senses" (597). Many things might seem to be true without possessing the Stoic mark of certainty. What Cicero argued for might be false, but at least the doctrines of scepticism were not detestable. In speaking of things only as appearing, "we don't rob you of daylight" (601). Cicero himself claimed only opinion, not wisdom. He was critical of people who formed judgments early in life, especially students, accepting the opinions of their first lecturer then clinging to them as to a rock.

The last known sceptic in antiquity was *Sextus Empiricus (late second, early third century A.D.)*, a Greek from Alexandria who possibly lived in Rome (or possibly the whole Empirical School of Medicine moved to Rome). The name Empiricus presumably came from some association with the Empirical school, but Sextus is known to have sided with the Methodic school; possibly he belonged to both. Three of his books on methodology survive, none on medicine. Nothing else is known of his life, not even approximate dates. He has typically been complimented as a faithful, if plodding, recorder of scepticism, but more recently has been credited with original work as well. Stough called his philosophy the "most consistent statement" of an empiricist theory of knowledge in Greek philosophy.[103] It was he who noted the consequences of basing rational knowledge in the senses: since every idea must be preceded by sense experience, if "sensibles" were abolished so would all conceptual thought. Sextus also opposed phenomenalism, arguing that a real object is more than the sum of its perceptible properties and exists independently of whatever is perceived.

STOICISM AND FUNCTIONALISM

Stoicism is the last of the great schools of antiquity, a synthesis of empiricist and idealist elements of methodology plus some new political theory. For some six centuries it was *the* school to which all others addressed themselves. Stoicism was as anti-sceptical as any idealism, purporting to offer a methodology of certain knowledge, at least for "the wise." Stoics opposed the two pro-empirical schools, Epicureanism and scepticism, yet by continuing the materialism of Ionian and Hippocratic science, countered Platonic and Aristotelian idealism. When new models were in demand in early modern Europe, Stoicism became a source. Descartes, Leibniz, and Adam Smith all show its influence.

Stoicism contributed some refinement to the understanding of causation and laws of nature.[104] Its teaching that the distinction between slave and free was artificial made it a mildly radical political force in its early days. Neither the radicalism nor the interest in natural science or methodology, however, lasted. In time Stoicism became a purely ethical system teaching acquiescence to established authority. More recently environmentalists have rediscovered Stoicism for its holistic, everything-is-connected-to-everything conceptualization of nature. Against this, however, the hierarchical tendencies and anthropocentrism of Stoicism might be remembered. The great body of nature served the interests of its sole rational members: *us*.

As with many an ancient, fragments only remain from the work of the founder of Stoicism, *Zeno of Cittium, Cyprus (336–264 B.C.)*, while major secondary sources on him were hostile. Stoic logic consisted of two parts, a materialist theory of sensation and a "dialectical" theory of reasoning to insure that "the truth" was reached. The logical process began with sensation, a passive stage, for which the Stoics used the image of a seal and wax. Error was possible here, but could be rectified at the active, "dialectical" stage. Impressions were not to be assented to indiscriminately, but only those in accord with "right reason." The wise mind was able to resist unreasonable impressions and refuse assent. Acquiring "right reason," then, becomes crucial, but the Stoics were light on detail as to how this was done.

"Common notions" were part of the answer. Not innate ideas, they were acquired by experience, normally between the ages of seven and fourteen. Thus instead of believing that we are all born with some common ideas, we must believe that we all have the right experiences at the right age to develop them. For the Stoics this was evidently not difficult, for they believed in a fully determined world, permeated with Reason/God. Moreover they did not believe in the reality of evil. All things working together for good was their creed and, if that were true, why not also certain, perfect, knowledge?

The Stoics used the analogy of a hand grasping something for the mental process of grasping. The hand was open as sensation began, passively ready to receive the object. The active assent process began with the fingers lightly squeezing the object. When the hand closed completely on it there was "complete representation" or "perception," understood as correct perception. To insure that perception continued permanently, the free hand took the closed hand and shook it firmly. These final, verified perceptions were the Stoic object of science. Mere impressions could be wrong without the active checking operation in place. "False presentations," like dreams or drunken ravings, would be weaker than true, hence could be distinguished. Complete knowledge, of objectively correct facts and the connections between them, was possible. The Stoics were not shy of the concept of infallibility.

They also refined and extended understanding of causation, opposing the Epicurean doctrine of free will. In the Stoic universe everything was caused, everything related to everything else through a long series of cause-effect links. The old Greek "fate" now came to be clearly understood as cause. The term actually meant "string beads," so that fate/cause was the stringing together of things.[105] The Stoics added two new types of cause, "intensifying" for something not able to act as a cause itself and "joint" causes. The inter-connectedness of everything in Stoicism makes it the original functionalism of the West.

This new understanding of causation has been interpreted as a reflection of the greater powers of the new empires, Macedonian and Roman. When the gods and the city-states were relatively weak, so also were people's concepts of causation. As the city-state was replaced by a kingdom, and then an empire, so also were weaker conceptualizations of causation replaced by stronger.[106] The Stoics then can be seen as prime contributors to the notion of laws of nature. Peoples and nature alike came to be seen as governed in a regular, law-like fashion after the concrete experience of rule by a stronger power. Stoic political theory similarly reflects the broader horizons of empires; Alexander reached India, and the Roman Empire covered nearly all the known world.

The world was one in Stoicism, so that all people were fellow citizens. In early writing the distinction between slave and free was artificial, contrary to Platonic and Aristotelian views.[107] Nevertheless, the Stoics did not go the next step of urging the abolition of slavery. A few Stoics are known to have had socialist views and Stoic advisers in Sparta urged the redistribution of land and admission of foreigners to citizenship. Stoics are known to have been involved in several later slave revolts, one of which put forward Stoic ideas for a new society. Stoicism never was a reform movement, however, and the radicalism soon disappeared from its theory. Stoic ethics came to teach resignation, which is what the term now means. Stoic officials were appreciated for their self-restraint and respect for the law and some had a moderating effect.

THE CHRISTIAN ERA

The great events of Christianity were slow to affect intellectual life, important as those effects were eventually to be. They expected an early return of Jesus and an end to ordinary human-run history. There were practical problems of persecution and poverty and the commission to spread the good news. The sort of people who might have become scholars in Greek or Roman society became missionaries, priests, or church administrators. When scholarly writing began in the second century A.D., the church "fathers" distanced themselves from "pagan" sources to show their loyalty to the new faith. For Tertullian, at the extreme, knowledge was to be disdained. Even for Augustine knowledge served at best to help people to lead the good life; it was not valued for itself.

The differences in world view between the Greeks and Christians are staggering in both the natural and the social sciences, so that we should not be surprised at the odd combinations that emerged. For the Greeks the cosmos was an animated, intelligent being, alive with soul or thought. The Judaeo-Christian view of a transcendent God creating inert matter, and then breathing life into it, is quite different. This view is at least as old as the Greek conception, but only with Christianity did it enter the European world. The activity or passivity of matter will recur as an issue with the recovery of Greek thought in the Renaissance and the early development of modern science. Whether as "vitalism" then or "the death of nature" now, the issue is still with us. For some Greeks, notably Aristotle, matter/the world was eternal. The Judaeo-Christian notion of a beginning and end is quite different from every known Greek cosmogony. The abstract Aristotelian notion of God as "unmoved mover" is again a far cry from the active Jahweh/Creator.

In the social world the differences are at least as great. For some Greeks human character was immutable, so that no notion of character development was possible. For others change was possible through education, at least for the elite. The Judaeo-Christian view differs from both in that all of us are sinners, yet all are called to repentance, change, and growth. Since there is grace there is hope, both for individuals and nations. In place of the many, capricious gods of Greece and Rome, or effectively none at all in Epicureanism and Stoicism, now there is one God, who both cares and intervenes.

The social sciences are possible since human nature, if sinful, is essentially the same everywhere and God has the same high purpose for all. Christians now divided history into periods depending on God's plan, the main division being before and after Christ's life on earth.[108] This new dating system was in use by the third and fourth centuries A.D. For some centuries God's actions were seen as so overwhelming, and the human contribution as so ·puny, that no social explanations were advanced. The details of human activity simply seemed irrelevant. On this point the pendulum has swung widely from a one-sided humanism in classical history to an abstract theocracy in the Middle Ages. When the human element again came to be highly valued, social science writing was revived, now showing the impact of Christian thinking and Christian dating. Instead of the vantage point being Greece *vs.* Persia or Rome *vs.* Carthage, with a universal God the focus became a generalized posterity. Isidore of Seville integrated events into a single chronology. With the influence of the venerable Bede the practice became more common.

The first Christian writer, *Eusebius (c.260–339/340 A.D.)*, saw much persecution and was himself imprisoned and nearly martyred. Yet he lived to see the Emperor Constantine accept Christianity and make it the official religion (and to wrongly conclude that the days of persecution were over forever). Eusebius' *History of the Church from Christ to Constantine* is the first work to show the impact of Christian thought. The purpose was to justify the ways of God to people. "From first page to last the writer's theme is the working of Providence, to be demonstrated not by moral tales but by historical facts."[109] Eusebius used more than 100 books other than the Bible in his research, including Herodotus, Thucydides, Plato, Aristotle, and the Hippocratics. He was not praised for good style, but his vast knowledge was respected. He demonstrated God's justice by describing a succession of punishments that interrupted human history. God was constantly coming to the aid of the apostles with swift retribution and marvellous acts. Similar explanations became commonplace in European scholarship, occurring in extreme form in the Middle Ages, but remaining well into the modern era.

The influences between Greek philosophy and Christian teaching were mutual. At the same time that writers like Eusebius were incorporating Christian ideas into the explanation of historical events, others were revising Christian teaching in the light of Greek, especially idealist, philosophy. Clement of Alexandria and Origen "spiritualized" Christian teachings about the poor. The obligation to feed the poor became a teaching about attitudes; the kingdom of God became a far-off, future event unrelated to present injustices. The gospel for the poor and lowly became one for the rich and prominent.

NEO-PLATONISM

The idealism that dominated Europe throughout the Middle Ages was Augustinian neo-Platonism, and Augustine's main source was *Plotinus* (c. 205–270 A.D.).[110] The bishop of Hippo himself Christianized Plato (or Platonized Christianity), but it was Plotinus' version of Plato from which he worked. Plotinus' system took all the most idealist, hierarchical, and conservative features of Plato and magnified them; where Plato was down-to-earth, sensible, and radical, Plotinus ignored him. As Plato's works were gradually lost to western Europe, Augustine continued to be read, continuing the influence of Plotinus.

The title of his one book, *The Enneads*, simply means nine, from the division of the material into nine sections. The work dates from lectures Plotinus gave late in life when he was in declining health. Apparently his eyesight was poor so that he could not read and correct his work. His pupils are said to have loved it when his meaning was inscrutable; this apparently indicated some deeper significance.[111] Consequently ambiguities and inconsistencies remain. Even supporters admit *The Enneads* is a confused work, although they usually insist that it has moments of soaring genius or justify its style as "stream of consciousness." There are fundamental difficulties as well with Plotinus' sources. He seems to have known the pre-Socratics only by secondary sources, and even his knowledge of Plato may have been second hand. Central to his system was an elaborate hierarchy of levels of existence.

The physical universe in Plotinus' system was the product of the blending of form and matter. As in the Aristotelian tradition, it had existed forever. As in the Stoic, it constituted one organic whole, with all its members united by one bond of sympathy. All parts were shaped by Reason-Principle, with no one having the power to alter it. Matter was privation, alienation, utter destitution of sense, virtue, beauty, pattern, quality. "This is surely ugliness, utter disgracefulness, unredeemed evil."[112] An odd feature of matter was that it could not be discerned by the senses but only by an act of the mind. There was no place for evil in the divine realm. If evil existed at all it must be in the realm of Non-Being. Note that it was not the world of *bodies* that was evil – that is another development of idealism – but *unformed* matter. Creation was as good as God could make it.

Plotinus' description of creation was of active, fruitful Mind acting on inert, barren matter. Plotinus' theory of knowledge included a denunciation of the materialist theory of sensation. Lower things could not act upon higher, so mere external objects could not act on the senses or the senses on the soul. Rather the soul itself went out to objects, giving out a light from itself. Perception of every kind seemed to depend on the fact that the universe was a living whole sympathetic to itself (338).

Dialectic abandoned deceit and falsity for the "Meadows of Truth" (38). It was the most noble method and science that existed, the precious part of philosophy. It did not consist of bare theories and rules but dealt with verities. Wisdom and Dialectic had the task of presenting all things as Universals, stripped of matter, for treatment by the Understanding.

Plotinus' system poses a number of difficulties for the non-mystical Anglo-Saxon mind. Some of these at least have the ring of familiarity, as Parmenides' identity of the mind or thinker with the object. Plotinus added an identity of being and necessity. Thus it means the same thing that "the One" is what it is, and must be what it is. Yet "unity-in-multiplicity" and "unity *and* multiplicity" are distinguished. It is not to be said that "the One" *causes* himself, but *is* his own cause.[113] For the reader who is baffled by this I have no advice.

Augustine of Hippo (354–430 A.D.), the pre-eminent theoretical influence on the Middle Ages, remains influential. His theory of knowledge was used in the seventeenth-century struggles against the revival of empiricism. It was a major, if not always conscious source for Descartes. For the next generation of Cartesians, thanks to Malebranche, Augustine was the highest authority. Augustine has also been said to have "anticipated" Kant. Or, thirteen centuries later, Augustine's methodology was still such a part of idealist thinking that the anti-mystical Kant would show its influence. Now, two centuries later, Augustine still has to be treated as one of the most powerful shapers of the idealist tradition.

Augustine never wrote a systematic treatise on methodology but he did take up the issue in his various theological and philosophical works. *On the Trinity* (written between 400 and 428) is a major source for his methodology, *The City of God* (413-427) for his political and social views. Probably the best way to approach the methodology is through the scepticism Augustine rejected en route to it.[114] This sceptical period was brief, the few years between Augustine's disillusionment with Manicheism and conversion to Christianity. The process is described in *Against the Academics*, his first work as an enthusiastic, born-again Christian. In it Augustine described the sceptical doctrine of probability as insufficient and even dangerous.[115] Platonism was truth shining forth in Plotinus. Augustine conceded that this thesis was only probable, but acceptable even if false. At least he believed that truth could be found. Positively, authority and reason help us to learn, he maintains. Why? Because no one doubts this (150).

There is much concern with classification. Augustine distinguished three types of objects of perception and three types of sensation. The lowest was the sensation of physical bodies, which humans shared with animals.[116] The highest was "intellection," or knowledge acquired through higher reason. Intellection was knowledge of forms, the eternal standards of truth which exist in the mind of God. The error-free product of intellection was "wisdom," directed to contemplation. There was also a middle-level of perception unique to humans: science or knowledge. The objects of this kind of perception were temporal and mutable. The end was action. In Augustine's early accounts of sensation the corporeal object produced an impression on the sense organ, which reported it to the "interior sense," and then to reason. His later writings simplified this, but clearly Augustine felt the need for some kind of intermediate step to keep mind and matter apart. It was the soul that perceived; the sense organs were only agents of perception.

Truth was not just a quality of propositions but really existent. In so far as creatures embodied the form in the mind of God they possessed onto-logical truth. Reality was knowable because it was created by God after the pattern of divine ideas. "To this wisdom every rational soul gives heed, but to each is given only so much as he is able to receive, according to his own good or evil will. If anyone is ever deceived it is not the fault of Truth, any more than it is the fault of the common light of day that the bodily eyes are often deceived."[117] So the acquisition of truth became, as for Plato, a moral problem, of goodness or evil of the *will*, not of the sense organs or intellect. Augustine often used the imagery of illumination, as in the truth illuminating the inner person. This was continued by his successors, Male-branche especially.

The Platonic primacy of knowing over being received its Christian form in Augustine. God does not know his creatures because they are, they are because he knows them. There was also the Parmenidean identification of being and knowing. God's knowledge was also his essence, or essence altogether. "It is not one thing to be wise and another to be, but to be wise is to be."[118] Subject and object of knowledge were similarly identified. Mind knows itself, and so knows its own substance.

The issue of reliability of knowledge was of crucial importance to Augus-tine and his tortured soul: how could there be certain knowledge of God and Christian doctrine if there is no certain knowledge of anything? His general point was that certain, if limited, knowledge by the senses was possible, while through reason it was hardly problematic. "Far be it from us to doubt the truth of what we have learned by the bodily senses – by them, we know heaven and earth" (7:404). Academic scepticism was "insane" by doubting all things. Philosophers babbled much against the bodily senses, but were never able to throw doubt upon those most certain perceptions of things true which the mind knows by itself. Augustine begged the question here, as he did everywhere else he addressed it. In *The City of God* his condemnation of the uncertainty of the New Academy was scathing: "The Church of God detests these doubts as madness, having a most certain knowledge of the things it apprehends, although but in small quantity, because of the corruptible body which is a burden to the soul."[119]

Augustine's answer to doubt was the "I think, therefore I am" usually associated with Descartes: "Who ever doubts that he himself lives, and remembers, and understands, and wills, and thinks, and knows, and judges? Seeing that even if he doubts, he lives; if he doubts, he remembers why he doubts ... Whosoever therefore doubts about anything else, ought not to doubt of all these things; which if they were not, he would not be able to doubt of anything."[120]

Augustine's conservative social and political views were as firmly grounded in theology as was his methodology.[121] Since the majority of people were corrupt the state had to use fear of punishment to control them. Rulers, no matter how wicked or cruel, were ordained by God to rule; the state was a divine institution, no matter how corrupt. Justifications for the use of torture, war, and slavery were elaborated.

THE EMPIRICIST CRITIQUE REVISITED

As we leave the classical period it is clear that some of the stereotypes in the critique of empiricism do not apply. Not only did natural scientists not apply their models to the social sciences, the first known borrowing was in the opposite direction. More often the borrowing went both ways, as scholars themselves worked in both the natural and social fields. Technology influenced both, as did medicine. The association between the social sciences and social reform goes back to the sixth century B.C. Solon's calls for reform were early social analysis, while the reforms themselves promoted an understanding of law as social convention. History in this early period was not separate from or an alternative to the search for general explanation. Thucydides' *History of the Peloponnesian Wars* was an attempt to explain a great single event with reference to enduring, underlying conditions. Differences in the success of the two sides were accounted for in causal chains, and social institutions were prominent as causal agents.

Environmentalist critics of empiricist methodology often look back to the classical period's "more fitting" conceptualization of nature. In practice a great deal of environmental degradation took place in this period, with deforestation, over-grazing, and soil exhaustion. Yet the dominant view of nature – atomism was an exception – was as a living, breathing whole, even as Gaia, goddess or life force. This is thought to have excluded a human/ animal or human/rest-of-the-world dichotomy otherwise prevalent. But did it? More often those who took the organicist view subscribed enthusiastically to a ranking of humans over animals. The Platonic theory of forms made for a rigid hierarchy and separation between the ideal and material worlds. So did the Aristotelian form/matter dichotomy. Both systems relegated women to a lower level of value, identified with matter and body, and granted men a higher status identified with intellect and soul. The neo-

Platonists, extreme organicists, espoused a hierarchy of levels of being, including a mind/body dualism not normally conducive to environmental ethics. The Stoics combined a holistic conceptualization with a sturdy anthropocentrism. The only significant challenge to anthropocentrism came from Lucretius, an ardent materialist.

Convenient as it would be to be able to blame a particular methodology for our environmental woes, this just does not stand up to scrutiny. Attitudes and beliefs conducive to the exploitation of nature existed in *all* the ancient methodologies. The organicist, holistic conceptualization then dominant did not serve to protect nature, while its accompanying mind/body dualism and hierarchical relations probably, if unintentionally, harmed it.

3 Empiricism and Scepticism Recovered

The human understanding is like a false mirror, which, receiving rays irregularly, distorts and discolours the nature of things by mingling its own nature with it.
Francis Bacon[1]

Is our knowledge so adequately commensurate with the nature of things as to justify our affirmation, that that cannot be, which we comprehend not?
Joseph Glanvill[2]

I have a great reverence for experience in comparison of authority.
Robert Boyle[3]

All the words and definitions in this world will not give any man without sensation a true conception of a sensible object.
Richard Baxter[4]

We are born ignorant of everything.
John Locke[5]

God has made the intellectual world harmonious and beautiful without us; but it will never come into our heads all at once; we must bring it home piecemeal, and there set it up by our own industry, or else we shall have nothing but darkness and chaos within, whatever order and light there be in things without us.
John Locke[6]

There is no error to be named, which has not had its professors.
John Locke[7]

We shou'd not be deceived by the report of our senses, the prejudices of education, our own private interest and readiness to receive the opinions, whether true or false, of those we love.
Mary Astell[8]

Medieval Europe experienced technological innovation, economic growth, some development in natural science, but scarcely any in the social sciences. The Greek schools had all disappeared, the Roman libraries had been sacked. Knowledge of Greek was lost, so that those manuscripts that survived in monasteries could not be read. The reigning social theory was Augustinian, which permitted no place to either social convention or scepticism. Revealed truth, certified by ecclesiastical authority, replaced the former, a firm certainty the latter. Neo-Platonic mysticism infused the whole. Alchemy and astrology spread.

The recovery of the ancient Greek schools was slow and gradual. In the twelfth century books by Plato and Aristotle again became available, often via Arabic, then Latin translation. Nominalism reappeared in the work of Roscellinus of Compiègne (b. 1050), Peter Abelard (1079–1142) and, in the fourteenth century, William of Ockham (c. 1285–1349). Ockham's scepticism was highly qualified, but his claims for knowledge were modest and cautious, indicating at least a sceptical spirit. Albertus Magnus (1206?– 1280) and Roger Bacon (1561–1626) contributed enormously to the revival of natural science. Robert Grosseteste (c. 1175–1253), although with much neo-Platonic imagery, proposed a notion of falsification through the testing of theory. Nicolas of Autrecourt (c. 1300–1350+) revived ancient atomism and a notion of probability. This flowering of scepticism, however, was brief. Nicolas' work literally went up in flames in one of the most successful book burnings of intellectual history. Machiavelli (1469–1527) can be seen as reviving the concepts of ancient sophism. His treatment of social conflict as natural was revolutionary.

The one identifiable social scientist of the Middle Ages was Ibn Khaldun (1332–1406), whose *Muqaddimah*, or *Introduction to History*, analyzed society in the fashion of Thucydides. Ibn Khaldun was critical of poor standards of historical research and conscious of his own imperfections, exhaustive as his research had been. He had a sense of the collective nature of research and hoped that other scholars would correct his work. In fact no students came forward to continue his research, and not until Francesco Guicciardini (1483–1540) do we see another advance. His *History of Italy* is the first modern work recognizably in the mould of Thucydides, at once sceptical and cautious. It was based on original documents, which were carefully checked. (Thomas Blundeville's *True Order of Writing and Reading Histories*, [1574] is another example in this tradition.) Jean Bodin (1530– 96) not only wrote on the methodology of history but contributed some early modern social and political theory, along with – this is the sixteenth century – a defence of astrology and witchcraft.

There was an enormous increase of interest in the classics in the Renaissance. Higher standards of scholarship were achieved, more accurate translations produced. Substantively, however, the focus was on Plato and on literary and rhetorical works, not the social nor even the natural sciences. The early impact of the Reformation, similarly, did nothing for scientific methodology or actual social research. Martin Luther (1483–1546) was an avowed asserter, opposing scepticism for reasons of faith. The Catholic Erasmus (1465–1536), by contrast, promoted scepticism. A more sceptical approach to knowledge was proposed by a follower, later opponent, of Jean Calvin (1509–1564). Castellion (1515–63), in *De l'Art de douter*, advanced a notion of levels of knowledge depending on the quality of evidence, with much tolerance for ambiguity. The subject was how to save one's soul, but the same approach was soon to be argued for science generally. The Catholic saint and martyr, Thomas More (1478–1535), more than anyone of this time, proposed a methodology with empirical observation, nominalism, probability, and the use of social conventions. Radical as *Utopia* was, it seemed to threaten neither state nor church because it was published in Latin.

Scepticism was the last of the ancient schools to be revived in western Europe, and it was not until its recovery that anything recognizable as social science re-emerged. Although ancient scepticism was not totally lost (manuscripts of Sextus Empiricus are known of in Europe in the fifteenth century),[9] it seems that scepticism was misunderstood or feared. Further, the first writings using sceptical arguments did not promote science but religion, arguing variously against pagan philosophy or Protestantism. It was not until late in the sixteenth century that Michel de Montaigne (1533–92) advanced a constructive scepticism, indeed that of Sextus Empiricus. Montaigne published the first of his *Essays* in 1580, the most significant for methodology in 1588.

The term "essay," literally a "try," was new at the time. Montaigne's essays posed questions and mused; they offer few conclusions and seem disorganized. The early essays show his stoicism, which gradually gave way to scepticism, which lasted. Montaigne actually had phrases from Sextus carved into the beams of his study. "Que sais-je?" became his motto, "What do I know?" His major methodological essay, "Apology of Raimon Sébond" (written 1575–6), was largely an attack on Sébond's rational theology. Montaigne argued that faith, not rationalist arguments, should be the foundation for belief, a position referred as "fideism." Rationalist reasoning Montaigne found invalid, in any event, and here he brought in all the old arguments of scepticism. There were errors in sense perception and reasoning; reason could never be an adequate check on the senses. The diversity of theories claiming to be the truth showed the futility of rationalism. Montaigne criticized both idealists and materialists who used speculative arguments, giving his kindest words to the sceptics.

A major theme of the *Essays* was a comparison of humans with animals, much to the advantage of the latter, whose strength, faithfulness, generosity, ingenuity, and social organization were recounted. Here also Montaigne included a remarkable early plea for kind treatment both of animals and of trees and plants.[10] Montaigne was fortunate to have as his editor Marie de Gournay, an early feminist poet and essayist, who for years after his death put out new and better editions of the *Essays*.

Francis Bacon was not content to ask "What do I know?" but set out to answer the question with vast schemes of research. If Montaigne's separation of matters of faith and knowledge freed his mind for philosophical inquiry, Bacon's energetic puritanism pressed forward to the building of the kingdom of God on earth – with the help of science. Empiricist methodology's next development took place in England, where Bacon took over from Montaigne, devising his own answers to Montaigne's questions. Constructive scepticism was proposed also in France at the same time, but it met there with quite a different reception.[11]

The impetus in both countries was religious, the need to answer Pilate's question "What is truth?" Constructive scepticism in science was an adaptation of answers first developed to questions concerning the repose of one's eternal soul. That questions of hellfire should fan the flames of scientific inquiry was doubtless unintentional. Yet the threat of earthly fire remained. Witch burnings were frequent in the seventeenth century, and even a few published authors met the fate accorded so many of their books. In short, the methodological stakes remained the stake.

Natural science's Copernican revolution was to upset intellectual life far more in the seventeenth century than in the sixteenth. Nor was it only the reversal of what was the centre of the universe that shocked, important as that question was. The possessors of revealed truth could no longer simply condemn a theorist for wrongful speculation. Galileo's empirical evidence in favour of Copernicus was an even more fundamental challenge to Church authority. Cardinal Bellarmine correctly argued that if the Copernican theory were truly demonstrated, theologians would have to reinterpret Scripture and admit that they had been wrong.[12] Yet Galileo was not content to argue his conclusion in the accepted medieval fashion. Not only was Ptolemy wrong about the earth being the centre of the universe, he argued, so also was the whole endeavour of "saving the phenomena." Galileo's observations were not part of an exercise in speculative philosophy but an attempt to explain a real, external world. The only way "to save the phenomena" was to explain this world correctly, with a theory that accurately reflects what goes on in it.[13] It has been argued that if Galileo had been content to qualify his conclusion as speculation he would not have been prosecuted. He refused, even with the threat of the stake.

The seventeenth-century understanding of hypothesis retained an openness to disconfirmation, with methodologists varying from the more certain and confident to the more sceptical and diffident. But a Copernican revolution shifted methodological intent to efforts to explain the real world. For Galileo, that two different hypotheses might be equally valid was a sign of ignorance. A host of empiricist methodologists soon agreed.

Historical method continued to be discussed, with concerns for accuracy in report, and knowledge for both general application and better conduct. Unity of method was stressed with modesty in aspiration; we should not strive to outstep nature in the investigation of natural things. "History" at this time still meant simply "research," applying equally well to human and physical affairs. John Ray's great work on botany was called the *History of*

Plants, and Bacon planned histories of the air, taste, touch, clouds, salt, etc.

The profound differences between seventeenth-century England and France in religious institutions and church-state relations had their impact in the development of methodology. Briefly, diversity in religious belief and expression was much greater in Britain. Officially Protestant, there were still Catholics claiming the throne and the possibility of counter-Reformation was not to be ignored. There was a vast range of doctrine in Protestantism, both within the established church and among the sects. The continental solution – join the dominant group, accept martyrdom, or leave – was not feasible in England. To the people of England the problem of deciding "what is truth" must have been greater than anywhere on the Continent. The objective conditions for scepticism were then much greater. So also was the need for accommodation that scepticism provides. The different groups from high Roman Catholics to low Anglicans, Presbyterians, and Baptists had to live together to a greater extent than anywhere on the Continent.

Not surprisingly, some thinkers advanced a moderate scepticism as a solution to the problem of determining religious truth. These ideas were not only broadly accepted, but in a short time moved to other areas of thought, especially science. The criteria for determining the correctness of a religious doctrine became the criteria for determining correctness in scientific theory. Tolerance, advocated in religious matters in view of human fallibility, became in science the tendency to view all theories as hypothetical and all findings as tentative. The leeway allowed people who changed sides in religion had also to be permitted to scientists.

England and France soon parted company in the treatment accorded the new methodology. In France constructive scepticism never took hold. Cartesian rationalism, initially resisted, gradually won acceptance. The more sceptical and material elements were played down by Descartes' successors, the certainty and intuitive elements stressed. Malebranche's version of Cartesianism, which drew heavily on Augustine, took over. The empiricists Gassendi and Mersenne sank into oblivion. In England precisely the opposite happened. The brief revival of neo-Platonism remained a minority movement, and the empiricism of the Royal Society became *the* scientific method.

For all their differences, the British and French were still closer to each other than to methodologists in any other country. Both developed *some* form of empiricism, for *some* period, while no other country did. Idealist methodology remained the norm in Europe. The English and French had come the closest to developing empiricism in the medieval period, with Roger Bacon and Grosseteste in England, and William of Ockham and Nicolas of Autrecourt in France. In the sixteenth century Thomas More brought England considerably along the empiricist path, while France produced Castellion and Montaigne.

The survival of religious diversity in Britain, and not in France, reflects basic political and economic differences between the two countries. The anti-Royalist Puritans gained control of Parliament and waged war against the king. Charles I was beheaded in 1640, whereas it took France another century and a half to behead a king. In France, the Counter Reformation meant the suppression of liberal views of Catholic and Protestant alike. The Edict of Nantes was finally revoked in 1685 after years of declining rights for Protestants. Protestants were persecuted and many went into exile. Even Descartes, a Catholic, took the precaution of doing his methodological work in Protestant Holland. The Catholic Church was re-established as the arbiter of true philosophy, and true philosophy in seventeenth-century France meant Aristotle. The scepticism allowed in the sixteenth century became dangerous in the seventeenth. Parliament, on Church prodding, made it a capital offence to teach any philosophy contrary to Aristotle. Several people were in fact burned at the stake for not recanting their dissident views. The political and social environment of seventeenth-century France was clearly not one to encourage the basic notions of scepticism. Intellectual questioning is not facilitated by an absolute, divine-right monarchy, or an absolute, the-truth-is-ours-alone church. France had both.

The situation was worse again in Catholic Italy with the Inquisition. While in France only lower-class people were burned at the stake, in Italy even respectable scholars were imprisoned, tortured, and executed. Galileo, even after recanting, spent the last eight years of his life under house arrest and his burial was without monument or epitaph. His humiliating renunciation was sent to the professors of mathematics and astronomy across Europe. The academic community responded as they were meant to, by publishing wimpishly in support of Ptolemy. Not until 1822 did the Catholic Church permit discussion of Galileo and not until 1992 did it take back the condemnation.

The English Civil War has been described as a war between two schools of astronomy, the Royalists for the Ptolemaic and Parliament for the Copernican. With the defeat of the Royalists, Ptolemaic theory perished too. The Puritan victory resulted more generally in the defeat of the "ancients" in theory of knowledge. It has also been claimed as ending belief in fairies, spirits, and witches but this, unfortunately, was not so – the Puritans continued to burn witches at the stake. Recent scholarship stresses the diversity of political and religious involvements of the new scientists, with some royalists and many Latitudinarians as well as Puritans.

Whatever the causes of the English Revolution and the role of ideas in it, certain consequences are obvious. The Cromwell Protectorate increased expenditure on universities, opened schools, and established a new university at Durham. Francis Bacon's works were republished and read to a greater extent than before. Though Bacon had supported the king, his materialist views were much more appreciated by the Puritans. The small Puritan sects explored radical new ways of organizing society. What had appeared to be natural and unquestionable now came to be seen as conventional. Moreover, one could learn from these new experiences and apply the knowledge.

The Revolution was eventually quelled, the more radical sects suppressed. The hope of establishing a kingdom of God on earth was given up. The fiery social writings of the Diggers and Levellers that helped to found modern political science came to an end. But the Restoration was never complete. Charles II in assuming the throne did not make all the mistakes of the earlier Stuarts. Most importantly he accepted the new science. While James I had only been puzzled by Bacon's plea for funding the sciences, Charles II chartered the Royal Society. Natural science then continued to advance after the Restoration. With the Restoration there was even more reason to treat social institutions as conventional, for there were further changes in social arrangements, more negotiations and compromises in church, state, education, law, and economy.

James II had become a threat both in trying to reclaim divine right prerogatives and, with a devout Catholic queen, in making the accession of another Catholic possible. A nearly bloodless coup replaced James with William and Mary of Orange. The arrangements confirmed the sharing of power between monarchy and Parliament. By 1688 the English had had two revolutions, while the French had another century to go before their first. While in England power and authority were being dispersed, in France they were being centralized. While the English were chasing out their second king, the French were building Versailles. Not just the unpredictable weather but also unpredictable social reality made the English sceptical. With conflicting sects, political theories, and kings, how could they accept a theory that made knowledge singular and certain?

Throughout this period idealist philosophy maintained its stronghold, taught from university chair to cathedral pulpit. In Britain there was another Platonic revival, centred in Cambridge and led by Ralph Cudworth (1617–88) and Henry More (1614–87). On the Continent three major, original, contributors to idealism emerged after Descartes: Malebranche, Spinoza, and Leibniz. Of the many lesser contributors one, the school of Port Royal, will be covered here.

Medical influences on the development of methodology, seen in every preceding period, continued. Plague was the impetus for the first collection of mortality statistics, the "bills of mortality" analyzed by Graunt, Petty, and Halley. Locke, another user of these early statistics, was himself trained as a physician. So was Petty, who used the anatomy analogy in studying the body politic.

By the end of the century we come to the first woman who contributed in her own name. Mary Astell was a Lockean unrecognized in the methodological literature, one can only suppose, for reasons of sexist prejudice. Her work was original and important, her style so clear and witty as to invite a wide readership. I suspect that the radicalness of her claim for women's equality made her unwelcome in the male scholarly establishment. Astell's relegation to the status of methodological nonentity marks yet another successful suppression of dissident ideas. It should strike a cautionary note that, for her, it did not take physical obliteration of her work. A woman scholar could be discredited and forgotten, her books remaining after her, unread.

THE FOUNDATIONS OF MODERN EMPIRICISM

Francis Bacon (1561–1626)[14] founded modern empiricism both by formulating most of what have become the standard rules of empirical method and by formulating its practical purpose: knowledge for the betterment of human life. Legally trained, after a stint in France with the French Embassy Bacon became an M.P., Solicitor-General, then Lord Chancellor. His early scientific work was squeezed into slack times at Court and between House sittings. Later, after being banished from Court and sentenced to the Tower for corruption, he turned full time to research and writing. Bacon was a compassionate man moved by the wretchedness of the human condition. Science and technology, as the means of increasing productivity and thus the material basis of life, were central to his scheme. His vision was no less than the restoration of human control over nature lost since the Garden of Eden. The rules of scientific method, with inference from observation and experiment, were a means to this end.

A materialist and an outspoken critic of Plato, Aristotle, and the scholastics, Bacon was nevertheless a Christian with strong Puritan leanings. The spiritual realm was higher than the material, but there was no rigid separation between the two as with Descartes. Life on earth was dignified, sacred.[15] I take Bacon's contribution to empiricism in the social sciences to be of the highest importance, marking the first real advance over the ancients. Significantly, he was a student of the pre-Socratic materialists, especially Democritus. Where Locke built on his work he did so in a fashion consistent with the basis Bacon laid. Yet Bacon never made any scientific discoveries himself, was no mathematician, and failed to understand the Copernican revolution.

Bacon's conception of the rebuilding of the sciences included research institutes, libraries, museums of natural history, laboratories, and universities with research facilities and incentives for professors to do research. The scheme clearly required major government support, for which Bacon argued long and hard. It was only after years of failure that he turned in earnest to writing. The project was first presented to Queen Elizabeth as part of a Court spectacle, but she was unimpressed. Bacon renewed his efforts with James I, an amateur scientist, dedicating the *Advancement of Learning* (1605) to him. The work is exceedingly cautious, introducing only the most presentable aspects of the project. It is also his only book written in English, for Bacon wanted it to be accessible to administrators. Otherwise he published in Latin, apparently considering English an upstart language that might not survive. The king was never converted to Bacon's scheme but sought his advice on state affairs and promoted his career. The "Wisdom of the Ancients" (1609) advanced Baconian ideas in the guise of fables. The king never commented on the work to Bacon but to someone else joked that it, like the peace of God, "passeth all understanding." *The Great Instauration* (1620), considered Bacon's finest work, was again dedicated to the king.

Bacon's earliest essays, published in 1594, contain only the barest mention of his real concerns. By 1603 his ideas on impediments to learning were appearing, with denunciations of Aristotle and the ancient approach to knowledge. He stressed need for natural history, facts, and causal understanding. Still, Bacon published only the most innocuous of his essays of this period.[16] The famous imagery of Nature in the service of humanity appears in one of the bolder, unpublished essays. Here he stated that his purpose was not to impart the figments of his own brain, "nor the shadows thrown by words, nor a mixture of religion and science, nor a few commonplace observations or notorious experiments ... No; I am come in very truth leading to you Nature with all her children to bind her to your service and make her your slave." Bacon hoped he would succeed in his only earthly wish, "to stretch the deplorably narrow limits of man's dominion over the universe to their promised bounds."[17]

Aristotle was "the worst of sophists stupefied by his own unprofitable subtlety, the cheap dupe of words." Just when the human mind had found rest in a little truth he presumed to "cast fetters" on our understanding, composing a "manual of madness" and making us "slaves of words" (63). Plato fared equally badly:

That mocking wit, that swelling poet, that deluded theologian. Your philosophy, Plato, was but scraps of borrowed information polished and strung together ...

When, however, you gave out the falsehood that truth is, as it were, the native inhabitant of the human mind, and need not come in from outside to take up its abode there, when you turned our minds away from observation ... when you taught us to turn our mind's eye inward and grovel before our own blind and confused idols under the name of contemplative philosophy; then truly you dealt us a mortal blow. (64)

Heraclitus, Democritus, Pythagoras, Anaxagoras, and Empedocles were mentioned as possibly better writers, known unfortunately only through inferior, surviving, writers of antiquity. Democritus Bacon singled out as having made a genuine contribution to knowledge.

In another early essay Bacon regretted the effects of blinding authority in preventing fruitful research. The whole scientific process had become "a succession of teachers and pupils and not of inventors and improvers of inventions" (76). The brief flowering of natural philosophy among the Greeks had been ended by love of argument and novelty. The human mind was biased against an active, productive kind of natural philosophy. Again the pre-Socratics were praised. Alchemists did some good, for in digging up a garden one might not turn up a pot of gold but at least improved the soil.

It was wrong to impugn the senses for mistakes on particular facts, which Bacon admitted there would be. These did not affect the final outcome for errors could be uncovered by an intellect "furnished with reliable information" (88). It was the intellect by itself that was thoroughly unequal to the "subtlety of things." How the intellect might acquire reliable facts was a question Bacon never solved, although he continued to make the claim throughout his writing. He was willing to admit numerous sources of error in his methodology but never gave up the belief that true knowledge could ultimately be found. Every individual, on account of differing education, interests, and constitution, was attended by a "delusive power" that mocked the mind (89). The mind was an uneven mirror, distorting the rays that fell on it by its angularities. Yet this was no excuse for scepticism, for instruments could be constructed to make up for the deficiencies of the naked eye and hand.

The importance of the mechanical arts could be seen, Bacon asserted, in the three great inventions that had occurred since ancient times: printing, gunpowder, and the nautical needle. No empire or school had exerted a greater influence on human life than these. Discoveries were made on occasion without deliberate effort; they would occur at a much greater rate when systematically sought. The mechanical arts were an even more important source of information than natural history, for nature betrayed her secrets more fully when in the "enjoyment of her natural liberty" (99).

Like a number of other methodologists Bacon saw his work as bridging empiricism and rationalism. Empiricists were like ants, gathering and consuming; rationalists were like spiders, spinning webs out of themselves. Bees combined both functions, gathering their material from garden and field, digesting and transforming it by a faculty of their own. True philosophy took its matter from natural history and experience and transformed it with understanding.

The kingdom of nature was, like the kingdom of heaven, to be approached humbly, by becoming like a little child. A great storehouse of facts had to be accumulated, sorted into orderly tables, and used to ascend to generalizations. The impulse to jump to first principles had to be checked. One should stick close to the facts, then move to generalizations of the "middle sort," and so progress up the ladder of the intellect. Conclusions drawn from a limited number of facts would be considered valid only on proof that no contradictory instance could be found.

The sacredness of the scientist's task and Bacon's fideism ring through in "The Refutation of Philosophies." God reserved faith for belief but gave the world over to the senses. God did not provide reliable and trustworthy senses so that we could study a few writings, but to study his *works*, heaven and earth, and celebrate his praises. The old philosophies should be used when convenient, but they were not to possess us. Again the ancient materialists were preferred to Aristotle for, as dedicated to experience, they penetrated more shrewdly and deeply into nature. Intellectual differences counted for little more than differences between the senses. We were "far from realizing how strict and disciplined" was research and how little it left to judgment (118). Elsewhere, as in "New Atlantis," the requirements for research were to be more rigorous. Pride was the reason that more discoveries had not been made in the past. People even imagined that they *made*, not *discovered*, the arts (120)! Not one achievement enriching the human estate could be credited to speculation. The practice of medicine, for example, came first, then theory. While the abstract sciences had remained at the same level for 2,000 years, with only some polishing, the mechanical arts had always been on the move.

After the early essays, the *Advancement of Learning* comes as something of a disappointment. It is long and rambling and shows the signs of hasty composition. There are nice turns of phrase – Bacon did aim to please – but the message is so watered down as not to seem worth the effort. The first fifty pages are taken up with a defence of learning at all; "pure knowledge" was not sinful but rather "proud knowledge." A superficial tincture of philosophy might incline one to atheism, but further study brought one back to religion. Further, learning was a better use of time than idle pleasure. That Bacon should have to go to such lengths to prove that learning was consistent with a good Christian life tells us something of the climate of opinion in which he had to work.

The finer points of Bacon's complex classification are only of antiquarian interest, but the major demarcations are important in the development of empiricism. The first division of knowledge was based on its source: divine revelation for divinity, the light of nature for philosophy. There is no reason to doubt Bacon's sincerity about revelation, but the separation of the two spheres could not have been more convenient for his empiricism. Philosophy was concerned only with knowledge that could be acquired through human effort, in the senses and reason. Revelation was the source for judgments of good and evil. People could philosophize about God, but Bacon thought little of the results. We should not presume to attain to the mysteries of God by contemplating nature. Note also that Bacon's commitment to value-free philosophy presupposes a sphere of knowledge based on revelation. It is not up to people but God to make judgments of right and wrong.

The "justest" division of learning was derived from the three different functions of the soul: history from memory, poetry from imagination, and philosophy from reason.[18] For history Bacon stressed the prosaic task of recalling what actually had happened. If poetry fell under the domain of the imagination, history was to be ruled by the memory. History, like philosophy, was properly concerned with individuals, but philosophy left individuals behind for general notions. The senses, as the source of individual data, led to the understanding, where images were ruminated on and impressions formed into classes. The division between the natural and social spheres was a division of subject matter. The sources of knowledge were the same for each, and Bacon went back and forth easily between them in giving examples. Natural philosophy divided into speculative and practical – the search for causes and the production of effects (92). The two were connected so that an advance in one helped the other. The "soul" of civil history was the coupling of events with their causes, the nature of countries and their people. The purpose must not be the gratification of curiosity only but to make the learned wise, not just to uncover how states run but to derive the best government. In *De Augmentis Scientarum* (1623), Bacon went further to include as tasks of civil history no less than the commotions of times, the character of persons, the instability of counsels, the courses of actions, the bottoms of pretences, and the secrets of state (432).

Empirical social science to Bacon did not mean confinement to trivial problems. He also conceded that there were great difficulties in taking on so much; no writing was so rare as true and perfect civil history. The purpose of knowledge in both social and natural philosophy was application. The greatest error of all was mistaking the ultimate end of knowledge; some coveted it for curiosity or entertainment, to win victory or lucre, few for employing the gift of reason to the use and benefit of humankind.

The *Advancement of Learning* throughout has an aura of sweet reasonableness about it. The doctrines of Plato and Aristotle were curiosities to be wondered at but not condemned. The pitch for educational reform was uncharacteristically mild, the need for research institutes and equipment mentioned only in passing. Yet the proposal comes through as the only possible conclusion of an eminently reasonable chain of thought. Errors begin with the mind hastily imbibing the first notices of things. These remain uncorrected. With the original notions confused, secondary notions were no less rashly formed. Human knowledge was not well put together but resembled a magnificent structure with no foundation. There was no other course but to begin the work anew, to rebuild the sciences, arts, and all human knowledge from a firm and solid base. Bacon's course was steep and rugged at the outset, but ended on a plain, while the then accepted method was at first view smooth and easy, but led to rocks and precipices.

Problems in acquiring true knowledge were all, with due effort, solvable. Bacon was sympathetic to the Academic sceptics, who included "many excellent philosophers." They denied certainty of knowledge with reason, holding that human knowledge extended only to appearances and probabilities. "Here was their chief error; they charged the deceit upon the Senses; which in my judgement ... are very sufficient to certify and report truth ... But they ought to have charged the deceit upon *the weakness of the intellectual powers, and upon the manner of collecting and concluding upon the reports of the senses*" (114–15). Instruments could make up for the deficiencies of the senses and correct methods of collecting data could be designed.

The Great Instauration is Bacon's masterpiece and a classic of methodology. With the benefit of some twelve drafts in as many years, it is his mature statement on the subject. Where it is repetitive one must be indulgent; Bacon was still writing for an unreceptive audience. He was also, for a change, direct, explaining the need for a new methodology and the faults of the old. He specified precisely his required methodological rules – induction – and gave examples of the necessary data base for natural science. There was the usual, but brief, criticism of Plato and Aristotle. Praise for Democritus was not hidden behind fables. Bacon published the work when he was fifty-nine and conscious that he would probably never finish the whole project. The only major section he finished was the book-length "Novum Organum" (1621), the name by which the whole work is known. There was to be a substantial section of natural and experimental "histories," meaning compilations of all the relevant facts. The "Novum Organum" was a series of aphorisms, succinct statements about a paragraph each. Bacon considered the aphorism conducive to science, its shortness getting to the "pith and heart" of science. The brokenness itself invites further inquiry and makes the "Novum Organum" eminently quotable.

The opening aphorisms give the central driving purpose of empiricist methodology, knowledge for application: "Human knowledge and human power meet in one; for where the cause is not known the effect cannot be produced. Nature to be commanded must be obeyed."[19] The empiricist sense of the hiddenness of knowledge reflects Bacon's forceful insistence that the "subtlety of nature" is many times greater than the subtlety of the senses,

understanding, and argument. The distinction between Bacon's new methodology and idealist speculation involves no crude sense/reason dichotomy
but different *degrees* of reliance on empirical data and different *processes*
of inference from data to theory:

There are and can only be two ways of searching into and discovering truth. The
one flies from the senses and particulars to the most general axioms, and from these
principles, the truth of which it takes for settled and immoveable, proceeds to
judgment and to the discovery of middle axioms. And this way is now in fashion.
The other derives axioms from the senses and particulars, rising by a gradual and
unbroken ascent, so that it arrives at the most general axioms last of all. This is the
true way, but as yet untried. (261)

"Literate" experience was needed, not just facts. The lower axioms differ
little from bare experience while the highest were most general and abstract.
Bacon even made a plea for middle-range theory, "the true and solid and
living axioms, on which depend the affairs and fortunes of men" (290). The
ant, spider, and bee analogies were again related, Bacon keen to make the
point that his methodology required not only the gathering of data but its
manipulation and digestion by the mind.

Bacon's analysis of the impediments to knowledge, more extensive than
anywhere in his earlier writings, is superb. The terms, the four idols, are
obsolete but the substance of his remarks not: "For it is a false assertion
that the sense of man is the measure of things. On the contrary, all perceptions as well of the sense as of the mind are according to the measure of
the individual and not according to the measure of the universe" (264). The
human understanding is prone, of its own nature, to suppose greater order
and regularity in the world than it finds. Once it has adopted an opinion it
draws all other things to support it. There might be more and weightier
contrary instances, but these it neglects, or somehow manages to set aside
as exceptions. It was the "peculiar and perpetual" error of the intellect to
be more moved by affirmatives than negatives when it should be indiffer-
ently disposed toward both alike. The human understanding cannot stop or
rest, conceive of an end or limit. In always struggling for something prior
it falls back on what is nigh at hand, final causes, which reflect human
nature rather than the nature of the universe. "By far the greatest hindrance
and aberration of the human understanding proceeds from the dulness,
incompetency, and deceptions of the senses; in that things which strike the
sense outweigh things which do not immediately strike it, though they be
more important." We know almost nothing about the nature of air, or of
the less dense bodies, for their workings are hidden and subtle changes are
not seen. Finally, human understanding is given to abstraction, according a
"substance and reality to things which are fleeting" (267).

The "idols of the cave" refer to errors introduced by individuals' variations in perception because of differences in education, associations, reading, and esteemed authorities. Everyone had a cave or den refracting and discolouring the light of nature. The "idols of the market-place" were the false or vague notions acquired from others, in the market-place as it were. The "idols of the theatre" come into people's minds from the various dogmas of philosophy, so named because "received systems are but so many stage-plays, representing worlds of their own creation" (264).

The Great Instauration gave little detail about how induction works, but it did lay down a few rules. "Simple enumeration" is not enough, its conclusions are "precarious" because based on too few facts, those close at hand. Properly, one went through "rejections and exclusions" and, only after a sufficient number of negatives, came to a conclusion on the affirmative instances. There was, in short, some kind of falsification process. Propositions so established were next to be tested to see if they applied more widely or fit only the particular instances from which they were derived. It was a question of proportion; one should neither "stick fast" to those things already known or "loosely grasp at shadows" (291). The problem was, upon a review of instances, "to find such a nature as is always present or absent with the given nature, and always increases and decreases with it" (320). "Since truth will sooner come out from error than from confusion" it was expedient to attempt to interpret nature in the affirmative (323).

Bacon ultimately believed that the laws of nature were knowable, but he sympathized with the doubts of Academic scepticism. Certainly he preferred that school to Plato and Aristotle. Doubt was useful when it encouraged a diffident approach to the subtleties of nature. The doctrine of those who denied certain knowledge had some initial agreement with his own, but ended in being opposed. "For the holders of that doctrine assert simply that nothing can be known; I also assert that not much can be known in nature by the way which is now in use. But then they go on to destroy the authority of the senses and understanding; whereas I proceed to devise and supply helps for the same" (263). The New Academy made a dogma of doubt. Unfortunately, Bacon contended, the human mind loses interest on despairing of the truth, so that despair is the greatest obstacle to scientific progress.

The sorts of helps Bacon envisaged were objective methods of measurement, including instruments and whole processes for making observations. It was necessary to separate the stages of sensation and judgment so that, in effect, the senses had only to make simple judgments. Bacon made clear that his methodology applies to all the sciences: logic, ethics, and politics as well as natural philosophy. His catalogue of particular histories begins with astronomy and goes on to physical and biological sciences, psychology, technology, industry, and the professions. He was always more profuse in natural science examples, but he went back and forth easily between the natural and social spheres.

We no doubt miss much of the excitement of the seventeenth-century war against the syllogism, but Bacon's attack ranks with the best of them. Thanks to the pithy aphorism form it is also one of the briefest.

The syllogism is not applied to the first principles of sciences, and is applied in vain to intermediate axioms; being no match for the subtlety of nature. It commands assent therefore to the proposition, but does not take hold of the thing.

The syllogism consists of propositions, propositions consist of words, words are symbols of notions. Therefore if the notions themselves (which is the root of the matter) are confused and over-hastily abstracted from the facts, there can be no firmness in the superstructure. (260)

To add insult to injury, Bacon later suggested that animals had some power of syllogizing (342).

Bacon was perhaps the first methodologist to stipulate the need for openness and clarity of method, which later became the rule that scientists must describe their procedures in sufficient detail for them to be replicated. He expressed this simply as the practice of presenting things "naked and open," so "that my errors can be marked and set aside before the mass of knowledge be further infected by them; and it will be easy also for others to continue and carry on my labours" (246).

Some commentators have considered Bacon's last work to be an abandonment of his logic.[20] It can perhaps better be described as an attempt at application with bizarre results. The *Sylva Sylvarum* (*Forest of Materials*, 1627) consists of more than 320 pages of scientific "facts," with a brief explanation of their usefulness. Intended to be a base from which scientific generalizations would be formed, it vividly demonstrates Bacon's commitment to induction. Unfortunately Bacon was pressed for time and had to rely on existing material. Thus citations from ancient and medieval sources appear with his own observations and those of his contemporaries.

There would have been something very wrong if someone with Bacon's vision had not at some point written a utopian essay. In fact Bacon wrote his late, and the "New Atlantis" was published posthumously in 1627. It is delightful in style, showing his literary powers at their best. The plot involves a ship landing accidentally at an unknown island, whose inhabitants go to a great deal of trouble to keep their existence a secret. The way of life of New Atlantis was civilized if authoritarian. Material conditions were prosperous. Science and technology, with the requisite social organization behind them, were the key to both the civilization and its prosperity. There was a college to promote scientific work, divided into sections on the sciences, mathematics, and the mechanical arts. Different people were assigned to different functions, including experimentation, compilation, and synthesis of data. In addition the island regularly sent off investigators to catch up with the technological advances of other scientists. Products of the island were taken along for trade, and new, model equipment bought with the proceeds (731). Altogether "New Atlantis" is a charming piece of utopian literature, showing how fine society might be if only Bacon's schemes were implemented.

With the benefit of hindsight it is easy to see that Bacon was one the most important influences on modern scientific method, the unity of the social and natural sciences, and their application to improve the world. Long before others he understood the importance of the material base to a society and the role of technology. Yet not until the foundation of the Royal Society, half a century after his death, was there any implementation of his ideas. It was not until the eighteenth century, with Adam Smith and Diderot, that Bacon was really understood, and more years still until his ideas were seriously implemented.

EMPIRICISM IN HISTORY

The resurgence of historical writing during the sixteenth century continued in the seventeenth, as will be seen with one major example, *Richard Brathwaite (1588–1673)*. *A Survey of History* (1638) was Baconian with its stress on accuracy in reporting the facts and knowledge for application. Like Bacon, Brathwaite held to a unity of method as being between "civil" and "physical" history.[21] The chief purpose of history was to give "a true Narration of what is done" or has been done, both for foreign and domestic affairs (2). "Invention" was the quality least needful to a historian. "It is sufficient for an Historian to express what he hath read or seene, truly, without concealing anything ... making truth the period of his discourse" (12). Methodologically this meant subjecting "inward" speculation to "outward" perception, preferring "the eye of the body before the light of the mind." Brathwaite counselled modesty in aspirations for knowledge. We should not affect to know more than nature has prescribed (163). The exact map of human affairs discovered was then to be put to use, to commend or reprehend, to know what was to be done and what avoided (27). The historian would make use of what had been done for advice for later times. The causes or probable causes of decay, for cities and empires, could be derived and useful lessons learned (222).

Although people have not, in fact, excelled in learning from the past to prevent mistakes in the future, this hope remains. Certainly throughout the seventeenth century there were to be improvements in the quality of historical writing. Yet both for quality and quantity of production we must wait until the eighteenth century for the really great advances.

HOBBESIAN ATOMISM

Thomas Hobbes (1588–1679)[22] worked at one time as a secretary and translator to Bacon, but Bacon's influence, if any, did not last. Rather Hobbes comes down to us as a deductionist and systemizer, important in empiricism for "mechanical philosophy." It was he who took atomism from physics and applied it to political science. Hobbes joked that his birth had been brought on prematurely by the invasion of the Spanish Armada (which in fact occurred two months later). Whatever the cause, he claimed to be a twin brother to fear, and his political philosophy bears this out. Hobbes' methodology brings together a most peculiar mixture of elements. His mechanism and nominalism, which were widely accepted, were coupled with a deductionism (which was not) and a determinism more characteristic of German idealism or later French positivism than anything British. His theory of knowledge was based on sense perception but was opposed to experimentation. Altogether Hobbes presents much more against the empiricist tradition than for it. In this history of methodology he can be seen as a transitional figure.

Hobbes formulated his mechanical philosophy about the same time as Descartes, but his contained no parallel idealism. Ideas were not inconsequential in his view, indeed he considered the false ideas of Puritanism to have been responsible for the civil war. But ideas were in turn explained as motion, the product of one body hitting another. Hobbesian motion was always externally caused by direct contact. There could be no action-at-a-distance. The force was a push, in contrast with the pull of gravitation. All existence in Hobbes' methodology was material. He conceded the existence of God and spirits but, like the Epicureans, held them to be material. They were too fine a material to act on other bodies, and hence could not be sensed.

Atoms were the basic unit, but – a view different from the ancient one – they were infinitely divisible. They had no properties except motion, so ultimately could be studied as geometrical figures. Human beings and the societies they form were ultimately mechanical bodies whose behaviour is determined in the same fashion as the motion of inanimate objects. The human body was a mechanical apparatus of sense organs – nerves, muscles, imagination, memory, and reason – moving in response to the impact of external bodies on it. Harvey's discovery of the circulation of blood in 1628 reinforced this conception by treating the body as a mechanism; the circulation of blood paralleled the revolution of planets as another case of motion.

A society was a giant body, Leviathan, whose organs were the government, army, and banks.

This back-to-the atoms approach, shocking in its day, marks another revival of an ancient endeavour. Democritus had constructed his theory of society from the basic units of atoms/individuals. Hobbes was now the first modern theorist to pose the question, "What if the atomists were right?" What if everything is nothing but atoms in motion? How will the state be constructed? In fact he also used Scripture as a source of first principles but he held that it was at least *possible* to derive the principles of political organization from atoms in motion.

The origin of all thought was sense, "for there is no conception in a man's mind, which hath not at first, totally, or by parts, been begotten upon the organs of sense."[23] The cause of sense was the external body or object pressing the sense organ, directly for touch and taste, or indirectly for the other senses. Sensation occurred when the "species" of external objects (the effluences of the ancient atomists) moved, directly or indirectly, the "spirits" of the animal.[24] Hobbes' account of sensation was identical with that of the ancient materialists. The will could not move the spirits, it was simply the last stage of the causal chain, itself the product of previous motions. Imagination was the obscure sense that remained after the sensation passed.[25] Creatures other than humans possessed it as well. Experience meant simply the accumulation of experiments, or the remembrance of specific antecedents and their consequences.

Hobbesian psychology can be seen as a new and radical version of the constancy-of-nature theme of the Hippocratics, sophists, and others. Authoritarian and hierarchical as Hobbes otherwise was, there is a radical equality in his psychology. He considered all persons to be objectively equal because all possess the same passions. The objects of those passions would differ depending on people's life experiences, but there is a fundamental democracy in Hobbes' understanding of human nature.

Hobbes was a strict nominalist, insisting that the senses give us knowledge only of particulars and that this did not give us authority for believing in the independent existence of universals or absolute ideas. The only universal was names, which are the product of thought and serve to guide us through the labyrinth of sense impressions. The painter of "man in general" was in fact painting a particular man.[26] The application of the same name, as "man" to many different men made people think, erroneously, that there was such a thing as "man in general." Equivocation of names made it difficult to recover the conception for which the name was ordained – the essence of understanding. Thus, while Hobbes' mechanist bent made him conceive of scientific knowledge in terms of causal relations, there is also a sense in which knowledge is definitional. Reasoning, or ratiocination, was equated with the making of syllogisms. True knowledge consisted in reasoning correctly about names. Conclusions were in accord with "right reason" when deduced from principles "found indubitable by experience, all deceptions of sense and equivocations of words avoided" (22).

An interesting reversal on certainty of knowledge occurs, Hobbes maintained, between the natural and social sciences. Demonstrative knowledge is possible in geometry because we ourselves draw the figures, and in politics and ethics for we make the laws to be studied. The motions involved were complex, Hobbes conceded, but certain knowledge is possible. In natural science, on the other hand, only hypothetical knowledge is possible, for we do not make the objects concerned and can only infer causes from effects.

Hobbes' methodological writings include frequent disparaging remarks about experimental method, so that scientists have blamed him for holding back science with his deductionism. This hostility to experimentation, however, is not the whole story.[27] Hobbes himself did amateur experiments in physics. Work he sent the Royal Society would be acknowledged but not published. He was never invited to join, and Society reviews of his work were hostile. Further, Hobbes abandoned his own deductionism in psychology and ethics.

Of the two stages in Hobbes' methodology, only the second was deductive. Propositions eventually reached ultimately rest on the principles arrived at through the first stage. In the case of mathematics these were definitions, but in the case of politics and psychology the process was more complicated. The thing to be explained had to be assumed to be the effect of unobservable factors. One had to search one's imagination for such factors as would, by strict logic, necessarily produce that result. Imagined, hypothetical forces had to be self-evident to any reasonable inquirer on introspection. Introspection, then, was essential to the process, and the imagination consulted was based on impressions. In political theory this means that characteristics of people in the state of nature are derived from observation of people in the real world. This, of course, raises the whole problem of deductive methodology. Except in pure mathematics the process has to start with some kind of induction. Hobbes' deductionism is further exaggerated by the fact that, in his practical writings, he described only the deductive stage.

Perhaps Hobbes' most important claim was that he founded the science of politics. He conceded that political thought dated back to the Greeks, but what they called philosophy was only each individual's opinion. The political philosophers Hobbes rejected were all idealists, however, so that his dismissal of earlier work was of only one tradition. The sophist tradition, Epicurus, and the Academic sceptics simply did not exist for him. Hobbes' claim to have invented the science of politics has not been allowed even by his most enthusiastic defenders, but he is generally credited with a couple of important developments. First, he shifted the basis of political theory from law to right, thereby instituting a major characteristic of the whole liberal tradition. This is one of the great ironies of his work: he drew authoritarian conclusions from decidedly liberal postulates. People kept back very little in entering the social compact, but what they did keep was the unconditional right to survive. They had onerous duties to the sovereign, but these were conditional on the sovereign's ability to protect them. This emphasis on rights marks a decisive break with ancient idealism, with its focus on virtue.[28]

The second radical feature of Hobbes' politics was its individualism. The fundamental units were individuals (referred to as "men," and probably only men were meant) who enter into a political compact. The sovereign's authority, great as it was, derived from their consent. Later writers would put quite a different twist on the "consent of the governed." The extremity of Hobbes' individualism had a number of nefarious implications at any time. Society was a market of bargaining individuals. "A man's worth was his price," by definition. People (or men at least) were seen as their own proprietors, owing nothing to society. Macpherson's critique of modern liberal theory goes back to the possessive individualism of Hobbes' formulation.

Hobbes' conception of natural law was secular, as deduced from human rather than divine, nature.[29] Strictly speaking, they were not laws, but methods suggested by reason to insure civil peace. The basis of natural law was to be sought not in ends, as the ancient idealists believed, but in beginnings, the passions that determine behaviour. Hobbes' theory was also secularized by replacing hell fire with death as the greatest evil in the world. The authority of the Scriptures even depended on the *civil* sovereign, for truths of revelation require interpretation. Hobbes was roundly attacked by the church for subordinating church to state. He was also attacked as a sceptic despite his extreme determinism; his theory in fact undermined faith.

When he died Hobbes left no school and no real followers, and he continued to be reviled as a corrupter of youth and a bad moral influence. *Leviathan* (1651) and *On the Citizen* (1642) were banned and publicly burned at Oxford in 1683. This was much too late to stop their being known, and they inspired many denunciations and refutations. Hobbes was given scholarly attention only when his views were well past being a threat, and then his influence on the Continent was somewhat greater than in Britain. Spinoza took over his theory on natural rights and the social compact. Leibniz for a short time adopted his materialism, and continued to admire him even when he reverted to idealism. Perhaps most important, people who did not accept his views came to use his method of argument. A Hobbes revival occurred in the nineteenth century, when the Utilitarians used his mechanistic determinism and individualism although in a quite different, liberal fashion.

EMPIRICISM IN FRANCE: RESISTANCE, COMPROMISE, AND DUALISM

The dualism of *René Descartes (1596–1650)* reflects the acute anxiety of the Counter Reformation world with the new materialist, anti-scholastic philosophy.[30] It was clearly a compromise and an unstable one at that. For example, the body was a machine but one made by God. In his own time Descartes was attacked for his materialism, although he always subordinated the material sphere to the ideal, and made other concessions to Catholicism. Thus Voltaire joked in his *English Letters* (1734) that Descartes was condemned in France for the only propositions of his philosophy that were true. And, while frequently taken to be a modernist fighting scholasticism, there is persuasive evidence that he was a good Catholic who correctly assessed the threat of scepticism. Descartes' own doubt then became an instrument with which certainty was re-asserted. Thus, for our purposes Descartes is primarily an idealist, although one who contributed to the development of empiricism. He is important also as the discoverer of co-ordinate geometry. The notation still used in algebra, letters at the end of the alphabet for variables, letters at the beginning for constants, came from him.

Reality for Descartes was divided into two radically different spheres each with its own independent existence. The spirit world consisted of God and immortal souls, the bodily world of stars, planets, the earth, plants, animals, and human beings. The main attribute of the spirit world was thought, that of the bodily world was extension. Thought was not dependent on any material substance. The spirit world was more knowable than the bodily, for the mind has some kinship with ideal phenomena. Yet, though he gave greater ultimate reality to the ideal world, Descartes was personally interested in the material world and devoted years of effort to studying it. Despairing of the knowledge he had acquired in school, he resolved to turn to the "great book of the world" and spent some twenty years travelling and observing. There is an anecdote that when a visitor asked to see his library, Descartes showed the man an animal he was dissecting. Yet references to "experience" in his work are rare, while "reason" and "judgment" recur on page after page.

The determination of truth lay in a "clear and distinct" understanding of phenomena, in the case of both the ideal and the corporeal. Certain knowledge was possible, for it was not in the nature of God to deny human creatures the necessary faculties for reasoning. Error was *never* the result of faulty reasoning but of mistaken or inadequate experience. It was necessary to go out into the world to study it, but this procedure was fraught with error, and reasoning alone sufficed for the discovery of many important truths. Descartes' system also includes *a priori* elements, or "common notions" acquired without experience. God insured not only an underlying order to the universe but also human faculties suitable to apprehending it. Astell exposed the fallacy of this point with a parody where she proved by "demonstration" that Columbus could not have discovered America. It was inconsistent with the goodness of God, she jested, to have allowed such "rich and delicious countries" and such improvements to have been so long concealed from us.[31]

However conservative idealist methodology usually is, Descartes' fundamentally democratic notion of reason was radical for his time. His theory that everyone was equally endowed with reason and that all should consult their own judgment rather than rely on traditional authorities obviously threatened established church and state. Descartes took the precaution of deferring to the Catholic Church, explaining in his *Méditations métaphysiques* (1641) that he submitted all his opinions to its authority, but Church officials were right to treat his emphasis on reason as a menace to their authority. Cartesian reason was never a challenge to belief as such, for Descartes held belief to be reasonable. He made every attempt to placate the hierarchy, leading a retiring life and not attracting attention to himself.

The "Discourse on Method" (1637) was just about to be printed when Galileo was convicted by the Inquisition. Descartes withdrew it, for the sun-centred theory was essential to his physics. When he did publish, he explained that he saw no challenge in Galileo to religion or state, and pious utterances permeate the "Discourse." The *Meditations on Metaphysics* was dedicated to the dean and doctors of the Sacred College of Theology of Paris. Many of the early Cartesians were clerics, including not only members of progressive institutions like the Oratoire but even certain Jesuits. Opposition was strongest among the Jesuits, who in 1663 succeeded in having Descartes' publications placed on the *Index*. This meant that they could not be used in schools and colleges in France, but by then it was too late to stop the spread of Descartes' influence. The Archbishop of Paris also issued a verbal ban on his teaching.

The "Discourse on the Method of Rightly Conducting the Reason" is Descartes' statement of his resolution to the problem of acquiring knowledge. It is what the French so aptly call a "genial" book, and so utterly charming as to touch the hardest positivist heart. Cartesian doubt is there given its most impressive exposition and there the democracy of rationalism rings its boldest challenge. It was written in French, "the language of my country," making it accessible to women as well as men (1:80). The "Discourse" was clearly intended to win friends for the "new philosophy." Unlike the

Principles of Philosophy it did not give a comprehensive account of the methodology, and has accordingly been considered a "vulgarization."[32]

The "Discourse" begins with an ironical statement on the equal distribution of reason: "Good sense is of all things in the world the most equally distributed, for everybody thinks himself so abundantly provided with it, that even those most difficult to please in all other matters do not commonly desire more of it than they already possess."[33] Good sense, or reason, was naturally equal in all people. It was not that some people are more rational than others, but that our thoughts pass through different channels and consider different things. Descartes' insistence on people's prerogative to make their own decisions concerning the truth or falseness of anything has fed both empiricism and idealism. The negative side of his democratic approach meant scepticism of everything derived from established authorities.

Descartes' indictment of the state of knowledge of his time had all the more power for the excellence of his own progressive education. He found himself encumbered with so many doubts and errors there seemed to have been no other result from his instruction. Literature encouraged good judgment and poetry revealed ravishing delicacies, but eloquence was more the gift of the soul than the fruit of study. Mathematics had been responsible for subtle inventions, contenting the curious and diminishing work. Despite its solid foundations, however, nothing more advanced had been built on it. Law, medicine, and other sciences were noted only for having brought honours and riches to those who cultivated them. Religious truths were revealed, apart from intelligence, to the most ignorant as much as to the most instructed. Philosophy was cultivated by the best minds but it had succeeded in propounding nothing that was not disputed. In so far as other sciences borrowed from it the same condemnation held. Descartes concluded that he would have to take as false all that was but probable, outdoing the sceptics at their own game, the better to attack them later. He resolved, as a result, to search no further than what he could find in himself, or which came from the "great book of the world," from travelling and experience: "I learned to believe nothing too certainly of which I had only been convinced by example and custom. Thus little by little I was delivered from many errors which might have obscured our natural vision and rendered us less capable of listening to Reason" (1:87). While Bacon's response to the same dismal assessment of the state of knowledge was an outward turning to experience, Descartes' was dual. Experience was one part of the answer, introspection another, and it was the latter that he most developed.

Cartesian doubt led in a few short steps back to certainty. As soon as Descartes realized that he must consider everything false, it was obvious that whoever thought this must be something: *"I think, therefore I am"* became a conclusion so "certain and assured that all the most extravagant suppositions brought forward by the sceptics were incapable of shaking it" (1:101). This "truth" he accepted without scruple as the first principle of philosophy. Descartes never admitted the difficulty he brought on with so fundamental a doubt. For, if one accepts the principle of treating everything as false that appears only to be probable, how can one have any confidence in one's subsequent conjecture, "I think, therefore I am"? It seems that Descartes hoped to win over sceptics by initially accepting their premises, but the problem remains. Descartes has accordingly been called a sceptic in spite of himself. In the *Meditations on Philosophy* he went so far with the sceptics as to entertain the possibility of a mischievous genie who made everything appear different from what it really was (1:148). Descartes was then unable to refute this possibility on rational grounds, but took recourse in faith; God was no deceiver. Descartes was also one with the ancient sceptics in accepting the religion, laws, and customs of his country.

The "Discourse" advances only four precepts, all resolutions Descartes determined to follow himself. The first was "to accept nothing as true which I did not clearly recognise to be so; that is to say, carefully to avoid precipitation and prejudice in judgments, and to accept in them nothing more than what was presented to my mind so clearly and distinctly that I could have no occasion to doubt it" (1:92). Here is the subjectivist core of idealism in its modern form. Rather than defining truth in relation to objective criteria, truth was what was clear and distinct in the mind of the thinker. "Clear" in turn was defined in the *Principles of Philosophy* in terms of what was "present and apparent" to an attentive mind, "precise and different from all other objects so that it contains within itself nothing but what is clear" (1:237). Something might be clear without being distinct (pain for example), but nothing could be distinct without being clear. The precept itself was devastatingly attacked by Descartes' pro-empiricist contemporary, Gassendi, who pointed out that we have often been deceived in matters we believed "as plain as daylight."[34] The precept also reveals the first betrayal of doubt, intimating the possibility of knowledge free of doubt.

The second precept was "to divide up each of the difficulties which I examined into as many parts as possible, and as seemed requisite" to solve them (1:92). The proposal itself resembles Bacon's reduction of phenomena to a manageable scale for purposes of study. Its purpose, however, reveals the idealist quest for certainty. Objects of study reduced to a suitably small scale are more easily understood intuitively, they more readily seem "clear and distinct." Certain knowledge will thus be more readily achieved. The precept also reveals a staggering assumption – that phenomena *can* be divided into units of appropriate size for thorough comprehension. There is no such expectation in empiricism. Descartes had a solution to the problem in faith: God, who created all phenomena, including the mind, could be trusted not to have created the mind unequal to the tasks set it.[35]

The third precept was "to carry on my reflections in due order, commencing with objects that were the most simple and easy to understand, in order to rise little by little, or by degrees, to knowledge of the most complex" (1:92). Again there is an assumption that God so arranged the world that such reasonable procedures would work.

The fourth precept was complementary, an enumeration of components. After dismantling problems into simple components there must be a reassembly, with careful examination to ensure that all components are accounted for and all inter-connections considered. Descartes elsewhere described this as induction following a long series of deductions. The process was of continuous, uninterrupted movement over the particular parts. Again the rationale was certainty. By reviewing everything together, reflecting on relationships and, as much as possible, distinctly conceiving of several things at the same time, our knowledge acquires greater certainty and breadth. Another of the purposes for the precept was more in keeping with empirical science, for review assists in the discovery of new things.

Descartes next showed how he had resolved to apply the precepts to his own life. Here, too, the quest for certainty is plain, as well as other more pious goals. He determined to employ his life cultivating reason, advancing as he could in knowledge and truth, following his method. He would not for a moment concern himself with the opinions of others but use his own judgment (2:106). To seek truth required rejecting as absolutely false all that one could doubt, in order to see whether anything remained that was entirely indubitable.

Proofs for the existence of God and the independence of the soul were essential components to the Cartesian system, for it was God who insured the adequacy of reasoning for the discovery of truth. The soul's independence was necessary for Descartes' position on the superiority of the ideal. Both proofs were based on reason as opposed to revealed truth or the authoritative teaching of the church, and both were resented as challenges to church authority. The "Discourse" proper was then followed by three substantive essays on optics, meteors, and geometry, which served as concrete examples of the efficacy of the method.

The *Principles of Philosophy* is the most complete and orderly presentation of Cartesian methodology. Written in Latin, and obviously intended for a professional audience, it provided operational details omitted in the more popular "Discourse." The methodology was presented in the form of 207 succinct principles, each with a paragraph or so of explanation. As in the "Discourse" application followed the methodology proper, in this case to the visible world (sun, planets, and elements) and the earth (heat, light, etc.). The accompanying substantive papers were intended not as exhaustive treatments but as examples. Descartes explained that full treatment would require numerous experiments, which could only be undertaken at public expense. He decided to content himself instead with study for his own instruction, and hoped posterity would see the eventual happy issue. Note the contrast with Bacon.

The object of Descartes' methodology here was the same betterment of the material and moral condition of humanity as in empiricism. Philosophy signified the study of wisdom, not only for prudence in affairs, but for a perfect knowledge of all things for the conduct of life, the conservation of health, and the invention of the arts. Again, as in empiricism, knowledge of underlying causes was necessary for application and was possible only after an orderly acquisition of basic knowledge.

It was in the *Principles* that Descartes accorded a place to what is for some people the most attractive feature of Cartesian thought: free will in the acquisition of knowledge. Principle 6 asserted that we have a free will which causes us to abstain from giving assent to what is doubtful. This is crucial, for it is this power that gives us the possibility of avoiding error. We do not have to assent to what we do not perceive clearly and distinctly, and accordingly we do not have to assent to what is untrue. But the same free will is also the source of error, for we are as free to assent to error as to refuse to. Sartre pointed out that no one before Descartes had stressed so much the relationship between liberty and negativity. The Cartesian, as the Christian, is free for evil, not for good, for error, not truth.[36]

A method of certainty would not be complete without the means to eliminate error, and Descartes provided his in the *Principles of Philosophy*.[37] The primary source of error was prejudices acquired in childhood when reliance on the senses is greatest and on reason least, where there is a tendency to confuse the properties of external objects with the sensations and reflections of one's own mind. Thus children think the sun is small because it looks small to them. Bad habits acquired in childhood are then difficult to forget. Fatigue was the next problem, for our minds tire when attention is required. Descartes believed it harmful to reflect on metaphysical principles for long periods of time. Finally, we attach our thoughts to words that do not express them exactly. Descartes never wavered in insisting that what was clearly and distinctly perceived was true. God gave us adequate faculties of reasoning, and error came exclusively from our failure to use them. Errors acquired in childhood, before one's reasoning capacity had matured, could be eradicated through the process of methodical doubt and the re-acquisition of what was clearly and distinctly perceived. By keeping to clear and distinct perception one could not err, for God was no deceiver.

In his letter to the French translator of the *Principles*, Descartes specified four degrees of knowledge. The highest degree was of "notions of themselves so clear that they may be acquired without meditation" (1:205). Descartes did not use the term "innate notions," but this must be close to what he intended. In the text he referred to notions "perfectly clear in themselves," not acquired by study (1:222). The second level was knowledge from sense experience. One would not expect it to have ranked first, of course, but that it came second of four perhaps deserves noting. The third was what "conversation of other men teaches us," the fourth reading as a type of conversation (1:205). Descartes here specified the writings of capable persons. Knowledge from experience, in other words, was to be preferred to the teaching of established authorities. Further, Descartes would rely more on the teaching of conversation than of reading. Proponents of the oral tradition may be pleased.

The Cartesian conceptualization of the material world largely resembled the empiricist. God had created matter and established the laws of nature that determined its subsequent evolution to the present. The notion of God as legislator of the universe was to become common enough later in the seventeenth century, but Descartes' expression of it was novel.[38] Copernicus and Galileo, for example, used no such term. It has been noted that the law-maker expression occurred some forty years after Bodin's (1566) theory of sovereignty, and arguably reflects the rise of royal power and the decline of feudalism. Again we see terminology from the *social* world being applied to the natural.

Cartesian laws of nature were unmistakably mechanical, much as Descartes tried to pass off his views as Aristotelian and contrary to Democritus. This was a sore point for the Church, and Descartes was blamed for eighteenth-century mechanical philosophy. The blame was only partially deserved, for his system included a "rational soul" in humans alone, which makes us radically different from animals. This soul, Descartes asserted, was entirely independent and could not be acted on by material bodies. The sharp distinction made between humans and animals typifies the whole idealist tradition.

Descartes ingeniously pursued the inevitable problem of connecting the material and ideal worlds in "The Passions of the Soul," which he wrote at the urging of Princess Elisabeth of Bohemia. Descartes was nowhere bolder or more original but, nonetheless his dualism cracks. His solution was to invent a new function for the pineal gland for the mediation of body and soul (1:345). There are pages of explanation as to the functioning of the "animal spirits," emotions, and so forth. Cartesian physiology, however, is a subject only for the dedicated, and will not be related here. Suffice it to say that Malebranche had a good point in insisting that Descartes' system stands or falls on the pineal gland. Malebranche was not to make the same mistake, nor was Leibniz or Spinoza, but all were to return to a pure idealism.

Princess Elisabeth herself was not convinced of the dualism. In a letter to Descartes she explained that she could not understand how an unextended and immaterial soul or mind could move a material, extended body. "It would be easier for me to concede the materiality and extension of the soul than give the capacity to move a body and to be moved by an immaterial body."[39] How also, if the soul/mind had no communication with the body, could it lose its faculty of reasoning through material conditions, as occurs in illness? Descartes answered these criticisms by repeating his earlier arguments. His compromise, in dualism, ultimately satisfies no one. By giving primacy to the ideal world, and insisting on the independence of the soul, Descartes grouped himself with the idealists. But since his materialism would not entirely go away, he continued to offend the guardians of orthodox idealism.

Descartes' machine imagery is often cited in the environmentalist critique of scientific method, which condemns him as having justified vivisection and cruel experiments by reputedly stating that animals could not feel pleasure or pain. Such critics, unfortunately, omit exact references, and my own and others' searches have failed to come up with any such statement in his published works.[40] Certainly Cartesians, and especially Malebranche, held that animals were unfeeling automata.

Descartes' views on the unity of science resemble Bacon's and those of other empiricists. In the *Rules* Descartes pointed out that facility in one area of applied work, for example painting, might not be congruent with facility in another, like working in a field. But it was erroneous, he believed, to think that the same held for science, for the sciences taken together were all identical with human wisdom, however different their objects.[41] Knowledge of one truth did not prevent us from discovering another, but in fact helped. Descartes then went on to an inference quite at variance with empiricism, making up for the deviation by being more Cartesian than ever. All the sciences are so interconnected that it is much easier to study them all together than to isolate one from the others!

Descartes also parted company with empiricists with his assertion that substances all have one main attribute which defines their essence or nature.[42] There is no such optimism in empiricism, either that any substance can be defined in any depth by only one attribute, or that the essence of any substance can ever be determined. We will see Locke arguing this point later. Descartes admitted that there were attributes other than the principal one, but one principal property of a substance always constituted its nature and essence, and all the others depended on it. Descartes' ambition with respect to level of knowledge, as is characteristic of idealists generally, was much greater than that ever intimated by any known empiricist. Not only was certainty within the power of human reason, but so was certainty about the very essence of things. It requires assumptions about the scope of human faculties empiricists feel are *unreasonable*. And this is the basis of my argument with idealism: it requires too many unreasonable assumptions.

Marin Mersenne (1588–1648), a good friend of Descartes, was probably the most important advocate of constructive scepticism in seventeenth-century France. Respected as a member of the scientific elite, his practical scepticism went against the French love of system. After his death his ideas, as Gassendi's, were eclipsed by Cartesian rationalism. In recent years appreciation for his cautious but hopeful methodology has grown,[43] but his work has yet to re-issued or translated.

Mersenne's chief methodological work was a massive, ungainly, and ill-written tome, *La vérité des sciences*, published in 1625. Its main point of constructive scepticism is reached in traditional dialogue form, via a tortured, circuitous route. A sceptic demolishes the case of the alchemist, with the usual sceptical arguments. The Christian (Mersenne) goes along thus far, but stops at the claim that there can be no knowledge whatsoever. Much is known, he maintains, at least well enough to be the basis for practice, which Mersenne then demonstrated with 800 pages of examples, largely from mathematics and physics. The argument is excellent, but tedious. Constructive, cautious, but hopeful empiricism is only reached by way of a treatise against *negative* scepticism.

Mersenne's model of the mind gave first place to the external senses, without which nothing can be known. There are also "internal senses" and a "common sense," or some kind of unifying or co-ordinating faculty, above both. Finally there is "the understanding" or "reason," the ultimate faculty of judgment, which assesses the reliability of data, takes care to insure not to be deceived by sense illusions, and decides when further or better measures are needed. The understanding did not pass absolute judgment until it had taken into consideration everything that could cause deception. For example, when he perceived a tower that appeared round, reason commanded the eye to look more closely, or the hand to take a compass, ruler or some other instrument to look and experiment. Then, "having made all sorts of experiments necessary to have certitude, it judges in a manner that it cannot be deceived. The knowledge it has is in conformity with the truth of the object."[44] Further, "the truth herself is judge of the understanding, for as soon as we learn something, and we believe it true, if the truth shows afterwards the contrary, as often happens, the understanding leaves the opinion it had and accepts the truth in question" (195).

In a much more modest way than the Augustinians, Mersenne attributed a kind of divine light to the understanding. Meditation was one way to activate it, but so were study, experience, and the sciences. Interestingly this "natural light of the mind" would not complete its task in this world but required the "supernatural light" of eternal glory. Certain knowledge, even with the aid of divine illumination, was not a thing of this world.

Mersenne criticized Bacon for being both too sceptical and not sceptical enough. Bacon's criticism of sense knowledge, the four idols, he saw as imitating the detested Pyrrhonists. Bacon himself made errors; he failed to consult other scientists; he recommended many things that had already been done. Our senses were limited to exterior knowledge. We could dissect things up to a point, but we would never manage to make our intellect equal to the nature of things, and that is why Mersenne considered Bacon's model impossible. The result would only be some new experiments, which ordinary philosophy could easily explain.

Mersenne anticipated Descartes' "I think, therefore I am" with a characteristically wordier, less lively phrase (204). He was also familiar with Augustine's centuries-earlier version, and reminded Descartes of it. Whether or not Mersenne influenced Descartes here is not known. Mersenne never favoured Cartesian philosophy and argued lucidly against it, but to no avail. He continued to serve his friend loyally, circulating the *Méditations métaphysiques* for comments; these Descartes then published as "objections," adding his own replies, which largely repeat his earlier arguments. The amiable Mersenne was one of those rare philosophers who never quarrelled with anyone.

Mersenne's friend *Pierre Gassendi (1592–1655)*,[45] a similarly ascetic priest, was bold enough to take on the task of reviving Epicurus. This was an unlikely project for a priest, and Gassendi was not consistent in carrying it out. Dissidence required courage in those days; Vanini was burned at the stake in Toulouse, and the Parliament of Paris forbade teaching contrary to Aristotle on pain of death. Gassendi got around the Aristotle problem by quoting nonsense from commentators and criticizing *them*, not the philosopher himself. Even then he published only half his work, and that anonymously. Another successful tactic (although not for Galileo) was to couch half his points for Aristotle, half against.

Gassendi's positive methodological views have to be culled from their protective trappings. In his paradoxes on Aristotle, he argued for a methodology of direct observation of phenomena. Reason was simply the force of the mind, nothing more, and nothing especially reliable. The dialectic was neither necessary nor even useful. To learn something one should turn directly to the art or science that treats it, not the dialectic.[46] In 1500 years of the dialectic no one had found any errors in Aristotle! Atomism appeared in Gassendi's philosophy as the best explanation of the world of appearances. Epicurus gave first place to the senses for acquiring knowledge, while Aristotle only paid lip service. Epicurus had also given reason an active role, in making inferences from sense data, in comparing and contrasting observations. More general ideas were formed from less general. The result was a kind of science that went beyond mere appearances, but without making claims to "the nature of things." We cannot know essences, so that in this sense knowledge was impossible. The senses can accurately report the qualities of things, and science is the explication of these qualities. With the sceptics Gassendi insisted that we can attain nothing but appearances and relationships. These we acquire well, relations as constant and valuable as the essences of the metaphysical. The sceptics were right to prohibit us from what *is*, fortunately leaving us sufficient assurances as to what appears to be.

Gassendi's revisionism was most flagrant in Epicurean physics. Eternal and indestructible atoms now lasted only between creation and destruction.[47] They had been created by God as the building blocks through which all things were made. Gassendi also gave the human body a second soul, for the first, Epicurean, soul was wholly materialistic and died with the body. He consistently opposed Cartesian idealism. His lengthy objections to the *Méditations* led to a break with Descartes (who cagily left these objections out of the French edition), but Mersenne later worked out a reconciliation. Gassendi's most salient point was that we often think we have a clear and distinct idea which we subsequently come to believe is wrong.[48] Although this is hard to dispute, Descartes remained unconvinced. Truth to Gassendi was singular and hard to find. Ordinary human beings could rarely be confident any particular idea was right. He was content to stick with a lower level of probable knowledge. Subjective judgment was not an adequate criterion for truth, yet Gassendi insisted that much could be known with it; negative scepticism remained the chief enemy.

Neither induction nor deduction offered any easy solutions to the problem of knowledge. Induction, based on what was better known, effects, was better. Deduction, based on what was less known, if more general, might not be so reliable. In either case, though, experience must be the judge.[49] After making inferences and deductions one must go back to experience and test them, a rare view for 1624.

Gassendi was well known by the scientists of his day, when the circulation of Latin manuscripts was the means of communication. That he did not publish in French undoubtedly hurt him later. Indeed, a generation after his death Gassendi was forgotten. The first major thesis on him, written in Latin, only appeared in 1898, and the modest revival of interest has been recent. His following now includes partisans who claim he invented empiricism fifty years before Locke.[50] At the other extreme is Marx, who shared Gassendi's interest in Epicurus, but dismissed him as a priest outside the realm of science. Yet even if Gassendi had written with the grace of Descartes, with brevity and consistency, there still would have been problems. There was just too much against constructive scepticism in France at that time. As we will see, the English climate was much more favourable to empiricism.

The fate of early seventeenth-century work on political economy shows the hostility in France. The *Traité sur l'économie* by *Antoine de Montchrétien (c. 1575–1621)*[51] seems less subversive than most banned books, but its author was a Huguenot, killed in the Huguenot revolts, his body mutilated and burned. With the revocation of the Edict of Nantes, the followers of Calvin lost their few precarious rights to French publication. Like many banned works, the *Traité* was known to experts in the field, but suppression meant scant availability and little public discussion.

Montchrétien's economic treatise, published in 1615, contains much that is unrecognizable as economics, but it did pioneer a few basic points. Montchrétien distinguished the estate of labourers, artisans, and merchants from that of the nobility and clergy. The popular estate, the "fingers of the hand" was the only productive one of the three. He condemned the contemplative life for its laziness, the nobility for fondness for luxuries. Instead he urged industry and the creation of productive capacity. He argued that a greater use of machines and finer division of labour would increase production. A good 150 years before Adam Smith, Montchrétien advocated a large degree of freedom of commerce and an end to monopolies. He himself learned the cutlery business while in exile in England (for killing his opponent in a duel). Montchrétien had an early conception of the relationship between politics and the economy. All of this makes him a precursor to the Encyclopedists, especially Diderot, and the line of French materialists through the nineteenth century to Marx. These developments were many years in coming, though, for Montchrétien's work was not carried on in France after his death.

Cartesian dualism proved to be highly unstable; it quickly broke down into its two components, at which point its dominate idealism took over. *Nicolas Malebranche (1638–1715)* was perhaps the most influential Cartesian in seventeenth-century France, and his version of Cartesianism, notably in *La recherche de la vérité* (1674–5), gained an official acceptance the original never achieved.[52] Malebranche proclaimed himself to be a follower of Descartes, quoting the master's "indubitable demonstrations." His version of Cartesianism, however, eliminated almost everything it shared with empiricism, notably the scepticism. Malebranche considered Descartes to be a master on the body, but St Augustine was better on the soul. Accordingly, he took Augustine's Platonism into Cartesianism, making it more idealist than ever. Augustine became an unquestionable authority, reference to whom ended all discussion on a point.[53] Malebranche was hardly exceptional in going back to ancient sources, but he made much greater use of scholastic sources than did others of his time. The question of how immaterial entities (our minds) acquire knowledge of material objects was a variant of a common scholastic problem: how angels acquire knowledge. Malebranche's aim was a Christian philosophy, including a philosophy of knowledge in harmony with revealed Christian doctrine. This had to be possible, for truth was ultimately unified. I do not much favour his solution, but it is interesting for its boldness. And it was popular. As empiricism began to gain ground Malebranche became *the* philosopher to defend the old beliefs.[54] He had only minimal interest in the physical sciences, which he disparaged as futile and even impossible.

Malebranche's methodology assumes an absolute division between the ideal and material realms. He extensively discussed the errors of sense data, making the usual points, which need not be repeated here. The problem was the bridge between the two realms, especially how ideas, which are immaterial, may be acquired of material objects. Malebranche considered all the standard available accounts wanting. Ideas could not come from effluences thrown off by objects; our minds could not produce them; they were not born with us; nor were they found by reflection on the mind's own qualities.

Malebranche's solution was the "vision in God," a distinctive Malebranchist doctrine. We see all things in God, at least all ordinary created objects. The argument was that God must have had in him the ideas of all things he created, because he could not have made them otherwise. God did not do anything without a reason, thus he would not have made our minds without intending to know us. He was more closely related to our souls than our bodies were. (This leaves unanswered the basic dilemma as to how an immaterial God could be intimately related to or united with anything material. As Locke pointed out in his critique of Malebranche, these notions all imply bodily relations, as between connecting surfaces, but God is not a body and has no surfaces.[55]) The mind could see ideas in God, representing created things, so long as God wished to reveal them.[56] Not only would God not deceive us, he would positively reveal information to us.

Malebranche initially described this theory as an explanation more reasonable than other current "hypotheses." Elsewhere he claimed that it was "more than probable." This, Malebranche insisted, was in an "intelligible" way. How matter could be "intelligible" was something we could not understand, a point which also perplexed Locke. Not fond of scholarly rows, however, Locke did not publish the essay he wrote criticizing the methodology.

Malebranche did not stint with practical advice as to how to put his methodology to use. The mind became purer and more luminous in union with God, but corrupted, blind, and weak in association with the body; "when a man judges things only by the pure ideas of the spirit, when he avoids with care the confused noise of creatures, and going into himself, he listens to his sovereign Master in the silence of his senses and his passions, it is impossible that he will fall into error" (1:16). The advice in *Entretiens sur la métaphysique* (1688) was to go into your office, pull down the blinds, reject everything that enters by the senses, silence the imagination, and forget, if you can, that you have a body (12:32). The barriers to knowledge, in brief, were sin and pleasure. Thus, the pursuit of knowledge requires privation of pleasure, distance from the world, and disdain for all things sensible. This view would obviously strain intellectual exchanges, for it is sin that keeps one's opponent from "seeing the light." Because Malebranche was too decent to accuse anyone of being a sinner, he avoided scholarly exchanges. His forty-year correspondence with Leibniz was at the latter's initiative, Malebranche flagging all the way.

Working with the vision was an "inner voice," which acted as a check on the decision to accept or reject a judgment (1:55). Properly speaking it was not the senses that err, but we make incorrect use of our liberty, too hastily accepting or rejecting a proposition. Again it was sin, wilfulness, that was responsible for error. Malebranche held that the most beautiful, the most dignified study was that of "man" (1:20). He was also fairly contemptuous of natural science, although he had studied it as a young man and went back to it after his first book was put on the Index. He was an honourary member of the Academy of Sciences. Much of his criticism of natural science concerned thoroughly legitimate points: sloppiness in research technique, triviality of subject matter, preference for novelty over more important but mundane subjects, and the choice of subjects for personal profit rather than scientific interest. He also displayed an ambivalence to the very enterprise of seeking knowledge of the physical world. From the perspective of empiricism, Malebranche appears decidedly as a step backwards. Cartesian dualism was hardly empiricism, but its scepticism and break with scholasticism both encouraged the empiricist cause. Malebranche revived the scholasticism, removed the scepticism, and downplayed the science.

There are defects in Malebranchism, even as an idealist philosophy. Most notable are the contradictions in the notions of intelligible extension and substance. Malebranche used "place" and "space" for immaterial entities, rather missing the point. He used circular arguments in his "demonstrations." His reasons often amount only to the elimination of possible alternatives, but hardly *all* those possible, so that *non sequiturs* abound. Strict rationalists would be offended by the frequency of his reversions to authority. He aimed at the reconciliation of religion and philosophy, which he did by integrating Catholicism with neo-Platonism.

Malebranche is also the major source of the contention that animals cannot feel, hence a rationalization for their ill treatment. His source was Augustine of Hippo, who had always taught the reverse, that animals can feel. Malebranche in effect revised his predecessor, using Augustinian doctrine on the soul to rewrite the point on sensation. If animals do feel they obviously suffer pain, contrary to the teaching that only those deserving it suffer (3:236). Thus the conclusion that animals lack sense derives not from the application of scientific method but from wholly speculative arguments based on authority.

To *Antoine Arnauld (1621–94)* and *Pierre Nicole (1625–95)*, Malebranche's methodology was "the worst invented and most unintelligible of hypotheses."[57] Their school of Port Royal advanced another, less Platonic but no less anti-sceptical version of Cartesianism. Philosophically more correct, it relied on reason without recourse to the vision-in-God. There were no such contradictions as intelligible matter. Yet Augustine was cited as an authority, reference to whom settled the point (267). The *Logique du Port Royal* (1662) was highly dogmatic, pronouncing axioms with unshaking confidence. Axiom 1 set the tone from which the others followed: "All that is comprised in a clear and distinct idea of a thing can be affirmed with truth" (294).

Arnauld and Nicole did not go so far as Malebranche in treating sin as the barrier to knowledge, but they did link scepticism in methodology with moral laxity. People who doubted in a general way fell into religious uncertainty. Doubt became a convenient escape for conscience. It is implied that the doubter perversely *chose* to doubt, to avoid religious duty. The school of Port Royal also begs important questions. Discerning the true from the false is obviously crucial, yet Arnauld and Nicole could utter such platitudes as, "Those who choose well are those who have the right mind [esprit juste]; those who take the wrong position are those who have the wrong mind [esprit faux]" (3). Who could argue, but what does this tell us? Yet the Port Royal revision of Descartes found a wide following in France.

Some decades after Mersenne and Gassendi's constructive, if convoluted, scepticism, the next major French contribution was the reverse: lucid, indeed witty and scathing, but negative. Unlike the two cautious Catholics, *Pierre Bayle (1647–1706)*[58] was a Protestant who suffered persecution after the revocation of the Edict of Nantes. Similar to the constructive sceptics and Cartesians, religion and moral concerns remained central to Bayle, but he added a defence of tolerance similar to Locke's. Bayle's vigour and clarity, if not his negativism, were a source for Voltaire and the Encyclopedists. His "*Dictionary* is a graveyard of ideological systems ... He dismantles totems, treats heterodox notions with impartiality, ridicules theologians and their anathemas, reveals the bankruptcy of received ideas, and yet leaves the foundations of morality intact."[59] Both the *Système de philosophie* and *Dictionnaire historique et critique* (1696) cut through obfuscation and qualification. It would be difficult to better his exposé of the claim to certainty of the major schools. The very diversity of schools proved that no certain principle was evident, "for if one were, the philosophers would all have agreed to it."[60] Yet Bayle's acceptance of Cartesian dualism and his belief that absolute monarchy was necessary limited his appeal for eighteenth-century theorists.

It is easy to see how the *Dictionnaire historique et critique* would be a banned work. Its three volumes were a source of acerbic commentary on major thinkers and periods. It covered ancient scepticism, the materialists, religion, and history. Bayle stated what was increasingly becoming obvious, that scepticism was a threat to religion, not the state. Church authorities detested Pyrrhonism, and with reason, because religion required certainty, a position not shared by the English divines of the time. Yet it was not a threat in civil life for it taught conformity with custom even without certain knowledge.[61] For its exposé of ignorance and intolerance, the *Dictionnaire* became a tool in the struggle for religious tolerance.

There are elements of the sixteenth century in Bayle, even if his expression is much more developed. A fideist like Montaigne, he argued for faith as a source of truth, given the failure of reason. His criticism focused on the weakness of reason, not sense perception. In retrospect, it seems ironic that this advocate of faith and underminer of reason should have been an inspiration for a period that was so soon again to construct systems and denounce faith. Such ironies are common enough in this history that it is perhaps more telling that scholars still debate what Bayle believed at all.

CONTINENTAL IDEALISM

If some philosophers have been slow to publish, *Benedict Spinoza (1632–77)*[62] was a case of reluctance in the extreme. He wrote in Latin, for he preferred that his work not be read widely than be read and misunderstood. In fact, his methodology goes back to esoteric notions reminiscent of Parmenides and the Cabbala. Being and knowing are again identified, as in a true idea's knowing itself to be true. Spinoza published only two works in his lifetime, a critical account of Descartes (1663) and, anonymously, *A Theologic Political Treatise* (1670). The latter argued that freedom of opinion was not only consistent with piety and public peace but essential for both. Most of Spinoza's writing was published by his friends after his death.

Spinoza's theory of knowledge began with a classification of modes of "perception," or means of acquiring knowledge.[63] He gave four initially, which he later collapsed into three. "Hearsay" or "report" was the first, a means only of uncertain knowledge, affording no insight into the thing itself. Next was the perception of "mere experience," or experience not yet classified by the intellect. This was the source of most practical knowledge in everyday life, but it provided only uncertain knowledge and no insight into essences. The third mode of perception entailed some, but inadequate, knowledge of the object's essence or cause. Thus one could have an idea of a thing, draw conclusions about it without error, but fall short of perfect knowledge.[64] This knowledge could occur by inference from an effect to a cause which, since the knowledge of the essence was not direct, could not be perfect. Finally, there was the certain "perception" of the essence or cause of an object without danger of error. It also constituted perfect knowledge, but few things could be known in this way. Mathematical propositions were an example, as the "knowledge" that two lines parallel to a third were parallel to each other. Knowledge of this sort could not involve pictorial images but only pure definitions. As to how this knowledge was achieved Spinoza gave scant detail. An important step was the recognition and elimination of "false ideas," which basically means those that are not necessary or are problematic because they depend on some other causal information.

Spinoza's identification of being and knowing meant the exclusion of any requirement of verification. Truth needs no sign; it manifests itself. One who has a true idea simultaneously knows it without doubt.[65] How this occurs is not clear, for Spinoza elsewhere conceded the possibility of human error. He indeed acknowledged the possibility of his own and had no confidence in the masses' doing any better. Yet, "for the certitude of truth," he declaimed, "no further sign is necessary beyond the possession of the true idea."[66] But how do we know we possess the true idea? One begins to suspect a tautology here, as in the next example. A "true idea" is distinguished from a false idea by its "intrinsic nature" more than its extrinsic object. The actual example was an architect's conception of a "properly-constructed building." Such conception would constitute a "true idea" even if the building were never constructed. But Spinoza never asked some central questions. What if the building fell down? What if the conception was good but, say, the builder used shoddy materials, or the building was felled by a hurricane or explosives?

Much of the discussion throughout Spinoza's works concerns entities described in the singular, which in the real world exist in large numbers and great diversity. Spinoza defined, for example, an attribute of a substance as that which the intellect perceives as constituting the essence of substance (2:45). My question is, Whose intellect? God exists because the nature of God can only be conceived of as existent. By whom? The human mind has an adequate knowledge of the eternal and infinite essence of God. Again, Whose mind? The "true aim of government is liberty."[67] But for what government is this true? Whose liberty? Clearly different people/intellects/ minds have different conceptions of God and different perceptions of various substances. The fact that Spinoza wrote in Latin, which has no definite or indefinite articles, does not help, but the problem would seem to be more basic. My impression is that Spinoza had some Platonic vision of "the mind," that his methodology has no reference to the actual world of many, differing intellects. To my mind this is the most fundamental error of

Spinoza's approach to knowledge. It is not just that one cannot prove propositions about natural phenomena by deduction. Rather Spinoza has removed himself from the contest, for he was not talking about how real people acquire knowledge, but only how some abstract "the intellect" would. I have gone to some trouble here, for this error is general in idealist methodology, including Malebranche, Leibniz, and even Kant, who was himself severely critical of Spinoza. Through Kant and Hegel this conceptualization continued in idealist versions of Marxism.

"The human mind is part of the infinite intellect of God; thus when we say, that the human mind perceives this or that, we make the assertion, that God has this or that idea."[68] "The" human mind perceives what happens to objects, because knowledge of such happening is necessarily in God, and in so far as God constitutes the human mind, knowledge of the thing will necessarily be in "the" mind. If this is so, how can Spinoza account for error, at least without blaming God for it? (Malebranche's theory that we see all things in God is an improvement here, for human sin becomes the barrier to knowledge.) For Spinoza, every idea in us that is absolute or adequate and perfect is true; the only source of falsity is knowledge by report or mere "experience" (2:108). But why, given that bodies – which experience – are part of God, should there be error in their perception? If all our ideas are true because they are of God, should not all our perceptions be true as well, for are not our sense organs and the objects we perceive also of God? If extension and thought are only different ways of conceiving of the same substance why should the one be thoroughly prone to error and the other perfectly free of it? Spinoza rejected dualism in ontology (what things are) but insisted on it in epistemology (how we know things).

Spinoza has often been described as the last of the medievals, but there are also modern elements in his thought. Defending freedom of opinion, he held that only deeds, not opinions, should be grounds for charges. His strongly Hobbesian political theory was defended on rationalist grounds. Thus the very teaching to obey authorities was offered in a manner disdainful of authority. It would be dangerous for the sovereign to deprive people absolutely of their rights, but Spinoza contested even less than Hobbes the sovereign's *right* to do so. His extreme determinism was bold in its day.

In the century after his death Spinoza was actively slandered. Empiricists rejected him for his idealist intuitionism and authoritarianism. For idealists his unorthodox theology made him seem an atheist. Descartes had been difficult enough; Spinoza was too extreme. It was not until the nineteenth century that Spinoza gained a respectable following. The German romantics led the way, English romantics followed. He then became popular in the Soviet Union, where he was written about more than any other pre-Marxist philosopher with the possible exception of Hegel. For the Soviets he was a materialist for recognizing matter as an attribute of God, and an atheist for depriving God of the functions of creation, miracles, judgment, and purpose. His doctrine of nature as self-caused and eternal found favour, while there was little comment on his authoritarianism.

Gottfried Wilhelm Leibniz (1646–1716)[69] was curmudgeonly as a courtier, his writing was graceless, and in academic politics he was hopelessly out-manoeuvred by Newton. Yet there remains something attractive about this seventeenth-century idealist. The uncompromising nature of his deter-minism and essentialism may not convince, but they cannot fail to impress. His theodicy endures as one of the most charitable ever, whether or not this *is* the best of all possible worlds. Evil exists in the world, Leibniz admitted, but only to the least degree possible to permit ordinary functioning through the laws of nature. Voltaire replied to Leibniz's optimism with a comic novel, *Candide*. Leibniz is also a major counter-example to the environ-mentalist critique of empiricism, coupling his opposition to empiricism with the most mechanistic determinism ever to appear.

Leibniz maintained a vast network of collegial contacts, including the most distinguished scientists and philosophers of his day. In Paris he met Malebranche, Colbert, Bayle, and Arnauld, Spinoza in Holland, and later also Locke in England. He had a strong sense of the social nature of knowledge, especially of the need for institutions to promote co-ordinated scientific work. He planned the Prussian Academy and was involved also in attempts to establish a scientific academy in St Petersburg. Leibniz did not publish systematically. His motives for publishing, according to Bertrand Russell, were opportunistic: to please a prince or refute a rival.[70] A lesser-known interest of Leibniz's, deliberately kept quiet, was cabalism.[71] Appar-ently his views were influenced by Anne, Countess of Conway, a prominent seventeenth-century mystic.

Methodology for Leibniz was never a central interest and was always subject to metaphysical concerns. Although his metaphysics were well known, much of his methodological work remained unpublished during his lifetime.[72] His failure to publish may have been due to a genuine reluctance to commit himself. His work certainly contains major contradictions and many ambiguities. Between 1700 and 1704 he wrote, in French, a book-length critique of Locke's *Essay concerning Human Understanding*, pub-lished in 1765 as the *Nouveaux essais*. The Lockean position is sympathet-ically presented, and it is clear also that Leibniz had a better grasp of empiricism than most idealist philosophers. He used a dialogue form, with a character each presenting Locke's and Leibniz's views. The pro-Leibniz character makes some concessions, but for the most part the two talk past each other.

The central thesis of idealism, essentialism, appears in Leibniz's meth-odology in full vigour, coupled with a determinism sturdier even than the usual in idealism. The essentialism came naturally enough through Leibniz's scholastic education. Plato was his favourite author, he also held Aristotle in high esteem. As a young man he had rebelled briefly to espouse the materialism of Gassendi and Hobbes. Largely for religious reasons, however, Leibniz repudiated the "new philosophy," and never again left the fold. (Materialism could not explain transubstantiation.) The Platonic influence is pronounced throughout Leibniz's work. There is a God, whose existence is the only knowledge we have. God holds all knowledge in his mind, so that to know all things would be to know the mind of God.[73] Knowledge in Leibniz's system was essentially definitional. To know something was to have a clear and adequate definition of it or, in his terminology, to be able to identify the complete predicate with the complete subject. This identification implies knowledge of the terms or processes of change, which Leibniz saw as completely predetermined. The image of a wound-up clock applies here; the universe and all its component parts were fully wound up and set in motion at creation, to unwind gradually over time. God's initial action done, no further intervention was necessary. Leibniz indeed argued against the Newtonian view of God's sustaining the universe. This was to suggest that God's work had been imperfect. Environmentalist critics of empiricism might note that the methodologist with the most mechanistic determinism was an idealist who had vehemently rejected empiricism.

Again rejecting empiricism, Leibniz held it to be possible to know the essences, not simply nominal definitions, of things. The basis of knowledge, he maintained, lay in "clear ideas," meaning those for which the terms could be expressed in a finite number of steps. Humans were capable of knowledge of this kind, but for many matters an infinite number of steps was required, which only God could manage. Thus for God all knowledge was analytic. Practically speaking, people would often have to be satisfied with less than the knowledge of essences, or only empirical knowledge. If, for Descartes, knowledge entailed a chain of intuitions, for Leibniz it was a chain of definitions.[74] In the "Elements of Natural Science" (1684) Leibniz argued the validity of *a priori* reasoning, even to arrive at the principle of sensible things. The process entailed demonstrating "from the known nature of God" the structure of the world which is in agreement with divine reason. From this structure, one could finally arrive at the principles of sensible things. Why this confidence? Since the *a priori* method was the "most excellent," it did not seem to be "entirely impossible."[75]

Difficulties are greater and abuses more likely with the *a posteriori* method, because it rests on analogies and induction. Leibniz admitted that the *a priori* method was difficult and that not everyone should undertake it. As time went on he became more modest in his expectations of attainable knowledge. Later in life he came to hold many things as hypothetical which he had earlier believed to be capable of certain knowledge. Most, if not all, knowledge of phenomena was only hypothetical. Observation and experiment were required to fill in the gaps of knowledge.

Body and mind in Leibniz's methodology were radically separated, characteristically for reasons of religious doctrine. To allow for interaction between them would be to accept the heretical notion that matter could think, which Locke was prepared to entertain, and which many materialists boldly asserted. Instead, to Leibniz, the mind was "windowless," unable to receive sensations from outside. His device for reconciling the two spheres was the original doctrine of "pre-established harmony." Both spheres were completely determined in such a way as to coincide. The mind's perception of an external object was not caused by the object, but was an act of the mind itself, at the same time. The separation of body and mind in Leibniz's terminology was part of a greater separation of discrete units, monads in his terminology, the "effective atoms" of the universe. Monads did not interact with each other but were separately pre-determined.

Leibniz made much, though not always consistently, of the important idealist methodological parallel distinction between mind and body and truths of fact and reason. Like Kant a century later, Leibniz was always careful to insist on the necessity of the senses for all knowledge. Like all idealists, however, he preferred truths of reason to truths of fact, which were much more subject to error. Reason was associated with the operation of the mind, although sense data were always somehow involved. Leibniz noted that it was impossible for the senses to convey knowledge of universality or necessity, a notion much more associated with Kant. Kant also followed Leibniz in inferring from this that although the senses could not supply such information, reason would. Both confounded possession of the *notions* of universality and necessity with *actual* universality and necessity, or the correct application of these notions. The inferiority of ideas based on sense impressions lay in their lack of clarity: "Ideas which come from the senses are confused, and the truths that are based on them are as well, at least in part. On the other hand, intellectual ideas, and the truths based on them are distinct, and neither have their origin in the senses, although it is true that we could not ever think without the senses."[76] The inconsistencies are readily apparent. Sense impressions obviously play some, although unspecified, role even in ideas of reason, so the potential for error and confusion hold also here. Leibniz never gave any detailed account of the role of the senses in the process, and frequently simply ignored the point of their always being involved.

Perhaps the most famous, or infamous, element of Leibniz's philosophy was his doctrine of the "best of all possible worlds." God, in determining the nature of the world, or in selecting the set of natural laws that would govern it, naturally chose the best possible. In effect, God had achieved the

Utilitarians' objective, the greatest good for the greatest number. Evil existed in the world, but only the minimum possible commensurate with the best possible total. God willed only what was good, merely accepting the evil inevitable with it; even God could not violate natural laws. The best of all possible worlds also had to be the fullest, for a vacuum would suggest lack of divine capacity. If God were greedy in this respect he was parsimonious in others, preferring the simple and general in laws of nature. Leibniz even argued that a hypothesis became more probable as it was easy to understand and wide in force.[77]

Like so many other idealist philosophers, Leibniz was in some doubt as to the existence of the material world. It seems that he started out with a common-sense acceptance of matter. After his break with godless materialism, he developed his idealism, ultimately going to the extreme of denying the existence of matter. Certain fragments of his writing suggest there was no actual creation, but that what we know of existence consists of essences existing in God's mind. Yet Leibniz continued to do historical research and advised on numerous scientific and technological matters. As a courtier he was constantly involved in the real world of war and intrigue.

Leibniz also gave practical methodological advice, anticipating points in C. Wright Mills' "On Intellectual Craftsmanship." For example, Leibniz noted in "Elements of Natural Science" that one who dealt with a limited field rarely discovered anything new since the subject was soon exhausted. But, he added, "from those who investigate many different things and are gifted with a combinatorial genius we may expect many new and useful interconnections of things" (281). Two centuries later Mills recommended a thorough review of one's complete file of notes, including those with no obvious relevance to the topic at hand. "Imagination is often successfully invited by putting together hitherto isolated items, by finding unsuspected connexions."[78] Even Leibniz's greatest partisans have conceded inadequacies in his position on error.[79] While Locke devoted chapters to the subject, Leibniz gave it only short, peculiar, mention. Leibniz's merits earned him the interest of the great methodologists, including such British empiricists as Bertrand Russell. Yet his methodology ultimately fails. His assertions in defence of certainty are unsupported. The inconsistencies remain crucial, as does his failure to deal with error, the existence of which he increasingly conceded.

NATURAL LAW THEORY

Natural law theory comes into this history more for the assumptions made in it than any explicit methodological stance. The two theorists to be considered here, *Hugo Grotius (1583–1645)*[80] and *Samuel Pufendorf (1632–94)*, did not write on methodology *per se*. Both believed it was possible to develop prescriptive ethical systems on which positive laws would be based.

A discernible relationship between *is* and *ought* was assumed, such that a consistent set of ethical principles could be grasped from intellectual effort. The fideist view, that revelation and faith are needed to ascertain what ought to be, is rejected. Proponents of natural law theory, given this understanding, come closer to the idealist tradition, especially with their confidence. Yet both Grotius and Pufendorf contributed good empirical work. Both believed that real social and political institutions had to be studied in order to develop rules. They added considerably to the substantive body of social science research in history and law, demonstrating high standards of thoroughness and accuracy.

Natural law theory had been a familiar enough form throughout the Middle Ages. John of Salisbury's medieval version was extremely conservative. In the seventeenth century the modern, liberal form began to appear although with the same methodological assumptions. (With "natural law" should also be understood "natural right.") Political activists will know the temptation of believing one's cause right in the nature of things. It has been the same throughout history. For Grotius and Pufendorf the cause was law reform. Locke was a notorious exponent of natural law in his political writing, quite forgetting his empiricism to argue his case. Of course those who argued the conservative cause also claimed natural law on their side, as in the divine right of kings. This, ultimately, is natural law's downfall. It can be, has been, and still is used to argue any principle and its opposite.

Kelsen has argued that there never has been a natural law theory of any importance which was not religious.[81] The whole approach presupposes that natural phenomena are directed to an end determined by final causes. Nature is conceived of as the supreme legislator, a kind of super-human, but personal, being to which we owe obedience. The nominal difference between scientific laws of nature and rules or ethics is obliterated. Positive laws are still needed because people do not always obey the laws of nature. The conservative bent of natural law theory comes from the view that nature contains a just social order. As the "is" and the "ought" become blurred there is a tendency to sanctify the *status quo*.

Grotius set out the religious underpinnings of natural law theory in his influential work. Laws of nature, as the dictate of rational nature, were the means God used to forbid or enjoin certain acts. God, the author of nature, willed certain acts in us, implanting them in us in a way we could understand. Some restraint on the conduct of war was at the time much in Europe's interests. The Thirty Years' War was taking its toll on military and civilian alike while Grotius was writing *On the Rights of War and Peace* (1620–5). In it he examined the ancient notion of a just war and advanced cogent arguments for rules to limit the slaughter. As liberal social contract theory specified rights within a society, Grotius advanced rights for nations within the wider world. Just as mutual rights had to be recognized for a society's survival, so had international rights to be recognized for mutual national survival. No state is so strong that it does not sometimes need the aid of others. Grotius had all the confidence of an idealist, asserting it "to be most certain that among nations a common law of Rights" holds with regard to war.[82] These notions of natural law were so certain that no one could deny them without doing violence to their own nature. Human nature was the grandmother of civil laws, the social compact the mother (xxvii). Natural law was reinforced by utility, but not established for it. God would punish those who disobeyed.

Yet Grotius' *Annals and History of the Low-Country-Warrs* (1665) is a conventional history, full of factual detail followed by explanations as to why a particular tactic did or did not work. For "On the Origins of the Native Races of America" Grotius had to resort to much less reliable information. Yet this eccentric paper is also an honest attempt at scholarship, and no empiricist could have ended it better: "These are the facts which I have been able to collect, some of them from conjecture, regarding the origin of the American races; and if anyone has more accurate knowledge to communicate, I shall enjoy the advantage of an exchange of thought, and for that advantage will return thanks" (20). In the *Freedom of the Seas* (1608) Grotius declared his distance from a fundamental principle of empiricism: "The delusion is as old as it is detestable with which many men ... persuade themselves ... that justice and injustice are distinguished the one from the other not by their nature, but in some fashion merely by the opinion and the custom of mankind."[83] Grotius' immediate purpose in writing was commercial advantage, the right of the Dutch to the East Indian trade then under British control. The common use of the seas he argued to be enjoined by nature herself. The principles to which he appealed in making the case were as lofty as any in natural law history: "The law by which our case must be decided is not difficult to find, seeing that it is the same among all nations; and it is easy to understand, seeing that it is innate in every individual and implanted in his mind ... For it is a law derived from nature, the common mother of us all" (5). Grotius was at once more graceful in expression and liberal in outlook than his successor.

Pufendorf's more plodding style foretold a more autocratic ethic, but in work that also made a substantive contribution to the social sciences. *The Law of Nature and Nations* (1672) begins with a historical, critical account of the "science of morality." Revelation was not needed, for the principles of this science were easily discernible. The most common experience of life sufficed, including an examination of one's own nature.[84] Consistent with this "easy knowledge" approach, Pufendorf denounced the sceptics as dangerous to religion and morality. Natural law was the rule to which "man" as a reasonable creature was obliged to conform (114). Natural law was universal and perpetual, while positive laws made people think, incorrectly according to Pufendorf, that there was no natural law. He allowed for the possibility of conflict between natural and positive law, but held such circumstances to be rare. He did not go so far as Hobbes in identifying the two, but their positions were not all that different.

Less illiberal than Hobbes, Pufendorf was still far from the progressive interpretations of natural law of people like Locke. A woman, for example, was obliged by natural law to be faithful and bound to her husband, even if she had been married to him contrary to her will (114). Yet Pufendorf also acknowledged a "natural equality" of the sexes (565). Slavery was a natural law institution with origins in contract. (The weakness of natural law, that it can be used to justify slavery or equality, democracy, anarchy, tyranny, socialism, or the divine right of kings (variously including or excluding queens), is obvious. By the end of the next century it would be employed to argue for *all* of these political aims.)

It has been suggested that by raising questions about the institution of law, Pufendorf's authoritarian version of natural law had a liberating effect. The very process of clarification required decisions on new issues.[85] Be that as it may, one can be charitable about Pufendorf's empirical work. His historical scholarship was painstaking. He used the best sources available, including the statistics, set out in an Aristotelian framework, of Hermann Conring.[86] If Pufendorf's systematizing failed, he nevertheless contributed as a historian. History belonged to the realm of fact, where truth was categorically different from the necessary truths of reason. He also studied contemporary social institutions. We may reject his view that rules can be derived from the study of what *is*, but we can still use the empirical observations obtained in his quest for natural law.

THE SOCIAL SCIENCES AND THE PURITAN MISSION

While the Huguenots were defeated and routed in France, in Britain their Puritan counterparts took power and made changes that have never been entirely undone. Thus began the Puritan experiment in which the sciences, natural and social, became aids in the establishment of the kingdom. The Puritan mission was no less than the building of the kingdom of God on earth. This meant completely overturning existing society and rethinking basic social institutions. For some Puritans, Scripture, or some personal revelation, sufficed as direction for this intrepid project, but others required some kind of scientific method. Societies were to be observed and experiments tried. Social laws had to be discovered in the same way as physical, to be made use of for the betterment of the commonwealth. Puritan theology was a stimulus also to natural science, giving it a noble purpose. Creation revealed divine nature, so that God could be better understood.

Gerrard Winstanley (1609–after 1660)[87] was leader of a radical sect, the Diggers (because they dug up the common lands), pamphleteer, and author of "The New Law of Righteousness" (1649). Most of his religious experiences were typical of the Puritan fervour of the time, but the revelation, in a trance, of the merits of communism goes beyond the usual. Within months he gathered together a group of people to dig and plant the commons. There was to be no expropriation of "particular property," cursed though it was. Rather the people were to take over the third of England's land held in common, or waste land. People were not to own more land than they could work themselves, a point Locke would take up later to quite different purposes. Both the hiring and selling of labour power were forbidden. There were to be a common treasury, common stores, and no buying or selling. All this depended on a transformation of human nature, which Winstanley saw as possible through the Holy Spirit. His radical social views included equality between the sexes, based on revelation in Scripture. "Man" in creation was made male and female, and there was to be no community of wives in the new society.[88]

Winstanley's Digger band near Cobham, Surrey, was never more than fifty people. Unarmed, they were beaten, their houses burned, and their plantings of parsnips and beans destroyed. Local landlords took them to court, where they were fined. The Digger experiment was over in a matter of months.

Winstanley's next major writing reflects some of the lessons of that sorry debacle. *The Laws of Freedom in a Platform* (1652) was dedicated to Cromwell as the leader of a people who had cast out an oppressing pharaoh. Cromwell was now to establish the communist society. There followed much more philosophical discussion which is still exciting by social science standards. Common ownership was defended not on grounds of personal revelation but by reasoned argument, with examples drawn from the Bible and English history. Requisite laws for the orderly running of the new society were outlined. There were to be no lawyers and no commerce. Basic education for all was specified. Ignorance was partly the result of bondage, for people kept knowledge secret to save their livelihoods. Experience had to be the basis for knowledge, not official position. People would be ready to delve into the secrets of creation when sure of food and clothing: "Fear of want, and care to pay Rent to Task-masters, hath hindered many rare Inventions" (580). Winstanley was a this-worldly Puritan, asserting that "To know the secrets of nature, is to know the works of God; and to know the works of God within the Creation, is to know God himself, for God dwells in every visible work or body" (565). To know God in creation was a worthy thing indeed. Speculation beyond that was not. Authority and intuition were both firmly rejected as means of knowledge.

The Law of Freedom's causal analysis makes it a milestone in the development of the social sciences. Instead of just railing at Norman oppression,

Winstanley gave a detailed analysis of its consequences. He set out the connections among social, economic, legal, military, and ecclesiastical institutions. His theory of the causes of crime linked law and social and economic conditions in a sophisticated way. One of the defences for digging the commons was that it would reduce crime, for destitution was a major cause of crime.

James Harrington (1611–77)[89] has been even more under-estimated as a theorist than Winstanley. Harrington's views were complicated, but his principles were simple and this, too, got him into trouble. His political analysis shows a Machiavellian influence. A society was a moving mechanism, and the first duty of the political scientist was not to praise or denounce it, but to explain it. There were impersonal, constant, and measurable forces at work, which to be controlled must be understood. Institutions were not accidental or arbitrary, nor were they changeable at will. Rather necessary consequences were to be discovered by patient analysis. Expediency was a surer basis for government than natural right, and interests than ideas. Harrington considered himself a "political anatomist" and compared himself with Harvey, discoverer of the circulation of blood.

Oceana (1656) is a sorry failure as a literary work but is nonetheless important for its ideas. Harrington was one of the first people to use the concepts of foundation and superstructure. The fundamental division in society was property, the foundation. The nature of "empire" followed the nature of property; where property institutions were not fixed, neither would be political ones. There was an imbalance between the property foundation and the political superstructure throughout Europe. The imbalance was most severe in England, "Oceana," where the Commons could buy out the Lords thrice over. Politically, of course, the House of Lords was stronger. The change in ownership had come about since the time of Henry VIII, but new political institutions had not yet been settled on. Harrington's thesis was in time accepted. Marxist analysis draws on it more than any other theoretical school, and its basic notions are commonplace throughout social science.

Harrington sought to use his thesis to insure both the right foundation *and* superstructure. Clearly there was to be no going back to the old "balance." There had to be equality in the commonwealth so that there would be no strife in either the foundation or superstructure. Agrarian laws were needed to keep property from being "swerved" out of the hands of the many. No person or class should be able to overpower the people by their possessions in land.[90] Thus popular government required a bar to the accumulation of land. Succession laws were one way of accomplishing this. There should be equal "rotation" in government, or succession into the magistracy by popular election. The ballot served to convey the "equal sap" from the roots upwards. There would be three orders in an equal commonwealth, the senate debating and proposing, the people resolving, and the magistrates executing.

The Puritan leader *Richard Baxter (1615–91)* completes my discussion of commitment to empiricist methodology as a matter of faith and to scepticism as a Christian virtue. Calamitous conflicts in the church resulted from unjustified claims to knowledge. The cure, if calamity had one, was "to know as much as we can; but withal to know how little we know, and to take on us to know no more than we do know, nor to be certain of our uncertainties."[91] Baxter accused the "licentious professors" of Christianity of mixing Platonic philosophy with the faith. The apostle Paul had vilified the "wisdom of this world," or Greek philosophy, not to prohibit it but to insure that it was not overly valued (2). Knowledge was valuable according to its use, and too much was used for riches and trifles. "Real Physicks and Pneumatology," or psychology, were useful. Clearly Baxter was after a balance, opposing the sceptical doubt of all, but realizing how great are the things we do not know. In decided contrast with the idealists, he declared: "It is sinful folly to pretend that we *know* or *receive any* thing by *Divine Faith* (or *Revelation*) when we have it but by *Humane Faith*, or probable conjecture from natural evidence" (14).

It was also sinful folly not to be a nominalist, to claiming knowledge of a thing or matter by words or notions, "which are separable from the knowledge of the thing." No human knowledge was perfect, and no evidence infallible: "A very great, if not the far greatest part of ... *Physicks*, is *uncertain* (or certainly false)" (46). Here Baxter cited Descartes and Gassendi along with the Greek schools. He set out his own classification of the degrees of certainty for both objective and subjective matters. Yet even "objective certainty" has a subjective definition, "such a degree of Perceptibility or Evidence as may aptly satisfie the doubting Intellect" (31). The uncertainties held in the same way for the natural and social worlds. The poor world paid for the lamentable uncertainties of medicine, more still for errors in politics. With hearsay and uncertain reports in history, "how shall strangers and posterity know when they read a History, whether the Writer was an honest Man or a Knave?" (52). As had the earlier materialists, Baxter stressed the continuities between humans and animals rather than their differences. His theology also stressed the continuities, noting the goodness of both as part of all creation. There are hints here of environmental ethics, again contrary to the expectations of the environmentalist critics of empiricist methodology.

CONSTRUCTIVE SCEPTICISM AND RELIGIOUS DOUBT

If Winstanley, Harrington, and Baxter were enthusiastic Puritans, convinced that social science knowledge was both possible and useful, the next methodologists were more cautious. Chillingworth, Wilkins, Glanvill, Boyle, and Locke complete the main line of development of scepticism that grew into British empiricism. While constructive scepticism failed in France, in Britain the same tentative, probing approach to knowledge gained support. This took time, but even as the new upstart it had strong backing. Idealism might be taught by the leading philosophers of the ancient universities, but the new empiricism had its own institutions in Gresham College and the Royal Society. While the empiricism of Gassendi and Mersenne succumbed to Cartesianism in the late seventeenth century, in England it became the method of the Royal Society.

In the eighteenth century the French had to relearn empiricism from Locke. I suspect that the greater diversity in religious belief is the major explanation for the success of empiricism in Britain. Although the country was officially Protestant, there were still Catholics in high places. The possibility of a Catholic on the throne, and a counter-Reformation, was not to be ignored. There was also a great range of doctrine among Protestants in both the established church and the sects. It was not possible for England to do as European governments had: force members of minority churches or sects to join the dominant group or accept martyrdom or exile. English people had to live with greater diversity, and the problem of determining "what is truth" became complicated accordingly. The objective conditions for a more open, sceptical methodology were thus excellent.

It is fitting that the earliest English advocate of scepticism, *William Chillingworth (1602–43)*, was an Anglican cleric who converted to Catholicism and then converted back. Chillingworth was a fellow of Oxford and an ordained priest when he was converted by a French Jesuit in England illegally for just such purposes. Chillingworth was persuaded in part by the need for an "infallible judge" to decide doctrinal controversies. He duly studied at a Jesuit college in Belgium, but after a year returned disappointed to England. The problem of the infallible judge remained. A few years later he declared himself a Protestant again. He published *The Religion of Protestants, a Safe Way to Salvation* (1638) on whether or not Protestants could have assurance of salvation outside the Catholic Church. He thought they could. In the course of argument "infallibility" became a matter of degree, absolute infallibility was beyond human reach.[92] Even geometricians were not infallible in their own science, certain as they may be of things they saw demonstrated. Fortunately, salvation required few correct beliefs, or there were few "damnable" errors (158). Chillingworth's arguments here are much like Castellion's. He was clear also on the subjectivity of certainty. Assurance from the spirit of God was not rational, but supernatural. What gave happy assurance to one might be no argument to another. Theological anxiety dates *The Religion*; few people today are so concerned about the state of their souls. The arguments, however, are still appealing for their moderation and common sense. Chillingworth was widely read and even made Locke's list of recommended books for the education of a gentleman.

The next English advocate of a moderate scepticism similarly developed his criteria for knowledge for theological use. *John Wilkins (1614–68)* was a bishop, a gifted amateur scientist, and an important advocate of science. With no scientific discoveries to his name, he conducted laboratory experiments and is credited with some inventions. He is said to have been the person most responsible for the creation of the Royal Society.

As a preliminary step to establishing the principles of natural religion, Wilkins considered the problem of evidence and assent. He wanted his criteria to be broadly acceptable to everyone who had "but an ordinary capacity and an honest mind," or the qualifications to do the arts and sciences.[93] Revelation must not be a requirement for understanding. Like Chillingworth, Wilkins considered "absolutely infallible" knowledge to be impossible; indeed the notion was blasphemous. The "conditionally infallible" was the only certainty of which most things were capable. This involved propositions that did not admit of any reasonable cause of doubting. Below the level of knowledge or certainty, even as qualified above, was "opinion" or "probability." This occurs "when though the Proofs for a Thing may preponderate any thing to be said against it, yet they are not so weighty and perspicuous as to exclude all reasonable doubt and fear of the contrary" (9). Assent was related to the kind of evidence available, whether of knowledge or certainty, probability, or opinion. Wilkins also argued the *usefulness* of religion. It was in people's interest to follow the precepts of the Christian life, for honesty and frugality were conducive to success in business, as well as being Christian virtues (293). The Protestant ethic-spirit of capitalism thesis had at least one keen supporter in the bishop.

By far the best exponent of a constructive sceptical empiricism, in my opinion, was *Joseph Glanvill (1636–80)*,[94] Anglican cleric, Fellow of the Royal Society, and author of *The Vanity of Dogmatizing* (1665), later revised as *Scepsis Scientifica* (1668). Glanvill continued to defend the middle ground, attacking both negative scepticism and dogmatism. His *Plus Ultra* (1668), on the advancement of knowledge since Aristotle, argued that science was developing, against sceptical criticism.

Glanvill deserves the credit, typically accorded Hume, for showing that observation cannot establish causation. Nicolas of Autrecourt and Malebranche had both argued the point earlier, but Glanvill's statement is much better developed. The argument began with good, sceptical empiricism as to the scantness and limitation of the senses relative to the subtlety and variety of Nature. Only Nature's grosser ways of working are sensible, her "finer threads" are out of the reach of our dull perception.[95] The senses cannot reach remote objects; we make errors in perception and judgment.

Knowledge comes from the senses but things may not be as our individual senses represent them; Glanvill speculates, for example, that white as perceived by white people might be black to Negroes (160). We obviously ascribe effects to causes: "All knowledge of Causes is *deductive*; for we know none by simple intuition; but through the mediation of their effects. So that we cannot conclude, any thing to be the cause of another; but from its continual accompanying it: for the *causality* itself is *insensible*. But now to argue from a concomitancy to a causality, is not infallibly conclusive: Yea in this way lies notorious delusion" (142). What seem to be the most palpable causes may be but "uninfluential attendants." The world is too heterogeneous and causes too "blended" to be able to sort them out. We would have to know everything back to initial causes, which is impossible. The object of science, nevertheless, was causal knowledge: "to profound to the bottom of these *diversities*, to assign each cause its distant effects, and to limit them by their *just* and *true* proportions." But it was "*flatulent vanity*" to call knowledge those few indistinct representations made by our grosser faculties (143). Glanvill confined to demonstration propositions for which the opposite is impossible. This, however, should not be discounted: "Methinks, did we but compare the miserable *scantness* of our *capacities*, with the vast *profundity of things*; both truth and modesty would teach us a more wary and becoming language ... Our demonstrations are levyed upon Principles our *own*, not *universal Nature*" (144). Are there not many things certain by one's principles which are impossible to another's? The best principles, except divine and mathematical, were but hypotheses. Thus we might affirm that things are thus and thus according to the principles we espouse, but should not plead their being so in nature or impossible otherwise.

Glanvill knew ancient scepticism; he approved of the constructive variety, disapproved of the negative. He reminded readers that scepticism meant to "speculate, look about, deliberate," and he referred to Sceptics as "seekers" and "doubters."[96] Glanvill's advice was to search, in the "book of nature," to establish maxims and positive doctrines. We should propose our opinions as hypotheses that may probably be true accounts, without peremptorily affirming that they are. This was the method of Bacon, Descartes, and the Royal Society: "This is *Scepticism* with some; and it if be so indeed 'tis such Scepticism, as is the only way to sure and grounded Knowledge, to which confidence in uncertain Opinions is the most fatal Enemy" (44). To believe that everything is certain is as great a disinterest to science as to conceive that nothing is, but the confident belief is the more dangerous evil.

Despite all the problems of perception, the senses are the only and, with due care, a reasonably reliable way to knowledge. The mere *possibility* that our senses may deceive us is not a *probability* that they will. Descartes'

mischievous demon could be safely ignored. Our senses might be so contrived that things are not what they appear, "but we fear not this, and the
bare possibility doth not move us." Similarly, we can believe the testimony
of others when it is "general, uninterested, full, plain and constant." We
believe Rome exists though we have not seen it, because of a simple
principle: "That *Mankind cannot be supposed to combine to deceive, in
things, wherein they can have no design or interest to do it*. Though the
Thing have a remote Possibility, yet no Man in his Wits can believe it ever
was, or will be so." Thus we do not suspect our senses are deceiving us,
although we may say that it is utterly possible. That kind of certainty is
only for God. Short of that, we may be certain of many things without
claiming "absolute infallibility." Still, the bare possibility does not weaken
our assent to what we "clearly and distinctly" perceive (49).

  Robert Boyle (1627–91) had the bad luck to publish his major work on
methodology, *The Christian Virtuoso* (1690), the same year as Locke's *Essay
Concerning Human Understanding*. The result is that Boyle is known for
Boyle's law while the virtues of his methodology go unsung. The two men
were friends and collaborators and there is a strong similarity in their
methodologies. If to promote Boyle's originality is to detract from Locke's,
then so be it. The point to be argued on Locke is not his originality, but
his giving the best expression of the empirical method.

  Boyle's "Sceptical Chemist" (1661) was a plea for a modest, phenomenal,
notion of knowledge. Though a "great lover of chymical experiments," and
with "no mean esteem of divers chymical remedies," he would distinguish
such from "notions about the causes of things and their manner of generation."[97] Carneades' warning on the limits of knowledge should be heeded.
Some philosophers deceived themselves, thinking they had satisfied inquiry
when they had given only the nearest and most immediate cause of a thing.
Yet the underlying cause and nature of a thing are obscure and one should
not stop the inquiry too soon. Causal knowledge should be the aim, although
it is difficult to establish. Here Boyle is in mainstream empiricism, as is
his concern for the applicability of knowledge in *The Usefulness of Experimental Knowledge*. He would not value physiology nearly so much if he
thought it only taught how to "discourse of nature, but not at all to master
her," if it served only "to entertain" the understanding without increasing
its "power" (2:64). He would not dare think of himself as a true naturalist
unless he grew a better garden than someone without scientific knowledge.
Knowledge must be shown to be useful, as Thales had, but philosophy as
taught in the schools had been sterile. One must have knowledge of the
natural world for "empire over it" (2:65). As the nerves extended the power
of the brain to all parts of the body, so also should scientific knowledge be
extended into the world.

Boyle's three kinds of demonstration follow the schemes of the earlier Puritan scientists, stressing the best evidence possible. Propositions should not be denied just because there might be some objections or their causes not fully explained. We must not conclude anything to be contrary to reason because the learned were not able to comprehend it clearly, so long as there are "competent" or "positive" proofs for them.[98] (4:173-4). Suspending judgment in the face of inadequate or conflicting evidence is not possible, either in science or religion, for in both cases decisions have to be made. Less than absolute criteria have to be resorted to. Boyle was a strong opponent of idealism in both scientific and religious questions. Neither the central truths of Christianity nor scientific theories could be proved by reason. Descartes' proofs on matters of religion were inadequate. Boyle added his own, but without claiming absolute certainty for them. Descartes, whose mechanical philosophy he greatly admired, was yet "a rigid philosopher, if ever there were any."[99] Boyle's references to earlier methodologists are consistent with this, favourable for materialists and sceptics, unfavourable for idealists.

The Christian Virtuoso contains Boyle's most thorough and enthusiastic defence of the experimental method. Always careful to point out the compatibility of religion and science, Boyle argued that "addiction to experimental philosophy" assisted rather than hindered being a good Christian. He stressed the superiority of experience, which he allied to reason, over authority. Corpuscular or mechanical philosophy was built on reason and experience. The Aristotelians also claimed this, but in fact made little use of experience, "contenting themselves for the most part to employ but few and obvious experiments, and vulgar traditions, usually uncertain, and oftentimes false; and superstructing almost their whole physics upon abstracted reason; by which I mean the rational faculty, endowed but with its ... common notions and ideas."[100] On the other hand, the virtuosi "consult experience both frequently and heedfully; and, not content with the phaenomena that nature spontaneously affords them, they are solicitous ... to enlarge their experience by trials purposely devised; and ... reflecting upon it, they are careful to conform their opinions to it; or, if there be just cause, reform their opinions by it" (5:513-4). The orientation had always to be external, to the real world: "Reason, furnished with no other notions than it can supply itself with, is so narrow and deceitful a thing that he that seeks for knowledge only within himself shall be sure to be quite ignorant of the greatest part of things" (5:539).

Sharing Boyle's view that scientific method should produce a better garden was *John Evelyn (1620–1706)*, FRS. In 1661 Evelyn published an analysis of the problem of air pollution in London, together with recommendations for remedy. The next year he published another ecological classic, *Silva:*

or, a Discourse of Forest-Trees, documenting the loss of forests in England well before the emergence of scientific method. Other credits include a translation of Lucretius, a telling link with ancient materialism. For Evelyn scientific method was both part of the solution to environmental problems and essential to their accurate description: "The design of this Discourse is not to persuade men to sit still, and let Nature work alone, but to aid and assist her as much as they are able."[101] Contemporary critics may disagree, but they should recognize that there is a history of environmentalism associated with the use of empiricist methodology.

THE SOCIAL SCIENCES FALL BEHIND NATURAL SCIENCE

In the late seventeenth century the social sciences, although advancing, began to fall decidedly behind the natural sciences, at least in the minds of the actors of the day. After an early period when natural scientists followed social science models, and then both kinds of science declined, we now see social scientists apologizing somewhat abjectly for imitating natural science. Unity of method was still the order of the day, so that some members of the Royal Society were doing both natural and social science. Yet the downward plunge had begun. *John Graunt (1620–74)* is an excellent example as a social scientist deferring to natural science and medicine. Although he was of humble origins, Graunt owned his own business and became a Fellow of the Royal Society. He was responsible for the first state collection of demographic data and the first analysis of the "bills of mortality," in 1662. As in ancient Greece, now again in the seventeenth century medical questions influenced social science methodology. The first collection of population data in England was prompted by outbreak of the plague. Graunt sought to use the bills of mortality like the "Noble Virtuosi" at Gresham, the college most associated with the Royal Society, not for idle and useless speculation, but "downright mechanical uses."[102] Clear knowledge of the particulars of population, especially occupational distribution, was needed for "good, certain and easie Government" (397).

The early circumstances of *William Petty (1623–87)* were as humble as Graunt's.[103] He then made his fortune in Ireland, was knighted, became an MP in Cromwell's Parliament, but survived nicely after the Restoration. Petty estimated the population of London without a census by using data on births and deaths. His work also is an early example of the use of the social sciences for purposes of imperialism, in this case England's occupation of Ireland. In his *Political Anatomy of Ireland* (published posthumously in 1691), he argued that one should not practice on the body politic without knowing its symmetry, fabric, and proportion.[104] Petty designed the forms for the collection of national statistics in Ireland. The influence of medical methodology and that of Hobbes are both evident in his own methodology.

Petty's demographic analysis used the labour theory of value.[105] People were wealth, and his writing abounds with figures on population per acre as well as amounts of commodities shipped. *Political Arithmetick* (1690) is hard-core quantification, and so intended. Instead of using only comparative and superlative words, and intellectual arguments, Petty expressed himself in "number, weight and measure" (1:244). He committed himself to using only arguments based on sense, to consider only causes with a visible foundation in nature. Those who identify social science with quantification will want to note how late this development occurred.

With the benefit of hindsight we can see the dangers of Petty's extreme anthropocentrism, which was made worse by his sexism. His *Treatise on Taxes* (1662) refers to labour as the "father and active principle" of wealth and land as the mother (1:68). This Aristotelian, male-supremacist division of labour means an over-valuing of the "active," male contribution and an under-valuing of the female, a so-called passive Mother Nature to be taken for granted. Locke followed Petty in vastly overstating the human part in the creation of wealth, minimizing the contribution of natural resources. Marx, who knew Petty's work well, went even further in *Capital*, attributing *all* value to social labour.

Edmund Halley (1656–1742), who is more known for discovering Halley's comet than for his work on probability, took Petty and Graunt's political arithmetic a step further in "An Estimate of the Degrees of Mortality" (1692). For his statistics he used, instead of London or Ireland, Breslau, where data on births and deaths were collected monthly and were relatively uncontaminated by migration. Breslau was far from the sea, where "the confluence of strangers is but small" and "proper for a standard."[106] Halley also showed how the degrees of mortality "or rather vitality" could be computed for each age, hence used for accurate calculations of annuities. Insurance companies did not adopt his method for a good half century. In a later paper, "Some Further Considerations on the Breslau Bills of Mortality," after recovering from the shock of realizing that half the population died before age seventeen, Halley reflected on the lowness of birth rates. The poor were not to be blamed, for besides supporting themselves and their families they had "also to work for those who own the ground that feeds them" (510). He recommended measures for job creation.

Sir William Temple (1628–98)[107] wrote some early political theory spelling out methodological principles much in line with modern empiricism. Although he was not at all conversant with natural science, his principles resembled those of the Royal Society virtuosi. Temple's approach to social science began with the same constancy assumptions about human nature as

Thucydides and the Hippocratics, using climate to explain variation: "The nature of man seems to be the same in all times and places, but varied, like their statures, complexions, and features, by the force and influence of the several climates where they are born and bred."[108] By a different mixture of humours and air this produces different "imaginations and passions," and thus "discourses and actions," which in turn (unless interrupted by some great force from without, or faction within) incline to different "customs, educations, opinions and law." Again there are medical analogies, for the faction, like a great blow or disease, may change or destroy the very frame of a body. Countries in the extremes of north or south, like Tartary and Muscovy, Africa and India, thanks to climate became single and arbitrary dominions, while in temperate Europe, more moderate, law-abiding commonwealths developed. Temple noted that where the gentry was braver than the peasantry, it might be because of diet.[109] England might be stronger than other countries because its yeomanry was better fed. Non-material factors in his explanations include custom, opinion, and the spirits of the heart. Most national customs were the effect of some unseen or unobserved natural cause. Temple's research problems, including causes of revolution, were anything but trivial.[110]

A stay in the Netherlands as ambassador resulted in an excellent case analysis à la Thucydides and Weber, *Observations upon the United Provinces* (1673). Here Temple sought to explain, arguing from observation, the rise and progress of the Dutch state, the causes of its greatness, and the steps to its fall. He noted that Holland's success in trade resulted from its religion, manners, disposition, situation, and form of government. Temple's aim in research was useful knowledge to benefit humanity. He searched for causes to show what is, as opposed to what ought to be. Macpherson credited him with asking good questions but failing to explore alternative hypotheses. Temple was an indolent inductionist whose intentions were right, if his delivery inadequate.[111]

The work of *Isaac Newton*, FRS, *(1642–1727)*[112] is perhaps the best fuel for the argument that the social sciences are more difficult than the natural. In both the natural and human worlds Newton's driving concern was to reduce phenomena to simple, highly general principles. But whereas his results in physics and mathematics dominated those subjects for more than 200 years, in the social sphere Newton can only be regarded as a curiosity. Newton's induction was immensely important in his methodology, largely because of his prestige as a physicist and mathematician. He was the first scientist to be knighted. He wrote only a few terse paragraphs explicitly on methodology, but enough to become gospel and, like other gospels, to be quoted in defence of contrary views. Social scientists in the eighteenth century became Newtonians hoping to find equivalents to the laws of motion in human affairs. Thus there was an "Age of Newton" in both the natural and social worlds.

It is not well known that throughout this time Newton was doing parallel work in history, mainly ancient, religion, and anthropology. He was, then, a social science researcher, devising practical rules of investigation for that work similar to those for natural science. Newton published none of this historical/theological work – some twenty volumes altogether – during his lifetime. His reluctance to publish seems to have been due not to any change of opinion but to his generally cautious nature; he hated to publish even his natural science and mathematics. He also disliked controversy, which this material would have caused, to put it mildly. What scandal for the Master of Trinity to be revealed a Unitarian at heart! Newton's publications on optics in the *Philosophical Transactions* marks the first use of a journal as the means of scholarly communication.[113] Edmund Halley persuaded Newton to write up the material in book form, the famous *Mathematical Principles of Natural Philosophy*. Yet while he was doing conventional work in physics and chemistry, Newton was engaged in what can only be called alchemy, trying to turn base metals into gold in the furnace in the college basement.

Newton's view of the world was mechanistic to a point. There was infinite, absolute space, within which was matter, ultimately composed of hard, moveable, virtually indivisible atoms, usually called particles. Newton's space was close to the void of the ancient materialists, but the concept of gravitational force made him equivocate. The attraction of one body for another in a complete vacuum would mean action-at-a-distance, uncomfortable to a mechanist. Newton never solved the dilemma satisfactorily to himself. He posited a fine ether as the medium between bodies in space, kept fine by a tendency for the particles to move away from each other. This meant a substance that could not be observed and a problem for an empiricist.

Newton departed completely from the Epicureans on the origin of the universe. He could conceive of no way that the world, organized as it is, could have occurred by chance. Even if one could accept that chance meetings of particles formed planets, there was no way they could get into orbit without being placed there by some intelligent Being. A planet falling toward the sun, for example, would be going too fast to go into orbit, even if it passed into the correct zone for its ellipse.[114] The laws of motion accounted for the movement of the planets *after* being set in place, it did not account for their getting into orbit. God had been a good mathematician, chemist, and physicist at creation, but the work was not then over. It was necessary for God to intervene from time to time, to keep comets from destroying the earth and to repeople the world after geological disasters. It was not that creation was inadequate, but the master of the world chose to keep it running by direct intervention. Newton roundly rejected Leibniz's view of the world as being wound up at creation.

Newton did not share the strong scepticism of his friend Locke, and indeed probably had less of it than most empiricists. But he did consider there to be serious limitations to knowledge in the incapacities of our sense organs. Pure thought, or speculation, was not remotely a reliable source of knowledge. God's superior knowledge occurred through his superior capacities for *perception*. This was an analogy, for God did not literally have eyes or ears or occupy space; space was "sensorium."

Newton's methodology above all else was an argument for induction. He gave the first clear exposition of the principles of induction, fitted onto an empiricist base. The process begins, at least in theory, with experiment and observation of phenomena. Regularities and patterns must be noted and the attempt made to formulate laws. It is impossible to observe everything, hence one must assume that unobserved phenomena behave in a way similar to observed ones. The object was causal explanation of the behaviour of phenomena, even if this is not always possible. Where simpler, descriptive laws alone are possible, this description must suffice. It was not scientific to speculate rather than observe, hence it is better to stop short of causal explanation. Mere suppositions should not be substituted. That, in a nutshell, is Newton's methodology, or at least the majority view of it. The extent to which he, or anyone else, actually followed those steps, of course, is quite a different matter.

The four "rules of reasoning" are considered to be Newton's attempt to replace Descartes' rules:

1. *We are to admit no more causes of natural things than such as are both true and sufficient to explain their appearances.* To this purpose the philosophers say that Nature does nothing in vain, and more is in vain when less will serve; for Nature is pleased with simplicity, and affects not the pomp of superfluous causes.

2. *Therefore to the same natural effects we must, as far as possible, assign the same causes.*[115]

The examples were of respiration in people and animals, the falling of stones in Europe and America, the light of fire and sun, and the reflection of light in the earth and the planets. This was required so that the argument of "induction not be evaded by hypotheses," meaning the substitution of mere supposition. A third rule was added to the second edition of *Mathematical Principles*:

3. *The qualities of bodies, which admit neither intensification nor remission of degrees, and which are found to belong to all bodies within the reach of our*

experiments, are to be esteemed the universal qualities of all bodies whatsoever.
(398)

We are not to relinquish the evidence of experiments for the sake of dreams and vain fictions of our own devising.

The last rule, which appeared only in the third edition, shortly before Newton's death, has been the most disputed:

4. *In experimental philosophy we are to look upon propositions inferred by general induction from phenomena as accurately or very nearly true, notwithstanding any contrary hypotheses that may be imagined, till such time as other phenomena occur, by which they may either be made more accurate or liable to exceptions.* (400)

An extreme interpretation of this rule makes empiricism a closed, untestable system; once a proposition is accepted it cannot be rejected but only slightly modified. Possible contrary hypotheses should be ignored, so that experimental and observational work on them would never be done. Of course this is not the only plausible reading of the passage. How much observation was required before an induction could be regarded as established, Newton did not say. Thus at what stage propositions would become immovable is not clear.

There has been some controversy as to what Newton understood by the term "hypothesis." He was obviously against hypotheses in the sense that he preferred experimental evidence. Thus, hypotheses mean something not deduced from phenomena but assumed without experimental proof. Newton evidently had little appreciation of the *psychological* role of hypotheses in scientific discovery. Somehow, the scientist was to investigate the properties of things directly by experiment. Hypotheses were then to be applied in the explanation of those properties. Yet, however much he disapproved of them, Newton himself used hypotheses.

In the "Queries" to the *Opticks* induction is preferred to deduction. Arguments from experiment and observation by induction were not demonstration but the best possible way to argue. Newton's faith in the possibility of certain knowledge was obviously greater than other empiricists would allow. Yet his correspondence with other scientists shows him generally to have been modest and tentative in his assertions. He insisted that experiments not mere supposition, be the basis for objections to his theories. He was content that a theory be called a "hypothesis" if it had not been proved to the satisfaction of his critic.[116]

Newton's work on history and theology includes the origin of the state, written language, polytheism, monotheism, cultural diffusion, and the relation between the family and state. What he did on these questions would not be called social science by most practising social scientists, but its methodology is of considerable interest. Briefly, Newton was a believer in prophecy in history. It was not possible to interpret prophecies *before* events happened, but the signs could be understood later. The same parsimony as in the laws of motion would hold here as well. All major events were forecast in Daniel and Revelations, and all the events described in those books were forecasts of real events to come. Newton was actually writing the *Mathematical Principles of Natural Philosophy* at just the time his predictions indicated the end of the world!

Since Newton's published writing contains scarcely a word about human affairs, commentators have made much of what little there is. The end of the "Queries" expresses the pious hope that "if natural Philosophy in all its Parts, by pursuing this Method, shall at length be perfected, the Bounds of Moral Philosophy will be also enlarged."[117] From today's perspective it is hard to appreciate how long it took for Newton's work to be understood. It was to be thirty years before the leading mathematicians understood it and sixty years before the leading universities taught it, and as usual, Oxbridge lagged behind the Scottish universities. It was through Voltaire, at best an amateur scientist, that Newton was popularized on the Continent. Britain and Europe made up for their slowness in appreciation by exaggerated praise. Newton became the "first and greatest of the modern age of science," a view to be challenged only recently when his historical works became better known. Keynes noted that Newton might better be called "the last of the magicians, the last of the Babylonians and Sumerians, the last great mind which looked out on the visible and intellectual world with the same eyes as those who began to build our intellectual inheritance rather less than 10,000 years ago."[118]

LOCKEAN EMPIRICISM

An Essay Concerning Human Understanding (1690) marks the culmination of seventeenth-century empiricism and the foundation for that of the eighteenth. *John Locke (1632–1704)*[119] was both natural and social scientist: a medical doctor and writer on education, politics, economics, psychology, religion, and methodology. Well versed in the classics, he knew ancient scepticism and materialism and was involved in the practical politics of his own day. The more one learns of earlier methodologists the less original Locke appears. Yet it was Locke who drew the principles of empiricism together and gave them their most polished and persuasive presentation.

Locke is the bridge also to the eighteenth-century social sciences, both British and French. *All* the French Encyclopedists were avowed Lockeans, although some of them more because of the natural law theory of *Two Treatises of Government* (1690) than the cautious empiricism of *An Essay*.

The continuities with Hume, Adam Smith, and Scottish moral philosophy are even more obvious. The feminist critiques of Wortley Montagu, Macaulay, and Wollstonecraft depend as much on Locke as on his feminist contemporary Mary Astell. In fact, *all* subsequent feminist critiques of male-supremacy theory are based on Locke. At the same time, his work provoked much opposition. Much German idealism was directed against it, beginning with Leibniz's *Nouveaux essais*, discussed above.

Locke's own opposition to idealism is clear throughout his writing. The first book of *An Essay* was largely an attack on the Cartesian doctrine of innate ideas, the third book a lengthy case for nominalism. Locke's lengthy critique of Malebranche has already been noted. It was Descartes' *certainty* and *system* that Locke rejected; he accepted the Cartesian components of knowledge. *An Essay Concerning Human Understanding* is far from a perfect book. It is long winded, poorly organized, and some of its definitions can only be described as unhelpful. It contains irritating inconsistencies and there are worse contradictions between *An Essay* and *Two Treatises of Government*. Nevertheless, the message of *An Essay* is clear enough to be one of the soundest statements ever of empiricism.

Locke studied botany and medicine (the latter to avoid ordination) at Oxford. His political and methodological work arose out of his service to the Whig leader, Lord Shaftesbury, initially as physician. (He even saved his employer's life with a bold operation.) Locke's intellectual development was further aided by a stay in France. He travelled widely, observing and taking extensive notes on French agriculture, technology, social life, religion, and scientific and philosophical developments. He also started to note mortality statistics, which were about the only social data then published.

Locke's association with his patron put him in danger when Shaftesbury fled the country after the failure of a plot to dethrone James II. Locke probably witnessed the last public book burning in England, at Oxford University. He left soon after for Holland. In exile and without his library, Locke did his greatest work. This includes most of the writing of *An Essay Concerning Human Understanding*, the "Letters on Tolerance," his educational writings, and probably the final work on *Two Treatises of Government*. He was fired from his position at Oxford and the Dutch government ignored an attempt made to extradite him. Locke was worried enough to change his address and even use a false name for a while. He was involved in the negotiations with William and Mary to assume the English throne, and returned to England in the same fleet as Mary.

An Essay Concerning Human Understanding is a careful exposition of the basic principles of British empiricism. Its most basic theses are not original and Locke did not properly acknowledge his intellectual debts.[120] The work advances no system but rather develops a few propositions with arguments based on observation. In this sense it reflects its practical origins

– discussions with friends on moral and religious matters – which raised basic questions as to the nature of knowledge. Locke was encouraged to reflect on these questions and report back. But neither then nor in the first two drafts of *An Essay* did he appreciate the difficulty of the questions he had begun to entertain. He early rejected the notion of innate ideas for that of experience acquired through the senses, the subjects of the first two books of the final *Essay*. By comparison, the early drafts take up little else. Over the years Locke filled out the documentation on these basic points, developing his own formulation as systematically as an empiricist could.

The purpose of *An Essay Concerning Human Understanding* was to inquire into "the original, certainty, and extent of *human knowledge*, together with the grounds and degrees of *belief, opinion,* and *assent.*"[121] The method to be used was the "historical, plain method," an examination of facts, as opposed to logical structure. Locke considered that he would not have wholly misemployed himself if he could give "any account of the ways whereby our understandings come to attain those notions of things we have; and can set down any measures of the certainty of our knowledge, or the grounds of those persuasions" (1:27). It was worthwhile to search out the bounds between opinion and knowledge and to examine how we ought to regulate our assent and moderate our persuasion where we cannot have certainty:

If by this enquiry into the nature of the understanding, I can discover the powers thereof; how far they reach; to what things they are in any degree proportionate; and where they fail us, I suppose it may be of use to prevail with the busy mind of man to be more cautious in meddling with things exceeding its comprehension; to stop, when it is at the utmost extent of its tether; and to sit down in a quiet ignorance of those things which, upon examination, are found to be beyond the reach of our capacities. (1:28)

Locke was careful to balance his case on the limits to knowledge with a positive declaration of what *can* be known. A servant has no excuse for not working in candlelight: "The Candle that is set up in us shines bright enough for all our purposes" (1:30). Note the modesty of the light analogy, while Augustinian idealists claimed the full brightness of sunshine, Locke's metaphor was only a candle in the dark.

When we know our own strength we should better know what we might undertake with hope of success. When we have surveyed the *powers* of our minds we shall not be inclined to sit still and not set our thoughts at work at all, in despair of knowing anything, nor question everything and disclaim all knowledge because some things are not to be understood. Locke discussed the careful balancing of what can and cannot be known in the exact terms used by Glanvill, Wilkins, and Boyle. He never expressly mentioned them, but he did distinguish his inquiry from those of the philosophers of "Being." It was of great use to a sailor to know the length of his line, though he could not fathom all the depths of the ocean. We should not let loose our thoughts into the vast ocean of Being, as if all that boundless extent were the natural and undoubted possession of our understanding. It was no wonder that questions arose, disputes multiplied, and people were confirmed in perfect scepticism. Such extremes of doubt were to be avoided as much as over-confidence.

Locke would not meddle with the physical consideration of the mind. He troubled himself neither about its essence nor about the spirits or alterations of our bodies which cause sensations or ideas and whether or not they depend on matter. Such speculations were out of his design. Similarly, he ruled out such favourite issues as how spirits acquire knowledge of material substances.

If ancient scepticism was one main source of Locke's theory of knowledge, ancient atomism was another. He had already worked on an atomic theory of chemistry with Boyle, and this is clearly behind his theory of knowledge. The ultimate constituent of the physical world was atoms – minute, insensible particles. The particles of a grain split in two still had solidity and occupied space, although they might change in "secondary qualities" of colour and taste. A whole almond, for example, was white and sweet; pulverized, its texture became powdery, its taste acidic, and colour grey. The "primary" or original qualities were confined to bulk, figure, texture, and motion of parts (1:173). The secondary qualities, colour, taste, and smell had an unknown relationship to the primary. The relation between the primary and secondary qualities was undiscoverable, so that this part of our ignorance is incurable. How well the secondary qualities might represent the primary could never be known, for the ultimate atoms are too small to be observed. Thus Locke said that the "real essences" of objects could never be known (2:27).

Locke's depiction of sensation was effectively no different from that of the early materialists. With the benefit of hindsight, however, he avoided going into embarrassing details. Rather he mentioned only briefly the basic operations of external objects on the sense organs which conveyed impressions to the brain. The mind was passive in this initial phase. Later it would reflect on its own operations, compare, generalize, and abstract ideas. This required basic sense data with which to start, which could only come from outside. Sensation and reflection were the two sources of knowledge, providing the understanding with ideas of sense objects and its own operations respectively. The mind was a "white paper" until furnished with ideas (1:121). Locke conceived of the ideas produced in sensation as dealing with only one quality each. Thus a snowball conveyed the ideas of white, cold, and round, all as distinct ideas. The mind might manipulate ideas, form abstractions, or join simple ideas together into complex, to an almost infinite variety. It could not, however, *invent* a single, simple idea.

So far, Locke's is at least a plausible account of the processes of sensation and reflection. It stands up well against much later neurological research. At the next stage, however, even the most sympathetic empiricist must balk. Locke's definition of knowledge, in terms of the perception of agreement or disagreement of ideas, is at best unhelpful. Knowledge in Locke's conceptualization was ultimately intuitive. The mind considered ideas and judged their agreement or disagreement. It might do this directly, and immediate intuition was the clearest, most certain knowledge of which human frailty was capable. Locke's examples of immediate intuition were that blue is not red, a man is not a horse, and one and one are equal to two. His examples of *certain* knowledge were always *very* cautious. Knowledge might require a series of steps or "proofs" for demonstration before one's understanding was convinced that the two ideas agreed or disagreed.[122]

Knowledge as the agreement, or not, of ideas poses problems of the knowledge of real objects. To be consistent, if understanding consists of ideas, which Locke said in Book 2, nothing can be known of objects. Yet in Book 4, when Locke dealt with real existences, he added sensation as another means of the perception of agreement or disagreement of ideas. With immediate intuition, and reason, or intervening proofs, there was the perception of the existence of particular things. The contradiction with the definition and his earlier treatment of the subject goes unremarked. Whatever the inconsistencies within *An Essay Concerning Human Understanding*, there are worse between *An Essay* and *Two Treatises of Government*. If not so irreconcilable as those of Descartes, Berkeley, Gassendi, or Aristotle, they are flagrant.

The *Two Treatises* were an important source for later theory on the separation of powers and the social compact. People formed civil society, or a "commonwealth," for the better protection of themselves and their property. In coming together people could not give away more rights than they had. They did not have the right to take their own lives, hence could not give it away that right. Similarly people could not consent to slavery. A king who threatened the lives of his subjects instituted a state of war, which gave the people the right to take his life.[123] As to who was to judge whether a state of war existed, Locke could not have been clearer: the people (312).[124]

Locke's state of nature was not especially warlike. Not anarchy but the tyranny of rulers was the worst thing to be feared – anarchy need never be a threat. His treatment of property can be objected to on many grounds but it began as an argument for people's rights to the products of their labour. Killing a deer and gathering acorns thus were the origins of private property. Locke apparently could not imagine a hunter killing a deer and the whole community eating it as *their* game, and he knew of no such societies. Thus he had the hunter make the deer his private property before eating it (chap. 5). There was a proviso, which has been typically ignored, that although labour was the unquestionable property of the labourer, no one had a right to resources except when enough was left in common for all. Locke, we can now see, exaggerated the value labour added to goods, and underestimated both scarcity and the value of the land itself. There was always more land, he asserted, not only in the Americas but even in Spain. Locke estimated that land cultivated European-style was a hundred times more productive than North American hunting and gathering. Later ecologists would regret that Locke so seriously underestimated the value of the land and primary resources.

However critical one may be of Locke, much of what he said about methodology is still good advice. His presentation of nominalism, if tedious, is commendable for its precision. He was careful to offer his definitions as his own and explain how they differed from those of others. He offered to change his definitions if anyone could give him a good reason to. Apart from the *Two Treatises*, he showed a healthy sense of the subjectivity of judgments. He typically gave his conclusions and the reasons for them in terms of experience. His judgments were grounded on the available data and would be changed if new data warranted. His treatment of the obstacles to knowledge is superb. Again, except in the *Two Treatises*, he acted on his own cautions. Knowledge really is difficult to find; one must be modest in what one claims. Locke's claims for knowledge were highly qualified. Even so, he was too optimistic in some places.

Locke acquired much technical and social data first hand in his travels. He was an avid reader of travel books, the seventeenth century's closest approximation to ethnographic monographs. He consulted the best available statistics. He had an excellent library in philosophy, natural science, and what social science there was. He learned a great deal about economics and politics through working on Shaftesbury's committees. He was, altogether, as good a social scientist as one could have been at the time. Perhaps the last word on him should be Russell's equivocal: "No one has yet succeeded in inventing a philosophy at once credible and self-consistent. Locke aimed at credibility, and achieved it at the expense of consistency. Most of the great philosophers have done the opposite."[125]

FEMINISM AND METHODOLOGY

Mary Astell (1668–1731)[126] made a serious contribution to methodology yet, probably because of her sex, is little recognized in the professional literature. Her major work, admittedly, has a misleading title: *A Serious Proposal to the Ladies for the advancement of their true and greatest interest*

(1694). Yet male contributors whose titles were no less misleading have been recognized.[127] A *Serious Proposal* is a devastating critique of male privilege, especially in education, where the exclusion of women was nearly complete. Intellectual equality between the sexes was a central argument, raising the basic methodological concerns of the day. Astell asked why, since God had given women as well as men intelligent souls, they should be forbidden to improve them? Why should women not employ their thinking on the noblest objects, instead of trifles? It was unjust and cruel to exclude women from knowledge since the soul was created for the contemplation of truth. "And as Exercise enlarges and exalts any Faculty, so thro' want of using it becomes crampt and lessened."[128] Astell's object was not to overturn lawful authority but to demand self-determination for women. Although it stops short of such matters as women as teachers in church, this theory was no less than revolutionary for the time.

Astell's understanding of methodology shows both Cartesian and Lockean influences. However much she condemned Locke's liberal political views and religious toleration, she shared his tentative, probabilistic approach to knowledge. On matters of theology she was more Cartesian, but she broke with both Descartes and Malebranche on key points of methodology. She used, as had Locke, much Cartesian terminology, defining knowledge in terms of clear and distinct ideas firmly assented to. Yet she accorded considerable scope for "opinion," when "the Nature of the thing be such that it admits of no undoubted Premises to argue from, or at least we don't at present know of any, or that the Conclusion does not so necessarily follow as to give a perfect satisfaction to the Mind and to free it from all hesitation" (81). The subjective nature of judgments of probability, the weighing and comparing of evidence, was a persistent theme. For all her Cartesian "clear and distincts" very few things could be seen by intuition. Nor could we demonstrate truths with adequate mediums, as Descartes had proposed. Astell issued a flat denial of the opening argument of the "Discourse" on the ubiquity of reason. Good sense was not the birth right of all, "tho' more are Born to, than make Use of it."[129] Propositions accepted on the basis of authority belong to yet another category, faith. Yet the differences concerned the way of proof, not the degree of certainty. Degrees of certainty varied for all categories of knowledge, and were a matter of judgment. "Moral Certainty is a Species of Knowledge whose Proofs are of a compounded Nature, with proofs partly resembling those which belong to Science, and partly those of Faith."[130] Sometimes we reject truths that are morally certain, considering them only conjectural and probable, because they lack a physical and mathematical certainty. Here Astell took up the language of constructive scepticism.

Astell amply warned of the possibilities of error in sense perception. She gave full play to private interests, regard for the opinion of friends, ambition, and greed along with the usual mechanical failings of the senses, weak judgment, and inattention. There were innumerable errors against one single truth. Yet she held to the ancient empiricist belief that we have enough knowledge for all the purposes of life, though we cannot fathom all the depths. It was the property of a wise person to know the limits of knowledge: "Ignorance then can't be avoided but Error may, we cannot Judge of things of which we have no Idea, but we can suspend our Judgment about those of which we have, till clearness and evidence oblige us to pass it" (90). In the search for truth we have "to examine her Counterfeits, to distinguish between Evidence and Probability, Realities and Appearances" (92). We should not stop at first appearances but search to the bottom to pull off all disguises.

Astell curiously took up one Malebranchist point, that "unruly passions" keep us from observing intellectual errors. The "animal spirits" had to be made "calm and manageable." The vision in God itself received the dubious compliment of being "commendable for its Piety" whatever may be "the Truth of it" (96). Nowhere is the idealist mistrust of body/female to extol mind/male to be found. Instead, there is an assertion of mutual influence between the two. Both mind and body can be the occasion for error, and both the means of correcting it. Astell's break with male supremacist dualism is original but was neither understood nor heeded. Later idealists, up to and including Kant, never refuted her; they ignored her.

Astell was one of the strongest asserters in the empiricist tradition of the democracy of knowledge. The higher our station in life, she warned, the greater the danger to believe what we want to. "The mean and inconsiderable" often stumble on truth while it remains concealed from "the Great and mighty" (95–6). "The Meanest Person should Think as *Justly* tho' not as *Capaciously*, as the greatest Philosopher" (98). Also in line with a long tradition, she was concerned with knowledge for application. It served little purpose to think and speak well unless we live well. Since she was especially concerned with the education of women, she stressed application of her ideas in the family for the raising of children. In the case of single women, Astell's arguments are an early anticipation of "maternal feminism": the whole world was their family (129).

In *Some Reflections Upon Marriage* (1700) Astell set out the disadvantages of marriage for women. The analysis shows a sophisticated understanding of the power of institutions and customs in a time when "nature" was commonly held to be the source of sex-role differences. Since Astell based her arguments on experience, the work is another example of the application of empiricist methodology. Men's arguments for the *status quo* were suspect because men did not *feel* the disabilities of marriage.[131] Her critique of the standard "reasons" for the subordination of women is thorough, shrewd, and witty. Nearly three centuries before there were feminist professors of theology, she exposed the flaws in male-supremacist interpretations of the Bible (104–19).

Lamentably, Astell has been neglected not only in the history of methodology but in social history, including the struggle for equal rights. Her writing is incisive, ironic, and, despite all the sexist prejudice against her, kind. Her religious beliefs and practice were orthodox Anglican. Hence the usual reasons for consignment to the back shelves – inscrutable tomes, heresy, or scandal – do not apply.

Soon after Astell published *A Serious Proposal*, another anonymous writer, probably Judith Drake, published *An Essay in defence of the Female Sex*, (1696) also dedicated to Princess Anne of Denmark. This work is in the courageous style of Astell, just as outspoken in its feminism, and as full of apt putdowns of masculine academic pretensions. Drake, if the writer was Drake, was even more an empiricist than Astell and quite explicit in her praise of Bacon and Locke. Like Astell, the author of *An Essay in defence of the Female Sex* set herself the task, formidable for the time, "to reduce the Sexes to a Level, and by Arguments to raise Ours to an Equality ... with the Men."[132] Here she argued that social institutions, especially education, were responsible for the *de facto* superiority of men. She would not dispute whether men or women were generally more ingenious, only that the great disparities in education, freedom of converse, business, and company gave the advantage to men. We will see these arguments used again in the late eighteenth century. By the late nineteenth century they would become the basis of an active movement for women's education.

Women, *An Essay* pointed out, used their natural and rational faculties as well as men. There were no male/female differences among animals in the senses or understanding, that is when there were no constraints of custom, laws, education, and prejudice (13). A female fox was as wily as a male. The frequent statements of superiority by men could be rejected as partisan (23). Often such arguments depended on case examples, although "tis very ill *Logick* to argue from Particulars to Generals, and where Premisses are singular, to conclude Universally" (117).

It is quite possible there were still other women who broke the barriers of education and publication to make a significant contribution to methodology, but who have dropped out of sight completely. If book burning extinguished radical ideas – and it did – prejudice against women's scholarship seems to have been as effective. Without an accepting intellectual community, university positions, patrons, or fellowships, women lacked the support system enjoyed by men. No schools formed to carry on their work. Those few women who did get into print were seldom reissued, and there were even fewer collected works, critical editions, essays in honour, and *Festschriften*. Centuries later these women's writing would have to be redis-

rediscovered by readers who wondered why they had been so long deprived of such excellent work.

THE CRITIQUE OF EMPIRICISM REVISITED

As empiricist and idealist methodologists went back and forth easily between the natural and social sciences, they saw no rigid division between particular historical study and the search for general laws. Hobbes, for all his mechanistic approach, both translated history (Thucydides) and wrote it (*Behemoth*, on the civil war). The natural law writers Grotius and Pufendorf both published extensive histories. Harrington considered that one had to be a historian or traveller to do good political analysis, and himself was both. Thomas More, who is not discussed in detail here, wrote history as well as advocating an empiricist approach. Leibniz wrote histories. Some of Locke's work might be considered contemporary history; certainly he wrote on particular topics apart from his methodological concerns. Newton wrote both on history and theology. The barriers between social science and the arts were no greater. Thomas More's methodology was couched in a utopian form. So also was one of Bacon's works. Montchrétien wrote a tragedy before he wrote anything on economics. Grotius wrote poetry as well as law and history. Astell was a poet. Even Locke wrote poetry as a young student. Bayle published poetry before philosophy.

The view that empiricists align themselves with the powers that be survives scrutiny no better. Rather the advocates of empirical methodology were on the side of the challengers to power. Montchrétien was a dissident Huguenot who suffered first exile, and eventually a violent death. Thomas More was a martyr. Descartes went into voluntary exile, held back on some of his writing, and took elaborate measures to placate the authorities. The Puritans were threats as revolutionaries, and were punished accordingly. Harrington and Baxter went to prison, Winstanley probably did too. Locke was never jailed, but he went hastily into exile and was threatened with extradition.

This period gives the environmentalist critics of empiricism, on the other hand, much to support their argument. Bacon's goal of dominating nature, whatever its intention, meant rough treatment, even the "shaking of nature." Few people of *any* philosophical persuasion showed any sensitivity to cruelty to animals. Henry More is often held up as a model for his vitalist, organic model of the world, explicitly rejecting atomism. Yet More, no less than the empiricists he opposed, accepted a hierarchical view of creation, with humans at the top having the right to use all those below for our own purposes.[133] The eminent naturalist, John Ray, rejected the atomic approach in no less uncertain terms. Yet he, too, while arguing some independent worth to animals, ranked them for their usefulness for human use.[134] Leibniz also rejected empiricism but his world view was even more deterministic and mechanical – complete with wound-up clock – than that of any empiricist. On the other hand, empiricist advocates like the Puritan Baxter argued expressly for kinder treatment of animals, contrary to the contentions of environmentalist critics. Also on the positive side, this period saw the pioneer application of the scientific method to environmentalist projects, reforestation and air quality improvement, by John Evelyn, FRS.

Descartes has become the most popular target in the environmentalist critique of scientific method. He is vehemently attacked for his denial of sensation to animals, thus justifying any treatment, including vivisection. Yet numerous of his writings show him to have stated perfectly clearly that animals have feeling. He even assigned a soul to animals to ensure that they could feel, since it was believed during his time that there had to be some seat of sensation. His "animal-machine" metaphor applied to both humans and animals. It was the anti-empiricist Malebranche who, because of his theodicy, actually made the argument of no feeling in animals.

Hindsight shows the labour theory of value, which emerged in this period, to have fostered a serious undervaluing of natural resources and complacency concerning their care and stewardship. Petty's early statement of this theory explicitly credited the active "male" role to labour and a merely passive, "female" role to nature. Women's work, it seems, is never fully appreciated. Locke was similarly to downplay the role of natural resources relative to that of human labour in the creation of wealth. Undoubtedly this undervaluing of nature has had dire consequences for the environment, but it seems that the culprit here is not empiricism as such, but ancient, sexist prejudice. Both anthropocentrism and male supremacy would be challenged in the eighteenth century, to which we now turn.

4 The French Enlightenment

Scepticism is the first step towards the truth.   Denis Diderot[1]

It is to the mechanical instinct of the great majority of human beings
that we owe all the arts, and not at all to sound philosophy.   Voltaire[2]

Philosophy is of every estate and both sexes; it is compatible with the
cultivation of literature and even with the most brilliant imagination,
so long as one does not permit this imagination to become accustomed
to gilding falsities, nor to fly over the surface of things.   Voltaire[3]

Everywhere one must reach the same results with the same methods
for the truth is one for everybody, because nature is everywhere subject to the same laws.   Condorcet[4]

Theory without experience is nothing but a phrase, experience without
theory but a prejudice.   Germaine de Staël[5]

Advances in learning in eighteenth-century France were as great as those
anywhere in the world; still, that this period should be called the Enlightenment never ceases to amaze. The eighteenth century was an age of great
economic expansion, colonizing, and war. There were achievements in architecture, music, and the arts generally. New schools, academies, and research
institutes were created; old ones expanded. Scholarly publications in books
and journals increased enormously. The fame of the salons attests to the
respect intellectual life acquired in this period. Important methodological
advances were made, but in my view they were no greater than those of
the seventeenth century. Further, the eighteenth century was a period of
intellectual repression. Censorship in France cursed the life of all the major
methodologists. Book burnings were frequent, and the punishments for
unauthorized publication made more severe. A number of methodologists
took the precaution of publishing outside the country, anonymously, or both.
Some fled and several spent time behind bars for their enlightened thoughts.[6]

Meanwhile, witch burnings continued all over Europe. Slavery had been
abolished there but was still strong in the Americas. Europeans profited
from the slave trade, and European ports were used in the transportation
of slaves from Africa to new world plantations. Peasants suffered severe
poverty and powerlessness. Their occasional uprisings were harshly put
down. Criminal penalties were brutal. Torture was widely used in the
interrogation of suspects as well as in the punishment of the guilty. The
legal disabilities women suffered continued unabated. The exclusion of

women from educational institutions meant that only those few with exceptional private means and good luck could get any education beyond reading, writing, conversational Italian, and singing lessons. That even a few women made a contribution to methodology is newsworthy. The century ended with the French Revolution and the Terror. One of the greatest methodologists, Condorcet, died in prison while under sentence of death, and his work was to be ignored for decades after his death.

The "Enlightenment," especially the French Enlightenment, is often sharply demarcated in the history of ideas, sometimes as the most important period for the development of modern society. To me such singling out is not warranted. The continuities with the seventeenth century are much in evidence, and this split is arbitrary. Locke, then Newton, was the greatest influence of the eighteenth century. Both were seventeenth-century thinkers in a long continuous line of gradual developments. Montesquieu and Voltaire both spent significant periods in Britain (as did most French writers) and both were greatly influenced by seventeenth-century British work.

In Britain, the Puritan revolution had run its course, altering the country economically, socially, and politically. In France, by comparison, reformers/revolutionaries were still waiting and writing. The *ancien régime* remained strong, repression continued to be harsh. Censorship was a serious threat in a regime that took ideas seriously enough to insure that many did not see the light of day. The Sun King was not a dazzling example of Enlightenment.

People analyzed the ills of the current regime, the poverty, waste, cruelty, religious intolerance, and injustices to women. Alternatives were proposed and comparisons made with other societies, real or fictional. There is a remarkable degree of common belief among the methodologists examined here that knowledge can be applied for human good. With the exception of Rousseau (so often the exception), these people believed that problems could be studied and better solutions found. Poverty, cruelty, and injustice, these people believed, were not natural but the result of conditions that could be changed.

Mathematical knowledge advanced in the eighteenth century and with it useful notions of probability. Understanding of the role of hypotheses and theory evolved. The anthropological data available were still quite basic, but superior to the travellers' reports on which seventeenth-century writers had to depend. Historical research improved greatly both in quantity and quality. Libraries and archives improved although access to scholars remained a challenge. The sense of unity of method continued into the eighteenth century in France especially. The *Encyclopédie* covered both the natural and social sciences, and its authors insisted on their common methodology. The main author and editor of the *Encyclopédie*, Diderot, made significant contributions in both departments.

MAINSTREAM SOCIOLOGY

The first person actually to apply the new methodology of Bacon, Locke, and Newton to social phenonema was *Charles Secondat, Baron de Montesquieu (1689–1755)*.[7] Never in prison or exile, Montesquieu took care to publish anonymously out of the country. He was politically more conservative than the Encyclopedists but supported their work and contributed several articles to the *Encyclopédie*. His *The Spirit of Laws* is the first modern, mainstream work of sociology in the world. Published in 1748, it was placed on the *Index* in 1751. The principles of empiricism in *The Spirit* are unmistakable: the social world is determined in the same way as the physical, its laws are discoverable by observation and comparison. The magnitude of Montesquieu's achievement is still debated. Some scholars prefer to treat him as a "precursor" to sociology or the social sciences, which then requires the designation of someone else as the first "real" social scientist. Yet the choice of anyone else would arguably present problems. The pioneering nature of Montesquieu's contribution was recognized in his own lifetime. It was said that, as Newton had discovered the basic laws of the material world, so had Montesquieu discovered those of the intellectual. At the end of the century Mme de Staël recognized the significance of his work: "If the social art in France attains the certainty of a science in its principles and application, it is to Montesquieu we owe credit for the first steps."[8]

The process of writing *The Spirit of Laws* is worth recounting. Montesquieu had already been gathering material casually for years when, about 1734, he began the project in earnest. He used secretaries for note taking but did all the reading, cataloguing, and summarizing himself. He had a large library at his chateau and good access to other libraries, including the king's. Montesquieu could also count on the baroness to run the estates when he was off doing research.

After some ten years of work the first draft was completed. Montesquieu's own revision took another year, incorporation of the suggestions of his friends another. In 1747 the book was "finished" and its author exhausted. Montesquieu visited the Polish court at Lunéville to recuperate, and there added a few more chapters. His publisher urged him to tone down a few sections, but Montesquieu refused. The work was published anonymously in Switzerland, but soon came to be known as his.

In the preface Montesquieu described the book as a work of twenty years and asked the reader not to judge it by a few sentences but to look at the whole design. He was careful to note – the book opened with his most general conclusions – that he had not drawn his "principles" from "prejudices" but from "the nature of things." Whether or not this is true we shall never know, but it seems that he used inductive methods as far as possible.

Book 1 began with Montesquieu's definition of laws, as "the necessary relations arising from the nature of things."[9] In this sense, he explained, all beings had their laws. It would be absurd that blind fate could have produced intelligent beings. There must then have been a "primitive reason," and laws were the relations found both between that reason and different beings and among these various beings themselves. The world was formed of movement and matter. Deprived of intelligence it yet continued to exist, which suggests that there must be some invariable laws directing these movements. God was related to the universe as creator and preserver, using the same laws for both functions.

Law for Montesquieu meant *invariable relations*. He was aware of the problems with this position but found no solution for them; the notion of cybernetic relations was not developed until the nineteenth century. There are contradictions in his work, for people did change and positive laws were broken. Montesquieu deserves credit, though, for not producing a false solution to the problem. His laws were static, or at least linear, but he probably misled fewer people than Kant or Comte with their dynamic laws. It was in relating positive laws to natural that Montesquieu ran into greater difficulties, for he used the same word "law" to refer to a piece of legislation and a law of nature like gravity. The one could be broken, the other not, as he fully realized. Nevertheless he conceived of them as being similar, and would apply characteristics of physical laws to the positive, where they did not remotely fit. Law, in general, he asserted, was "human reason." "Civil and political" laws must be particular cases of the application of human reason (1:8). Perhaps they *should be*, but clearly they often are not. Montesquieu himself criticized numerous "civil and political" laws, notably on slavery, as being unjust, unnecessary, and contrary to reason. He admitted the dilemma most directly in discussing the behaviour of individuals. "Man" as a physical being was, like other bodies, governed by invariable laws. Yet he violated laws God had established and changed "man-made" ones. As a sensible creature "man" was subject to a "thousand passions," so there were religion and philosophy to remind him of moral laws and legislators to remind him of political and civil ones (1:4). That one does not have to be reminded of the laws of gravity Montesquieu ignored here. Rather he emphasized the similarities – that positive laws support moral laws, and that both are part of the primitive reason that runs the universe.

A good part of *The Spirit of Laws* deals with the origins of slavery, demolishing the traditional arguments used to justify it. The major portion of the book, however, deals with *types* of government, which Montesquieu classified according to their "spirit" or guiding principles: republic, monarchy, and despotism. Montesquieu's types of government were his own construction, "ideal types" did not correspond to any actual governments of the time. In contrast with Aristotle's typology, it was not *who* rules that was crucial, but the type of human passion that set the government in motion. The type of society, in turn, determined the nature of the laws needed. Next, an implicit functionalism led to a tendency for what was needed in fact to occur. Thus there was a correspondence between actual, positive laws and the characteristics of a society.

Many determining elements interact, sometimes through several stages. Climate was an important factor, which acts on disposition or passions. Montesquieu's arguments here resemble those of Thucydides and the Hippocratics of the fifth century B.C. Laws had to be harsher in countries with cold climates, for people were hardened by severe conditions. In countries with mild climates, people's sensibilities were softened, so that they could be controlled by weaker penalties. Montesquieu actually cited experimental evidence in support of this proposition. He also made a plea for moderation of penalties. Excessive harshness could have a brutalizing effect rather than deterring crime. Climate interacted with social phenomena like *mores*. Over time physical factors like climate decline in importance as causes, while the social factors gain. Yet the prominence he gives to climate indicates Montesquieu's commitment to the notion of law in natural science. Human behaviour, individual and social, was explicable with laws similar to those for physical phenomena.

Perhaps what has most made Montesquieu a "precursor" of social science rather than a practioner of it was his ambivalence about the nature of social units. Individuals, as physical bodies, were clearly determined by laws, for they are part of nature. Societies, however, he considered somewhat artificial. Properly speaking, human beings should be studied *before* societies were formed. Montesquieu, however, was not interested in mere speculation, and clearly there could be nothing else for any pre-social period. He postulated a primitive equality, another argument against the "naturalness" of slavery, but quickly returned to the observable world. Ethnographic materials of any quality were then scarce. Montesquieu had a notion of the comparative method, as the social science equivalent of experimentation; the problem was lack of data. Legal materials were more available, and these he used with considerable facility. Indeed he has been credited with inaugurating the field of comparative law. *The Spirit of Laws* is pre-social science also in the amount of space it gives to normative discussion. Further, Montesquieu took no pains to distinguish between the normative and empirical.

The Spirit of Laws was a highly influential book, Montesquieu's concept of laws became *the* concept in the social sciences. Marx and other theorists dropped his linearity for abrupt junctures and stages, but still kept the essential notion of necessary relations. While in no way solving the problem of free will, Montesquieu led in refusing to accept it as a complete barrier to social science. His mildly framed proposals for reform were to give way to more radical demands, but can still be seen as a model of the use of social science knowledge for the betterment of humanity. Montesquieu's political conservatism limited his appeal to the next generation. His functionalist conceptualization was another conservative limitation. Even when acutely aware of the need for change he was concerned about interfering with the delicate balance of a society. The ill consequences of rapid change could be serious, far ranging, and long lasting. It would take a long time for the necessary new social *mores* to become accepted. The next generation of the Enlightenment learned much from Montesquieu, but he could not be their model in the struggle for reform.

FROM THE ENGLISH LETTERS TO THE FRENCH REVOLUTION

François-Marie Arouet, Voltaire (1694–1778)[10] is the link between eighteenth-century French empiricism and seventeenth-century British in ways even more direct than Montesquieu. With *Gabrielle-Emilie Le Tonnelier-Breteuil, marquise du Châtelet-Lomont (1706–49)*,[11] he helped make Newton widely known on the Continent. Had Voltaire not made Locke known in France, the eighteenth century would not have been the age of Locke. Note that this stage of French empiricism drew from British roots, not Mersenne or Gassendi. The pious priests were perhaps too clerical and moderate to be models for the unchaste, flamboyant French methodologists of the eighteenth century. Perhaps their style disqualified them. One can imagine Voltaire and Diderot reading Bacon and Locke with pleasure, and being repelled by the circumlocutions of Mersenne and Gassendi.

Two stays in the Bastille were formative for Voltaire's intellectual development. He was released early the second time on condition that he leave the country, whereupon he went to England for two years and learned English, English institutions, and tolerance. There, in 1733, he wrote and published his *English Letters*, which were so crucial in bringing British empiricism to France. A French version, considered dangerous to religious and civil order, was published a year later as *Lettres philosophiques*.

Châtelet and Voltaire were collaborators for fifteen years in methodology, history, mathematics, and natural science. A better mathematician and physicist than Voltaire, Châtelet merits attention in her own right. The two established a laboratory at her chateau at Cirey, a retreat where they both worked and received eminent scientists, mathematicians, and writers. She helped him with his popularized account of Newton, published in 1738 as *Élémens de la philosophie de Newton*. Châtelet published her *Institutions de physique* in 1740, an abridged account of Leibnizian philosophy, with her own introduction. She translated Mandeville's *Fable of the Bees*, the work that influenced Voltaire's materialistic poem, "Le mondain." An essay,

"Discours sur le bonheur," written c. 1747 and published in 1779, argues the need for women to study. Work she did on linguistics surfaced in the 1940s among some Voltaire papers in Leningrad. The two worked together on Biblical criticism and the early history of religion. Châtelet is probably the author of *Doutes sur les religions révélées*, a sceptical work much more negative than anything Voltaire wrote on religion. She is known to have influenced his historical writing, notably the move to more general "universal history." He wrote the *Philosophie d'histoire* for her, and did some of the work for the *Essai sur les moeurs* while at Cirey. He also wrote the *Traité de métaphysique* for her, which gives his position on basic methodological questions. Châtelet's last work was a translation into French of Newton's *Mathematical Principles of Natural Philosophy* (1759), which she finished only just before her untimely death, at age forty-three, as a result of childbirth.

In the last period of his life Voltaire lived at Ferney, located conveniently close to Geneva and safety from French arrest. He improved the land, brought in small industry, and worked for political reform. He took up causes and defended victims of French criminal justice, in some cases working for their posthumous rehabilitation. There Voltaire wrote *Candide*, a splendid short novel in which the hero's Leibnizian philosophy – all for the best in the best of all possible worlds – is put to a series of unlikely tests. *Candide* ends on a practical, materialistic note as the characters begin to make their own life on a small farm.[12] Voltaire lived to become the grand old man of the French Enlightenment, recognizing and encouraging new talent. In 1778 he made one final, triumphant trip to Paris, where he died. Voltaire was one of the first "great men" whose remains were removed to the Panthéon in 1793.

That Voltaire's cautious *English Letters* should be burned by the official executioner on the steps of the Courts of Justice gives a measure of the censor's power in the *ancien régime*. The next generation of protesters were to be outright republicans and atheists, compared with whom Voltaire is meek and mild indeed. The first four letters, on the Quakers, reveal a sober, decent, people, without a clergy, living at peace with one another and respecting the established authorities if not deferring to them. The English, Voltaire noted, seem to think the more sects the better. Yet even with such competition the established church did not suffer. Voltaire's letters on politics and commerce show the English to have been considerably better off than the French. Free institutions were at least consistent with, if not positively conducive to, prosperity and stability. The letter on Bacon praises his preparing the way to the new philosophy with the "Novum Organon."[13] Discoveries before Bacon had been made only by chance, but after he founded experimental philosophy others were encouraged to unearth the hidden treasure of findings. The next letter, on Locke, reveals even more devotion. Although Voltaire was no great mathematician, there had probably never been either a mind so wise or methodical as his or a logician so exact.

Voltaire found fault with the ancient methodologists, materialist and idealist, and became even more severe with Descartes and Malebranche. There is a brilliant put-down of "our Descartes, born to discover the errors of antiquity, but to substitute his own." Descartes, said Voltaire, was led by system, the spirit "which blinds the greatest men." He imagined himself to have demonstrated that the "mind was the same thing as thought, as matter ... is the same thing as extension." The soul arrives in the body "provided with all the metaphysical notions knowing God, space, infinity, having all the abstract ideas, filled with beautiful knowledge that it unfortunately lost on leaving its mother's womb." Locke then set things straight: "So many reasoners having made a novel out of the mind, a wise man came along, who modestly made a history of it" by describing the growth of understanding from infancy, making comparisons with animals, and above all consulting evidence (63).

Cartesianism had by Voltaire's time become establishment philosophy, yet his only compliments for Descartes were two edged. Descartes had been born with a lively and strong imagination, which he could not hide in his philosophical works. He had had to flee his own country to be able to philosophize in liberty. "He was wrong about the nature of the soul, on proofs for the existence of God, on matter, on the laws of movement, on the nature of light; he admitted innate ideas, he invented new elements ... he made man to his taste, and one says with reason that Descartes' man is, in effect, just his, and far removed from the real" (75–6). Voltaire wrote an essay on Newton as well, but at this stage he did not know enough physics to do his subject justice.

Convinced empiricist that he was, Voltaire gave little advice on how actually to do empirical work. His own experiments never rose above the amateur. He argued that careful observation, repeated experiments, and mathematical measurement were required, and even then only a degree of probability could be reached. Doubt was important, for even Newton and Boyle erred in experiments. The spirit of system was always to be resisted. One should not attempt to know first principles. Yet Voltaire shared with Locke, and many methodologists to come, the confidence that introspection was a valid way of collecting data, or at least no worse than other ways.

Châtelet did not go any further than Voltaire on how science was to be advanced, but she provided one of the best early statements on the use of hypotheses. The book was addressed to her son, to encourage him to pursue scientific studies and to introduce him to some basic principles (the son was one of the early victims of the Terror). "One of the errors of some philosophers of this time is to want to ban hypotheses from physics, which are as necessary as the scaffolding to a house one builds. It is true that when the building is finished the scaffolding is no longer needed, but one could never have put it up without its help."[14] She then warned that hypotheses may become the poison of philosophy when people try to pass them off for the truth. They may even be more dangerous than the unintelligible jargon of the scholastics, which was absolutely devoid of sense. An ingenious hypothesis with some initial probability encourages human pride to believe it; the mind is pleased to have discovered some subtle principles, and then uses all its powers to defend them. The majority of the great system builders have been of that type. "Their systems are great boats taken away by the currents – they make the most beautiful manoeuvres in the world, but the current carries them off." Her final advice to her son was to remember "that experience is the guide which nature has given us blind people, to lead us in our research; we cannot be sure with its help to find the right way, but we cannot but fail if we stop using it; it is by experience that we are made to know physical qualities, and it is by our reason that we use it and draw new knowledge from it" (10; my translation).

Châtelet is one of a small number of people who did original work in both the natural and social sciences. Her natural science contribution has begun to be recognized as feminist historians of science recover this past. Her work in the social sciences is still ignored, although it includes some of the earliest theory on sympathy as the means of developing law and morality. She used Mandeville, an early eighteenth-century British writer, as a base, preferring his *positive* bonds over Hobbesian force and fear. She is an excellent example of how women theorists make a difference. Her translation and commentary of Mandeville's *Fable of the Bees*, completed in 1737–8 although not published until 1947,[15] well predate Hume's *Enquiry concerning the Principles of Morals* (1751), Smith's *Theory of Moral Sentiments* (1759), and Helvétius' *De l'esprit* (1758).

The one place where Voltaire decisively parted company with Locke's essay was on espousing an inborn disposition, sometimes qualified as instinct, for justice. Voltaire insisted that there was a common sense of morality across all peoples, although the details as to what was right and wrong would vary. This was not to admit innate *ideas*, but rather dispositions of pity and remorse that led to a notion of justice. God gave us these sentiments in giving us a brain and a heart. The fundamental rule was not to do to others what one would not want done to oneself. This Voltaire maintained was the organizing principle of codes of justice. It made torture and all kinds of intolerance inadmissible, for people could not want these things done to themselves. Natural right was what nature showed to all people, including the right to the products of one's own labour.[16] Law could not but be founded on natural law, or human laws contrary to it were invalid. His notion of pity was akin to that developed later by the Scottish moral philosophers. Pity and justice were the sentiments on which society was founded. Evidently Voltaire needed to appeal to some kind of natural law principle. The *ancien régime* with which he did battle had the divine right of kings and revealed religion on its side. He needed a higher principle, too, something absolute and universal. Although he did not do it easily, for a cause as important as justice Voltaire went against Locke's methodology, as did Locke himself in *Two Treatises*.

Voltaire was one of the first people to write history "objectively," although he wrote highly polemical work as well, especially in his later years.[17] His early *Vie de Charles XII* (1731) was a factual account with little extraneous comment. For it Voltaire interviewed actual participants in the events concerned. He was critical of documentary sources. His universal histories are noteworthy for their attention to broad social and economic factors. Voltaire still accorded pre-eminence to great individuals, but long before it became common he included social matters. He has been described as an "idealist historian," for he considered ideas the motivating forces of great individuals. Human progress figures largely in his writing along with a concrete notion of progress. Voltaire's view of human nature, too, was at odds with that of traditional idealism. His human beings differ only in degree from animals. They exhibit neither the perfection idealists have considered their due, nor the wickedness of the human lot since the fall.

Voltaire's social and political views evolved over his mature years. Although he came from a privileged background (even in the Bastille he was not badly treated), he gradually became aware of the suffering others endured. At first he wrote of specific cases of injustice with some accompanying analysis. As he learned more, through other cases or more systematic reading, his analysis broadened accordingly. In the case of criminal justice he began by pointing out failures in due process, arguing for better safeguards to insure that innocent people were not convicted. In time he was persuaded of the injustice of the whole system, not just that there were occasional excesses. Although Beccaria was the main influence here, Voltaire never became as radical as his source.[18] Voltaire's views on slavery evolved, too, until finally he came to believe that all forms of slavery were wrong. He was never the exponent of equality that Rousseau was, and he maintained certain elitist ideas all his life. Progress was something to be imposed from above, while education presupposed a leisure class. Nevertheless, he did believe in an underlying equality: all people had the right to consider themselves the equals of anyone else. How inequalities arose did not much interest Voltaire. Class inequalities, as in serfdom or slavery, he described as the result of some desperate economic need.[19]

Voltaire's actual influence on the French Revolution has been much debated. Certainly a number of the causes he championed were taken up by revolutionaries who claimed to be his followers. It is thought that criminal law reform would not have been such a priority if Voltaire had not championed it. His abhorrence of war – he opposed all war – found fewer followers.

The one Italian contributor to empiricism to be considered in this history, *Cesare Beccaria (1738–94)*,[20] lived in the region of Italy with the greatest ties with France and Britain, Milan. Beccaria was much influenced by the Encyclopedists, and they in turn quoted him, with noisy praise, to the world. His *On Crimes and Punishments* (1764) had an enormous impact on the movement for criminal law and penal reform. The little book's timing could not have been better. Voltaire had begun to convince the enlightened world of the errors and barbarism of the existing system. Now Beccaria both made the case as to just how great, and unnecessary, that cruelty was and provided precise proposals for reform. The book was promptly attacked by lawyers and judges and put on the *Index* by the Catholic Church. One of the condemnations called Beccaria a "socialist," the first modern use of the term, in 1765.[21]

Beccaria's opening citation of Bacon and compliments to Montesquieu place *On Crimes and Punishments* in the tradition of French and British empiricism. Methodologically, the work is eclectic, combining an assumed natural law approach, progressive social contract theory, utilitarianism, empirical observation, and a great deal of reforming zeal. Beccaria seems to have *felt* the cruelty of criminal repression the way Adam Smith believed we feel the pain of our "brother on the rack." The groans of the tortured resound through his descriptions of the filth and horror of prison.

Beccaria used social contract theory to limit the power of the state, specifically to exclude torture and capital punishment. People could not give away such powers over their lives, nor indeed did they give away any liberty for the good of others. The sovereign's authority consisted of the sum of all the portions of liberty sacrificed by each person for that person's own good. "The aggregate of these least possible portions constitutes the right to punish; all that exceeds this is abuse and not justice."[22] Neither could torture, or other severe punishments, be justified on grounds of utility. (Here Beccaria's work was highly original and much copied.) It was the certainty and promptness of punishment that deterred, not severity. Severe punishments were counter productive, weakening social and moral bonds. Further, by becoming common, even cruel punishments lost any deterrent power they might otherwise have had. Much of the book was taken up with an analysis of particular abuses, with prevention as the focus.

Beccaria included much discussion of the proper scale of punishments, a matter taken up with a vengeance by the British Utilitarians in the next century. "For a punishment to attain its end, the evil which it inflicts has only to exceed the advantage derivable from the crime ... All beyond this is superfluous and for that reason tyrannical" (43). In retrospect, this is the only part of Beccaria's work that had negative results. He himself was never so crass as to suggest that criminals were totally rational, calculating machines weighing the anticipated gains of any crime with the possible punishment; later Utilitarians would go to such a logical extreme. Otherwise, Beccaria's work stimulated humanitarian reform of a barbaric criminal justice system. Reformers used his arguments, and kings and queens acted on them. Some of his advice remains unimplemented, for example, that theft without violence should be punished by a fine and not prison. Beccaria may still be cited in arguments for not letting off prominent people for their crimes: disgrace is not a sufficient punishment.

Those who think of Utilitarians as heartless quantifiers will find an exception in Beccaria. His commitment to empiricism is evident, if often submerged under plain moral outrage. He makes lofty appeals to reason, but uses scarcely a number or statistic. Nonetheless, the Utilitarian goal is expressly stated, as "*the greatest happiness shared by the greatest number*" (8). *On Crimes and Punishments* ends with a succinct statement of a general theorem of considerable utility, though it hardly conforms with custom: "*In order for punishment not to be, in every instance, an act of violence of one or many against a private citizen, it must be essentially public, prompt, necessary, the least possible in the given circumstances, proportionate to the crimes, dictated by the laws*" (99).

Beccaria's other social science work, *A Discourse on Public Economy and Commerce* (1769), was equally liberal but less influential. Except in his treatment of industry as well as agriculture as productive, Beccaria's political economy aligned with that of the physiocrats. He advocated free trade within the country and protective barriers against other countries. He proposed reforms in agriculture and forestry. He advocated public education and medicare. Property rights were to be limited in accordance with the common good, for property was the daughter of society, not the mother. The science of political economy was intended to increase the riches of the state for useful application.[23] Beccaria's economic reforms included a new, metric system of weights and measures, which the French National Assembly adopted in 1790. Followers of Canadian politics may be amused that the abolition of capital punishment *and* the introduction of the metric system came from the same source.

THE *ENCYCLOPEDIE*

Denis Diderot (1713–84)[24] is one of the most attractive figures in the history of methodology. After years of adversity, he developed a nobility of character to match his genius. He stands squarely in the middle of the empiricist tradition, carrying forward the central themes of seventeenth-century empiricism and laying the groundwork for the nineteenth century. He was remarkably faithful to the empiricism of Locke, which cannot be said for most of the professed Lockeans of his day. His materialism and atheism won him the praise of Marx, again showing the common ground between empiricism and Marxism. Yet his atheism was never so anti-clerical as Rousseau's or Condorcet's, and his materialism stopped far short of of the extremes of Holbach and Helvétius. His great achievement was the twenty-volume *Encyclopédie*, which he edited with d'Alembert. It was Diderot who shaped the work into a reasoned, co-ordinated whole. Diderot himself wrote much of it, fought with the censors, and kept going through two suppressions on the part of the authorities. Diderot's work is now available in a thirty-three volume collected works.

Diderot's philosophical work began with the translation of Shaftesbury's *Inquiry concerning Virtue*, from which he borrowed considerably in his own first writing, *Pensées philosophiques* (1746). This work scandalized the authorities by placing Christianity on the same basis as other religions. Published clandestinely and sold under the counter, the *Pensées* were condemned to be burned by the Parliament of Paris as contrary to religion and morals. Another early methodological work, *Promenade d'un sceptic*, was confiscated by the police and not published until 1830. When Diderot began work on the *Encyclopédie* it was only as an expanded French version of Chambers' Dictionary. He wrote a "Prospectus" in 1745 to obtain paid subscribers; d'Alembert wrote the lengthier *Discours préliminaire*.

Diderot's first work of importance in methodology, the *Lettre sur les aveugles* (1749), was secretly printed without authorization. The Lockean doctrine that all knowledge comes through the senses informed the work. The question was how knowledge, and especially moral ideas, could occur when one sense – vision – was absent. Much of the book was presented as an interview (which it was not) with a blind British mathematician. A fictitious death-bed scene, in which the dying man denied the existence of God, was especially scandalous. English academe never forgave Diderot, and this may be the reason for his never being admitted to the Royal Society. Voltaire wrote Diderot with praise for the essay in general, but disagreed with the concluding atheism.

The *Lettre sur les aveugles* and a short fictional piece resulted in Diderot's imprisonment in the Château de Vincennes. After a month in the dungeon conditions were improved thanks to the interventions of the Marquise du Châtelet, a relative of the prison governor. Diderot was given a room and was allowed to walk in the garden and receive visitors. He devised a way to make ink of wine and ground stone, writing the recipe on the wall for the benefit of the next prisoner. Although he refused to name the printer of his books, for which the penalty was life in the galleys, after four months he was released. Thereafter he sought authorization for his publications or left them for posthumous publication. If the *Encyclopédie* seems cautious, there was good reason.

Catherine II courted Diderot. After finishing the *Encyclopédie* he made the long trip to St Petersburg to thank her for her financial help. He stayed five months and urged on her all kinds of political and economic advice. Catherine apparently enjoyed his simple openness, but never took her philosophers seriously. "If I had believed him, everything would have been turned upside down in my kingdom," she said.[25] Diderot gave up discussing reform with the empress when he realized she wanted *glasnost* only, not *perestroika*. So they discussed literature, and she supplied him with information – much of it inadequate and frivolous – on social and economic conditions in Russia. In time she lost interest in Diderot. She bought additional copies of his work from his daughter and had the complete collection safely stored behind locked doors. Diderot's work was well preserved, then, but Catherine's inattentiveness impeded both his work and its publication. These unpublished works did not appear until the end of the nineteenth century.

The main work of Diderot's mature years consisted of selecting the contributors, editing, and arranging for the vast and complex array of engravings that accompanied the *Encyclopédie*.[26] What made the project an encyclopedia, as opposed to a mere dictionary, was its integration. Definitions and short explanations formed a large part of the work, which was alphabetically arranged. Links between the parts and more broadly the branches of knowledge were stated. The first crisis in the production of the *Encyclopédie* occurred apparently at the instigation of the Jesuits in 1751, after the publication of volume 2. Sales and reprinting of the existing volumes were forbidden. Diderot was ordered to hand over all relevant materials. His genius, however, could not be confiscated, and the work continued. The materials were returned, but the official ban kept over his head.

The next crisis came after volume 8 was published in 1759, when the *Encyclopédie* was condemned both by the Pope and Parliament. Helvétius' publication of the aggressively anti-clerical and materialistic *Esprit de l'homme* the previous year had enraged Parliament, and Diderot was incorrectly blamed for this book. Voltaire's article on Geneva also caused offence. A committee to investigate the *Encyclopédie* was established, but before it finished its work the royal privilege was withdrawn. The Church maintained that advantages to learning in the arts and sciences did not compensate for the damage the *Encyclopédie* did to morality and religion. Punishments were already death for writing or printing anything tending to attack religion, rouse opinion, impair the king's authority, or trouble the order and tranquility of his state, all of which the *Encyclopédie* was endeavouring to do. For technical infractions the penalty was the galleys for life.

Typesetting on the *Encyclopédie* never stopped, but contributors understandably became harder to find. Diderot had to do even more of the writing at this point, and for the next years he literally worked behind locked doors. One of the worst consequences of the pressure was that the publisher lost his nerve and undertook his own preventive censorship. He left entire sections incomprehensible and threw away the originals. Diderot kept going, however, convinced that the work would eventually appear. Advice, such as Voltaire's, to publish out of the country he refused in the best philosophical tradition: courageously despise the foe and take advantage of the feebleness of the censors. One must work and give a good account of one's gifts. In 1765 the last ten volumes were published. Subscribers were ordered to turn them over to the police, but the copies were returned with only petty amendments. Financially the *Encyclopédie* was a success. More copies were sold outside France than in, but the work made money even from the original subscribers and provided Diderot with a modest income for many years.

The *Encyclopédie* endeavoured to treat all the sciences, including the "liberal arts" and "the mechanical arts." A good deal of its popularity was due to its coverage of practical subjects. In the "Prospectus" Diderot noted the difficulties in covering the "mechanical arts," which required as much care as the sciences and the liberal arts, but on which almost nothing had been written. On the sciences and liberals arts, by contrast, too much had been written, most of it error. It was necessary to go out to the craftspeople themselves, in their workshops, for information. Diderot himself took chemistry classes to be able to cover the technical topics. A great deal of care was taken in the engravings of machinery, instruments, and so forth.

The volumes accorded relatively little space to traditional philosophy. The history of philosophy was covered competently, if with little originality. There was a highly favourable account of Epicurus, Gassendi and the early materialists generally. Scepticism was treated only as a negative approach. Idealism, as "rational philosophy," and especially the search for final causes, was judged unhelpful for science. Abuses and evils were noted, and where practices in other countries were better their reforms were praised. The section on agriculture described modern methods of farming. In discussing almshouses and hospitals, the *Encyclopédie* stressed the need to eliminate the causes of misery, not just provide refuge. It also attacked the corvée system of forced labour.

While the official line on religion had to be respected, a number of ruses conveyed an anti-clerical message. Pagan practices similar to Christian ones were criticized through skilfull use of irony and juxtaposition. Under the heading "Jesus Christ" for example, the reader was referred to the "History of Ancient and Modern Superstitions." Christianity, it was noted, as the true religion, was not really philosophy. The apostle Paul ceased to be a philosopher as soon as he began to preach. The Sorbonne, the theological faculty of the University of Paris, was described as able to contribute only on "theology, sacred history and superstitions." As a result of an outcry in Parliament an *erratum* was published. Now the Sorbonne could contribute to "theology, sacred history and the history of superstitions"![27] Unable to attack king and church directly, the *Encyclopédie* set out to undermine the philosophy and institutional framework that supported them. Language as a problem for philosophy never existed for Diderot. The "Prospectus" explained that in each article what was important would be set out. No assumption of prior knowledge on the part of the reader would be made. No problem of terminology, consequently, would arise.

Diderot's major paper on methodology, "Pensées sur l'interprétation de la nature," was an outgrowth of the work for the *Encyclopédie*. Four volumes of the *Encyclopédie* had been published, and Diderot wanted to give readers a short, non-technical explanation of its rationale. The "Interprétation" was published anonymously in 1754, with tacit permission (it was not authorized, but the censors gave the understanding that they would not prosecute, a provision to keep too many authors from publishing out of the country and ruining the printing industry). The "Interprétation de la nature" is the most Baconian of Diderot's works; it argues the same points as *The Great Instauration*, and also uses aphorisms. The disjunctive style was deliberate, to reflect breaks in the current state of knowledge. A radical distinction between the real world of empirical investigation and the imaginary world of mathematics was drawn right at the beginning. Mathematics was part of a wholly intellectual world, but its "rigorous truths" lost this advantage when introduced into the ordinary world. Diderot would write about the world of nature, where a great revolution in learning could be expected thanks to particular work. Mathematics, he predicted, would decline in comparative importance. Diderot was no opponent of mathematics but simply thought detailed empirical work more useful for the foreseeable future. Advances in mathematics would help little in understanding the real world.

The "Interprétation" expresses a strong sense of the limitations of human capacities in Lockean fashion: "The understanding has its prejudices, the senses incertitude, memory its limits, imagination its flashes, instruments their imperfections. Phenomena are infinite, causes hidden, forms perhaps transitory. We have so many obstacles we find in ourselves and in nature outside, that experience is slow and reflection constrained. These are the levers with which philosophy proposes to move the world."[28] Three related means of organising knowledge are described: observation of nature, reflection, and experience: "Observation collects facts; reflection combines them; experience verifies the result of the combination. It is necessary that observations of nature be assiduous, reflection deep, and experience exact" (9:39). Rarely did one see these means combined. Facts were the true riches of philosophy. "Rational philosophy," unfortunately, had been occupied much more with the relation between the facts it possessed than with collecting new ones. The backwardness of science was not due so much to lack of genius but to the fact that the best minds had hardly studied what was important to know. Words multiplied, but knowledge remained behind. Experimental philosophy took what came to it, while rational philosophy claimed learning, even when what it taught failed to happen (9:45). Experimental philosophy here included the social as well as the natural sciences, although most of Diderot's examples were of the latter.

Much would be made of the democratic streak in Diderot's methodology in the next century. He held that knowledge was to be useful in concrete ways to ordinary people and suspected that knowledge had been deliberately and unnecessarily kept from the people. The great philosophers had drawn a veil between the people and nature, while Diderot wanted philosophy made accessible. "Has not nature enough of a veil without lining it further with that of mystery?" (9:69) He stressed practical utility to ordinary people without any glorification of human beings. The idealist conception of "man" in the centre of the universe Diderot rejected completely. The world would be very dull without people, but it was preposterous, and a religious superstition, to go further than that. In a letter to Voltaire, Diderot joked that ants thanked God for giving them the world and putting everything they needed in it.

The "Interprétation de la nature" included some practical advice on how precisely the senses and reflection acquire knowledge. While Condillac was content to criticize Locke, Diderot offered help and advice. He warned against too rapid a dismissal of hypotheses in empirical testing. People sometimes think a conjecture is false when it is simply that the correct measures have not been taken to find it true. It is worse to abandon a hypothesis lightly than to hold on to it obstinately. The person who continues to look for verification might at least find out something, and perhaps something better. "Never is the time spent interrogating nature entirely lost" (9:71). Bizarre ideas perhaps deserve only one try, those with a greater initial probability more. Hypotheses that promise an important discovery should not be renounced until one has exhausted all testable possibilities. Altogether the amount of effort one gives to research would naturally reflect the interest of the subject. Tests should be repeated, extended to different objects, and combined in as many ways as possible. One must work to separate causes, decompose the results of actions, and reduce complicated phenomena to the simple. The testing had to be free, for to "keep it captive" was to show the side that proved one's hypothesis and to hide evidence to the contrary. Practically, the solution was to keep pushing the experiment further. If one's hypothesis or conjectures were true, more positive evidence would appear, if they were false, contradictory information would arise. Thus, while the sense of the difficulties of research is strong, there is still a confidence that recognizable truth will out.

The threat of censorship rendered the *Encyclopédie* not always a reliable guide to Diderot's political and economic views. His later, unpublished work was more radical.[29] Accumulation in social science is a process of small steps, however, and a few points from Diderot deserve inclusion here. Roughly he was a Lockean liberal. He had fairly close ties with the French physiocrats of the period, but differed from them in insisting that not just the land but both people and the earth produce riches. Property was as sacred as anything in Diderot's beliefs, signifying the effort people put into production. He consistently argued for free market conditions and against feudal privilege. His stress on the role of technology in productivity is obvious throughout the *Encyclopédie*. Socialists who have drawn on Diderot have emphasized his practical materialism. No ascetic, he distinguished between expenditure on frivolous luxuries and investment to generate greater benefits. He has been credited with advancing economic research by the quality of his observations. This is most evident in the reports of his travels in Holland and Russia. His questionnaire to Catherine II on social, economic, and political conditions in Russia deals with concerns which are still of primary interest to social scientists in those fields.

For Diderot sovereignty lay in the people. Even in the *Encyclopédie* the king's authority was said to be derived from the people, and the legitimacy of the monarchy was bound in time. Power acquired by violence or usurpation would last only so long as those who commanded could force others to obey. "The same law that has made *authority* unmakes it – the law of the strongest."[30] Strict limits on the sovereign were made clear. "It is not the state that belongs to the prince, but the prince who belongs to the state" (5:540). No social compact permitting abuse could be legitimate, for such implied either ignorance or folly on the part of the people and could be revoked when they came to their senses. Diderot approved of the American Revolution, as he did of revolution in general. He had no idea that there would be a revolution so soon in France (he died five years before it began).

Diderot was no utopian looking either to the future or the past. He did not idealize the "so-called state of nature," nor did he consider society any guarantee of peace. The happiest portrayal of society to appear anywhere in his writings was of a contemporary primitive society, and there the tone of the writing was humorous.[31] In his last years on the *Encyclopédie* Diderot also wrote some of his most brilliant works. There was a fine novel, *The Nun* (written 1761, published 1796); philosophy in dialogue form, *D'Alembert's Dream* (written 1769, published 1830), *Jacques the Fatalist* (written

1773, published 1796), and *Rameau's Nephew* (written 1762, published 1823); and a critique of Helvétius' *L'esprit de l'homme* (written 1773/4). Diderot now wrote for posterity, and posterity has much for which to be grateful.

Recognition of Diderot's genius was slow in coming. After the Revolution his work seemed too cautious, the result of compromises with censors; to the Restoration he was a godless materialist. Some of his books were not published until the Napoleonic era, the worst possible time for wider European circulation. He was scarcely known in Germany except as a literary critic; one edition of his "philosophical works" even omits the philosophical works! Diderot has typically been treated by Marxists as the best eighteenth-century materialist. He has been described as one of Marx's favourite writers, and certainly won the compliments of Engels and Lenin.[32] There is a substantial Marxist scholarship on Diderot. Marxists have liked Diderot's plebian background, glimpses of evolution, his atheism (ignoring his fondness for religious processions!), and the sense of relationship between theory and practice.

FROM THE MAN-MACHINE TO PSYCHIATRY

While Diderot and d'Alembert were struggling to get out the first volumes of the *Encyclopédie*, *Julien Offray de La Méttrie (1709–51)*[33] published a work that caused one of the greatest scandals in the French Enlightenment. His *Man-Machine* (1747) was an audacious development of a Cartesian idea. In retrospect it can also be seen as an early contribution to psychiatry. While Descartes' animal-machine was the most direct source for the concept, animal-human analogies had become increasingly acceptable throughout the eighteenth century. Still, *Man-Machine* was a shocker, offending the otherwise materialist *philosophes* almost as much as the idealists. No one was prepared for a complete determinism that eliminated free will or the possibility of altruism. Human motivation was reduced to the pursuit of pleasure and the avoidance of pain. People, like animals, were machines whose behaviour could be explained entirely in terms of responses to sensation. Epistemologically, all thought processes were reduced to sensation. Ontologically, thought and matter were one.

The man-machine idea came to La Méttrie while he was working as a French Army doctor. Overcome by fever on a campaign, he hallucinated and then began to reflect on his aberrant thoughts. He became convinced of the importance of physical conditions in determining mental states. Drugs, food, and sleep in particular, he decided, affect mental response. The practical consequences were obvious to La Méttrie, although he was to do little more than suggest the possibility. In so far as mental illnesses are a function of bodily conditions, they can be treated by physical intervention.

Medicines can change minds; *mores*, or mental states, "follow" the progress of the body.[34]

La Méttrie saw humans as only slightly removed from animals. Before language, humans were just animals with fewer natural instincts. The link was through sensation, and it was essential to his whole scheme that there not be any abrupt break. Thus the arts, the work of humans, could be described as "the child of nature," although they followed after a long gap in time. La Méttrie was one of the first writers to give prominence to imagination in methodology, crediting it with a crucial role in the evolution of the arts and sciences. It was through imagination that the "cold skeleton of reason" took on living flesh (165). Through imagination the sciences blossomed, the arts were embellished, the woods spoke, and marble breathed. Imagination, beautiful, great, and powerful, was as appropriate for the sciences as for the arts.

The stress on sensation, far from leading to hedonism, was the basis for social behaviour. La Méttrie suggested a kind of natural law as a learned feeling not to do to others what we would not want done to ourselves. This is an elementary notion of the "moral sentiment" much used by the Scottish moral philosophers. If pleasure was the link between humans and animals, it was also the link to social good. The moral philosophers, and later the Utilitarians, were to follow suit. It is ironic that by the time La Méttrie published *Man-Machine*, Descartes himself was just being rehabilitated. From being on the *Index* and banned by the Sorbonne, Descartes was again being openly taught. By 1755 the turn-about was complete. The French Academy gave a prize to a Jesuit who praised Descartes for his refutation of Aristotle and his services to Christianity![35]

De l'esprit by *Claude Helvétius (1715–71)*[36] caused at least as much trouble as the *Man-Machine*. In fact it was the spark that fired the censor's campaign against the *Encyclopédie*. *De l'esprit*, published in 1758, was condemned by Parliament, the Sorbonne, and the Jansenists, publicly burned in Paris, and put on the *Index* in Rome. The Encylopedists were almost as outraged much but kept their criticism private. Helvétius was forced to publish three retractions, each more humble than the last. Part of the offence was to have published with official approval; Helvétius tricked the censor by giving him the work in pieces, out of order, and by applying flattery and pressure. The censor lost his job for the mistake.

As in the *Man-Machine*, all mental processes were reduced to sensation, understood as the passive reception of impressions. Thus there was no room for free will. Judgment was simply a type of sensation. No different from animals, people responded to sensation, seeking pleasure and avoiding pain. This much is unoriginal, but Helvétius next developed a utilitarian ethics based on sensation. The object was to make people behave morally while acting in self-interest: "The whole art of the legislator consists in forcing men by the sentiment of self love always to be just to others. Thus, to compose laws one must know the human heart."[37] People were born neither good nor bad, but were ready to go in either direction as their interests took them. By saying that people were not naturally wicked, Helvétius offended traditional Christian doctrine. Yet by not seeing people as naturally good he offended the *philosophes*. That people should be appealed to frankly on the basis of calculated self-interest scandalized nearly everyone. Helvétius was also perverse enough to treat democracy sympathetically, including rights for women. He criticized the nobility and the Church for their exploitation of people, and hurled many insults at the Church. He claimed that people were born with equal potential for education, a most radical notion for this period.[38] Differences in accomplishment were largely due to differences in education, not innate capacities. Yet Helvétius was dogmatic in his arguments. He pronounced that he had "proved" propositions when all he had done was provide plausible reasons. He gave examples for which counter-examples were equally plausible. Helvétius took on all the sensationalism of empiricism, but without the hypothetical methodology, doubt, and search for alternatives.

The career of *Paul Thiry d'Holbach (1723–89)*[39] resembles that of Helvétius in many respects of background, extreme determination in methodology, and outraged sensibilities all round. When the royal prosecutor-general appeared before the Parliament of Paris in 1770 with indictments for seven books, five were by Holbach, including his methodology. All were duly condemned to be burned by the public executioner. All deserved the charge: "Impious, blasphemous, and seditious literature, tending to destroy all ideas of divinity, to rouse the people to revolt against religion and government, to overthrow all the principles of public security and uprightness, and to turn subjects away from the obedience due to their sovereign."[40] Holbach put all his advantages of wealth, education, and domestic happiness to use for the cause of philosophy. The Holbach salon (dinners twice a week) was one of the main meeting places for the *philosophes* and visiting intellectuals. Sceptics and clerics, deists and atheists, were welcome, for Holbach got along with everybody. He translated scientific and technical works, largely from German to French. He wrote some 400 pieces on science and technology for the *Encyclopédie*.

Holbach's major work on methodology, *Système de la nature* (1770), interrupted a spate of anti-religious writing and translations (which, to avoid problems, he published outside France). Not the least reason for the scandal was that he had *Système* published in England under the name of the secretary of the French Academy! Holbach next published two books on social and political questions, *Politique naturelle* (1773) and *Système social* (1773). He translated Hobbes' *De Cive* and *De Homine* and then went on to liven the field of natural religion. One of his last books, provocatively dedicated to Louis XVI, presumed to give advice that only a constitutional monarch could welcome. *Ethocratie* (1776) was published anonymously in Amsterdam. Curiously, the anti-religious books have been reprinted, while the methodology and politics have been unduly neglected.

Système de la nature moved quickly from an expression of the usual elements of empiricism to a contentious statement about the nature of human beings, called "man" (l'homme). Human beings were physical, and only physical, beings. "Moral man" meant only "this bodily being considered from a certain point of view ... relative to his way of acting."[41] "Man is the work of nature, he exists in nature, is subject to her laws, and cannot go beyond her even in thought" (1:1–2). While other methodologists have supported endeavours to escape bodily limitations, Holbach was unsympathetic: "It is in vain that his mind wants to soar beyond the boundaries of the visible world, he is always forced to come back" (1:2). Political, social, and moral questions could only be approached with this understanding of people as material beings in a material world. To forget this was to court all kinds of trouble. It was from not knowing nature that humans created gods and superstitious cults, the source of all their woes. People were unhappy only when they misunderstood their nature, wanting to do "metaphysics" before doing "physics," pretending to know their destiny in an imaginary other world before dreaming of making themselves happy in the here and now (1:v–vi). Once this material basis was accepted there was cause for much hope, for the material world was knowable through experience, and knowledge could be applied for the betterment of all.

The social and natural sciences and the practical arts were mingled together. "It is therefore to nature and experience that man must have recourse in all his research ... in religion, morality, legislation, government, politics, the sciences and the arts, pleasures and pain" (1:6). Relationships within this material world were absolutely determined, as much so for human beings as for the most inert material objects. The universe consists of nothing but matter and movement, in an immense, uninterrupted chain of causes and effects. "All that we do or think, all that we are and shall be, is but the consequence of what universal nature has made us: all our ideas, wills, and actions are the necessary effects of the ... qualities nature has put in us" (1:3–4). Holbach did not mince words about the fatalism of his methodology. People were always responding to outside stimuli and always did what they could not help doing. "The will of man is moved or determined secretly by external forces which produce a change in him; we believe that it moves of itself because we neither see the cause which determines it nor the way in which it acts" (1:19). Clearly there could be no place for a soul, or god, for that would be to admit a source of influence outside the natural sphere of cause and effect. Or, in Holbach's words, to believe that the soul was capable of determining its own will was to "pretend that man was free" (1:224).

A logical consequence of this determinism was that people could not be blamed for their conduct, and Holbach quite consistently did not blame anybody. Criminals, he believed, should be dealt with in the least severe manner possible consistent with deterrence. Holbach was one of the first French writers to advocate less cruel punishments. Education, just laws, and good government would insure desirable social behaviour. Virtue and vice were viewed in a completely utilitarian fashion. A virtuous person is one whose actions constantly tend to the welfare of others, a vicious person makes others unhappy. Nature makes people "neither good nor bad; it makes them machines more or less active, moving, energetic" (1:178). What is implicit in all determinism, but which Holbach actually said, is that self-interest is the "sole motive in human action" (1:375). People's interest in virtuous, social conduct was to obtain approval from others, a theme worked out further in *Politique naturelle*. The other *philosophes* remained unconvinced, however, and even Diderot, a life-long friend, was critical.

Holbach's insistence on the physical basis of mental functioning helped to lay the foundations of French psychiatry. Clearly, so long as an immaterial soul is responsible for guiding human behaviour there is no place for medical intervention. Holbach helped to destroy the old assumptions and offered an explicit alternative. He insisted that mental illness has a physical base, as does healthy functioning. Medicine, by consulting experience, can cure not only the body but the mind, in his view essentially the same thing. If we know the elements that form temperament we will know what needs to be done. It was not to be doubted that temperament could be "corrected, altered, modified by physical causes" (1:149–50). Holbach gave few details but indicated that diet, exercise, and alcohol use were important.

Holbach subscribed to the usual list of the sources of error of empiricism. He differs from the British, and especially Hume, whom he knew, in his robust optimism about eventually gaining access to the truth. The object was causal knowledge of the real, external world, not just phenomena, and not just associations. "Nature acts by simple, uniform, invariable laws, which experience puts us in a position to know" (1:6). How we can be sure that these laws are simple was not explained. There was no disorder in the universe, but what seemed to be disorder was simply our ignorance of the connections between things. Chance, similarly, was ignorance of cause (1:79).

Holbach's materialism has been criticized for its completely static, ahistorical character. Whereas Diderot revealed glimpses of evolution theory, and Condorcet had a vision of stages of history, Holbach viewed people, and indeed the whole natural world, as always the same. To admit change would be to deny the universality, the immutability of natural laws. Holbach was a middle-of-the-road social reformer, sceptical about democracy (as tending to anarchism), concerned about revolution (sometimes inevitable, but accomplishing more harm than good), and he was no believer in equality. He was aware of injustices to women, especially in family law, and favoured extending legal rights, if not also political participation, to them.[42] His Lockean notion of property was radical in its day. There would be no need for property if the earth produced without effort on our part all that was needed for existence. Since this was not so and people had to work, the laws of nature gave them the right to property. "A field becomes, in some fashion, a portion of him who cultivates it, because it is his will, his arms, effort, and industry ... that make the field what it is. This field, having absorbed his sweat, becomes part of him."[43] Holbach even recognized that the vast mass of the people who labour do not own property. "The majority of the peoples of the earth are forced to waste their sweat, blood and fortunes for those ingrates who have persuaded themselves that heaven wills that their equals work for them" (42).

Holbach was a thorough liberal on sovereignty, reason enough for anonymous publication in pre-revolutionary France. "No society on earth could have nor have wanted to confer irrevocably to its leaders the right to damage it."[44] "Divine right" was the outrageous claim of despots, usurpers, thieves, and brigands.[45]

LANGUAGE AND LEARNING

Although the abbé *Etienne Bonnot de Condillac (1714–80)*,[46] an aristocrat at home in the French court, was politically about as far from the firebrand as possible, he was a radical enough empiricist methodologist to appeal to the *philosophes*. He was a "sensationalist" only in the prosaic use of the term, as a proponent of Lockean, sensation-based methodology. Voltaire said that if Locke had not written *An Essay Concerning Human Understanding*, Condillac would have, and made it shorter. Voltaire, of course, must be granted poetic license, but Condillac was, at the least, a most concise and well-organized writer.

Condillac considered Locke's *Essay Concerning Human Understanding* to be the best work on methodology to date, but inconsistent and repetitious. His own *Essay on the Origins of Human Knowledge* (1746) is largely a restatement of Locke, with corrections. Condillac rejected Locke's use of the "understanding" as an unnecessary and mysterious element in the process. His analysis was a swift, Cartesian thrust to the heart of the matter. Reflection was not a distinctive faculty but simply the power to control one's attention.[47] The mind could distinguish, abstract, compare, judge, compose, and decompose. Substantively, the process of acquiring knowledge was very much as Locke had proposed. The key phase was the association of ideas, for which language was required beyond the simplest perceptions. Condillac's stress on terms here makes him an early founder of logical positivism. His second major work on methodology actually ends with the admonition: "Do you want to learn science with facility? Begin by learning your language."[48] By his third book on methodology, Condillac considered that he had over-stated the case for language. He now argued that the senses alone were sufficient for the development of all abstract ideas, including God, causation, quantity, and quality.[49]

Condillac was a mainstream empiricist in his stress on the continuities between humans and animals. He criticized the Cartesians for considering animals senseless automata. Not only do they have the capacity to feel, they can compare and judge, for they have ideas and memory.[50] Animals could even be said to have language in cries and gestures, and some live in society. Yet Condillac justified the study of animals as a means better to understand humans. His concept of knowledge for application was still only weakly developed compared with that of the Encyclopedists and the British empiricists. Condillac also saw that continuities were necessary between the different fields of science. The best method of study had to be the same for all.

Condillac vociferously opposed two kinds of systems. He argued against "metaphysical" systems, based on abstract principles, and those based on "hypotheses," which were mere suppositions but often taken for the truth.[51] He denounced Leibniz, Malebranche, and Spinoza, which pleased the Encyclopedists. Yet he succumbed to another form of system, that ostensibly based on "demonstrated" fact (1:194). A complete system could be built from such facts, he held, showing little awareness of the difficulty of *demonstrating* anything. He was blissfully unaware of even such a basic obstacle as differences in perception between observers. So long as one was careful in naming the terms in the process all would go well. After all, systems were part of nature, and people were themselves systems.

For all his naïvety on the problems of perception and processing, Condillac gave some good advice on hypothesis testing. To be sure of the truth of a hypothesis, one had to exhaust all other possible hypotheses. Hypotheses could not themselves be used as the basis for any system but, when properly tested, could become a source of truth. This involved the accumulation of observations adequate to permit no doubt. With the advice, then, there is still a confidence that truth can be found, doubt eliminated. Condillac adopted *all* of Locke's sensationalism, but he missed, or rejected, the scepticism. He denounced the idealists for their systems, yet matched their confidence of finding *the* truth and building systems on it.

Nor was Condillac entirely consistent in applying his philosophy of education, but his attempts constitute a good story. His goal was a careful adaptation of Locke's theory of education, the subject of the experiment a French prince. One crucial premise was that the education of the individual should follow in broad lines that of the human race. Thus, since people had first to produce food, the young prince was given a garden to learn to grow things. The acquisition of cultured taste and the ability to speculate followed, so the prince's schooling moved from gardening to French literature. Perhaps the most ingenious part of the scheme was that the prince was taught methodology at age seven! Obviously he had early to become aware of how he observed, constructed, and reflected on hypotheses. Thus the methodology of empiricism, or Condillac's version of it, was on the curriculum in the formative years. (Condillac considered appropriate experiments important agents of learning.) Like Locke, Condillac conceived the task of education as the feeding of facts to the mind. How, and in what order, become crucial questions.

Condillac's political views were conservative enough for the French court. They were also expressed in a functionalist framework, a frequent method in the nineteenth and twentieth centuries. To Condillac the ideal society was simply the old order with the worst abuses eliminated. The monarch, for example, should promote Catholicism as the true religion, but not persecute minorities or undertake crusades.

Some parallels between Condillac and *Georges-Louis Leclerc (comte) de Buffon (1707–88)*[52] will be immediately obvious. Both developed methodology from a Lockean base, and both nonetheless succumbed to the French love of system. Both enjoyed considerable success in their day, offended neither church nor state, yet were esteemed by the Encyclopedists. Buffon is noteworthy also for some truly original ideas on probability. This points to yet another contradiction, of course, for his systematizing was based on certainty, scepticism and probabilism for the moment forgotten. Intendant of the King's Garden, Buffon is often considered the founder of natural history, a precursor of Lamarck and Darwin.

Buffon in his *Histoire naturelle* (1749) advocated a thoroughly empiricist methodology. A solid data base was the beginning of knowledge; observations should be made without an initial design. It was dangerous to draw causal inferences too early, for one could fill the memory with prejudices difficult to get rid of later. The natural world was wholly determined by laws unchanging between creation and destruction. "Nature" meant the system of laws established by the Creator.[53] Causal knowledge as such was beyond our scope but we could know general or always occurring effects, which we call causes (1:40). The elementary parts of nature, some kind of atoms and void, were unobservable and beyond our knowledge.

Buffon offended the Church with his description of creation, which bore no resemblance to that in Genesis. He retracted fulsomely, one suspects insincerely. He explained that his object was modest, the measure of uncertain things. Absolutely certain knowledge could not be attained in either the social or physical world. One could get closer in the physical world, for more observations were possible in it than in the social. Buffon's notion of probability was based entirely on the number of observations, the more observations the higher the probability of accurate interpretation. The highest possibility was still only "virtual certainty," the probability that an event which has always occurred will occur again (1:457). The absolute was the province of neither Nature nor the human mind.

Buffon's originality lies in his attempt to establish concrete criteria for judging probabilities. Given that there can be no certain knowledge, at what point should we deem an event "virtually certain" to happen? The calculations appear in an essay on "moral arithmetic," a term we shall increasingly see. Buffon's ingenious demarcation point came at the probability that a mature man his age (fifty-six) would not die the next day. This probability in 1749 was 10,000 to one. The rationale was that if you knew your chances of dying in the next twenty-four hours were only one in 10,000, you would go about your normal routine. You would feel "morally certain" that your life would continue. Thus we feel morally certain that, among other things, the sun will rise tomorrow (1:460).

Buffon's treatment of the relations of humans to nature was at the aggressive end of the empiricist tradition. Raw nature was ugly and brutal, but humans made it alive and beautiful by activities such as clearing swamps and cultivating land (1:34). If people let up on the struggle, Nature took back her rights and destroyed their work. Buffon was inconsistent on human-animal differences. In places he was a strict materialist/empiricist, in others he agreed with the idealists, especially the Cartesians. Less understandable inconsistencies occur in his justification of systems of thought. Beginning with the Lockeans, he asserted that the mind could create nothing but could learn only by experience. Somehow, however, it could go on to build systems by reflection, "immortal monuments resting on unshakeable foundations."[54] Buffon had little to say either on the establishment of the initial data base or the process of reflection from it. Although he wrote science well, his advice on scientific writing was naïve. One must fully "possess" one's subject and reflect on it to see clearly the order of thoughts. Next one had to form a continuous chain in which every point represented an idea. Taking pen to hand one had to go from the beginning to end at one time without getting off track.

Materialist writers of the period respected Buffon as a biologist, but he could not be a model for them. Biological analogies were fashionable in the late eighteenth century, even more so in the nineteenth century, but Buffon's systematizing went too far. Again we see how difficult it was for French theorists to remain true to empiricism. Condorcet, giving the eulogy for Buffon, stressed his great contribution as a materialist but warned against the bent for systematization.

THE PHYSIOCRATS AND ATTEMPTS AT REFORM

The physiocrats were the first modern school of economics.[55] Free trade within a country was hardly a distinctive physiocratic demand, but it was part of the reform package. Feudal strictures on manufacturing and sales stifled enterprise and efficiency and were counter-productive. Economics, with the physiocrats, became the science of wealth, of the formation and distribution of capital. The growth of capital became synonymous with economic progress.

Physiocracy means "rule by nature." The constant theme of these would-be reformers was that the French economy was at odds with the laws of nature. With its backward laws and taxes the state prevented the vital flow of capital. Free trade, even only within the country, was a revolutionary idea in this period, threatening a massive redistribution of income and wealth. (England, ahead of France in moving to internal free trade, was Quesnay's model.) Physiocracy can be seen as a truncated section in the development of the social sciences. Its influence was greatest in the 1760s, and declined sharply by the late 1770s. Yet even in that short time the physiocrats contributed to methodology. They wrote for the *Encyclopédie* on methodology as well as on economics. They were all committed to Lockean empiricism, the unity of science, and, in the case of Turgot and to his ruin, knowledge for application.

The founder and leader of the physiocrats was the doctor *François Quesnay (1694–1774)*.[56] His first disciple was Victor de Riqueti, Marquis de Mirabeau, father of the revolutionary leader. Mirabeau senior was more conservative politically than the other physiocrats and more of an idealist methodologically. The school as such can be said to date from 1757 when Mirabeau began to collaborate with Quesnay and publicize his views. He then played Engels to Quesnay's Marx. Mirabeau published Quesnay's "Tableau économique" in his journal, *Ami des hommes*, in 1758, giving it wide circulation. Turgot was the school's best-known advocate, although he deviated from Quesnay's theory of agriculture as the *sole* means for creating a surplus. Turgot, as comptroller-general of France, was the physiocrat most involved in the application of the theory to practical reforms.

The physiocrats were better connected at court than the other encyclopedists. They were more diplomatic and not at all anti-clerical. Moreover, since the reforms they sought required a strong monarchy, they supported Louis XV and Louis XVI. The feudal aristocracy opposed any reform and successfully pressured Louis XVI to fire Turgot and stop his reforms. Many of his practical measures in public works, education, health care, and the abolition of the corvée and many unfair taxes, were gradually implemented after the revolution. If these reforms had been made in time, it has often been said, there would have been no revolution. Physiocracy advanced a mixture of often incompatible elements. It was progressive in economic theory but woefully lacking in political know-how. One apt theory considers physiocracy a heroic attempt to bring together the static and feudal strands of French political thought. Yet its aim of revolution, individual freedom, and social harmony proved to be as difficult to implement as liberty, equality, and fraternity.[57]

A specialist in economics and finance, Quesnay wrote the articles on farms and grain for the *Encyclopédie*, but his discretion saved him from difficulties with the censor. The first edition of his famous "Tableau économique" was printed on the king's own press, a decided change for an Encyclopedist. He wrote also on natural law, medicine, and surgery. The "Tableau économique" was a summary statement of the French economy by sector and showed the flow between sectors. Agriculture was the main focus, but "the land" also included forests, woods, mines, fishing, and processing of raw materials for manufacture.[58] Only the land yielded a "net product," that is produced beyond what was necessary to sustain the workers on it. Artisans, and all other members of society, live off the net product harvested from the land. The class of landowners "lives off the *net product* from agriculture," which is paid annually by the productive class after it has taken off the production needed to pay its annual advances and to maintain the capital stock for future exploitation of the land.[59]

The tableau was neither an abstract model nor a report of data. The quantities reported, in money terms, were estimates of the worth of the various sectors. The account began with micro-level estimates of a typical French farm, then on to national estimates both of annual revenues and expenditures and of the wealth of whole sectors of the economy. Thus, Quesnay estimated the value of the land of France at £40.33 billion. The total wealth of the "sterile classes" was estimated at £18 billion, and the grand total of all forms of wealth for France was £59 billion.[60] The original tableau was short, a chart with zig-zag lines between the columns of expenditures and revenues. The explanation was brief, although Quesnay himself defended and expanded his theory with further articles, as did his friends.

The most distinctive feature of physiocratic theory was also its downfall, a belief that only the land produces wealth. Quesnay was to remain true to this doctrine, but Turgot abandoned it. That agricultural production would be the source of the division of labour has an obvious intuitive appeal, for we all have to eat. No one, at least on a full-time basis, can be released for work in other arts or crafts unless there is a food surplus from which to be fed. That the other classes should be called "sterile," as productive of nothing, was resisted. The object of physiocracy is well described in the title of Quesnay's collaborative work with Mirabeau: *Rural philosophy, general and political economy of agriculture reduced to the unchanging order of physical and moral laws to assure the prosperity of empires* (1763).

Quesnay described two sources of knowledge: "Nature reveals herself only obscurely to our eyes; we must therefore scrupulously examine her ways, follow her in all her detours, and observe her effects. But in observing the mind is but a simple spectator, seeing the outside. With the help of physical experiments, we must try to penetrate to the very principles of nature ... to question her and force her to reveal herself."[61] He was careful to say the right things about religion, if briefly and at the end of the article. Thus there is an acknowledgment of divine illumination and a sharp juncture between humans and animals, where he departs markedly from the empiricist tradition. If Quesnay was the first modern economist he was certainly not one to focus narrowly on his subject. His article on evidence in the *Encyclopédie* competently discusses the acquisition of sensations and making judgments from them. It is standard Lockean fare, with swipes at Spinoza.

As intendant of Limoges *Anne-Robert Jacques Turgot (1727–81)*[62] saw the poverty, cruelty, and backwardness of the old order. He set out to correct every abuse within his power, and made headway in his thirteen energetic years in office. His efforts were recognized in 1774 when Louis XVI appointed him comptroller-general of France, in effect minister of finance, transport, natural resources, energy, and public works. He now had considerably more scope for his ambitious plans for reform. The corvée (peasants' forced labour) was abolished, taxes simplified, certain feudal privileges abolished, and taxes imposed on the nobility. Turgot began to organize local assemblies, poor relief, schools, and hospitals. His reforms were popular with the ordinary people, but the nobles moved against him, and after two years he was dismissed. Turgot spent his last years in writing and scholarly pursuits.

Turgot's first steps to physiocracy can be seen in his article on farmers in the *Encyclopédie*. By 1769, when his *Réflexions sur la formation et la distribution des richesses* was published, Turgot had fully accepted physiocracy. He describes the agricultural worker as the pre-eminent producer, the motor that drives society. "What his work produces from the soil over his personal needs is the sole source of the wages that all other members of society receive in exchange for their work ... The agricultural worker is the only one whose work produces above and beyond the wages of work. He is therefore the sole source of all riches" (2:537–8). The first division of labour was that between the productive, agricultural class and artisans.

Initially, landowners and cultivators were not distinguished, but gradually this division and then a class of slaves emerged. Other divisions included administrators and the military.

Turgot used his years as intendant of Limoges and the shorter period as comptroller-general of France to prepare and, as far as possible, implement a vast array of reforms. Agricultural research, education, land clearing, drainage, and roads were all needed to improve productivity. To finance these projects a more effective tax system was required. The peasants, at a near-starvation standard of living, could bear no more. Exorbitant taxes, special levies for war, and an archaic system of forced labour were all disincentives to productivity. The nobles had to be made to pay their share. Bringing together all these concerns, Turgot's goal was the single tax, on land. It was the perfect physiocratic solution, for land was the source of wealth. To the physiocrats, any other tax was indirect or misplaced.

For his intrepid reforms Turgot has been accused of being politically naïve. It was said that he had no plan for marshalling the forces to which he appealed. He seemed to believe that ideas derived their power from their quality.[63] He understood, however, that constitutional change was needed for the kind of France he envisaged. The prime beneficiaries of his policies were farmers and, second to them, artisans. Yet neither group had political power in pre-revolutionary France. The nobles, who had enormous powers, had much to lose from Turgot's reforms. Whether or not political power could have been redistributed from the nobility to the productive classes in some way short of revolution is still debated. In any event, the nobles managed to have Turgot removed from office and many of his reforms reversed. Within fifteen years, many of these same nobles were to die in the Revolution and the succeeding Terror. Feudal privileges were abolished and the great mass of Turgot's practical reforms were in time implemented.

Turgot's methodological articles and correspondence show that he sided with the Encyclopedists. His article on existence in the *Encyclopédie* was far more a discussion of sensation than of existence as such. He also used the article to berate idealists, especially Berkeley. It demonstrates that Turgot was equally at home with natural and social science material. He parted company from most of the Encyclopedists, though, in rejecting determinism in motivation as mechanistic. Here he sided with the idealists in asserting free will.[64]

SUBJECTIVITY IN METHODOLOGY

Against this development of empiricism in the social sciences, idealist philosphy continued to received official favour and support. That, of course, is not our subject here, but two theorists outside the empiricist camp made contributions that must be included: Vico and Rousseau. Both were critical of the emerging empiricism, but both had an impact on it. The alternative approaches they offered had to be considered, positively or negatively, by later methodologists. Rousseau also influenced the development of political theory.

Giambattista Vico (1668–1744)[65] is of interest not only as an idealist theorist but as an exponent of concepts that later came back into empiricism. He was an early founder of the "understanding" concept, which was to have both romantic/ idealist developments, as in Wordsworth and Herder, and empiricist ones, as in Weber. He is still cited in attacks on the empirical social sciences as the author of a better alternative. Vico can also be seen as an early structuralist. He contributed to philology as well as to his main subject, Roman law. If in these respects he seems modern, he can equally well be seen as a latter day Eleatic or neo-Platonist.

Vico arrived at his methodological position in a common enough way, through criticism of Descartes. This included such obvious points as that ideas could be clear and distinct, yet false. More profoundly Vico concluded that the Cartesian method could not be applied to the natural world, that only God, who had made the world, could know it. True knowledge could be had of the social world, Vico held, for it was humanly made, and thus humanly knowable. His imagery is quintessentially idealist: "In the night of thick darkness enveloping earliest antiquity shines the eternal and never failing light of a truth beyond all question: that the world of civil society has certainly been made by men, and that its principles are therefore to be found within ... our own human mind." This enunciation makes Vico the inventor of the concept of "understanding." Dilthey and Weber's later formulations were thoroughly secular and empiricist, yet it is interesting to note that the Vico original owed as much to theology as had Augustine, Descartes, Leibniz, or Malebranche. Vico marvelled that philosophers should have bent all their energies to studies of the natural world "which, since God made it, He alone knows."[66] He explained this aberration with the idealist hierarchy of mind over body. It was because the mind was buried in the body, and inclined to notice bodily things, that people gave more attention to natural science than human studies.

There is a common sense objection to Vico's greater confidence in the social sciences to natural. Laws and social institutions are scarcely, if ever, the work of one person. Thus knowledge of them can rarely, if ever, be achieved by a purely internal process, quite apart from any possible distortion from unconscious motives, self-interest, or false consciousness. To meet this objection Vico had to assume that all minds are alike, a supposition surely refuted in any meeting of philosophers. Vico, however, obviously thought otherwise. Indeed he continued to refer to "mind" in the singular, a device for avoiding the problem of diversity of opinions rather than solving it. "The mind" is only an abstraction, nowhere existing. Any real, functioning, mind must be connected to a person. Thus, it is difficult to see how his concept of "understanding" could ever be used in social science investigations. Ultimately, it means one person introspecting and making universal generalizations from that introspection. Another person might make completely different generalizations, and there is no way for anyone to judge which, if either, is correct.

Vico betrays a fundamental inconsistency in explaining his preference for social over natural sciences. He stated that the social world was knowable because it was humanly made. Yet in other places he described the social world as being as divinely ordered as the natural. The new science must be a "demonstration of what providence has wrought in history," often *against* human design (102). In a *non sequitur* Vico further insisted that, since social institutions were established by divine providence, their course was and had to be as "our science demonstrates" (104). Vico was here, as elsewhere, remarkably unsceptical. His work was laced with truths and certainties, and even "divine proofs." He was unsceptical in his substantive work as well, making vast generalizations from the scantiest of evidence. Evidence, of course, is not needed in a methodology which fundamentally rests on introspection.

A good part of *The New Science* (1744) is simply the assertion of "axioms," of miscellaneous facts, beliefs, or suppositions. Without further ado these are then drawn on for the enunciation of more complex principles and theories. Vico's philosophy of history follows logically enough from his theology. Since history was determined by one God, every nation would follow the same course, from rise and maturity to decline and fall. Certain notions and symbols were common to all nations, like ideas of God, patriarchy, marriage, and burial. An objective science of institutions was possible because these notions were universal, God given. "Uniform ideas originating among entire peoples unknown to each other must have a common ground of truth" (63). Vico's structuralism follows in turn. For all such common notions to be expressed, there must be a common language underlying them. "There must in the nature of human institutions be a mental language common to all nations, which uniformly grasps the substance of things feasible in human social life and expresses it" (67).

Vico can be seen as a transitional theorist, bridging the thousands of years between the ancient Eleatics and neo-Platonists, Augustine, and Malebranche and more recent romantics like Wordsworth. The Eleatic identification between being and knowing is part of his methodology. Knowing and creating, in God, were one and the same thing (105). The distinction between subject and object simply disappears. Vico also reveals a belief in the idealist confounding of knowledge and virtue. "He who is not pious cannot be truly wise" (339). Practical difficulties ensue as well from the identification of "is" and "ought." Obviously one cannot compare actual social institutions against any ideal standard. Vico could assert without apparent difficulty: "That which regulates all human justice is therefore divine justice, which is administered by divine providence to preserve human society" (102). What is is right, or, Might is right. But was there anything divine in the justice of the eighteenth century, when judges could be bought, "witches" burned, debtors thrown into stinking jails, and suspects tortured for confessions? With this confounding of is and ought, critical questions cannot even be raised. From the Hebrew prophets through the sophists to natural law theorists, critics of injustice have posed ideal justice against actual to expose and denounce real abuses. With the methodology of Vico this simply cannot be done. Instead the great work exposing the cruelty of European criminal justice was done by the empiricists Voltaire and Beccaria.

Jean-Jacques Rousseau (1712–78)[67] has been seen variously as a romantic and a rationalist opponent of empiricism, although he also made methodological statements in the tradition of Locke. Although he was a hero to the revolutionaries, many of his political and social views were conservative. To some people he was essentially a moralist, to others an educational reformer. Certainly he was a brilliant writer and an original political theorist. Rousseau himself insisted that his work constituted a coherent whole, that the inconsistencies were only superficial. A tortured soul, Rousseau gradually withdrew from society in his later years. There was always tension between the goodness of his intentions and unsavoury reality. Moralist and pedagogue, he abandoned his five children, and suffered guilt ever after.

To sociologists Rousseau is important for the concept of the "general will," a direct forerunner of Durkheim's "collective conscience" and through it to the concept of culture in structural-functionalism. His way of dealing with the relationship of the individual to society is not one many social scientists have accepted, but he was one of the first people to broach the problem. His insistence on equality as a precondition of liberty continues to have an immense impact on social and political thought. Kant was one of his greatest admirers, and through him Rousseau had an influence on nineteenth-century idealism. My criticism of his methodology will be severe, for Rousseau was a proponent of introspection as a means of acquiring general knowledge.

Rousseau's first work on methodology, *Discourse on the Sciences and Arts*, was written in 1750 for a contest of the Academy of Dijon. His *Discourse on Inequality* (1755), written for a similar contest, contained a bolder political analysis, but was still short of the extremism of *The Social Contract* (1762). He wrote the article on political economy for the *Encyclopédie*. Rousseau next wrote *Emile*, the *Nouvelle Héloïse* (1761), and the *Social Contract*. The *Social Contract* was promptly condemned by the Parliament of Paris as contrary to religion and government. Rousseau fled to Geneva, when the natural religion of *Emile* (1762) got him into as much trouble as he'd had in France. Under threat of arrest in both countries, he moved on. Voltaire published a vicious anonymous attack on Rousseau in 1764, supporting the Encyclopedists. This prompted Rousseau's famous *Confessions* (1782), memoirs in defence of his life. Rousseau died the same year as Voltaire, 1788, at Eamonville, where his tomb became a place of pilgrimage. After the revolution, and after an acrimonious debate in the Assembly, his remains were removed to the Panthéon.

There has been much dispute as to how serious Rousseau was in the *Discourse on the Sciences and the Arts*. Perhaps he was only playing devil's advocate to win the prize. One explanation has Diderot thus persuading him, and certainly Diderot did help him with the essay, suggesting revisions and later taking charge of publication. But this theory creates further problems, for Rousseau continued the same methodological approach in the second discourse and *Emile*. Rousseau himself claimed to have been inspired by a vision like Paul's on the road to Damascus. He had been literally on the road when he got the idea for the Discourse – the road to the prison of Vincennes to visit Diderot.[68]

Whatever its origins, the *Discourse* was weak in argument, in places illogical, and ended on a silly note. Rousseau's undoubted gift of style helped, and his appeal to the judges was clever. He was not about to mistreat science, he said, but to defend virtue – to judges who were men of virtue. A main argument was that societies that were advanced in the sciences and arts were corrupted by luxury and indolence and thus were morally weakened. Egypt, Greece, and Rome were learned nations, and look what happened to them. In later works Rousseau elaborated on this theme, especially in comparing the scientifically advanced Athens with the simpler, puritanical Sparta. Rome was strong in the time before it became learned; it lost everything when the Romans began to study.[69] Rousseau even articulated a law out of the relationship; morals and probity were as subject to the progress of the arts and sciences as the rising and falling of the tides to the moon (3:10). Astronomy had its roots in superstition, geometry in greed, physics in vain curiosity, and all in human pride. In a *non sequitur* Rousseau pointed out there would be no jurisprudence if there were no injustice, and no history if no tyrants, wars, or conspiracies. Error was not only frequent but a thousand times more dangerous than discovered truths were useful. By the late twentieth century we are more concerned with the dangers of truths than of errors, but even empiricists would grant Rousseau the point. With printing, dangerous works last, while in antiquity impious works often died with their authors. The progress of the arts and sciences added nothing to our real happiness (3:26).

Rousseau conceded that there had been, perhaps, a few great philosophers: Bacon, Descartes, and Newton. These, however, were not the products of the arts and sciences but of nature. They did not need teachers, but were destined by nature to become her disciples. If it was necessary to permit a few men to study the sciences and arts, it should be rare geniuses like these. That his three examples had all been well educated, and were well connected with other practising scientists, Rousseau ignored. The second part of the essay ends with a flowery address to virtue, which asks if so much trouble and apparatus are necessary in order to know it. "Are your principles not engraved in all hearts, and is it not sufficient to learn your laws ... to listen to the voice of one's conscience in the silence of the passions?" (3:30). So innate ideas re-emerge, not only as a reliable source of knowledge but as the only source for necessary knowledge. Virtue is itself a kind of science, the science of simple souls.

Rousseau's method of abstraction appeared for the first time in the *Discourse on Inequality*, although not until *Emile* was it fully elaborated. He explained that he had to proceed by hypotheses or conjectures, for there simply were no relevant facts. Scientific books did not teach us how "men" were made, but by *meditating* on the first and simplest operations of the human mind, Rousseau thought he had perceived principles anterior to reason.[70] "Let us begin then by setting aside all the facts, for they do not touch on the question" (3:132). Books lie, nature does not. How one was to distinguish between Nature's truth and human falsehoods was not explained. Elsewhere Rousseau admitted problems, for we were all corrupted by society. In the preface he noted that it was easier to show the "general cause" than to assign precise "true causes," and clearly his notion of a general cause was of a different order. It was not more than a sum of particular causes, any more than the general will was to be a sum of particular wills.

It was no easy task, Rousseau pointed out, to untangle the original from the artificial in present human nature or to know "a state which no longer exists, which perhaps never existed, and probably never will" (3:123). He drew on factual material to illustrate a point, but the basis of his state of nature was an abstract construction. The method of writing the *Discourse on Inequality* further shows that he practised what he preached. He prepared for the writing with a week's stay outside Paris, with Thérèse Levasseur, for meditation. He then returned to Paris to write, spending the nights alone walking and thinking in the Bois de Bologne. The essay was dedicated to the republic of Geneva as the state that came closest to natural law, and the most favourable to both the maintenance of public order and the welfare of individuals.

Rousseau's statement on the origin of inequality is one of the most radical and most influential "genesis" stories of western civilization.[71] I will begin with the *Discourse on Inequality*, and then briefly trace the more extreme development in the *Social Contract*. Physical inequalities (age, health, physical strength, and mental qualities) were the source of "consensual" inequalities (riches and honour). Thus Rousseau, like Aristotle, held that all social inequalities were based in nature. The initial state of nature was blissful. Then long harsh winters forced people to develop better clothing and shelter and new techniques to acquire and preserve food. In the process of doing this, people created new needs, desires, and modes of strength. From the habit of living together arose the desire for society. The development of metallurgy and agriculture produced revolutionary results. Agriculture required the division of land, and once property was recognized the first rules of justice were created. One of the more famous quotations from Rousseau follows from this: "The first person who, having enclosed a piece of land, took it into his head to say, '*This is mine*,' and found people simple enough to believe him was the real founder of civil society" (3:164). Yet Rousseau's notion of property was the right to the fruits of one's own labour. This right then evolved into a right of permanent possession and a host of other inequalities. There was now much to fight over. The rich discovered that the rights they had won by force could similarly be taken away. It was they who conceived the ingenious project of the state, to use the very forces that attacked them for their defence. Disunited and weak, the poor agreed. Once a society was formed people were gradually forced to join. "That was, or must have been, the origin of society and laws," Rousseau concluded (3:178). He adduced no evidence as to what was, and what must have been could only be conjecture. For de Staël, such tales of the origin of society were useless and counted only as "metaphysical novels."[72]

In the *Discourse on Inequality*, Rousseau still had a liberal view of the obedience due civil authorities. There was a strong statement on human liberty, although this did not apply equally to the two sexes. Rousseau here was absurd enough to claim knowledge of a natural law – that women were meant to obey men.[73] Social inequalities continued to grow with the establishment of the state, ultimately to tyranny, a despotism without law. Rousseau thus brings us full circle, from equality in the state of nature, through inequality in the state of society, to a new equality in which all have nothing. The only law is the law of the strongest, or a new state of nature.

Rousseau claimed not to know how, from being born free, people were everywhere in chains. He did claim to now how to make the chains legitimate. *The legitimation of the chains* became the extraordinary subject of *The Social Contract*. The general will is the key solution, and one of great importance for the development of structuralism and functionalism in the social sciences. The first problem was to find a form of association that protected its members and their goods, yet in which people would be obeying themselves, and thus free. The social contract entailed each putting "in common, his person and all its strengths under the direction of the general will," each thus becoming an indivisible part of the whole.[74] Individuals would no longer be guided by physical impulses or desires, as in the state of nature, but the "voice of duty," reason. From the "stupid, limited, animal" of the state of nature came an "intelligent being," "man." "Man" lost his unlimited right to everything he could get for civil freedom and property. The general will was the social equivalent of the forces of nature. The social contract, far from destroying the equality of the state of nature, substituted a new equality, by convention. Rousseau's extraordinary definition of freedom was obedience to law. Under this law the sovereign could require any service of a citizen and specify minimal religious belief. Kant followed him here, as on much else. Not even Hobbes gave the sovereign the power that Rousseau did.

The philosophy of education set out in *Emile* is one last, important, source for Rousseau's methodology. The lengthy speech of the Savoyard vicar is really Rousseau revealing his doubts as to the nature of knowledge and his own solution. The vicar went through the usual sceptical analysis, ending in a doubt "too violent for the human mind."[75] It was better to be wrong than to believe nothing at all. The process was Cartesian in its use of a purely interior, subjective standard of truth. Leibniz is nowhere cited, but his principle that the simplest ideas are also the most reasonable appears. There is also a fair dose of Lockean empiricism concerning the passive acquisition of sensation and active comparison and reflection. But Rousseau shared none of the empiricist's modesty and caution. He drew the boundaries to knowledge on the basis of perceived *needs*, not on an assessment of human faculties and their limitations. He made many assertions on the nature of matter, God, free will, justice, conscience, and virtue. Again, friend and foe alike were offended, for it was by *reason*, not revelation, that ideas of divinity occurred. Rousseau's "reason," it must be remembered, implied an intuitive, grasping process, not careful, disciplined inquiry. It is quite appropriate that he was a major source for nineteenth-century romanticism.

PROBABILITY, "SOCIAL MATHEMATICS," AND FEMINISM

Jean Antoine Nicolas Caritat (marquis) de Condorcet (1743–94),[76] one of the noblest and gentlest spirits of a great age, was the only Encyclopedist to take part in the Revolution. A committed democrat, he was also, most exceptionally for the time, a feminist. I believe that his work as a methodologist has been underrated. Condorcet had the bad luck to be outshone in all the various fields to which he contributed, by d'Alembert in mathematics, Montesquieu in political science, Rousseau in education, and Turgot in political economy.[77] Voltaire was more anti-clerical and a better writer. Even as a feminist Condorcet had Macaulay and Wollstonecraft as competition.

His revolutionary writings were read with respect but not heeded. It was Condorcet who said that "natural liberty consists in the right to do anything that does not injure the rights of others ... The only limit to this right is to do nothing that can injure the safety, liberty, property and, in general, the rights of another."[78] Yet J.S. Mill is still credited with this statement on liberty.

Condorcet's methodology remains truer to the spirit of Locke than of any other French theorist. His work on education was impressive and his treatment of probability brilliant. He was one of the first methodologists to address the practical problems of data organization. He showed how to apply probability theory in actual hypothesis testing. He carefully distinguished ethical and empirical components in his writing long before this became common. When Voltaire persuaded him to give up mathematics for human problems, Condorcet began to write on economics and for a while worked for the French mint. He wrote on natural science for the *Encyclopédie* and, through d'Alembert, got to know the Paris intellectual elite, including such visitors as Benjamin Franklin, Thomas Paine, and Adam Smith.

Condorcet was first active in the Revolution as a journalist. Later he was elected to the Municipal Council of Paris and the Constituent Assembly. He had no political alliance and was not a good speaker. His proposals for a new system of public education were not acted on. He opposed the expropriation, at least without compensation, of church property, urging that pensions be provided for nuns and priests left destitute. Condorcet's wife was more radical politically than he, demonstrating on the streets. He was a slow convert to republicanism, raising abstruse legalistic objections to the trial of the king. He opposed capital punishment in principle, and voted against it for Louis XVI. Despised by the Jacobins, Condorcet's status as the last of the *philosophes* saved him for some time. He chaired the committee that prepared the first draft constitution which, though a fairly liberal document, omitted the vote for women. The draft was shelved and another, less liberal, hastily accepted by the Assembly. Condorcet was condemned to death for treason for publicly criticizing this new constitution. He hid out in Paris for a year, during which he wrote the movingly optimistic *Esquisse d'un tableau historique* (1793–4). A law was then passed that stipulated the death penalty for anyone harbouring a proscribed person. Warned that his hideout had been discovered, Condorcet promptly left, poorly disguised and against the wishes of his benefactress. After wandering in the outskirts of Paris for several days and being turned away by friends, he was captured. He died in prison that same night, whether by suicide or exposure is not clear.

Condorcet wrote his earliest work on methodology, on probability theory, in simple language so that women, who had not had men's educational advantages, could read it. Many of his examples were the usual statistical white balls and black balls, and even the human examples were the familiar marriage and mortality statistics. Yet he also proposed innovations in the collection and coding of social science data.[79] A data bank should be established, based on mortality records, but adding information on occupation and marital status. As data were continuously added to astronomical tables, so should they be to social records. There is even an anticipation of primitive data processing equipment, of punch cards and card sorters if not computers.

Condorcet was content with mere probability, as opposed to certainty, for the usual empiricist reasons. Nothing was certain. Even our belief in the constancy of the "laws of nature" was based on no certainty. The proofs of geometry were no more than probable, for they depended on memory, whose accuracy was uncertain. Condorcet's hopes for science lay not in the achievement of certain, deduced, principles, but precise calculations of probability. Our grounds for believing something might not be sure, but we can know how firm they are. Condorcet here also gave some of the earliest advice on how to avoid incorrect sense impressions, a problem usually skipped over by French methodologists. The answer he advanced was to become a central principle of empiricism: the careful development of objective measures. Other things being equal, a deduction made from more exact observations should be taken as correcting a judgment "mixed with sensation" (87). Or, objective observations should take precedence over subjective. Similarly, we should not be unduly moved by the *intensity* of sense impressions, but should be influenced by their *number*. Intensity was a matter of subjective judgment.

Condorcet had a vision of mathematically based social science.[80] The possibility of such science was recent, for it required not only a mathematical base but conditions of liberty, tranquility, and enlightened support. He used the term "la mathématique sociale," in the singular, to indicate that it was but one branch of mathematics. He preferred "social" over "political" or "moral" for greater generality and precision. Condorcet believed that we risk error and prejudice by confining ourselves to reasoning without calculation: "We will soon arrive at the point where all progress will become impossible without the application of rigorous methods of calculation ... The progress of the moral and political sciences, like that of the physical, will soon be stopped."[81] Condorcet's work on probability was much influenced by Laplace, whose examples were confined to natural science, especially astronomy, and such abstract problems as throwing dice. Instead "la mathématique sociale" would be applied to "contribute to the happiness and perfecting of the human species" (173). Mathematics was a means to an end. Condorcet preferred the "moral pleasures" of direct action for humanity over the glories of geometry and philosophy. Although he had made original mathematical discoveries himself he valued the work he did as Turgot's assistant more highly.[82]

Condorcet's feminism first appeared in a paper comparing American democratic institutions with French absolutism.[83] He stressed the similarities of the two sexes and neatly rebuffed the usual arguments for male supremacy. He expanded his ideas in an essay calling for legal rights for women.[84] The rights of men, he argued, arose solely from the fact that they were sensible beings, capable of moral ideas and reason. So were women. Either everybody, men *and* women, had rights, or nobody did. Education, not sex, was responsible for most of the disadvantages of women. Women's different interests provided no excuse for depriving them of their rights. In effect this would be to deprive women of their rights because of their lack of rights. Women were incapacitated by pregnancy, but were men disfranchised for gout? Condorcet further argued for a significant role for women in scientific research, which he saw as a collective enterprise.[85] Women could contribute fine, precise work.

Condorcet is the source of one of the simplest and least problematic justifications for the submission of the individual to the state. For liberals it makes for a welcome contrast with Rousseau's. Condorcet held that even the unanimous will of the citizenry, with one exception, could not impose a legitimate obligation on that one exception, to act contrary to what he considered to be reasonable or useful. "Accordingly, when I submit my will to a law I do not approve of, I do not really act against my reason, but I obey it because it tells me that in this case it is not my particular reason that should guide me, but a rule common to all."[86]

Condorcet wrote his *Esquisse d'un tableau historique* in hiding (somewhere near the guillotine) and seemingly in defiance of his death sentence. The work is optimistic and generous, free of recriminations, bitterness, and even second thoughts. There are factual errors and inconsistencies with earlier writing. The factual difficulties are understandable, for the author was working without books or notes. The inconsistencies appear to be a response to the desperation of the situation. Condorcet seemed determined not to despair. Thus the *Esquisse* contains much more confidence about solving problems, including methodological difficulties, than he had ever before shown.

The *Esquisse* is both an intellectual history and the beginning of a sociology of knowledge, and it is competent on both counts. Charges that it claimed never-ending progress do not stand up to the most cursory reading of the work, for Condorcet maintained that progress included regress.[87] Errors as well as truths were part of our history. Condorcet was no Comte, Hegel, or Kant. The subject of the *Esquisse* was no less than the human mind, with methodology as a subtheme. He stressed western history, but paid some attention to the Arab world and China. History was divided into nine periods (compared with three for Comte), with a tenth period for the future. Condorcet's purpose was to explain why and how, not just to tell what happened. The rise and fall of specific ideas, theories, schools of thought, theorists, and empirical researchers were all chronicled. The conditions that favoured or retarded developments were described. Fundamental to the analysis was a belief in the unity of method. Natural science was based on the assumption of necessary and constant laws regulating phenonema. "By what reasons should this principle be less true for the development of human intellectual and moral faculties than for these other operations of nature?"[88]

The sorts of explanations Condorcet advanced have stood up fairly well in the light of subsequent research. The obvious exception is the heavy dose of anti-clericalism, for he denounced the faults of the Catholic Church on nearly every page. The role of observation in theory development was stressed, beginning with the early astronomers. "Empirical laws" became easier to discover as observations were extended, and were the key to general laws of the system (110). Aristotle had pointed out that all knowledge was acquired through the senses but had not realized that experiments requiring instruments were needed, that observation was not enough. The idea of "interrogating Nature" to "force her to respond" had not yet occurred.

Condorcet's assessments of the great methodologists were remarkably fair. He could find fault with Bacon and praise idealists, including priests and scholastics. The very "audacity of [Descartes'] errors served the progress of the human species" (202). Condorcet noted two great periods of intellectual flowering, one each among the early Greeks and Arabs. Both had been stopped by tyranny and superstition (164). Learning had lasted longer in the Eastern Empire than the Western but, when extinguished, had been harder to revive. Condorcet was optimistic that rapid progress would be made in this next stage of history. This hope, moreover, was based on an analysis of social conditions favourable to intellectual progress. The growth of educational institutions, publishing, and scientific institutes was noted. Condorcet believed that past experience provided no reason to believe in any natural limits to the development of the human mind.

The tenth stage of history could indeed be better than all earlier ones. People made their social institutions, and could make them for the better. Here Condorcet had concrete advice to give, including the need for population control (259). Quality of life considerations made it necessary to limit population growth in view of agricultural productivity. He put probability theory to use in recommending a system of social insurance.

Condorcet developed his theory of morality with his wife, *Sophie Grouchy (marquise) de Condorcet (1764–1822)*, who is also known for her translation of Adam Smith's *Theory of Moral Sentiments*.[89] The capacity to identify with the suffering of others was central. Morality arose through a sentiment of fellow feeling. Animals also had this capacity to identify, hence they also had real, if rudimentary, moral sentiments. The theory of evolution obviously requires strong continuities between humans and animals, with which both Condorcets agreed.

Condorcet may have coined the term "social science."[90] He certainly was one of the first to use the term. In 1791, his friend Garat addressed a pamphlet to him urging greater co-operation among scholars, as among the encyclopedists, to achieve a just social order. *"Art social"* was already current among the physiocrats; now *"science sociale"* and its data were needed as well. Condorcet used *"science sociale"* in 1792 in a draft plan to the Committee on Public Instruction. Tellingly, the chronology is *from* the practical *to* the theoretical, from social art to social science. Condorcet used the term originally in the singular, yet the English translator turned it into "the social sciences."[91]

Antoine-Laurent Lavoisier (1743–94) took a view similar to Condorcet's on the use of probability theory in *all* the sciences. Lavoisier is one of the few methodologists to fit the stereotype of the critique of empiricism: a natural scientist, indeed a founder of modern chemistry, he proposed transfering its method to the social sciences. Yet the expectation of empirical methodology's supporting the powers that be fails utterly. Lavoisier supported Turgot's reforms against his fellow nobles and later was a victim of the Terror. His scientific achievements were pointed out to the judge, who apparently replied that the Revolution did not need a chemist.

Lavoisier contributed to the social sciences the recognition of the need for good economic statistics in order to insure that everyone had enough to eat. In 1784 he began to collect quantitative data on the "territorial riches of the French kingdom." Extracts of this work, never finished, were presented to an agriculture committee of the National Assembly, which published them. A colleague, Lagrange, later published an essay on "political arithmetic" using Lavoisier's material and otherwise arguing for a public institution to collect centralized statistics.[92] Lavoisier also supported proposals for public education.

Pierre-Simon Laplace (1749–1827) similarly was a natural scientist and statistician who believed that the principles of probability applied in the social sciences. His examples were either overwhelmingly abstract – the usual games of dice – or came from natural science, especially astronomy. Yet the "law of large numbers" made it possible to distinguish statistically between chance anomalies and constant causes, whatever the subject matter.[93] One could use probability to choose between different kinds of medical treatment, and in other "conjectural sciences." Each branch of public administration needed an exact register of the results of the different methods used. Statistics could show the risks of mortality in different occupations (66). Regional comparisons might show particular causes of death, and then measures could be taken to eliminate them. Medical statisticians and epidemiologists in time would do just that. Laplace was an unabashed natural scientist arguing for the extension of a method he knew to the social sciences. In influencing Quetelet he influenced the development of mainstream sociology. Laplace's term "celestial mechanics" is probably the source of Quetelet's "social physics."

WOMEN CONTRIBUTORS TO THE SOCIAL SCIENCES

There were women political theorists and revolutionaries in France although the role of both has been neglected. The unfortunate Olympe de Gouges, executed in 1793, will only be mentioned in passing. She was a prolific and popular writer, especially of drama. Her Declaration of the Rights of Women in the Revolution was a remarkable achievement. Her courage was outstanding, but her poor education limited her contribution as a theorist.

The neglect of *Marie-Jeanne Roland (1754–93)*[94] is harder to justify. Apart from whatever of her work has been attributed to her husband – she worked with him – enough of her own ideas have survived to enable her inclusion here. She ran a salon known for its pro-democratic views. She and her husband sided with the Girondins in the Revolution; both were condemned to death. He escaped arrest, but she was guillotined at age thirty-nine.

Mme Roland's surviving political writing consists of short analyses, observations, and appeals. The excellence of her judgment shines through with the benefit of hindsight. Her sympathies generally extended to people well outside her own society, to Africans, Japanese, and Caribbeans. In "Pensées sur la morale" (written in 1775) she used arguments reminiscent of Adam Smith to describe the afflictions of these oppressed peoples. Roland's political prescriptions show eminent good sense. Slavery and virtue are incompatible; tyranny corrupts those who exercise it as well as its victims. "Political liberty consists, for each individual of a society, in doing whatever he judges right for his own good, so long as he does not injure others."[95] (Condorcet's similar statement on liberty has already been noted; both Condorcet and Roland wrote long before John Stuart Mill.) Roland is especially interesting for next adding to the definition of political liberty that "it is the power to be happy without harming anyone else." Roland is also noteworthy for being one of the few people to have predicted the scale of the Revolution: "If the system continues, with food remaining as dear as rents, and people continue to suffer, either a violent crisis will occur which could upset the Throne and give us a new form of government, or lethargy similar to death. How sad it is to foresee such a future" (2:141).

Mme Roland wrote her husband's letter to Louis XVI giving his last advice on leaving office as minister in 1792. In retrospect the letter can be seen to have been deadly accurate. It predicted crisis and revolution, and urged the king to act promptly to avert bloodshed by siding with the people against the reactionary aristocracy. The letter, read out loud to the National Assembly to bursts of applause, warned that it was too late to turn back, that the people had seen the advantages of reform and wanted a new constitution. Roland warned that, should the king try extreme measures of repression, "all of France would rise in indignation."[96]

Germaine Necker (baronne) de Staël-Holstein (1766–1817)[97] was a survivor of the French Revolution, shrewd and practical where Condorcet was a visionary and martyr. Sadly, she is known more for her personal life and literary commentary than as a methodologist, political theorist, or historian. Yet at the end of the eighteenth century she was writing social science and coining the words of the new political science. A full generation before Quetelet she described the fundamental distinction between individual and aggregate explanation and prediction. She is the first writer, to my knowledge, to have used such expressions as "public opinion," "established facts," and "predictable results" in what she termed "political science." Her political and historical writing have received more attention than her methodology proper, but they have yet to compete with interest in her love affairs. Her politics were too liberal and conciliatory to be of interest to hard-line radicals.

Reportedly a favourite of Marie Antoinette's, de Staël witnessed the removal of the king to Paris and his swearing of allegiance to the new Constitution. She took part in the attempted escape of the royal family, hid refugees, and organized the emigration of others. Her salon was a meeting place for the moderate revolutionary leaders. De Staël's best-known work in the social sciences, the *Influence of the Passions*, was published in 1796. She began her influential *Literature and Social Institutions* that same year. It was published anonymously in 1800, but was well known to be her work. She wrote *Circonstances actuelles* probably in the period 1796–8, but it was not published until long after her death. She wrote several novels that are still read. In 1803 she learned German, visited Germany and wrote *On Germany* which, while ostensibly about literature, included comments on German social institutions. She thought that by not mentioning Napoleon and packaging the material as literature she would be safe. Not to praise him, however, was unacceptable, and she compounded the crime by praising the institutions of the country he had just defeated. The police arrived, confiscated the manuscript, and gave her twenty-four hours to leave France. Naturally she had a spare copy and published the work in England. After Napoleon's defeat de Staël corresponded with the Duke of Wellington, urging an early end to the occupation. It was in fact ended before the full payment of reparations, and her pressure may have helped.[98] De Staël used the peace negotiations to plead for another of her lang-standing causes: the abolition of the slave trade.[99] She had met Wilberforce in England and helped to publicize his work in France. Her substantial treatise on the French Revolution appeared in 1816, the year before she died.

In the *Influence of the Passions*, de Staël dealt with the fundamental paradox of the social sciences: that despite the unpredictability of individuals, there are regularities or social laws. She noted that the same number of divorces was recorded in the city of Berne every decade. One could calculate exactly how many assassinations would be committed every year in Italy. Events that happen in large numbers have a periodic cycle, a fixed proportion, when observations are the result of a large number of chances. "That leads us to believe that political science can one day acquire geometric evidence."[100] One could be entirely mistaken in applying social laws to a particular individual, but constitutions are based on "fixed facts," for the great number of all genres yield similar, always predicatable, results. De Staël's intention was to examine ancient and modern governments regarding the influence they had on the natural passions, "to find the cause of the birth, duration, and destruction of governments." This ambitious undertaking, however, was not pursued.

De Staël showed herself to be scrupulously fair throughout her work. Her *Considerations of the Principal Events of the French Revolution*, apart from defending her father as minister of finance, steered a careful line. She pointed out faults of the *ancien régime*. She was remarkably kind to her old adversary Napoleon. She was interested in the effects of scientific discoveries on society, believing that the sciences had "an intimate connection with all the ideas on the moral and political state of nations." If, one day, "aerial navigation" was achieved, how many social relations would be different? Progress in the sciences made progress in morals necessary, for "on increasing the powers of man, we must strengthen the brakes that prevent abuse."[101] Evidently this pioneer of the expression "political science" was thoroughly aware of the moral consequences of scientific work.

An interest in public opinion appears early, right from the papers de Staël wrote in the heat of the Revolution. An article in 1792 asks, "By what signs can the opinion of the majority be known?"[102] Here she distinguished between the long and short term, opinion inspired by fear and by reason, and that fostered by hatred of the old government as opposed to regard for the new. This article also includes the germ of the notion of dialectics. De Staël argued that there are two forces in society as in nature, a tendency to repose and the impulsion to liberty. She made little use of the concept, instead specifying concrete causes without identifying which type they were. The paper was also daring in its praise (albeit it before Waterloo) for the Duke of Wellington's opposition to slavery.

Literature and Social Institutions has been called "an inspirational tract for left-of-centre liberals whose faith is weakening under the onslaught of reaction."[103] Not only did it serve this purpose, there is scarcely an idea of the eighteenth century it did not transmit, scarcely an idea of the nineteenth century it did not contain in germ. Where de Staël considered the differences between French and English philosophers, she sided with the English. She was especially pro-Bacon, stressing knowledge for application.

Des circonstances actuelles qui peuvent terminer la révolution et des principes qui doivent fonder la république en France (written in 1798 but not published until 1906) must be one of the most underrated books in the history of political theory. The title sets out the thesis, that the way to end the war was to establish a new, republican, constitution. Its author's very moderation caused problems. By arguing *for* the return of those royalists who would accept the new republic, she offended the Jacobins; by arguing *for* a republic and against all hereditary privilege, she lost the royalists. Her abhorrence of monarchy, especially the excessive powers of the Sun King, seemed to be a criticism of Napoleon. Yet *Circonstances actuelles* is a wise, tolerant book with amazingly prescient discussion of the political process.

De Staël sought to prove that the crimes of the Revolution were not a consequence of its republicanism, but indeed that only in such a system could any remedy be found.[104] The book then sets out the essential characteristics of a republic: plurality of powers, an elected legislature, and the merit principle. There is a chapter on public opinion. De Staël did not envision government by opinion polls but did have a sense that government has to be in accord with broad public concerns. It has to deal with its citizens' real needs: agriculture, commerce, the public debt, taxes, peace, and war (107).

De Staël believed that social science research could be a means to peace in a country torn apart by war. She was optimistic in arguing that the "peace of demonstration" could be attained by basing government on "geometrically true principles," developing the argument used originally in the *Influence of Passions*. When disputes were submitted to calculation, discussion ceased and passions abandoned for reason. However excessive her optimism, generations of social scientists since have agreed that interests and desires can be studied like other natural phenomena. People's passions are "as susceptible to calculation as the movements of machines ... The passions of a nation can be calculated by a legislator as births, deaths and marriages" (27). The final phase in the perfecting of the human mind was no less than the application of calculation to all branches of the moral system. "The calculation of probabilities is applied to human passions as to the throw of dice, when given a certain number of chances. Arithmetic is applicable to all knowledge of collectivities. Chance is for the individual, never for the species" (281). The same determinism held for physical and human laws.

De Staël even referred to "the small number of physical laws, if one can use the expression" as not being reversible. "The unjust finishes, as a stone falls by its own weight." Revolutions were the same. When enough of the unfortunate said "this can't go on!" a sort of "contagious opinion" inspired insubordination (134).

De Staël had no confidence in the export of revolution. Other countries would be led to political change by the example of France's happiness and the writing of her philosophers. "Armed propaganda" was nothing but conquest, and a conquered people did not have the energy to be free (6). People would fight for their own country even if they shared the opinions of the invader.

De Staël's astute political analysis can also be seen in her correspondence with Thomas Jefferson, president of the United States. It reveals profound differences of opinion concerning foreign policy, despite the common commitment to democratic principle and a personal link from Jefferson's stay in Paris. De Staël initiated the correspondence in 1807 when in exile from Paris and considering moving to the United States. In 1812 when the United States was at war with England (neither writer mentions Canada), de Staël argued that Napoleon "makes use of you now against England" (65). She reminded Jefferson that he had, early in the French Revolution, indeed in her father's own house, warned the "exaggerated radicals" that their demagogic principles would lead to despotism in France, and that his prediction had been fulfilled (66).

If by a misfortune which would plunge all the world into mourning, England were to be subjected and her navy were to fall into the hands of the conqueror of the earth, it is against you that he would turn, for your principles are the most in the world opposed to his and he would wish to efface from the very pages of history the time when men were not subjected to the despotism of one man ... You tell me that America has nothing to do with the continent of Europe. Has she nothing to do with the human race? Can you be indifferent to the cause of free nations, you the most republican of all? (66)

She justified the abuses England had committed with the argument that it had for ten years been "the sole barrier against this singular despotism," a nation of twelve million struggling against one hundred million, "coerced by one man" (66). She cited the basis for Anglo-American friendship in their mutual love of liberty and hatred of despotism:

All your old friends in Europe, all those who thought as you did when you upheld the independence of America, expect you to put an end to a war which seems to them a civil war, for free people are all of the same family. – Yes, the greatest misfortune which could come to the American people in the present war would be to do real damage to their enemies, for then the English would no longer be in a condition to serve you as a bulwark against the despotism of the Emperor of France or rather of Europe. When he shall have overthrown the liberty of England it will be yours that he will next attack. (66)

Jefferson countered that England was "the enemy of all maritime nations." Napoleon would die "and his tyrannies with him, but a Nation never dies." England's object was the *"permanent dominion of the ocean* and the *monopoly of the trade of the world"* (67).

In her last letter, in 1816, de Staël returned to an old concern: the abolition of slavery, although her correspondent was a slave owner: "If you should succeed in destroying slavery in the south there would be at least one government in the world as perfect as the human mind can conceive" (70). Jefferson's letters were published with his correspondence, but de Staël's lively and even more prescient letters did not appear until 1918.

Reflections on Suicide (1813) was not written in the ethically neutral style of social science but it includes, with moral advice, factual observations and theoretical speculation. Differences in rates of suicide by country were noted. De Staël then sought to explain these, drawing on the influence of public opinion. Nearly a century before Durkheim she understood the social pressures on the individual as an explanation for suicide.[105] She rejected simple explanations of differences in suicide rates by country by differences in climate. Public opinion, or the "empire" society held, was a more likely explanation.

De Staël's feminist qualifications include support for education for women, emphatic opposition to the double standard in sexual matters, and frank writing in her novels about injustices to women. She stopped short of demanding the vote or equal political participation for women. *On Germany* contains some astute analysis of the role of women as "other" in social relations.

De Staël is sometimes treated as a romantic writer, even as a founder of romanticism. She helped make German literature better known in France, did translations, and had plays produced. She considered that Germany had a literature the French ought to know. With the romantics she believed in the riches of diversity. Yet with the empiricists she assumed a common underlying human nature and laws to explain it. She insisted on criticism without pre-established criteria, opposing "tyranny in taste," but this is hardly enough to qualify her as a romantic. She used romanticism when it suited her purposes without ever fully accepting it.[106] She mistrusted German metaphysics.

THE EMPIRICIST CRITIQUE REVISITED

Despite the strongly held belief that the social sciences are a tool of conservatism, their very terminology was a product of the French Revolution, devised by supporters of the Revolution and, in turn, victims of the Terror. The encyclopedists, the major advocates of empirical social science in eighteenth-century France, did not hold political power. Many went to prison, including Voltaire, Diderot, and Condorcet. Others avoided prison only by leaving the country fast: Voltaire (on another occasion), de Staël, and probably Helvétius and La Méttrie. Mme Roland and Lavoisier were executed, Condorcet was under sentence of death when he died. The first person to be accused of being a "socialist" was Beccaria, an empiricist social reformer.

Most of the Encyclopedists had difficulties with state censors. Voltaire's problems were pressing and persistent, but even the mildly liberal Montesquieu had to publish anonymously in Switzerland. Even then his work was promptly placed on the *Index* and he was pressed on his deathbed to retract offensive passages. Diderot, after years of fights with the censors over the *Encyclopédie*, saved his last work for posthumous publication. La Méttrie published his *Man-Machine* anonymously in liberal Holland, but even he had to move on to Prussia and the protection of Frederick II. Helvétius lost only a minor court appointment for his scandalous book, which was publicly burned in Paris, but he left the country for extensive travel and, on return, lived discreetly in the country. He took the precaution of leaving his last book for posthumous publication. The public executioner burned many of Holbach's books, which had been published outside France, also anonymously. Holbach was protected by his status as a baron. Beccaria also published anonymously, was attacked, but was lucky in having an unusually liberal ruler in his district.

The overlap between the social and natural sciences continued, especially among the encyclopedists. Laplace fits the stereotype of a natural scientist urging the adoption of probability theory, first developed for natural science, in the social sciences. Other advocates of probability theory in the social sciences, Condorcet and Lavoisier, genuinely worked in both fields rather than borrowing from one to other. The overlap between history writing and the search for general explanation was also strong. Voltaire was a major writer of history as well as an advocate of empiricism and an amateur scientist. Condorcet and de Staël wrote histories, so, in a sense, did Buffon. At this time the overlap with the arts world increased. Voltaire was famous for his plays, novels, and poetry. Diderot's plays are still performed, his novels still read. De Staël's literary criticism is well known and her novels have been rediscovered. She wrote poetry and plays and translated German literature. Rousseau wrote on music for the *Encyclopédie* and composed an opera.

The encyclopedists supported a vast array of reform causes. Voltaire fostered the abolition of torture (sometimes the rehabilitation of the name of the dead victim), freedom of religion and expression, and improvements in small industry and farming. Beccaria, apart from opposing capital punishment and torture, promoted monetary and trade reform, fairer taxes, a health care system, job creation, and the metric system. The *Encyclopédie* showed the way to all kinds of social, economic, and legal reform: limits on the king's powers, tax reform, improved education, agriculture, industry, trade, institutions for the poor, and an end to peasants' forced labour. La Méttrie's condemned work was a step toward health care instead of punishment for the mentally ill. So was Holbach's. Condillac promoted educational reform. The physiocrat Quesnay, apart from advancing his major concern of the single tax, was active in agricultural reform. Turgot actually implemented many practical reforms before the nobles had him fired for improving the lot of the poor at their expense.

The encyclopedists appear also on that shorter list of advocates of women's rights. Condorcet is the shining example, but Holbach and Helvétius also qualify. De Staël, no feminist, yet wrote sensitively in her novels on the difficulties women face. She supported better education for women and, at age eighteen, criticized Rousseau's sexist approach to education. Diderot exposed injustices to women in property institutions in his hilarious satirical novel, *The Nun*. The empiricists also pioneered the struggle against slavery. Condorcet belonged to the first French anti-slavery society, Amis des nègres, while de Staël both translated Wilberforce and wrote passionate denunciations of slavery. Roland condemned racial discrimination.

Sensitivity to the environment, when it did rarely appear, was a concern of the empiricists. Stressing the continuities between humans and animals offended church and state alike; Voltaire, La Méttrie, and Condillac were chief culprits. Buffon was inconsistent, while the physiocrats were exceptional in being pro-empiricist but espousing a sharp human-animal divide. The next developments in environmental concerns took place in Britain, to which we now turn.

5 From Moral Philosophy to the Quantum of Happiness

As the senses are the only inlets to human knowledge, consequently human knowledge can only be gained by experience and observation.

Catharine Macaulay[1]

The progress of knowledge ... was very tardy in Europe because the men who studied were content to see nature through the medium of books, without making any actual experiments themselves.

Mary Wollstonecraft[2]

Scepticism, no doubt, by restraining credulity, may guard against one species of error but, carried to extreme, would discourage the search of truth, suspend the progress of knowledge, and become a species of palsy of all the mental powers.

Adam Ferguson[3]

What is agreeable to our moral faculties is fit, and right, and proper to be done; the contrary wrong, unfit and improper ... The very words right, wrong, fit, improper, graceful, unbecoming, mean only what pleases or displeases those faculties.

Adam Smith[4]

For many scholars the eighteenth century was the age of Hume. Leslie Stephen credited him with marking the great turning point of thought, the definite abandonment of the philosophical conceptions of the seventeenth century. Yet, if Hume was free of theological prepossessions, few of his contemporaries were, and eighteenth-century methodologists include Presbyterian divines, Unitarian ministers, and the founder of Methodism. Hume's contribution was prodigious, but I would still stress the continuities with the seventeenth century. The same Leslie Stephen, after all, called Locke the "intellectual ruler" of the eighteenth century.[5]

There was an enormous output of substantive work in Britain in history, ethnography, politics, and economics. Locke's influence through Hume, Joseph Priestley, and William Godwin is evident. Scottish moral philosophy led to the Utilitarians. British links with the French remain strong, notably through Hume and Adam Smith. With Smith we see the modern formulation of division of labour and the key concepts of capitalism. Smith's theory of moral sentiments was the chief source for modern functionalism. Hume established the main features of modern British empiricism. That it remained sceptical, in contrast with French empiricism, is largely due to his influence.

The same can be said for its constructive do-what-you-can approach. With Hume knowledge could be applied, even if it was not – and it *was* not – perfectly certain.

British women even more than French brought a feminist challenge to the intellectual foundations of male supremacy. From the lone Mary Astell at the end of the seventeenth century, we now have four impressive women contributors, all of them feminists as well. Wortley Montagu, a friend of Astell, produced an impressive analysis of Turkish society from a woman's perspective and defended the right of women to education. Mary Hays, apart from her biographies of women, contributed a dialectical under-standing of historical process two generations before Marx. At the end of the century Catharine Macaulay's *Letters on Education* used empiricist principles to argue for women's education. Mary Wollstonecraft, another radical, went the next step to propose the vote for women. For all these theorists methodological questions were crucial: convention versus nature, the use of evidence, and limits to knowledge. Yet *none* of these writers is treated in conventional intellectual histories of the period, although all were well known, published, read, and reprinted. Nor can any of them be dis-missed for having written "only" for half of humanity. Wortley Montagu was esteemed for her letters, and even published her one feminist tract anonymously. Macaulay's histories were popular. Hays published novels as well as scholarly work. Wollstonecraft was famous for her *Vindication of the Rights of Men* before she ever wrote her second *Vindication* for women.

In Britain two Jacobite rebellions were put down, while in France divine right ruled until the end of the century. Britain's industrial revolution and urban migration began in earnest. In France and elsewhere on the Continent comparable changes did not occur not until the nineteenth century. While intellectual opinion in France was flavoured with anti-clericalism and even atheism, in Britain there were no such extremes. David Hume, the worst atheist the British could muster, was mild in comparison with French athe-ists. Joseph Priestley, known as the discoverer of oxygen, was also a minister, Bible scholar, historian, and methodologist. Here the continuities with the seventeenth-century divines are obvious, although Priestley was politically more radical. The Puritan period was long over but many of its reforms lasted. Poor law administration improved, schools and colleges were built. Britain had a Parliament which, if weak and corrupt, was considerably better than anything in continental Europe.

John Wesley demonstrates further continuities with the seventeenth-cen-tury English divines in methodology. There is the same reverence for nature as the work of God, and knowledge of nature as a means to know God. The earlier Puritan mission to establish the kingdom of God on earth was replaced by concern for individual reform and campaigns on single issues. Reform movements developed in response to some of the worst abuses of

British society. These were now single issue causes, for law and prison reform, workers' education, Sunday schools, and the abolition of slavery. Wesley supported the abolition movement, run by evangelicals within the Church of England. John Howard and Elizabeth Fry led prison reform. John Millar, a Scottish moral philosopher, supported most of these reform movements. There was even some hint of concern for animal rights and human responsibility for animals.

The Puritans' holy mission had failed, and the secular struggle to establish the kingdom of God on earth through socialism had not yet begun. Revolution, for the British, was an academic matter, the American and French Revolutions providing examples for reflection and speculation. Methodologists and political commentators took sides for or against. Edmund Burke wrote the definitive denunciation of the French Revolution and the Terror, *Reflections on the Revolution in France* (1790). Priestley's and Godwin's work welcoming the Revolution soon came to be seen as hopelessly naïve panegyrics. The theoretical debate as to the possibility of fundamental social change was underway.

The story of socialism, as movement and party, begins in the nineteenth century, but many of the elements and ideas date from this earlier period. As in France, theoretical work on necessity, progress, and evolution fed into nineteenth-century formulations. British versions of necessity appeared in Priestley and Godwin. Godwin, an anarchist, predicted the gradual, predictable, and inevitable withering away of the state. Political writing on property and equality in the eighteenth century led to organization and action in the nineteenth.

The Utilitarian movement can be seen as a logical evolution of the belief in necessity. If criminal behaviour is not willed then it is unjust to punish it. Punishment then can only be justified for the good of society – for the greatest good of the greatest number. Our world does not give the Utilitarians good press, and certainly some of their proposals are chilling. Yet in their time they were humanitarian reformers. The system of criminal justice in Britain they condemned relied on capital punishment, transportation, and prisons with abominable conditions. This is the lesser known side of eighteenth-century "Enlightenment." While Handel was played in the drawing rooms of the rich and noble, misery was the lot of the great mass of the population.

Not the least of the good deeds of the Utilitarians was their inclusion of the needs of the least members of society in their equations. This calculation of the greatest good was a significant advance toward democracy. Elitist notions of "the good" were rejected with their vision of culture in which only the wealthy had education, and leisure for the better things of life. Utilitarianism was a radical commitment to the idea that ordinary people counted. Bentham's even more radical formulation included "the whole sensitive creation," bringing animals into the ethical debate.

Looking back over British methodology of this period, it is clearly the empiricists who triumphed: David Hume and Adam Smith are still flourishing, intellectually speaking. Their work is still in print, researched, cited, and debated. By comparison the Scottish idealists are out of print. Adam Ferguson is probably the best known of the group, but that is for his substantive work, not his methodology. Bishop Berkeley is still a methodological curiosity. Yet it was the Scottish idealists who held the university chairs. Hume never obtained a university appointment and even gave up trying to get one. Priestley taught only at the academies, as a Unitarian he was barred from the universities. Godwin, a radical, earned his living as a journalist and died poor. The idealist Berkeley became a bishop. Respectable appointments and adequate pay, in short, continued to be the reward of idealists. Acceptance of empiricism in the universities came slowly.

Scottish universities in the eighteenth century were more progressive than the English or French. Locke and Newton were taken up faster in Scotland than in their own country or France. But there was also an idealist backlash to this empiricism. The "common sense" school of methodology was even better represented in the universities than pro-empiricist moral philosophy. It was closely allied as well with the Church of Scotland and, as earlier opposition to empiricism had been, was largely motivated by religion. Hume was a notorious atheist and Adam Smith was seen smiling in divine service. Scepticism in methodology was too great a threat to religious belief.

The influence of the Scottish moral philosophers can be seen in the social sciences across the political spectrum. Marx's labour theory of value drew heavily on Smith. Modern functionalism is indebted to Smith for his conceptualization of the social system. There was a strong emphasis on application among all the Scottish writers, a concern which became even more explicit in nineteenth-century Utilitarianism. The term "moral philosophy," like the French "moral sciences," covered, as well as natural religion, the modern functions of the social sciences: politics, economics, law, sociology, and anthropology. The purpose was normative, usually the search for the right rules of ethical conduct. The field remained scientific, however: these rules had to be based on an understanding of *actual* conduct.

SCOTTISH MORAL PHILOSOPHY AND THE GREATEST GOOD

Since Utilitarian theory is so commonly associated with atheism and immorality, or at best with everyone-for-self ethics, it is noteworthy that one of its originators was a Scottish clergyman deeply concerned about morality,

Francis Hutcheson (1694–1746).[6] Utilitarian theory was devised in the quest to understand morality in order to improve people's conduct. The great dilemma of course lies in reconciling individual and social advantage. By the eighteenth century it was commonly believed that people acted on the basis of perceived good for themselves. Moralists then had to show how people's own advantage lay in acting for the public good. It was Hutcheson who took the argument this far, in *A System of Moral Philosophy* (1755). His student Adam Smith added the theory of the invisible hand. Hutcheson is of interest as well for supporting democracy and women's rights.

Hutcheson did not coin the phrase "the greatest good for the greatest number," but the notion is clear in his writing from 1725 on. The context, characteristically, was moral and religious: God's design for eliciting moral behaviour on the part of people. We can be deceived as to what is good, for what seems good might not be, or might be good for us but not for others. There has to be an *"Internal* or *Moral Sense,* which we call *Reason,* the rule by which we judge true and false, and moral good or evil."[7] Here Hutcheson insisted that things do not seem true or right because they are beautiful or please us because they seem true or right. He carefully distinguished private good and public or universal good. Moral behaviour obviously required what is needed for the *public good,* a matter each individual has to judge, possibly with a sense that his or her private good would be better served differently.

The "first Original of our moral Ideas" was a sense that arises from a *"Determination by the Author of Nature, which necessitates our Minds to approve of Publick Affections,* and of *consulting the Good of others."* Then our reason directs us to those actions that "produce the greatest and most extensive Good in our Power." To Hutcheson, this tendency to Utilitarianism was built into creation by God. The result of all those individual determinations, "the greatest and most extensive Good," would be confirmed "by Motives of *Self-Interest"* and would be proved "to be *reasonable* in that sense" (7:31). With only modest editing Hutcheson's "greatest and most extensive Good" would become "the greatest good for the greatest number."

The close identification of goodness and happiness is further evident in Hutcheson's *System of Moral Philosophy,* which also confounded later moralists who wanted Utilitarians to ignore virtue and adopt gratification or self-interest. The intention of moral philosophy was to direct people to that course of action which tends most effectively to promote their greatest happiness and perfection.[8] The method was secular; it used observations and conclusions discoverable from nature without the aid of supernatural revelation or rules of conduct reputed to be laws of nature. Further on there is unashamed reference to "publick happiness of the most extensive kind" (1:101). The public happiness and greatest good concepts are an early cry for democracy. Hutcheson held that natural rights belong equally to all.

Everyone was part of that great system "whose greatest interest is intended by all the laws of God and nature." God, in short, was a democrat. "These laws prohibit the greatest and wisest of mankind to inflict any misery on the meanest, or to deprive them of any of their natural rights" (1:299). Consistent with this was the justification of property rights by virtue of the labour theory of value. The public good remained the chief aim, so that the exercise of property rights was conditional on serving this higher good.

As well as extending the greatest happiness principle to all people, Hutcheson included animals as well, if not on an equal footing. "Human domination over the brutes" was justified on the basis that people had a moral, internal sense while animals, whose external senses are as acute as those of people, feel only immediate pain. Yet we must condemn "all unnecessary cruelty" and not create "any needless toil or suffering, or ... diminish their happiness" (1:311).

In a time when philosophers used natural law to keep women apolitical and subordinate, Hutcheson was an upstart who insisted on the equality of the sexes. Civil laws gave "monstrous" power to husbands over their wives, as the dues the conqueror extracted from the conquered. This, to Hutcheson, was "unjust and imprudent, as well as contrary to nature" (2:165). Males were generally "superior" to females in body and mind, he noted, but that did not give them any right to govern. In any event, this "superiority" did not hold universally, and females excelled in other respects. Marriage should be a partnership of equals. When the partners could not agree on some matter of importance they should submit to an independent arbitrator. Partners should jointly manage property. Alternatively, both could retain the power to manage their affairs separately. This might seem like a modest proposal today, but in the early eighteenth century it was radical feminism.

Probably no one better exemplifies eighteenth-century British empiricism than *David Hume (1711–76).*[9] His work follows directly from Locke's, and there are important links with Smith and the other moral philosophers. He spent significant periods of his life in France, was fed by French thought, and was a source, in turn, for French theorists. Fundamentally a constructive sceptic, Hume was both aware of the limits to human knowledge and committed to the search for knowledge. While many professional philosophers consider his early and negative *Treatise of Human Nature* (1739) his best work, he later disavowed it. His political and economic essays were well received, his multi-volume *History of England* (1754–62) a resounding success. Here Hume's contribution lay not in original research but in superb analysis. Both the *Essays* and the *History* are laced with causal explanations, whatever his doubts as to knowledge of causation might have been; *Inquiry concerning the Principles of Morals* is an early treatment of utility theory.

Hume's enduring contribution to methodology is his constructive scepticism, elegantly expressed in *An Inquiry concerning Human Understanding* (1751).[10] In it is all the wonder of the mysteries of Nature. "Nature has kept us at a great distance from all her secrets, and has afforded us only the knowledge of a few superficial qualities of objects; while she conceals from us those powers and principles on which the influence of these objects entirely depends."[11] Yet Hume was confident that much could be learned, even with "certainty and solidity," as was shown by the success of scientific inquiry. Scepticism was "entirely subversive of all speculation and even action," and had to be put away. It could not be doubted that the mind was endowed with several powers and faculties. More confidently yet, there were "a truth and falsehood which lie not beyond the compass of human understanding" (4:10). The purpose of *An Inquiry* was to show what the mind could and could not do, to provide a "mental geography" of the mind. Hume's own political and social analysis was full of observations, analysis, and conjecture, including much causal explanation. His *Essays* covered numerous contemporary problems, and his *History of England* was a massive work with explanations in the same vein as Thucydides.

An Inquiry concerning Human Understanding closed with a tribute to academic scepticism. Hume reached this conclusion after repudiating both the negative scepticism of Pyrrhonism and the equally fruitless Cartesianism, and considering the confusion of Berkeley. Fortunately, there was a "more *mitigated* scepticism, or *academical* philosophy," which might be both more durable and useful. Resulting from Pyrrhonism, its excessive doubts were "corrected by common sense and reflection" (4:183). Hume was a faithful and graphic exponent of the theory of sensation of Locke and the French materialists: "The most lively thought is still inferior to the dullest sensation ... When we reflect on our past sentiments and affections, our thought is a faithful mirror, and copies its objects truly; but the colors which it employs are faint and dull, in comparison of those in which our original perceptions were clothed" (4:15–16). Yet Hume seemed to have great confidence in the process. All was subjective, but distinctions between fact and fiction could readily be made. "*Belief* is something felt by the mind, which distinguishes the ideas of the judgement from the fictions of the imagination. It gives them more weight and influence; makes them appear of greater importance; enforces them in the mind; and renders them the governing principle of our actions" (4:57). Somehow "nature" saw to it that sensations based on real things would be more vivid than dreams or conjectures. Of course there was no appeal to God, but Hume showed no less confidence in nature than other philosophers have in divine guarantees.

The stress on sensation in methodology has a sociological corollary in the notion of sympathy. Hume was one of the first writers to treat sympathy as the fundamental bond of society. His discussion predates Adam Smith's

Theory of Moral Sentiments by twenty years and presumably influenced it. Hume then directly and through Adam Smith, was a source for the French theorists discussed in chapter 4.

In a period called the "Age of Reason," in a country with a strong intellectual tradition, Hume's stress on sensation and disrespect for mind must have offended. "What we call a *mind* is nothing but a heap or collection of different perceptions, united together by certain relations, and supposed, though falsely, to be endowed with a perfect simplicity and identity."[12] Idealists liked to segregate the mind, understanding or reason from the earthier senses. Hume put all sensations together although he criticized reasoning phase more than initial sensation. "The memory, senses, and understanding are therefore all of them founded on the imagination, or the vivacity of our ideas" (1:327). "Imagination is the ultimate judge of all systems of philosophy" (1:281). "Reason is nothing but a wonderful and unintelligible instinct in our souls, which carries us along a certain train of ideas" (1:227–8). With no appeal to mind, God or reason for certainty, all knowledge can only be probable. Hume was quite explicit that this included mathematical knowledge. While algebraists gained confidence in their proofs by going over them repeatedly and from the approbation of friends, the applause of the learned world, too, was derived from the constant union of causes and effects, from the experiences and proofs of earlier mathematicians, and from their colleagues' applause. This is much the same argument as Condorcet's.

Hume was far from the first methodologist to treat causation as a subjective judgment imposed by people on relationships. He follows the ancient sceptics, the medieval Nicolas of Autrecourt, and the seventeenth-century Malebranche and Glanvill. He deserves praise, nonetheless, for the lucidity and power of his account. The point is most forcefully made in *A Treatise of Human Nature*. No impression conveyed by the senses, Hume stated, could give rise to the "idea" of cause and effect. It is only by custom that we pass from an object to the idea usually associated with it as its cause or effect. When we frequently see a billiard ball move when another one hits it, we consider that the one *causes* the other to move. In similar games of billiards we will expect similar consequences, although there is no logical reason to believe that the future will resemble the past. "Necessity is something that exists in the mind, not in objects" (1:212–13). Causation is simply our thinking so, a habit formed from some impulse to seek connections.

Hume polished the argument in *An Inquiry*, stressing the natural impulse to impute cause to mere associations. Natural principles force us to conclusions of cause and effect, and these conclusions then become custom. "Whenever any object is presented to the memory or senses, it immediately, by the force of custom, carries the imagination to conceive that object which is usually conjoined to it."[13] When we see a watch on a deserted isle we conclude that people must have been there before. We infer from the effect, the watch, to a cause: someone must have put it there (4:32). It was only custom that made us do this, not logic. "Custom, then, is the great guide of human life. It is that principle alone which renders our experience useful to us, and makes us expect, for the future, a similar train of events" (4:52). This is also nicely put in the abstract Hume wrote to promote *A Treatise*. "'Tis not, therefore, *reason*, which is the guide to life, but custom. That alone determines the mind, in all instances, to suppose the future conformable to the past."[14] Yet experience of the past *proves* nothing for the future nor, in all eternity, could it.

For all his insistence on the subjective status of causal relations, Hume was no less a determinist. It would be almost impossible to engage in either science or action without acknowledging the doctrine of necessity. Liberty in any profound sense would require the violation of natural laws, which was inadmissible. Hume offended established opinion here as well, for belief in determinism over free will was considered harmful to religion and morals. His firm views on the continuities between human and animal life, even on the development of mental faculties constituted another affront.[15] He did not enunciate rights for animals – they were not equal to people – but he pleaded for "gentle usage" of these creatures.

Hume was a great believer in the unity of science. If it was a worthy labour to find the true system of the planets, was it not also worthwhile to discover the parts of the mind? Nor would description satisfy him, he wanted to find the "springs and principles" which activate the mind. In astronomy it was not just the order and magnitude of heavenly bodies science sought, but their "laws and forces." Moreover there was "no reason to despair of equal success in our inquiries concerning the mental powers and economy, if prosecuted with equal capacity and caution" (4:12). Hume made similar assumptions about the constancy of human nature as the ancient sophists and Hippocratics. How could politics be a science, he asked rhetorically, if laws and forms of government had not a uniform influence upon society? The "conjunction between motives and voluntary actions" was as "regular and uniform" as between cause and effect in any part of nature (4:100). Natural and moral evidence linked together to form a single chain of argument.

Hume's views of society were conservative and functionalist, a growing trend in the social sciences. The conservatism followed logically from his methodology, with its emphasis on custom. Revolutionary change had to be opposed, for habit was the basis of allegiance to society. His conservatism was moderate, however, permitting resistance to the sovereign under extreme, though unspecified, circumstances.[16] There is remarkable consistency between Hume's political, social, and historical work on the one hand

and the methodological/psychological work on the other. The two domains are complementary. There are, however, contradictions *within* the methodology, especially between the earlier, pessimistic, *Treatise* and the later, positive and practical, *Inquiry*. The author himself explained the differences in the "advertisement" introducing *An Inquiry*. Here the mature Hume repudiated *A Treatise* as the work of his youth "projected before he left college," and sent "to the press too early." This is an exaggeration: Hume spent three years on the book in France and at least a year revising it in London. Still, the repudiation was serious; he never published the *Treatise* with his name on it and left it out of his collected works. The *Inquiry* advertisement advises the reader that "henceforth the Author desires, that the following Pieces may alone be regarded as containing his philosophical sentiments and principles."[17] The change in title is also instructive. The young Hume presumed to offer a *treatise* to the world on no less a subject than human nature. The older Hume claimed only to have made an *inquiry*, and then into the narrower field of human understanding.

Hume's intentions for *A Treatise* seem to have been honest enough: a better foundation for the sciences, social and natural. Later he realized he had gone too far. *A Treatise* challenged knowledge of real existence: "If colors, sounds, tastes and smells be merely perceptions, nothing, we can conceive, is possessed of a real, continued, and independent existence; not even motion, extension, and solidity, which are the primary qualities insisted on."[18] Hume recognized that however provocative and logical negative scepticism might be, it would not help in the search for knowledge. In order to encourage scientific work, he would have to use constructive scepticism. Although he was aware of having made a narrow escape, he persisted. "Can I be sure that, in leaving all established opinions, I am following truth? and by what criterion shall I distinguish her, even if fortune should at last guide me on her footsteps?" (1:326)

Bertrand Russell perhaps deserves the last word. He credits Hume with starting with a belief that scientific method yields the truth and ending with a conviction that we know nothing. After setting forth the arguments for scepticism Hume falls back on "natural credulity" rather than refuting scepticism. One is eventually left with no reason for studying philosophy except that it is a reasonable way to pass time. Hume's philosophy represents no less than the "bankruptcy of eighteenth-century reasonableness."[19] Having started out, like Locke, being sensible and empirical, Hume arrived at the disastrous conclusion that *nothing* could be learned from experience and observations. No one line of action could be more rational than another. Hume had a better intellect than Locke and a greater capacity for consistency in his methodology. Yet even by the end of *A Treatise* Hume was writing like any enlightened moralist. His scepticism was "insincere," Russell held, not maintained in practice (672).

If Hume is the great sceptic of eighteenth-century methodology *Adam Smith (1723–90)*[20] is its materialist, with his revival of Stoic and Epicurean concepts. His treatment of sensation came from Locke, and there were more recent influences of the Scottish moral philosophy school. His machine model of society, complete with the invisible hand, had predecessors in Hobbes, Descartes, La Méttrie, and Newton, but it was Smith who established the concept in the social sciences, applying it to society as a whole. Smith, then, more than a century before Durkheim and almost two centuries before Parsons, becomes the first modern exponent of the theory of functionalism. This makes him a pivotal methodologist, a major link between the ancient Greek materialists and the modern social sciences. The Greek influence was deliberate, and Smith was an accomplished scholar although he never published his Greek research in his lifetime. He is, of course, much better known for his economic writing, which was enormously influential from the time it appeared. *The Wealth of Nations* (1776) had taken twelve years of contemplation, twelve more years of writing, then three years of revision. As soon it was quoted in Parliament it became the Bible of *laissez-faire* capitalism. For mainstream social scientists it was a major source on the division of labour; it was Marx's major source on labour theory of value.

The Theory of Moral Sentiments (1759) is the chief source for Smith's methodological views.[21] In it he sought to explain why some conduct is considered moral and other conduct not and how, whatever their content, some views came to be accepted as moral. The result was a remarkable system with careful linkages among the components: individuals, small groups, whole societies, and all rational creatures. Animals, it seems, were included among rational creatures, a point the discreet Smith did not develop in detail.[22] Moral rules, he held, evolved in a gradual process of interaction within face-to-face groups. The key was sympathy, which meant both pity and compassion for the suffering of others and an identification with them in good fortune. "Our brother on the rack" was Smith's opening example, the problem being how to identify with him when obviously not in his predicament. For good empiricist reasons Smith explained that our imaginations could copy impressions only of our own sensations. We had to "become in some measure the same person" to feel something of another's agony. This was possible, Smith argued, observing that we shrink when we see someone about to receive a blow and writhe watching a dancer on a tight rope. We react instinctively to such crimes as murder, naturally seeking vengeance on behalf of the victim. We feel injustices to other people and come to hate oppression suffered by ourselves or others.

People naturally and spontaneously make judgments of other people's conduct. Patterns become evident as judgments accumulate. We do not approve or condemn particular actions because, on examination, they are or are not consistent with a general rule. On the contrary, the general rule is a result of experience, of certain actions' being deemed acceptable or unacceptable (159). We later cite these standards as rules, which misleads some authors into thinking that the rule was formed first. Religious justifications for moral rules were a still later development, giving them an added sacredness. In the last edition of the book Smith developed the notion of an "impartial spectator," an abstraction from real life, to be appealed to on questions of right and wrong (262). The account is naturalistic throughout, depending on neither abstract reason nor revelation. The intent was normative, but since Smith believed in the possibility of a scientific ethics, his method was scientific.

Smith's social system depended on a benevolent God, a point *laissez-faire* advocates like to neglect. God was usually described as the administrator of the universe. His role as creator was not much stressed and he did not intervene as much as Newton's God. God's purposes, fortunately, were entirely benevolent: the greatest possible quantity of happiness. Smith had no particular liking for Leibniz's theology, but his assurance that only evil would be admitted which was "necessary for the universal good" is much the same thing as "the best of all possible worlds." God contrived and conducted "the immense machine of the universe" so as to produce the greatest possible happiness (236). Smith's more immediate source was probably his old teacher, Francis Hutcheson, whose own system was thoroughly optimistic and relied on divine guidance. Hutcheson, as well, drew on the same Stoic sources that attracted Smith.

In *The Theory of Moral Sentiments*, the care and happiness of all rational creatures is the business of God, not of people. To ascribe purpose to a mere component of the system, people, would be like confusing the watch with the watch-maker. "Man" was allotted a humbler department, the care of personal happiness and that of family, friends, and country (237). Thus, underlying the whole rationale for *laissez-faire* economics was a principle of faith – that an all-wise, great, and benevolent Being was in charge, governing the universe for the greatest possible happiness of all. Part of the management program was a system of checks and balances. God saw to it that the individualistic sentiments of self-interest and prudence were offset by collectivist sentiments, "the consciousness of ill desert, those terrors of merited punishment" (86).

The ultimate mechanism for insuring good operation of the system was the invisible hand. Further developed in *The Wealth of Nations*, Smith used it first in *The Theory of Moral Sentiments* to explain the distribution of wealth. The account tells us much about his economic and social views:

The rich only select from the heap what is most precious and agreeable. They consume little more than the poor, and in spite of their natural selfishness and rapacity ... they divide with the poor the produce of all their improvements. They are led by an invisible hand to make nearly the same distribution of the necessaries of life, which would have been made, had the earth been divided into equal portions among all its inhabitants, and thus without intending it, without knowing it, advance the interest of the society. (184–5)

Providence, Smith affirmed, had not forgotten those who seemed left: "The beggar, who suns himself by the side of the highway, possesses the security which kings are fighting for" (185).

The division of labour, treated at length in *The Wealth of Nations*,[23] was the source of increased productivity and all the ensuing changes in stratification. Not originally the effect of human wisdom, it occurred through a slow, gradual, and unintended human propensity to barter. The propensity to trade and exchange one thing for another was common to all peoples, but existed in no other species. "Nobody ever saw a dog make a fair and deliberate exchange of one bone for another with another dog."[24] Again, it was from the pursuit of individual advantage that this social good developed: "It is not from the benevolence of the butcher, the brewer, or the baker, that we expect our dinner, but from their regard to their own self-interest" (14).

The labour theory of value has been a matter of so much controversy that its formulation merits some attention. Apart from Petty and Locke, there is some brief mention of the notion in Hutcheson, but not until Smith was it well developed. "Labour, therefore, is the real measure of the exchangeable value of all commodities. The real price of every thing, what every thing really costs ... is the toil and trouble of acquiring it ... Labour was the first price, the original purchase-money that was paid for all things. It was not by gold or by silver, but by labour, that all the wealth of the world was originally purchased."[25] The notions of productive and unproductive labour are part of the early history of the theory of capital accumulation. One sort of labour added to the value of the object of labour, another not: "A man grows rich by employing a multitude of manufacturers: he grows poor, by maintaining a multitude of menial servants." The labour of the manufacturer fixed itself in a vendible commodity lasting after the labour is past. "It is, as it were, a certain quantity of labour stocked and stored up to be employed, if necessary, upon some other occasion."[26] The labour of a menial servant, by comparison, perishes in the very instant of its performance, although it also deserves its reward.

In Smith's view the obstacle to greater prosperity lay in mercantilism, hence his arguments against state intervention. He postulated the invisible hand without ever having the opportunity to see whether it worked. From all we know of him, he would have been horrified by nineteenth-century industry. We must remember that all the theory of *The Wealth of Nations* assumes a benevolent God directing human affairs for the common good. It would be harder to argue now that an invisible hand distributes goods almost as equally as if the land were equally divided. And do our moral sentiments correspond exactly to societal needs?

Smith's earlier methodological work, which was not known in his day, is of great interest. He revived the ancient materialist, especially Epicurean, use of theory as a means of calming fear. While the empiricists of his time stressed observation as the source of theory, Smith argued the use of bold conjectures in response to the need for explanation. Observed facts remained the *test* of theory, but the motivation for *discovery* was conjecture. Smith's essay on the history of astronomy provides an excellent example. It opens with the wonder and admiration people feel for natural phenomena. Surprise events, it goes on, can be horrifying and painful, so people began to develop explanations that would still fears of the unknown. Causal theories showed how seemingly unrelated events were bound together. Classification systems made it possible to fit new objects among the familiar.

The philosopher's task was to find a chain of invisible objects to join together two events. "Philosophy, by representing the invisible chains which bind together all these disjointed objects, endeavours to introduce order into this chaos of jarring and discordant appearances, to allay this tumult of the imagination, and to restore it ... to ... tranquility and composure."[27] When life had been more precarious, lesser incoherences escaped notice. For major happenings like comets and thunder, which were inescapable, religious explanations were created, superstition supplying the place of philosophy. (Smith was careful to associate superstition with polytheism, presumably so as not to offend Presbyterians and other monotheists.) With civilization people became less accepting of superstition, feeling their weaknesses less and becoming more cheerful. They were led to conceive that some chain connected all seemingly disjointed phenomena. With leisure to study, and the security of established law, people wished to know these links. Wonder and excitement, not the possibility of practical applications, were the initial impetus to study.

Smith now introduced a notion of system without any benevolent deity. "Systems in many respects resemble machines. A machine is a little system ... an imaginary machine invented to connect together in the fancy those different movements and effects which are already in reality performed" (66). Just as machines when first invented are unnecessarily complex, so are theories. Both are simplified over time. The essay betrays a fondness for Cartesian analysis, especially of the vortex. The ancient materialists are nowhere given explicit credit, obvious as their influence is. Smith may have been reluctant to be seen as unorthodox. The predilection for the vortex has been interpreted as a kind of general principle, that the vortex accounted for the building up and breaking down not only of physical particles but of their social equivalents as well.[28] There are Greek antecedents for this, for example in Empedocles, whose work Smith knew. It is worth noting that

Smith, who set off for London with his sole copy of *The Wealth of Nations*, took the precaution of keeping a spare copy of his astronomy essay in a safe place.

John Millar (1735–1801)[29] falls at the liberal end of the moral philosophy spectrum. As a student of Smith and the teacher of James Mill he is a direct link to the Utilitarians. Professor of civil law at Glasgow University, he was an active worker for electoral and Parliamentary reform, the abolition of slavery, prison improvement, and the education of the working class. Many of his students became leaders in the reform causes of the next century as well. His concern for workers' education arose directly out of a dominant social science issue, the division of labour. Education was needed to overcome the blunting, robotizing effects of an overly specialized division of labour. Again we see the empiricist concern for application.

The Origin of Ranks (1779) stressed study of society for purposes of practical application. We examine the manners and customs of nations, Millar maintained, to reap the benefit of their experience. We cannot form a just idea of the utility of any particular measure, or how far it is practicable, without knowing the circumstances that recommended it in the first place. Causal knowledge, in short, is needed. In searching for the causes of particular systems of law and government, we must consider such factors as soil fertility, production techniques, the labour required for subsistence, community size, and the state of the arts. All these factors influence habits and ways of thinking. The greater part of the political system is derived from the combined influence of the whole people, but individual factors, like the views of particular leaders, may play a minor role. Since leaders are usually educated within their society and influenced by it, they are not a distinctive force. Millar's discussion of all these points is sound but not particularly original; Montesquieu was an important source as well as Adam Smith.

Millar broke new ground in *The Origin of Ranks* with a lengthy chapter titled "on the rank and condition of women in different ages," which was a major source for John Stuart Mill. Its good comparative analysis aimed at discerning trends. Millar examined a great variety of societies: primitive, agricultural, medieval, and recent European. He not only described the situation of women in those societies but tried to account for changes in their status, influence, and economic roles.[30] His explanations included the level and social relations of production, the emergence of specifically female occupations, emphasis on sexual pleasure in the culture, and the cultivation of the arts. He reported cases of primitive societies in which women held real political and economic power, and where descent was reckoned and property and name transmitted through the female line. Monogamy he argued to be the "natural" condition, although he conceded that there had been a brief period before the family was established (198). He treated instances or vestiges of matriarchy as anomalies. Still, his very raising of specific cases helped to start the re-evaluation of patriarchal assumptions. *The Origin of Ranks* also examined relations between fathers and children, masters and servants, sovereigns and their subjects.

Joseph Priestley (1733–1804),[31] one of the eighteenth-century founders of Utilitarianism, is most widely known today as one of the discoverers of oxygen. He also did important scientific work on electricity and optics, was a historian, Bible scholar, grammarian, and political radical in addition to being a methodologist and discoverer of the process to put fizz in soft drinks. In short, Priestley is an able representative of both the use of theory in application and the unity of science. He caused an uproar over his contention that the powers of the mind derive from the structure of the brain. He denounced the Scottish idealists as reactionaries and defended the French Revolution. His social contract theory was more than liberal; he insisted on the *duty* of members of society to resist tyranny before abuses become so great that the whole system has to be subverted. Priestley firmly believed in necessity and progress. It was his "greatest happiness" which inspired Bentham's "greatest good for the greatest number."

Priestley's empiricism owed much to Locke, but Locke could be criticized for inconsistency and confusion. He was indeed guilty of prevarication on the touchy matter of where thinking took place and what exactly did it. Priestley had no such compunctions but argued that the brain did the thinking. In *Disquisitions on Matter and Spirit* (1777) he held that people were wholly material. Poisons, spirits, opiates, and injuries affected the mind by affecting that white "medullary substance," the brain. Arguments to the contrary were based on "incorrect notions" of the inertness of matter. Priestley ingeniously cited revealed religion in support: the Christian faith teaches the resurrection of the body. Not only does the body not fetter the soul, Christians believe that soul and body will be reunited. Greatly impressed with David Hartley's development of Lockean methodology, Priestley devoted an entire book to a paraphrase of the argument and an enthusiastic defence.[32] Both go into minute details long since abandoned or radically modified; both are part of the development of "association psychology."

Positions in the free will/determinism debate had hardened considerably by this time. At first glance Priestley's position is paradoxical, arguing for "philosophical necessity" as essential for any practical notion of free will. This "philosophical necessity" can be seen as the secular rejection of "gloomy" Calvinism.[33] It entails a naturalistic understanding of causation without any arbitrary divine interference. Predestination meant a denial of human free will, for crucial determinations were obviously made by God.

In order for free will to have any meaning, then, this intervention from above and beyond had to be eliminated, leaving the naturalistic causation of "philosophical necessity."

Priestley maintained that the causal process was the same for the natural and social sciences. In politics, "as every branch of study," Priestley held theory to be derived from the observation of causes and effects. He conceded the difficulty of determining causation in single instances: "Individuals may escape the influence of general passions, but multitudes are actuated by gross and sensible motives." Whatever depended upon a few persons might as often be ascribed to unknown causes, but for great numbers "determinate and known causes" (24:207). In any case, some form of hypothesis was preferable to none whatsoever.

Priestley's confidence in limitless progress is more often associated with the nineteenth century. In *First Principles of Government* (1771) he explained how the human species was capable of "unbounded improvement" through society and government. Citing Bacon that knowledge is power, he argued that human powers over nature can be enlarged, people's situation made easier and more comfortable, and existence prolonged and made happier (22:8).

Priestley is responsible for one of the classical formulations of the principle of utility, deriving it from liberal social contract. People, he held, live in society for their mutual advantage "so that the good and happiness of the members, that is, the majority of the members of any state, is the great standard by which every thing relating to that state must finally be determined" (22:13). As in later Utilitarian theory, when actual calculations were made, members of society were equal. There is a strong sense of equality in his writing. Every government, for example, was an "equal republic" in its original principles.

Priestley marks the end of the apostolic succession from Bacon, Boyle, Locke, and Newton.[34] With Priestley, as with Wesley, we see the persistence of the "holy alliance" between science and religion in the eighteenth century, despite Hume. Moving on to William Godwin we come to much more radical politics, indeed to the eighteenth-century beginnings of anarchism. Priestley and Godwin held similar notions of necessity, and both were important contributors to Utilitarianism. Yet while Priestley's rejection of Calvinism stopped at Unitarianism, Godwin followed the French into atheism.

William Godwin (1756–1836)[35] is the last and most radical of the eighteenth-century Utilitarians. If the greatest good to the greatest number suggested greater state intervention to many Utilitarians, to Godwin it did not. He concluded instead that government was evil, and the less of it the better. Change could only be brought about slowly and gradually by changing people's opinions. Godwin was also a strong advocate of equality, arguing for an original common ownership of property. Thus, in spite of his anarchism (the main source of which is his *Enquiry concerning Political Justice* [1790]), Godwin influenced the nineteenth-century development of socialism. His novels, as well, were widely read. His theory of crime reflected an extreme Utilitarianism, but probably had a salutary effect for stressing societal responsibility for the conditions that produce crime. In a time of cruel punishments this thinking appears decent and humane. The hero of Godwin's most popular novel, *Caleb Williams* (1794), was a common man, the victim of injustice. Caleb was innocent, yet his guilty employer's word was enough to have him hounded by magistrate and sheriff into prison and dungeon.

Thought, opinion, persuasion, and understanding were key elements in Godwin's political theory. Moral causes were stronger than physical ones in determining events. The actions and dispositions of people were the off-spring of circumstances and events, not of any original, innate, determination. These influences were made not directly by the senses but through decisions of the understanding. Godwin was an empiricist in the tradition of Locke and Hume. For him, moral principles followed from the succession of associations described in their methodology. The voluntary conduct of our neighbours entered into our calculations as well as material impulses and the mind passed from one to the other without distinguishing between types. Godwin wrote in *The Enquiry*: "The farmer calculates as securely upon the inclination of mankind to buy his corn when it is brought into the market; as upon the tendency of the seasons to ripen it."[36] Thus mind was a real factor in causation, as "a real principle, an indispensable link in the great chain of the universe" (1:386). Yet it was not a "first cause," but a medium through which operations were produced. With Godwin's robust determinism this makes for a thoroughly closed, and predictable, system: "In the life of every human being there is a chain of events, generated in the lapse of ages which preceded his birth, and going on in regular procession through the whole period of his existence, in consequence of which it was impossible for him to act in any instance otherwise than he has acted" (1:384). With this total determinism there is logically no place for guilt or crime, and Godwin was rigorously logical in excluding them. It would be "pernicious" to punish for what was past (2:327).

Godwin's Utilitarianism was grounded in the ancient view of people as having a common nature and led to the principles of socialism. What pleases one person will please another. Similarities among people are greater than their differences. It follows "upon the principles of equal and impartial justice, that the good things of the world are a common stock, upon which one man has as valid a title as another" (2:423). Godwin's determinism was as optimistic as any Marxist's. Change would come so surely that revolution was, in a profound sense, unnecessary. Marx had no liking for Godwin, but there are similarities in their beliefs in the inevitability of the revolution.

"Everything then is in order and succeeds at its appointed time" (1:259). When the crisis came the sword would not be needed but the chains would fall off by themselves. Revolutionaries were so misguided as to "propose to give us something for which we are not prepared, and which we cannot effectively use." They confounded "the process of nature and reason," suspending "the wholesome advancement of science" (1:274). Note how revolution can be explained both by nature and reason, for the two were intimately linked in eighteenth-century thought. Given the inevitability of change, there was little its proponents could do. Since opinions had to be changed, people could work for that. Truth had an effect for good, so advocates of change should work to enable people to see things as they are. Improvements in society depended on improvements in the understanding.

Jeremy Bentham (1748–1832)[37] took the Utilitarian principle – the greatest happiness of the greatest number – the next step to application by precise calculation. For our purposes he is a transitional figure only, for the idea itself came from Priestley and Helvétius, and Bentham's own application of it was so extreme as to be ridiculed rather than followed. Still he founded the school of philosophical radicalism, which gave direction to many social scientists. He is the link from the eighteenth century to John Stuart Mill. One of his merits was to include as appropriate objects of sympathy not just other human beings, "the whole nation," or even "human kind in general," but "the whole sensitive creation."[38] This was scarcely to be noticed in the next two centuries, nor did Bentham himself elaborate the point. It is, nonetheless, fundamental: all creatures of feeling count in the calculation of the greatest happiness of the greatest number. What brings pleasure or pain to dumb animals must be added or subtracted in calculations of utility.

In 1768, Bentham came upon Priestley's phrase "the greatest happiness of the greatest number"; a year later, on reading Helvetius, he discovered how to use it. For friend and foe alike this became the foundation of Utilitarianism. *An Introduction to the Principles of Morals and Legislation* (1780) opens with a plain assertion of the claim: "Nature has placed mankind under the governance of two sovereign masters, *pain and pleasure*. It is for them alone to point out what we ought to do, as well as to determine what we shall do ... They govern us in all we do, in all we say, in all we think: every effort we can make to throw off our subjection, will serve but to demonstrate and confirm it" (1:1).

The principle of utility recognized this stern fact and built it into the systems of law and government. The legislator's task was to design a system of pleasure and pain, or rewards and punishments, so as to promote the greatest happiness of the community and exclude what detracts from it (1:83). Punishments had to be carefully determined to ensure maximum deterrence. Punishment itself was a pain, hence to be minimized or administered only when it would exclude some greater evil. The greatest happiness principle would ultimately be applied to every area of government, but since pleasures and pains could be calculated most readily in the area of criminal law this is where Bentham chose to devote most of his attention.

Few philosophers have followed Bentham in any precise articulation and computation of pleasures and pains. Many resist, for excellent and obvious reasons, the identification of good and evil with feeling pleasure or pain respectively. Yet the contention that government and law ought to be directed to achieving the greatest happiness of the greatest number is surely basic to all democratic theory, and was clearly seen to be so in the nineteenth century. The Utilitarian principle came to be a convenient argument against aristocratic privilege and for every manner of reform. Bentham's reforming zeal was initially directed to those in power, who were meant to see the reasonableness of his proposals and enact them promptly. Later, when he realized that legislators and administrators resisted reform of any kind, he redirected his efforts to the people themselves.

The continuities in methodology – if differences in application – are clear in the work of religious reformer *John Wesley (1703–91)*.[39] Wesley is included in this history less for the originality of his methodology, reminiscent of that of the Puritans, than for the impact of his life and work. Several historians have credited Wesley with preventing revolution in Britain by diverting reforming zeal into religion that might have gone into politics. That is probably an exaggeration, but Wesley's preaching and organizational genius did lead to reform of both church and state. In France, those thinkers with similar concerns for the common people and disgust at political corruption became anti-clerical and politically more radical. Ironically the Tory Wesley is in the direct line of influence into nineteenth-century reform movements, up to and including democratic socialism. The routes to socialism differed in France and Britain, but both had links to the eighteenth century.

Wesley's *Compendium of Natural Philosophy* (1763) reflects all the love of nature of seventeenth-century British empiricism. The study of natural science, or a "full, plain account of the visible creation" would "display the invisible things of God; his power, wisdom, and goodness."[40] The *Compendium's* summary of available knowledge, it was hoped, would bring people to a reverence for the Creator. Thus scientific discoveries from psychology through botany to astronomy were reviewed, the difficulties in obtaining causal knowledge admitted. "The facts lie within the reach of our senses and understanding, the causes are more remote. That things are so we know with certainty, but why they are so we know not" (1:v). Yet as the ancient sceptics had held, available knowledge was sufficient for present wants. Wesley included the standard denunciation of Aristotle as obstructing, rather than promoting, knowledge of nature, "for he made philosophy as unintelligible by his abstract and metaphorical notions as Plato, Pythagoras and others did by their ideas, numbers and symbols" (1:2). Knowledge was for practical application. Even for the austere Reverend Wesley, scientific discoveries "tended very much to improve all the arts of life and add much to the comforts of society" (1:4). Yet reason could never serve as a substitute for faith. As for Montaigne, reason could not lead anyone to God, but faith depended on God's revelation to us, "*the faith once delivered to the saints*" (1:9).

Wesley's politics were outrageously conservative. He rejected the liberal social contract theory for the view that sovereignty lay in God, not in the people or the king. Theologically he has a point, but practically, since the king could not be criticized, his theory differed little from the divine-right doctrine. Unlike other conservatives, though, Wesley compensated for this diffidence with frequent and pointed criticism of corruption in high places. Except for the king, Wesley was no respecter of persons. Most important, Wesley was one of the first leaders of British society to oppose slavery. Although slavery as such had become illegal in Britain by this time, English ports were used in the transportation of slaves, and Britons still owned slaves in America and the West Indies and made money in the slave trade. Wesley's "Thoughts Upon Slavery" (1774) is an emotional denunciation of the treatment of slaves from their capture, transportation, and exploitation at work to cruel punishments on escape. The last letter he wrote before his death was to Wilberforce, the last book he read was by a freed slave.

In addition to his voluminous advice on personal conduct, Wesley wrote a few papers and letters analyzing social institutions. "Thoughts on the Present Scarcity of Provisions" (1772) includes a protracted causal analysis of the causes of poverty.[41] Wesley's recommendations included legislative prohibition of distilling, incentives to farmers to increase food production, and prohibitive taxes on horses. Yet he expressed little hope that any practical measures would be acted on. Wesley's "narrow Toryism" in political theory was contradicted by a lifetime of practice, and it was this practice whose results lasted. In everyday life Wesley was anti-aristocratic, irreverent to the rich, and a breaker of class barriers. In the days of rotten and pocket boroughs he was a vociferous opponent of political corruption. His listeners were miners, factory workers, farm labourers, and the unemployed, whom he helped to equip for political work. In fact, Methodists were prominent activists in the development of the Chartist movement, trade unions, and the Labour Party.

IDEALISM FROM COMMON SENSE TO KANT

The name of the Scottish school of "common sense philosophy" must appeal to any empiricist but, alas, the school fails by the very criteria its name announces. It is perhaps best seen as a British rejection of British empiricism, with parallels and influences on continental idealism. The main exponent of the school was a clergyman, Thomas Reid (1710–96), who held the chair of philosophy at Aberdeen University and later succeeded Adam Smith at Glasgow.[42] His work was carried on by Dugald Stewart (1753–1828), who succeeded Adam Ferguson as professor of moral philosophy at Edinburgh University. The school was popularized – some would say vulgarized – by James Beattie (1735–1803), a virulent opponent of Hume. His *Essay on the Nature and Immutability of Truth in opposition to Sophistry and Scepticism* (1770) was a particularly nasty attack, contributing much to the misunderstanding of Hume's work.

At the heart of Scottish "common sense" philosophy lies an inductivist empiricism as confident as any. *Thomas Reid*'s positive sources were Bacon, for inventing induction, and Newton, for applying it. We are connected to the real, external world directly in the case of the organs of touch and taste, and through media such as waves, rays, and effluvia in the case of hearing, sight, and smell. There is no action-at-a-distance. Reid insisted most strongly that we can, should, and must believe what we perceive. In the case of sensation, which referred to feeling or sentiment rather than perception, there could be no error, for sensation was what we felt it to be. Error in the perception of external objects was possible through disease in the sense organs, nerves, or brain. Such disorders, however, were rare enough to be ignored. So was the telling of lies.

The universe was run by fixed laws, determined by God, who assured us adequate means for discovering them. God intended a great part of our knowledge to come from experience, before we were capable of reasoning. Specifically, God implanted in us principles of veracity and credulity, so that we could speak the truth and believe others who did so.[43] Thus, common sense philosophy turns out to have the same theological foundation as Cartesian and Leibnizian idealism. Doubts as to the adequacy of our means of knowledge implied disrespect for God.[44] The process of acquiring knowledge was automatic and reliable. Every degree of evidence the mind perceived produced a proportional degree of assent or belief. The sign suggesting the thing signified and created belief in it.[45] The process by which scientific laws were induced from observation was similarly effortless.

The common sense philosophers criticized Locke for not being enough of an empiricist, for not breaking with the idealism of Descartes and earlier philosophers. Locke of course laid himself open to the charge with his definition of knowledge as the agreement of ideas. Reid simply ignored the real-world orientation of Locke's work. Yet Hume's *A Treatise of Human Nature* was the real enemy of the common sense school. Reid's attack, if immoderately long, was moderated by decency. It was also misguided, for Reid interpreted Hume as denying existence to both the spiritual and material worlds (1:96). Hume, of course, never denied the existence of the real world, arguing rather that we could not have *certain* knowledge of anything.

The similarities between common sense philosophy and continental idealism turn out to be negligible, for Reid's rejection of Hume and Locke was largely for reasons not central to their methodologies. Common sense philosophy was closer to idealism than empiricism in asserting confidence in the ability to attain true knowledge. Still, its expectations were more modest than those typical of idealism.

Adam Ferguson (1723–1816)[46] methodologically resembled Reid, from whom he borrowed considerably; sociologically he is of much greater interest than Reid. He is one of the many people to have been called the first sociologist and he was well thought of by the Encyclopedists. Marx, who mistakenly thought he was Adam Smith's teacher, praised Ferguson for his work on the division of labour. Ferguson himself complained that Smith had plagiarized his work, but was never convincing on that score. He opposed Hume's scepticism, believing it to be dangerous to society. Social order, according to Ferguson, required the enthusiastic commitment of citizens, whose vitality and self-respect would be sapped with sceptical doubt. Criticism of authorities was dangerous for similar reasons, for it too would weaken the bonds of commitment. The possibility of real knowledge, both natural and moral, was essential for the proper functioning of civil society. Knowledge by introspection was even surer than by the senses, carrying with it a conviction of reality unshaken by the assaults of scepticism. On this argument Ferguson became Cartesian.

Ferguson's lasting contribution to social science consists of three works: *A History of Civil Society* (1767), *Institutes of Moral Philosophy* (1769), and an expanded version of the latter, *Principles of Moral and Political Science* (1792). In them he expounded and applied methodological principles to particular subjects of study. Ferguson's goal was general explanation, always within the context of *moral* science. This is well demonstrated in his repudiation of *mere hypothesis*: "As, in physical science, our object is to investigate and comprehend the actual state of things, no mere hypothesis or supposition can be admitted among the laws of nature: And, in moral science, our object being to determine a choice of what is best, no mere fact can be adduced to preclude our endeavours to attain, in any subject, what is better than its actual state."[47] A moral objective, and confidence in its attainment, are both typical of the whole common sense school.

Ferguson is a good case study for those who like to believe that sociologists are politically conservative. He opposed both the French and the American revolutions. British authorities circulated a pamphlet he wrote against the American rebels. Despite his Highland origins he was anti-Jacobite. The Stoics were positive sources for Ferguson. His academic writing was popular at the time it appeared, and was cited on the Continent as well as in Britain. The recent search for sociological roots has resulted in a modest revival of interest in him, but Ferguson never had the originality or brilliant expression to warrant inclusion among the greats of social science history.

Bishop George Berkeley (1685–1753)[48] is often classified as a British empiricist, perhaps more for his Britishness than his empiricism. I am more inclined to follow Lenin and rank him with the idealists. Yet he did believe the world of sense data to be the normal source of knowledge, and he shared the empiricist concern for the application of knowledge. His conceptualization of nature was highly anthropocentric. While his religious views, which were Stoic and not very Anglican, pervaded his methodology, he also wrote on practical economic subjects where his views were liberal, even Keynesian.[49] In politics Berkeley was conservative, teaching passive acquiescence to constituted authority and opposing free speech.[50] He believed in the identity of truth and beauty so characteristic of idealist philosophers.

Berkeley's first published work was on that empiricist favourite, the psychology of vision. A year later, in 1710, he published "The Principles of Human Knowledge," his main work on methodology. This was later expanded in *Three Dialogues* (1713). In the course of developing his new methodology Berkeley had first to work through a process of rejecting Locke.[51] The result was his theory of a world divided into two components, ideas and spirits.[52] Ideas were inactive "things," existing only in the mind. Spirits, by contrast, were active beings, also known as mind, soul, or self. There were further subdivisions of both, which need not concern us here. What is of note in Berkeley's methodology is a resemblance to Malebranche. The things perceived by the senses could be termed *external* in respect of their origin. They are not generated from within, by the mind, but imprinted on the mind by a spirit distinct from that which perceived them. Our ideas come from God's will acting on us, exciting our minds. Imprinting was only a metaphor, implying no physical process such as the wax impressions used by the ancient Greek materialists.

Berkeley's denial of matter led to joking about his "idea wife" and "idea house." He went to great pains to insist that he never denied the existence of material objects in the ordinary sense of the term. This was to no avail to eighteenth- and nineteenth-century readers, but more recently his "realism" has been recognized. Berkeley insisted that what he was objecting to was the Lockean concept of matter as something distinct from sensible qualities, as something underlying "secondary" qualities. A cherry was real, for example, because he could see it, feel it, and taste it. "Take away the sensations of softness, moisture, redness, tartness, and you take away the cherry."[53] What to Lockeans were "only appearances," or "objects of perception," Berkeley took to be "the real things themselves" (2:244). "I am of a vulgar caste, simple enough to believe my senses and leave things as I find them ... real things are those very things I see and feel" (2:229). If we grant Berkeley his criticism of Locke we must yet see how quickly his alternative gets into worse trouble. Objects, like cherries, bread, and houses, have to be called "ideas" to convey the point that they exist in mind. It was not essential that they exist in any particular mind, though, so that there would be no such thing as a room's disappearing when you walked out of it. Yet *some* mind had to be perceiving objects for them to exist. This led Berkeley to a proof for the existence of God: since it is impossible for objects now to exist and now not, there must be some infinite mind insuring their continued existence. Note the contrast with Malebranche – God implants ideas in our minds instead of our seeing them in God's. There are similarities with Leibniz and other idealists in the stability of the world required for perception to work. For "illusion" and "reality" to be distinguished there could be only negligible interference from dreams, hallucinations, and flights of fancy. "Illusions" had to be weaker to be distinguished from normal sense impressions.[54] Here, as in so much idealism, enormous demands are put on God to guarantee the truthfulness of every perception.

Another difficulty with Berkeley's methodology is that each collection of sense impressions becomes a separate thing. Thus what appears as a bent oar in the water is a different thing from the straight oar out of the water. Berkeley had to insist on that, so contradicting his own stated criterion of respecting "plainest experience."[55] Unusual as his methodology was conceptually, though, in practical respects it resembled ordinary Lockean empiricism. The source of knowledge in both was observation of the real external world, followed by reflection. Regularities were to be noted and natural laws described accordingly. Information so acquired could then be used to guide one's own behaviour. The great difference between Locke and Berkeley lies in the possibility of error. While Locke belaboured the point at every stage, Berkeley scarcely raised the subject. His desire to put down scepticism, it seems, was so great that he could not make much of the potential for error. In one respect he defined away the possibility. Where Locke had many perceptions of a thing, only one of which could be correct, for Berkeley different perceptions were of different things.

Berkeley's purpose in working on methodology was frankly religious. He was concerned with growing atheism, which he viewed as closely connected with, and fed by, scepticism. Scepticism was in turn was a product of materialism. If Berkeley's principles were true, it followed that atheism and scepticism would be utterly destroyed.[56] Hobbists and Epicureans were particular culprits in Berkeley's thinking, but some of Locke's views, too, he found dangerous.[57]

Immanuel Kant (1724–1804)[58] was the major modern formulator of idealism. He lived through the French Revolution, dying early in the nineteenth century. There were no appeals to authority or divine revelation in his thoroughly secular idealism. His pietist origins show through perhaps in the force of his conviction of the dominance of mind over matter and certainty over probability. Secular and modern as his idealism was, though, the continuities with the past are considerable. Reason is reified, becoming an individual actor, with intentions and faculties similar to those of the Augustinian or Cartesian creator. Kant, further, was as teleological as Aristotle. History unfolds according to a principle of increasing freedom. Things happen; ergo they were meant to happen. Observed tendencies become principles of organization, fulfilling their destiny through evolution.

Kant shares all the sexism of the idealist tradition. His mind-over-matter hierarchy relegated women to the lower, material functions of domestic work. Even the tautology seems to have escaped him. Women could not have political rights because they were economically dependent. Yet they were economically dependent because of a legally enforced division of labour. In the 2200 years since Aristotle, little had changed. Kant's other political views were moderate. He rejected the radical social contract interpretations of the day but insisted on a right to critical *expression*, free speech. When we consider the authoritarian politics to succeed him, it is understandable that he should be looked back to with fondness.

After many years of work on the *Critique of Pure Reason* Kant despaired of solving every problem. He then wrote up the material in a matter of months for publication in 1781. Disappointed with the book's cool reception – even his friends found it unreadable – he set out to defend it with the *Prolegomena to any Future Metaphysics that will be able to present itself as a Science* (1783). As well as restating the main elements of *Critique of Pure Reason*, the *Prolegomena* gives Kant's views of such other major methodologists as Hume, Berkeley, and Descartes and, to a lesser extent, Plato and Aristotle.[59]

Kant's methodical quest seems at first to duplicate Locke's: finding the limits and extent of knowledge. It has been likened to our turning our attention to a telescope to find out how it works before turning it on the stars, a most reasonable thing to do. I shall argue that Kant changed the inquiry to something quite different, but to show this it is best to begin where he did. He wrote his *Critique of Pure Reason* roughly a century after Locke's *Essay concerning Human Understanding*, time enough to have seen "empiricism in morals" developing, or scepticism as to intellectual authority encouraging a dangerous scepticism about moral authority. The fruits of the illustrious Locke were "indifferentism" at best, and the nihilism of Hume at worst. Yet Kant had become critical of the dogmatic idealism of Leibniz and Wolf, the philosophy he had been taught, and which he himself taught. If he found Hume too atheistic, there was too much religion in Leibniz. Kant soon came to consider himself an opponent of idealism, and certainly he was on such points as the existence of the real world. But his own methodology remains in the idealist tradition.

Aware of the great strides being made in mathematics and natural science, Kant wanted an equally impressive methodology for dealing with metaphysical questions. Before embarking on the construction of yet another system, he determined to ascertain whether a scientific basis for one existed. He had no doubt of the importance of such questions. Human nature was called upon to consider questions of the nature of God, the soul, and mortality.[60] Unfortunately, Kant concluded, metaphysical questions transcend the faculty of the mind, which was confined to the world of experience. At this stage, then, there is no quarrel between Kant and empiricism.

Kant next turned his attention to another question: Within the world of possible experience, how is knowledge possible [that is, *synthetic* knowledge and not simply *analytic*, as in Leibniz]? Kant's point was not to reject the empiricist answer that knowledge was possible through the senses. Nor was he concerned with the problem of error in the process of perception, which empiricists pointed out on most possible occasions. Indeed Kant made very little of error in sensation. Rather the problem as he perceived it was that even the best observation could not supply knowledge of the *necessary* and *universal*. Hume had correctly pointed that out but had erred in concluding that such "knowledge" could never be more than the "delusion of habit." Kant would not make the same mistake as Hume, but would look further for a solution. Clearly no solution was to be had in perception, so attention must be directed to the operations of the mind.

The distinction Kant made between sensation and thought in order to ascertain the contribution of "pure" reason to knowledge was as radical as any by an idealist. In effect, he inquired how the mind, by virtue of its own powers, is able to make universal and necessary judgments without relying on actual experience of objects or anticipating experience. The answer was that the mind brings to perception certain concepts, or categories, which structure experience. Since these exist before any experience they may be thought of as a kind of innate idea. Rather than denoting a particular proposition, they were categories that helped to form experience.

One of the most serious defects in Kant's methodology appears at this point, the isolation of "pure reason." Pure reason is not something that anytime or anywhere exists but is an abstract concept. Kant himself admitted as much. Thoughts without content are empty, just as perceptions without conceptions would be blind. Sensibility and understanding were related like matter and form; one could no more conceive of matter with no form than form without matter. The *Critique of Pure Reason* indeed begins with a famous statement of the origin of knowledge in experience:

That all our knowledge begins with experience there can be no doubt. For how is it possible that the faculty of cognition should be awakened into exercise otherwise than by means of objects which affect our senses, and partly of themselves produce representations, partly rouse our powers of understanding into activity, to compare, to correct, or to separate these, and so to convert the raw material of our sensuous impressions into a knowledge of objects, which is called experience? In respect of time, therefore, no knowledge of ours is antecedent to experience, but begins with it. (1)

Kant then, however, ignored this very point for the rest of his inquiry. He referred frequently to reason "antecedent" to experience or to reason "without the aid of" experience, as if these were possible. Perception and thinking were fundamentally different processes in Kant's conceptualization, much further removed from each other than in either Locke or Leibniz. Since all knowledge begins with experience, this distinction between what the reason and the senses add might seems artificial. "Pure reason" is an abstract concept, not existing in practice, but Kant considered it important to isolate it.

Since the *Critique of Pure Reason* was an investigation of the *forms* of reason, Kant also used the analogy of matter and form. The *Critique* set out a list of universal and necessary forms whereby the chaos of sense stimuli could be converted into an orderly world. This to a great extent destroyed a straw man of empiricism – denial of intellectual functions. Certainly Locke described the mind as performing a range of manipulative tasks in the processing of sense data. Yet his followers persist in crediting him with the discovery of the mind's contribution to knowledge.

Kant's methodological work has given many people insights they would not otherwise have had. Yet it is a corrective that would not be needed if empiricism were better understood. Kant himself was ill informed. He did not read the two languages in which most of the work on empiricism was published, English and French. His discussion of Locke shows him to have seriously misunderstood main points. Kant had never read Hume's *Treatise of Human Nature*, his most sceptical work and fiercest attack on idealism. It was Hume's *Enquiry concerning Human Understanding* that allegedly wakened Kant from his philosophic slumber.[61] His quest was for certitude: "I have fully convinced myself that, in this sphere of thought, *opinion* is perfectly inadmissible, and that everything which bears the least semblance of a hypothesis must be excluded, as of no value in such discussions."[62] Fortunately, though, "Nothing can escape our notice; for what reason produces from itself cannot lie concealed, but must be brought to the light by reason itself" (xix). Others might worry about the inadequacies of the mind's capacity, but Kant was supremely confident. He claimed to have disposed of Humean doubt once and for all. He agreed with Hume that one could not have insight by reason into the possibility of reason. Then, rather than treat these concepts as taken from experience and "mere illusion imposed on us by long habit,"[63] Kant claimed to have shown that they stand *a priori*, before all experience. While these concepts have their undoubted objective accuracy in respect to experience, objective rightness simply means conformity to his theory. Here Kant apologizes that this "validity" holds *only* for experience. More precisely, it holds only for *his* theoretical construct of experience.

Kant argued that the criteria which justify the distinction between *a priori* and *a posteriori* knowledge are necessity and universality, which cannot be known from experience. Where he went wrong, in my opinion, was in confounding the existence of *judgments* of universality and necessity, with universal and necessary *knowledge* itself. Kant, in the *Prolegomena*, rejected "probability and conjecture" as "child's play" (138). "Knowledge," let us be clear, included simple judgments, which might be pure nonsense. The classical use of the term knowledge to denote *true* opinion has been entirely lost. Knowledge might be entirely wrong so far as empirical tests go, and need not even imply internal consistency. A person could make two contradictory judgments involving universal or necessary propositions, and both would constitute knowledge according to Kant's use of the term. The statement "all dogs are brown" would be a universal judgment in Kant's scheme, and thus knowledge, but wrong nonetheless. "Objective validity" similarly entailed no external references as is understood in empiricism. Rather Kant used it simply to mean a *judgment* of universal validity. Experience, he asserted, taught us all the same things! (58). Descartes and other idealists at least felt the compunction to provide some reason, for example that God guaranteed accurate perception.

Kant took on the labourious task of establishing a tribunal of self-examination for nothing less than the critical investigation of pure reason. He flattered himself to have discovered the cause of, and therefore how to remove, "all the errors which have set reason at variance with itself." And this he proposed to do to "perfect satisfaction."[64] He further claimed to have discovered the twelve categories used by the mind in approaching sense data.

Kant's "Copernican revolution," the reversal of relations between external objects and the mind, was another extraordinary claim. The empiricist goal of representing an external object as accurately in the mind as possible was too modest for him. Instead of forcing the mind to conform to the external object, his methodology proposed to make the object conform to the mind. Neither the merits of the proposal, nor the Copernican analogy, however, survive close inspection. Kant did not mean that the mind was literally capable of producing real objects, for that would be absurd. No one need ever go hungry if the imagination could produce food. Rather the mind produces mental images, or "phenomena," of which it can then have certain knowledge, for it has itself produced them. This removes the gap, which empiricism never successfully bridged, between an external object and our minds. But note that there is now no longer an external object. Kant has dispensed with it, to confine "knowledge" to a purely internal world of our own construction. He seems to have forgotten that this "knowledge" must be activated by sense objects from the external world.

Kant otherwise advised that reason must approach nature not as a pupil but as a judge, compelling nature to answer. The highest legislation of nature must lie in ourselves, that is, in our understanding. "*The understanding does not draw its laws* (a priori) *from nature, but prescribes them to nature.*"[65] But what if several of us, with our different understandings, all prescribe different laws to nature, as indeed we do. Is nature in any meaningful way the *recipient* of these various laws? Does it obey them? Did Ptolemy get the sun to race around the earth, and Copernicus and Galileo to stop them and switch places? Note the complete reversal with empiricism, where the scientist's task is to study nature, social or physical, to try to understand it and frame laws – as *regularities* rather than *orders.* Note also the misleading use of the singular. Earlier theorists were confident that God would not make nature more complicated than our minds could understand. But how can nature obey so many disparate "laws" as there were by Kant's time? How can the poor earth and sun cope with so many conflicting instructions?

Kant's methodology explicitly concedes defeat, as the empiricists had done, at the level of knowledge of real external objects. Things-in-themselves, while not necessarily unreason, remain unintelligible to us. Only phenomena can be "known," but what their relation to the real world is remains as much a mystery as in Locke. Our "knowledge" may be perfect, but it is utterly unreal. We know what an "object" is because we made it, although even this requires perfect memory!

Kant's social science entails a thorough rejection of Leibnizian determinism. History is not predetermined. Predictions can be made, but they will be of limited value, for the future is unknown.[66] Yet he espoused a theory of stages of history, with laws to account for the transition from one to the next. It was a highly optimistic history of increasing freedom for "man" (excluding women). The optimism was moderated, however, with the qualification that freedom involves the potential for evil. Here, as elsewhere, Kant plays the moderate Aristotle to Leibniz's Plato.[67] In retrospect, Kant's historical predictions must be seen as tragically over optimistic. There is the usual idealist confounding of is and ought, and the imputation of intention to abstract categories.[68]

When Kant is cited as a possible source for environmental ethics, the rigid idealist separation of "man" from nature and teleology should be recalled. Man was "certainly titular lord of nature ... born to be its ultimate end."[69] Nature becomes the *means* by which free men realize their ends. The teleology is of the same order as Aristotle's: "*All the natural capacities of a creature are destined sooner or later to be developed completely and in conformity with their end.*"[70] Kant was a liberal in deeming freedom to be the essential nature of "man," but excluding half the species from this beneficence. It was his observation that freedom was increasing, as was enlightenment. There was a regular process of improvement in political constitutions. Germs of enlightenment always survived, even with apparent setbacks, preparing the way for a higher level of enlightenment. Yet the history of ideas is full of recoveries after centuries of disappearance, and we have enough knowledge now of lost germs of enlightenment to realize what has been lost.

Lucien Goldmann credits Kant with being the first modern thinker to recognize anew the importance of totality as a fundamental criterion of existence.[71] (Kant thus opened the way to the nineteenth-century totalizers: Fichte, Hegel, and Marx.) However, saying it is so does not make it so. Announcing that everything has been considered and the truth is thus-and-so does not change external reality. In Kant's case totality left out both the female half of humanity and the entire non-European world. In matters of culture, who knows every language, religion, song, dance, and book? Clearly one must distinguish between totality as an *objective* and as a *result*.

Kant is finally of interest for his influence on Marx, both directly and through Hegel. The stress on totality as a focus of analysis is one obvious link. So is the teleology, which was optimistic in both cases. There is even a rough similarity between Kant's prediction of increasing freedom in the young Marx's projection of complete freedom in society after the withering away of the state. The Kantian antinomies, not discussed here, can also be seen as an early form of the Marxian dialectic.

For all the secular, modern mode of expression, Kant's methodology, as epistemology, remains in the tradition of idealism. It fails more than empiricism because it dares more. Claiming certitude, even infallibility, it rejects mere probability and opinion. Yet while Kant (unlike the empiricists) *argued* that certain knowledge is possible, he failed to *prove* that it is.

WOMEN METHODOLOGISTS

Mary Wortley Montagu (1689–1762)[72] was Astell's chosen successor. The two were friends and each learned from the other's work. Wortley Montagu was influenced by her early reading of Astell's *Serious Proposal to the Ladies*, and Astell wrote an enthusiastic preface to Wortley Montagu's *Turkish Letters* and helped publicize her friend's health promotion cause, inoculation against smallpox.

Wortley Montagu's indisputable contribution to the social sciences lies in her *Turkish Letters* (1763), written while travelling to and staying in Turkey as wife of the British ambassador. The letters were always intended for publication, but not in their aristocratic author's lifetime. In the absence of professionally trained social scientists and scholarly journals, travellers' reports served as the main source of comparative data. Wortley Montagu's observations are especially valuable for their account of Turkish women's society, a society not accessible to male visitors. Her biographer stresses the *Letters'* role in the exchange of ideas between Islamic Turkey and Christian Europe. "By virtue of their expansive tolerance, and their candid sympathy for an alien culture, they are Lady Mary's valid credential for a place in the European 'Enlightenment.'"[73]

Astell's praise of the letters was less restrained, praising their author's delicacy of sentiment and sublime genius. She regretted that Wortley Montagu would not publish in her lifetime, but wanted posterity to know that "among her contemporaries, *one woman*, at least, was just to her merit" (1:467). The letters were published the year after Wortley Montagu died, forty-six years after they had been written, and even then against the objections of her daughter.

Wortley Montagu as well, while still a young woman and a political wife, published nine issues of a political review. *The Nonsense of Common Sense* (1737–8) gave her views on political events, which were often at odds with those of her MP husband. One issue was devoted to the status of women. In it she argued, as had Astell, the necessity for women to develop their powers of reasoning. Wortley Montagu was an early user of the term "humankind" in making the argument: "Men that have not sense enough to shew any superiority in their arguments hope to be yielded to by a Faith that, as they are Men, all the Reason that has been allotted to human kind has fallen to their Share" (27). Wortley Montagu herself was of a different opinion.

Wortley Montagu learned of smallpox inoculation while in Turkey. She not only had her own two children inoculated, but persuaded the Princess of Wales to have hers done as well.[74] Voltaire in his *English Letters* credited her with saving large numbers of lives in England despite the opposition of the medical establishment. He urged for the adoption of inoculation in France. Wortley Montagu wrote an article, published anonymously, advocating the practice, and Astell published an article in the progressive *Plain Dealer* in 1724 which cited comparative mortality statistics in support of the practice.

It is not known whether Wortley Montagu was "Sophia, a person of quality," author of an intrepid feminist tract, "Woman not Inferior" (1739). (We will probably never know, for Wortley Montagu's daughter burned those parts of her journals and essays she deemed controversial or scandalous.) A number of the same arguments appear in this work as in Wortley Montagu's letters and the *Nonsense of Common Sense*, but "Woman not Inferior" is even more radical. The claim of men to superiority is dismissed as resting on "prejudice and custom." Men assumed that they were women's masters, yet were not able to demonstrate why. The only area in which "Sophia" conceded men any superiority was with brute strength. Yet, if this were the criterion, the lion had better title over the whole creation. If esteem were accorded on the basis of usefulness, women were "incomparably the greatest contributors to the public good." Princes, merchants, soldiers, and lawyers could be dispensed with, but not women who raise children: "In a peaceful, orderly state, the major part of Men are useless in their office, with all their authority."[75] Men prostituted reason to their groveling passions, suffering sense to be led away by prejudice. For an age that held men to be superior in reason and excluded women from public life because of their "lower" natures, Sophia's reversal was audacious.

The vicious circle was pointed out: women were denied an education because they were excluded from public offices, yet they were deemed unworthy of public office because of their lack of education. There were no differences in the soul, but differences in accomplishments came from differences in education, exercise, and external impressions. If women were given the same advantages of study as men, they would at least keep pace. "There is no *science*, *office*, or *dignity*, which *Women* have not an equal right to share in with the *Men*" (55). Sophia was consistent as well in insisting on women's right to exercise an office, not merely to be educated for it. Yet she also insisted on knowledge for private life, as did Wortley Montagu in her known letters.

The exclusion of women from medical practice was derided. Without the help of Galen or Hippocrates, women had in fact invented an infinity of reliefs. Their exact observations showed the "useless pedantry" of systems. "I hardly believe our sex would spend so many years to so little purpose as those *Men* do, who call themselves *philosophers*; were we to apply to the *study of nature*" (42). Male privilege was responsible for lazy, sloppy, and arrogant scholarship. Here Sophia criticized not empiricism *as such*, but inadequate work. Men held to their "undoubted truths" without being able to assign reasons for their opinions (3). Their suppositions lacked evidence. Idealist abstractions were another instance of masculine impracticality. Men wasted whole years, even entire lives, "on mere *Entia Rationis*, fictitious trifles, no where to be found but in their own noodles" (42). Women would find more useful employments than idly plodding to ascertain whether there was imaginary space beyond the utmost circumference of the universe. Instead the "chief fruit of learning" was a "just discernment of true from false," to find out what relates to us and "by what applications they may be beneficial or obnoxious to us" (42–3).

Catharine Macaulay (1731–91)[76] was a success in her day. Her books sold and other writers used her ideas. Macaulay indeed was the source for the radical feminist views associated with Wollstonecraft. Nonetheless she was soon forgotten after her death, and it has only been thanks to the zeal of feminist scholars and the establishment of women's studies that her work has been rediscovered. She deserves recognition also as a pioneer environmentalist. Macaulay published the first of her eight-volume *History of England* in 1763, the last in 1783. Her major methodological contribution was *Letters on Education* (1790). She also published an unusually accessible book on Hobbes, a reply to Burke on the French Revolution, a proposal on copyright, and a stirring appeal to the people of England on toleration and liberty.

The *Letters on Education* set out a comprehensive proposal for a liberal education based on Lockean principles. Holding that "experience ... is the only efficacious instructor,"[77] Macaulay outlined the nature of experience required from earliest infancy into the twenties. The two sexes were to be educated in the same way, except that girls would not be taught certain sports. Rousseau's *Emile* is a negative model throughout. Macaulay's demolition of this "entertaining performance" is sarcastic and brilliant (46). In pleading for equal education for girls Macaulay shows a firm grasp of the nature of sexism. Although her work predated use of the terms "sexism" and "patriarchy" by almost 200 years, her understanding of a comprehensive, interlocking system of prejudice, law, and education is clear, and she recognized that sex-role differentiation could be limiting to boys as well as girls. Thus she argued that boys should be taught more of the fine arts and crafts, as well as that girls should be taught the male academic curriculum. By comparison, idealists of this period still tended to treat all differences between the sexes as natural, immutable, and unquestionable.

Macaulay showed how insidious sexist thinking is. She quoted Alexander Pope's dictum that a perfect woman was but a softer man. She then showed how this could be reversed: a perfect man was but a woman from a coarser mould (204). Her prescribed curriculum was original in both content and order of instruction (134–5). It was longer and more ambitious than most curricula, including a European tour when the student, male or female, was capable of mature reflection. She herself had managed to break through the restriction against female travel and understood its importance for scholarly work.

Along with the usual belief in progress Macaulay accepted the empiricist conception of sympathy. Sympathy in human nature, with knowledge of the relation of things, causes people to put themselves in the place of the sufferer and thus to acquire ideas of equity. All human virtue arises from equity and all equity from the "useful affection" of sympathy. She condemned barbaric punishments, noting that they fail to excite sympathy. Yet Macaulay went much further than Adam Smith in extending this sentiment of sympathy to all creatures. Her sense of the unity of nature is keen, and unusual, for historians are so often humanists in the pejorative sense of that word.

Macaulay is a model environmentalist by contrast. Humans and animals are all part of creation, in which humans, thanks to their special gifts, have special responsibilities (125). Children should be taught to care for animals and actually be given animals to care for. The good of animals as well as of people should be considered in calculations for utility.

Like Mary Astell a century earlier, Macaulay rejected the mind/body hierarchy of idealism in favour of a view of mutual influence. Rather than treating body as a source of evil she considered that mind "was often more in fault than the body." Experience, she claimed, was her witness. Feminist critics of idealist ethics have their forerunner in Macaulay: "In the contempt with which the severe moralist regards the sensual part of man, he does not take into consideration, that the most sublime ideas we are capable of forming owe their origins to the impressions of sense" (295). Kant and company ought to have taken note, but failed to. Idealist philosophers were to continue the denigration of body, relegating women with it to the world of sensuality, impurity, and error. After Macaulay it could not be said that an alternative vision had never been offered.

Macaulay's histories are remarkable for their liberal view of human nature and trenchant criticism of Stuart and Jacobite conservatives. Her express motive for writing was the lack of liberal work available in spite of the efforts of "several ingenious and learned men."[78] She had gained her love of liberty at an early age from exposure to Roman history. Now she would not be mute in the cause of liberty while the doctrine of slavery found so many writers to defend it. She noted that in every society a number of people profit from tyranny. Having made her political point of view clear, her commitment as a historian was to adequate data and proper interpretation. Macaulay's well-documented histories referred to many original sources which she researched in the British Museum. Hume's histories, by contrast, contain much less adequate scholarship, quite apart from their conservative politics.

The historian, said Macaulay, had to digest voluminous collections to give the public a true and accurate sense of events. With this "just information of facts" there had to be a good understanding of the context: "Labour, to attain truth, integrity to set in its full light, are indispensable duties in an historian" (1:x). She claimed not to have been wanting in either duty. "Party prejudice" and "private interest" were to blame for bias in other, conservative histories (1:ix). Falsely painted memories of past times served to justify an illiberal regime. Macaulay, on the other hand, would relate events accurately, assigning blame or praise as merited. As the ancient Chinese historians held, the only punishment for the tyrant is "eternal infamy," while the reward of fame can be held out to the virtuous.

Macaulay's later single-volume history was at least as lively and liberal. When history has been so much a glorification of war her assessment of militarism bites: "I know of no real advantages ... which can accrue to any people from success in arms, but that of political security ... Victory only serves to facilitate the ends of domestic tyranny, and is purchased with the addition of accumulated taxes, with public debts, and public slavery, for my own part, I look on the military achievements of such a nation as so many badges of their servitude, or as glaring marks of their folly."[79]

Hobbes' authoritarian politics were an obvious target for the radical Macaulay. Her paraphrases reveal unresolved paradoxes. She herself provided counter examples from "nature and reason."[80] Edmund Burke, a contemporary, was another target. Macaulay was one of the first to respond to Burke's attack on the French Revolution. A false opinion could enslave minds into passive obedience and inflate the pride and arrogance of princes. In time, rectitude would give way to will, and thence to violence and anarchy. Opinions urging quiescence had to be resisted.[81] The moral was that rebellion, in time, resulted in less violence than indefinite submission.

Mary Wollstonecraft (1759–97)[82] merits her place in the history of the social sciences because of her application of methodology to reform ends, not for any original methodology as such. Her *Vindication of the Rights of Woman* was a comprehensive, articulate demand for equality for women, argued from a devastating exposé of legal, economic, and political injustices. Her earlier *Vindication of the Rights of Men*, now less known, was the first answer to Edmund Burke's attack on the French Revolution. (Virginia Woolf commented that Wollstonecraft's two vindications now seem "to contain nothing new in them – their originality has become our commonplace."[83]) Wollstonecraft's *Historical and Moral View of the French Revolution*, written several years later and after she had actually visited revolutionary France, is competent and brilliantly written.

Wollstonecraft's passionate *Vindication of the Rights of Men*, published anonymously in 1790, was hastily written and little researched. It won immediate acclaim, however, and was promptly reprinted with its author's name on it. Answering Burke's "servile reverence for antiquity, and prudent attention to self interest" it contains many fine turns of phrase.[84] It castigated the strong who gain their riches by sacrificing the many for their vices (10). It argued for a solidarity that could only be based on equality. It pointed out the absurdity, and class interest, of a criminal law that regarded the life of a deer as more sacred than that of a person. Since Burke made much use of feeling in defending tradition and royalty, Wollstonecraft countered with reason over passion. Feeling and physical affection had only a limited scope for regulating conduct, she maintained. It took time for humanity to learn that each person's happiness depends on the general happiness. A more enlightened, moral love would be based on principles. Yet, for all her appeals to reason, the *Vindication* was no idealist tract. There is a sombre sense of the limits to knowledge in the human understanding, especially for the determination of causes (77). Both *Vindications* contain methodological cautions. She points out, for example, that it is impossible to determine whether certain quick perceptions are reminiscences or rationalizations. We have little power over the "subtile electric fluid" in the brain.[85]

Most of Wollstonecraft's lengthier *Historical and Moral View of the French Revolution* (1794) consists of a side-by-step account of the events of 1789 and the dissolution and debauchery of the French court that led to them. It powerfully describes the "vile despotism, under the lash of which twenty-five millions of people groaned; till, unable to endure the increasing weight of oppression, they rose like a vast elephant, terrible in his anger, treading down with blind fury friends as well as foes."[86] Wollstonecraft carefully set out causal links. For example, misery was described as resulting from a corrupt, ineffective political system which made it necessary for the favourite of the day to amass riches against future losses. Thus, to save himself from oblivion, he must become a knavish tyrant (46). "Everything was effected by natural causes" (122). As empiricists were wont, Wollstonecraft condemned the study of nature through books, without experiments. "Labourious compilations of the wanderings of the human understanding" slowed the progress of knowledge (237). She linked progress in knowledge with civil liberties.

Wollstonecraft wrote *French Revolution* before the full horrors of the Terror. Yet enough blood had been shed to make her cautious in her judgments. She argued that the excesses were due to the degraded character of the French people, which was in turn the result of despotism (72). Whenever further convincing was required she again reviewed the oppression caused by court and clergy. While defending the revolution Wollstonecraft repeatedly affirmed the need for change of opinions to overtake the empire of tyranny. Revolutions of state ought to be gradual. Despite certain acts of "ferocious folly," Wollstonecraft continued to believe that the people were essentially good. It was natural for people to run to extremes. Time was required for things to find their level, when a fairer government would arise. In the progress of civilization Wollstonecraft saw the polishing of manners as a stage, and the "harbinger of reason" (497). Yet this polishing meant only "partial civilization," short of real morality and benevolence. She remained a believer in progress, succumbing to doubt only briefly, and then recovering. It was a "vulgar error" to believe that civilization could go no further than it had (19).

Contrary to Rousseau, Wollstonecraft held that nature made people unequal in bodily and mental powers. Thus the end of government ought to be to eliminate this inequality and protect the weak. Wollstonecraft was original and interesting here; it is regrettable that she has been routinely ignored in the literature on political equality. Her second *Vindication* pled also for equality as essential for morality.[87] Most of the evils of the world flowed, as from a poisoned fountain, from the respect paid to property. Her conclusions were cautious, postponing final judgment and calling for more research. "It is only the philosophical eye, which looks into nature and weighs the consequences of human actions, that will be able to discern the cause which has produced so many dreadful effects."[88]

A Vindication of the Rights of Woman is a cry from the heart with comparatively little factual information and analysis. "I plead for my sex, not for myself," said its author.[89] The book makes strange reading today for, unequal as women yet are, few doubt their capacity for intellectual and moral decision-making. Wollstonecraft had still to contend with an education system and a literature in which women were not considered fully human, hence the high sounding arguments appealing to reason. Equality, as fact, could hardly be proved, and Wollstonecraft did not try. Instead she pointed out the necessity for society as a whole to have educated women. Woman, "if not prepared by education to become the companion of man ... will stop the progress of knowledge and virtue, for truth must be common to all" (20). Plainly, many men wanted women not as companions in the search for truth, as rational mothers, or affectionate wives, but as "alluring mistresses." It would only be when women had been given the same education as men that we would know if they had equal power. Time would tell. "Men of genius and talents have started out of a class, in which women have never yet been placed" (170). Wollstonecraft rejected the benevolent subjugation of women, even if men firmly believed it to be in women's best interests. "Who made man the exclusive judge, if woman partake with him the gift of reason?" (22)

There were great *social* benefits to be had from educated and independent women, for individual and society are related. Very much in the moral philosophy tradition she pointed out that a truly benevolent legislator endeavoured to make it the interest of each individual to be virtuous. Private virtue thus becomes the cement of public happiness, consolidating all the parts towards a common centre (306). Without rights, there can be no duties. Here Wollstonecraft went well beyond Macaulay and all the radicals in calling for the vote for women. This first recorded demand for the vote was made almost apologetically: "Women ought to have representatives, instead of being arbitrarily governed without having any direct share allowed them in the deliberations of government" (311). *A Vindication of the Rights of Woman* is a classic in the history of feminism, ranking with Astell's *Serious Proposal to the Ladies*, Wortley Montagu or Sophia's "Woman not Inferior," and Macaulay's *Letters on Education*. Methodologically it is the least weighty of the four, but it is a part of the long process of redefinition of the role and capacities of half of humanity. In promoting an understanding of the importance of institutions, rather than nature, in shaping social reality, *A Vindication of the Rights of Woman* is part of the history of methodology.

The contribution of *Mary Hays (1760–1843)*[90] to the social sciences includes both astute observations on methodology proper and substantive work in social history, especially on the much neglected subject of women. Hays also pamphleteered, in 1798 publishing an anonymous *Appeal to the Men of Great Britain in Behalf of Women*. Her *Female Biography* (1803), six volumes of "Memoirs of Illustrious and Celebrated Women," is a signal contribution of great usefulness. The arrangement, as for the *Encyclopédie*, was alphabetical, so that Astell follows Aspasia, 2200 years her senior. The writing is succinct and witty. Hays throughout unabashedly promoted her cause, the benefit of her own sex. Yet she could claim to have disdained bigotry, for she was unconnected with any party, hence able to serve truth and virtue. Her own reflections were "sparingly interwoven ... such as naturally arose out of the subject," showing no favour to "sects or systems."[91] Her description of the petty scurrilous attacks on Catharine Macaulay are familiar to contemporary feminists. "Her talents and powers could not be denied; her beauty was therefore called in question, as if it was at all concerned with the subject; or that, to instruct our understandings it was necessary at the same time to charm our senses" (3:158).

In an essay on civil liberty Hays argued that truth would slowly win, resisted by the older generation but more accepted by the younger. Thomas Kuhn would undoubtedly agree that "novel truths, or rather truths represented in a new point of view, operate more forcibly on the rising generation, where the memory is not 'preoccupied.'"[92] Her empiricism shows also in the use of understanding*s* in the plural.

For Hays there was no inconsistency between moral commitment and acceptance of the mechanical philosophy. "Sympathy" was a key notion. Vice or virtue prevailed in a person in proportion to the feelings excited by sympathy. Hays gave no unqualified endorsement to materialism or necessity, but simply considered that these notions were better than the alternatives. There were, moreover, positive implications in the doctrine of mechanism, for it inspired "charity and forbearance. A necessarian may pity, but he cannot hate."[93] Hays' feminism includes a reference to God as "Parent of the universe" (169). The relegation of women to "frivolity and trifles" was "mental bondage" of "the most fatal" sort, an "absurd despotism" and "gothic barbarity that enslaved the female mind" (19–20). She correctly predicted that the name of Mary Wollstonecraft would be revered by posterity, "when the pointless sarcasms of witlings are forgotten" (21). That reverance took nearly two centuries is another story.

Hays' essay on civil liberty shows the insights of a woman observer. Women favoured liberty more than men, she argued, because they are sensitized by government partiality, which injures them more than men. Women were less often in the "vortex of influence."[94] Since they are excluded from the benefits of pensions and position, they are less likely to be partial. Two generations before Marx, Hays understood massive social change as propelled by inner contradictions. Monarchical and aristocratic governments "carry within themselves the seeds of their own dissolution; for when they become corrupt, and oppressive to a certain degree, the effects must necessarily be murmurs, remonstrances and revolt" (17). She was better able than others of her time to distinguish between short-term and long-term consequences of historical events. Posterity, she held, would reap the benefit of the French Revolution, which was ruinous for those involved in it. Hays was a cautious believer in progress. "Liberal attitudes" would produce "certain, though slow effects; the feeble efforts of prejudice and interest must in the end give way to truth, however gradual may be their declining struggle" (13).

THE LAST DECADE AND TRANSITIONS

Events of the last decade of the eighteenth century, especially the French Revolution and Terror, were to dominate life and thought well into the nineteenth century. As has already been seen with Burke, Bentham, Godwin, and Wollstonecraft, theorists showed their conservative or radical colours in taking sides for or against the Revolution. Two other less world-shaking events in this last decade were also to influence methodology well into the next century: the publication of Malthus' *Essay on the Principles of Population* in 1798, and Sinclair's *Statistical Account of Scotland*, 1791–9. This massive survey of Scotland took the moral philosophy with which this chapter began to its logical conclusion in a questionnaire to ascertain "the quantum of happiness" of actual people. A Church of Scotland clergyman, Francis Hutcheson, had first formulated the principle of the greatest happiness of the greatest number. Appropriately the clergy of the Church of Scotland collected data on the economic and social life of their parishes for this first social survey.

Thomas Malthus (1766–1834) was not interested in methodology as such, but virtually everyone in the nineteenth century who was had to address him. The classical economists accepted his pessimistic thesis and worked from it. Others sought a way out of his pessimism in the theory of evolution. Darwin himself got his idea of natural selection from musing over Malthusian images of struggle for survival. Radicals had to answer Malthus' contention that improvement in the human lot was not possible at all, apart from limiting population, before they could put forward their particular remedy.

The nature-versus-nurture debate that raged throughout the nineteenth century dates back to Malthus' thesis that the misery of the labouring class was due to an "inevitable" law of nature. Unfailingly polite to his opponents, the Reverend Thomas Malthus held that Godwin and the other prophets of improvement through social reform were wrong. It was erroneous to attribute all vice and misery to human institutions, as Godwin did. Thomas Paine, similarly, was wrong to attribute all evil to government. Malthus praised Condorcet for his nobility of mind, but held him to have been in error in the possibilities for progress. Robert Owen was a practical man who had done much to better the lot of his workers in New Lanark. Yet an economic system based on equality would not provide enough stimulus to exertion. The rich would become poorer while the poor would not become rich, deduced Malthus. He did not deny the misery of the poor – indeed he was a compassionate man and wished to help – but simply disagreed with the radical theorists as to the cause of poverty and, consequently, the possible remedies.

The major thesis of *An Essay on the Principles of Population* was that the population tended to increase geometrically while the food supply increased at a much lower, if variable, rate. The greatest impediment to human happiness was "the constant tendency in all animated life to increase beyond the nourishment prepared for it."[95] That some human beings would be "exposed to want" appeared from "the inevitable laws of human nature." The owners of surplus produce would hire people in need of food, who would be forced by necessity to offer their labour. "The fund appropriated to the maintenance of labour would be the aggregate quantity of food possessed by the owners of land beyond their own consumption" (316). The happiness or misery of the lower classes depended chiefly on the state of this fund. It was not the fault of human institutions that this suffering occurred. Even in a society constituted on the principles of benevolence, the same tendency would result. Nor should despair follow, for evil existed to create exertion and activity. By the second edition of the *Essay* Malthus was arguing that the lower classes could limit their growth through "moral restraint," the only means they had to increase their wages.

Malthus' essay was based on deductive reasoning from a few assumptions, with data of population and food increases cited in illustration. The year after publishing the first edition he travelled in Europe to collect more data, which were incorporated in subsequent editions. It was only near the end of his life that he became acquainted with Quetelet and his statistical methods, a subject to be taken up in the next chapter. Malthus indeed chaired the meeting that established the statistical section of the British Association for the Advancement of Science. He may have been preparing another version of his essay on this basis, but died before any such project could be realized.

The first mass survey in history was the work of Sir *John Sinclair (1754– 1835)*, M.P., assisted by the clergy of 938 parishes and other "friends of statistical inquiry." The result was *The Statistical Account of Scotland*

(1791–9), twenty-one volumes of economic, social, geographical, and cultural data. The motive was the usual one of moral philosophy: the happiness of the people. Sinclair explained his use of the "new" word "statistics" candidly as a means of attracting public attention. He distinguished his use from the German, which referred to inquiry engaged in by a *state* to ascertain its own strength.[96] William the Conqueror's survey for the Domesday Book had similarly been for purposes of state, not the welfare of the people. Sinclair's survey of Scotland rather was "*for the purpose of ascertaining the quantum of happiness enjoyed by its inhabitants and the means of its future improvements.*" He hoped that his term "statistics" would be "completely naturalised and incorporated with our language."[97]

Sinclair's questionnaire was apparently influenced by one published in 1755 in *The Gentleman's Magazine*, which focused on natural history and antiquities more than the economic and social (the number of hands in manufacturing, the price of manure). Sinclair expanded the social and economic section and retained such questions as "What is the nature of the air? Is it moist or dry, unhealthy or otherwise?" Numerous questions probed the state of farming, roads, fishing, kelp gathering, rents, land ownership, and the number of poor receiving alms. There were questions on the number of murders, suicides, and deaths from want. Some items were open ended: "Are they fond of a military life?" Do they enjoy to a reasonable degree "the comforts of society?" "Are they content?" Finally came "Are there any means by which their condition could be ameliorated?" (1:47) Sinclair then discovered he had omitted some key areas, so sent out a second letter with queries on schools, new housing, and prisoners.

The clergy who obtained information used informants to answer the questions. Many appended documents to their already extensive replies. To reduce non-response Sinclair sent out reminders stressing the importance and usefulness of the study. He also encouraged response by giving the profits from publication to the Society for the Benefit of the Sons of the Clergy. At this time the recipient of a letter had to pay the postage – a considerable sum – so that Sinclair's ability as an M.P. to use the mail at no cost to the recipient was a great advantage. When all else failed he had "Statistical Missionaries" to complete the task. Altogether he was most successful in eliciting co-operation.

The information, grouped by county, was published in the order and form in which it arrived with no attempt at aggregation or other analysis. Nonetheless it has proved to be a gold-mine for researchers ever since. The data of course reflect their source, a socially conservative and dependent clergy. Yet the study probably did help to increase happiness. Some local grievances were redressed, teachers' salaries were raised, and the British government was prompted to begin its own surveys on agriculture.

A study of the poor in England followed in 1794–5, also with respectable clergy as data collectors and a "set of Queries" shorter than Sinclair's. The Scottish survey was the model, the motives "benevolence and curiosity."[98] In the nineteenth century, to which we turn next, studies of the poor, the working class, criminals, prostitutes, and other unfortunates would become a prime concern in the social sciences.

BACK TO THE EMPIRICIST CRITIQUE

There are as many refutations of the critique of empiricism for this period in Britain as there were in France. Fewer methodologists were working in both the natural and social sciences but there is the example of Priestley. Methodologists advocating the search for general laws also turned out to be keen historians – Hume and Macaulay are major examples. Millar, Ferguson, Wortley Montagu, and Wollstonecraft as well qualify here. Hays wrote historical biography, Adam Smith a history of astronomy. Further, the social science/arts boundary was crossed notably by Wortley Montagu and Godwin. Wollstonecraft wrote children's stories, Mary Hays wrote novels.

Many of the advocates of empiricism were militants in good causes. Millar supported workers' education, prison reform, and the anti-slavery movement. A number were early feminists: in addition to Wollstonecraft there were Hutcheson, Hays, Macaulay, Bentham, and Godwin. Wesley encouraged the anti-slavery movement. Wortley Montagu fought the medical establishment on the introduction of smallpox vaccination. As supporters of democratic rights many empiricists, including Macaulay, Wollstonecraft, Godwin, and Bentham, defended the French Revolution. The Utilitarian approach was itself fundamentally egalitarian: the greatest happiness for the greatest number, with everybody – commoners as well as nobles – taken into account. More of the methodologists were middle-class people; a few of the Scots were actually poor. The aristocrat, Wortley Montagu, is an exception. Near the end of his life Smith was much consulted by political leaders. Apart from that neither he nor the other pro-empirical methodologists could be said to much identified with established power. Wesley's politics were conservative, but he also routinely berated the rich. Hume could not get an academic position because of his atheism. None of the women held positions of any sort. Priestley had to leave the country when his house and laboratory were attacked by a mob. The stereotype of empiricists as lackeys of the powerful simply does not hold.

Hutcheson, Bentham, and Macaulay number in a select group as environmentalists. No one at the time made much of including "the whole sensitive creation" in the calculation of utility, except in derision. Looking back we can see the concept as a step in the development of environmental ethics. Those who took sympathy as the basis of ethics were able to see the common bond in sensation. The question was not whether or not animals *reasoned*, although some would grant them that, but did they *suffer*. Those who took the argument further in the nineteenth century, notably John Stuart Mill, began from this point.

6 Sociology: Mainstream, Marxist, and Weberian

Sociology is "a convenient barbarism."   J.S. Mill[1]

The dictum that truth always triumphs over persecution is one of those pleasant falsehoods which men repeat after one another till they pass into commonplaces, but which all experience refutes.

J.S. Mill and Harriet Taylor Mill[2]

Perfect wisdom we can never attain, in sociology or in any other science; but this does not absolve us from using, in our action, the most authoritative exposition, for the time being, of what is known.

Beatrice Webb and Sidney Webb[3]

This is how to proceed if you want to appear German, profound and speculative. For example:

Fact: The cat eats the mouse.

Reflection: Cat = nature, Mouse = nature; consumption of mouse by cat = consumption of nature by nature = self-consumption of nature.

Marx and Engels[4]

> The land belongs to the Russians and French
> The English own the sea.
> But we in the airy realm of dreams
> Hold sovereign mastery.
> Our unity is perfect here,
> Our power beyond dispute;
> The other folk in solid earth
> Have meanwhile taken root.

Marx and Engels[5]

After the French Revolution came the Terror; after the Terror, Napoleon and the Napoleonic wars. For most of Europe the early part of the nineteenth century was a time of great misery. Invasion, occupation, and continuing industrialization and urbanization created brutal conditions. *Laissez-faire* economics prevailed. There was scant public protection for the poor against any kind of economic calamity. According to Malthus and the "political economists" intervention would not help in any event. When Marx and Engels began to write the rich were getting richer and the poor poorer. The lot of the poor did begin to improve at mid-century, at least in Britain and France, but misery and oppression were sufficient for Marx's thesis to be credible throughout the industrial world. Improvements in living conditions in Europe depended on even greater exploitation of the colonial poor. Peasants died in famines during which landlords continued to export crops for profit. Millions emigrated from Europe to the New World. Revolts broke out in the cities in 1820, 1830, 1848, and 1870.

Such conditions prompted national and social movements: utopian socialism, Marxism, co-operation, anarchy, Christian socialism, and movements to abolish serfdom in Russia and slavery in the United States. Social scientists fought the *laissez-faire* political economists, insisting that conditions could be changed, that governments could intervene for good, that there was no "iron law of wages." The great methodological advances of the century were made by people moved in some way or other by "the social question." The uprisings themselves prompted governments to collect data and people previously involved in other sciences to take up social issues. As the plague had prompted the first bills of mortality, so now cholera epidemics provoked new social investigations. But reforms posed their own demands; criminal statistics, for example became necessary when England eliminated hanging for minor thefts. Nationalist movements had a strong social/economic component of people wanting to control their own destinies, choosing meritocracy over aristocracy, mass education over education solely for the elite, wide definitions of citizenship over narrow. The questions raised provoked substantive research more than ever before.

The need to find the right answers inspired methodological reflection and innovation. In Britain reform-minded employers and politicians established statistical societies for the collection of data on social conditions.[6] The London Statistical Society was formed in 1831 and became the Royal Statistical Society in 1887. It is no coincidence that the other main city prompting a similar endeavour was industrial Manchester. The British Association for the Advancement of Science, formed in 1831, set up a statistical section two years later. The instigators were researchers opposed to theoretical economics and wanting real data. At the 1833 meeting of the British Association for the Advancement of Science, the term "scientist" was first used, apparently because members considered "philosopher" too lofty. Note that the official statistical agencies were formed *after* the non-governmental ones, the Board of Trade's statistical office in 1832 and the General Register Office in 1837. Government, as usual, lagged behind the social reformers. Later in the century government was still catching up. Charles Booth conducted his massive survey, *Life and Labour of the People in London*, as a purely private endeavour in the 1880s and 90s. He was given access to census data, however, and his findings stimulated further surveys, official and unofficial. The Fabian Society, founded in 1883, became a major source of research on social problems and alternative ways of organizing society.

Few numerical data were initially collected, and only later did "statistics" come to mean quantitative data. The United States had conducted the world's first census in 1790, and continued with decennial censuses thereafter.

Britain, Sweden, and other European countries soon followed. By the 1820s, many countries were establishing central statistical bureaus. Statistical information, again not necessarily quantitative, was seen as crucial for social reorganization and reconstruction. German economic historians joined with liberal Protestant theologians to study the social question and halt the move to socialism. Professors who researched and wrote about social issues – some of them even were socialists – got their name from their predilection for scientific work on socially relevant issues. Weber, the last methodologist in our history, did his first quantitative research for one of these reform-minded organizations, the Evangelical Social Union.

In the United States the social question similarly prompted methodological innovation along with concrete action. Socialists, social reformers, social workers, and social scientists overlapped considerably. Thus the "social worker" Jane Addams did the first quantitative research in the Chicago school of sociology, a feat usually but erroneously attributed to Burgess and Park in the 1920s and 1930s. By the turn of the century, and even more so in the twentieth century, academic respectability required a stiffening of the boundaries between social reform and academe. At its beginning, however, American sociology was as deeply rooted in the quest for human improvement as was European. The origins of Canadian sociology, a little later, show a similar overlap between concerns for knowledge and its application for good.[7] The first urban sociology dates from Ames' 1897 survey of below-the-hill Montreal, a much scaled-down version of Booth's study which contained no methodological commentary whatsoever.[8]

The French-British connection continued to be important, especially in the first half of the century. French experience was crucial for Mill, as were British and French experience for the Belgian Quetelet. Marx was strongly influenced by the French although he spent little time in France. Now British-American and French-American relations also became important. Tocqueville's travels in the United States are well enough known, those of Harriet Martineau, herself of an old Huguenot family, are not, although she published the first book on how to conduct sociological observations. The Scottish Frances Wright also produced a book with methodological reflections on the United States. Jane Addams got her idea to found Hull House after visiting an English university settlement.

German connections became increasingly important throughout this period. Marx published most of his work in German, and the most intellectual work on socialism was being done in Germany. By late in the century Americans were travelling there. German theology was a major attraction but, as theologians turned more and more to social questions, they continued to draw American students. Albion Small, Lester Ward, and Richard Ely all studied in Germany, then returned to the United States for their academic careers.

The chief theoretical competition to mainstream social science was a socially conservative theory of evolution. Auguste Comte and Herbert Spencer had already proposed theories of societal evolution when Charles Darwin published his *Origin of Species* in 1859. The very popularity of the book sparked interest in their theories. For those inclined to biological models – and there were many – the theory of evolution gave credibility to its social counterpart. Although Spencer and Comte were philosophers of history rather than social scientists, their influence on the social sciences assures their place in this account. Both men used the term "sociology" and Comte can even claim to have been first. For each, however, the theory of evolution was a theoretical framework that was not itself testable. Neither did anything to advance empiricist methodology, though both advocated social science research. The theory of evolution, of course, need not have harsh social corollaries, but both Spencer's and Comte's did. Spencer especially espoused an extreme form of *laissez-faire* "social Darwinism" to limit the role of government to running the police, courts, and armed forces. He is one of the few people who might have looked on Margaret Thatcher as a bleeding heart. A socially conscious theory of evolution later evolved to correct the imbalance. Darwin himself published work to show that co-operation and not just individual struggle plays a role in natural selection. The anarchist Peter Kropotkin gave copious examples in *Mutual Aid* (1902) of co-operation as crucial for both species survival *and* societal/community survival.

The theory of evolution also stimulated a whole new field of eugenics, including an applied eugenics intended to be the answer to Malthus. Eugenics research in turn was the link between the use of probability theory in the natural and social sciences. Francis Galton, Darwin's cousin, not only founded the science of eugenics but actively urged its implementation to improve the human stock. Karl Pearson, who combined socialism, imperialism, and women's rights with his passion for eugenics, pioneered the statistical methods most used in sociological research. George Yule made the first concrete application to social problems, using Booth's data on the London poor. It was late in the eighteenth century that Germaine de Staël had argued that probability theory could be applied to social data, not just dice and stars. It had been a long time coming.

Advances in empiricist methodology came overwhelmingly from people who were politically left of centre. There were numerous conservative philosophers and political theorists at all stages of this period, but they had only the most nebulous interest in empiricism. The one possible exception is Frédéric LePlay, a French mining engineer who for the best humanitarian reasons became interested in the "social question" in the 1830s. LePlay pioneered "direct observation," or the acquisition of social data on families by family members themselves, as opposed to statistics collected by an agency. He, however, excluded the majority of issues of social structure fundamental to most social scientists. Further, while criticizing researchers for generalizing from *a priori* considerations, LePlay was himself flagrantly guilty of it.[9] Thus, from a study of family budgets of European workers he concluded that the only reforms needed were not in social or economic institutions, but of morals. His work was published by the imperial printers with Napoleon's authorization.

The terms "sociology" and "social science" gradually replaced the older "moral philosophy" and "political arithmetic." Comte accused Quetelet of plagiarizing his "social physics," but then went on to coin the "bastard" term (it combines a Latin beginning with a Greek ending) "sociology." Nor did Weber's *Kulturwissenschaft*, with its French/Latin beginning and German ending, cause offence. The great social scientists, however, were not fussy in their usage: Mill used all of "sociology," "social science," and "moral science," as did Weber and Durkheim.

The nineteenth century used the words "positive" and "empirical" and their isms simply and interchangeably to indicate a base in the real, observed world. As "positive law" had denoted a law enacted by a legislature or monarch, as opposed to a divine law or assumed natural law, so "positive facts" signified the results of observation, as opposed, in Saint-Simon's formulation, to "the presumed facts of conjecture." There was no presumption of quantification, nor would there be as Comte, Marx, Mill, and Weber would use these terms. Marx and Engels contrasted "positive" with "speculation and mystification," again stressing the basis in real world observation and with no necessary implication of quantification. "Empirical," from the Greek word for experience, was used interchangeably with "positive." Weber's last set of lectures, exactly a century after Saint-Simon's first use of the term, was a "positive" critique of Marx's materialist interpretation of history, meaning a critique based on what had actually happened.

Women contributors to methodology again appear who have been left out of standard historical accounts. Harriet Taylor's contribution is still contested. For others there is not even the excuse that they did not publish in their own names. Harriet Martineau, author of the first text on social science research, is routinely missing from lists of the "founding fathers" of the subject. Frances Wright, contentious for her radicalism, was well known in her own day, but has since been ignored. Beatrice Webb tends to get brief mention in sociological histories, whereas she deserves full coverage as a major founder. Florence Nightingale is still the heroic war nurse and Jane Addams the pioneer social worker, but both are unrecognized for their early quantitative work in the social sciences.

As we come to the end of this narrative, religious considerations change in character and become less important. There were more agnostics and atheists in the nineteenth century who were frankly looking to the social sciences for an alternative model for understanding the world. Acknowledged agnostics/atheists include such major figures as Marx, Engels, J.S. Mill, Harriet Taylor, and Durkheim. Weber, despite his involvement with liberal Protestants, described himself as "religiously unmusical." For some, especially the early American social scientists like Albion Small, an early religious commitment was gradually replaced by social activism. Yet, if religion was less an independent variable for these methodologists, it became even more significant as a dependent variable. Religion was a major subject of study for Weber, Durkheim, and Charles Booth. Methodologists offended with their heresies great and small. Comte and company tried to found a new religion not unlike that of the Saint-Simonians.

MAINSTREAM SOCIOLOGY AND FRENCH CONNECTIONS

Henri (comte) de Saint-Simon (1760–1825)[10] makes an excellent starting point as a transitional figure. Born an eighteenth-century noble, he fought in the American Revolution and influenced all of mainstream sociology, functionalism, and Marxism. He lived through the French Revolution to address the problems of the industrial age, giving sociology some of its early vocabulary, including "industrialization," "social physiology," and "positivism." Saint-Simon's work is the first to deal with problems we recognize using terms much the same as our own. Thomas More, Bacon, and Diderot dealt with basic economic questions, but with Saint-Simon industrialists, business people, and scientists are recognizable as the prime determiners of a society. There are also major anomalies in Saint-Simon's work. He was an important influence on Marx, but he founded a new religion and saw religion as a means of reconciling class interests. He wrote pieces that could be used as public relations for any chamber of commerce. Yet for all his flattery of industrial leaders he had no influence on them, nor did he succeed in getting their support for his research schemes. International in his interests, Saint-Simon was also an extreme French patriot. Thus Locke and Newton became disciples of Descartes who, in order to be true to empiricism, Saint-Simon turned into a thorough empiricist!

Saint-Simon's methodological work began with rough hints in "Lettres d'un habitant de Genève" (1802). More thorough explication appears in *Introduction aux travaux scientifiques* (1807) and *Mémoire sur la science de l'homme* (1813). The basis of his methodology was the empiricism of Bacon and Locke: sensation was the means to all knowledge, and theories were to be tested against "observed and discussed facts." This held both for the natural and social worlds, between which Saint-Simon's discussion moved easily. There was a real, external world to be explained by causal laws. This, as in Locke, involved no denial of the existence of God, but an insistence that God did not intervene in events after the natural world had been set in operation. The purpose of causal laws was the betterment of humanity. An increase in knowledge would benefit the *whole* society, and indeed was the only activity of such collective utility.

Knowledge of the past was the basis for prediction of the future. Saint-Simon's repeated statement of this point indicates a solid determinism. Moreover, "each effect is necessarily proportionate to its cause."[11] This was not a passive determinism, but one which permitted and indeed encouraged human intervention. Saint-Simon's own work was highly interventionist, as was his methodology: "Real intelligence, positive intelligence, consists in predicting the progress of those phenomena with which we are related, to know how to guarantee ourselves protection from those which are harmful, and to profit from those which are useful. It consists in influencing the progress of those phenomena to turn them to our advantage" (11:182). We study the cause of disturbance to prevent it or make it disappear if we cannot stop it from happening.

Physiology was a science based on observed facts, holding within itself precepts applicable to those facts. "Physiology," or the "science of man," had not yet become positive, that is it was not yet based on facts (11:28). Hence it could not be applied. There had to be both a base in facts *and* connecting laws. Mere facts, isolated data, were not enough. Physiology, including the science of "man," would only become a part of public education when it became positive (11:187). History, which was the physiology of different ages, was still only a collection of facts, and not useful to kings or subjects for the prediction of the future. Clearly, when social physiology joined astronomy, chemistry, physics, and the like, it could be useful in prediction. The best use we could make of our intelligence would be to imprint on the science of "man" a "positive" character, basing it on observations and treating it by the same method as is used in other branches of physiology. When politics became positive, political issues would become questions of "hygiene" and would be dealt with as disinterestedly as other matters (11:29). Saint-Simon was naïve on the possibilities of accomplishment on all these points, expecting too rapid a development of science.

Saint-Simon used the term "positive" simply to signify actual, observed facts as opposed to conjecture. The sciences began by being conjectural because of inadequate examination of insufficient observations. Thus, there was nothing but "the presumed facts of conjecture" (11:26). Reasonings were to be based on facts examined, dismantled, and verified, instead of following the way of the conjectural sciences, where all facts were related to one reasoning. Saint-Simon was perfectly aware of the social context in which facts are gathered and assessed. Another description of "physiology" was the study of the relations of physical and moral phenomena. Again, this was not to oversimplify the relations but to point out the need for serious empirical work instead of mere conjecture. Clearly there is no suggestion of a simplistic economic, psychological, behaviouristic, or other reductionism. Neither is there any notion that values do not count. Indeed Saint-Simon so believed in the importance of values to a society that he founded a religion to promote them.

Saint-Simon's aim was for "general science," which he believed could not be achieved until all the particular sciences comprising it were positive. The fact that there were still only particular sciences was a sign of the weakness of human intelligence. Saint-Simon's notion of "alternance" involves certain distinctions of lasting interest, but poses a number of problems. There are two distinctive modes of thought, the *a priori* and *a posteriori*, from the general to the particular and vice versa respectively.[12] This distinction could also be seen as that between an exterior orientation, or external facts acting from the circumference in, and an internal orientation, or an intuitive perspective acting from the centre out. The two modes were components of a common methodology, both were essential for the growth of knowledge. *A priori* ideas had to be confirmed by observation and observed facts related to general theory. Note the difference with Kant. The two modes were not alternatives, from which to choose one or the other.

Saint-Simon's work was marred by sloppiness, inconsistency, repetition, and failure to follow up good ideas. His writing on the nature of society has all these faults, but is still good enough to make his contribution impressive. "Society" in Saint-Simon's terminology was not confined to the nation-state. Indeed he often referred to "European society" with the idea that the similarities among nations were greater than the differences. Much in advance of his time, he aspired to a real European union, particularly in "Social Physiology," the full title of which, characteristically, is "Physiology applied to the betterment of Social Institutions" (1813). The vitality of Saint-Simon's concept of society is evident:

Society is not a simple agglomeration of living beings in which actions, independent of any final goal, have no other cause than arbitrary individual wills, nor no other result than ephemeral accidents without importance; on the contrary, society is, above all, a real organized machine of which all the parts contribute to the functioning of the whole. The meeting of men constitutes a real BEING, of which the existence is more or less vigorous or tottering, according as its organs accomplish more or less regularly the functions assigned to them.[13]

Society was to be studied as an "animated being," with a different character at different stages of its life, as individuals vary between infancy and old age (10:178). History is then the study of social physiologies at different stages. Saint-Simon, however, made this a philosophy of history, insisting on continuing progress with no interruptions. He used organic, biological images, but these references should not be interpreted in any narrow fashion. He was neither a biological determinist nor a psychological reductionist.

What made Saint-Simon so attractive a forebear to radical sociologists was his stress on movement, anticipation, and purpose.[14] These were characteristics of ordinary people, and the interplay between their wishes and those of their rulers was an important force in history. Saint-Simon's recommended subjects of research included war, revolution, conflict resolution, peace, and the establishment of non-oppressive relations between ruler and ruled. There is some similarity with later functionalism in a notion of inter-related systems changing in accordance with the underlying system of thought.

Saint-Simon was impressed with Bacon's New Atlantis scheme, and his own proposals for the advancement of science were on a similar scale. His support for Napoleon and a substantial state apparatus is quite in keeping with this thinking. Here again the common ground between Marxist and mainstream sociology can be seen for the rationale of the ability of humans to dominate nature. As in nearly all European philosophies to that time, human beings were accorded every right to do with nature what they wanted.

Saint-Simon's views on animals resembled those of the early empiricists but placed even greater stress on continuity. The original differences between humans and animals amounted to only a slight advantage – ours – in intelligence or "organization." This slight advantage increased over time, for it gave humans the ability to weed out dangerous animals and to domesticate others.[15] Any other animal would have done the same; advantage, not any particular human quality, made the difference. Saint-Simon had the temerity even to make animals capable of mathematics, invading the idealist holy of holies. A dog who chooses a morsel of meat, he believed, is doing mathematics.

Marx's father-in-law introduced him to Saint-Simon's ideas. Not only did Saint-Simon's analysis of industry influence Marx, he adopted the terms "positive" and "positive science." Thus "where speculation ends – in real life – there real, positive science begins."[16] Marx, like mainstream social scientists, used the expression interchangeably with "empirical" to refer to actual experience. This makes Saint-Simon a common source to *all* the social science developments of the nineteenth century.

Auguste Comte (1798–1857),[17] author of the term "sociology," must appear in a history of methodology even if, as a philosopher more than a social scientist, he can make only a cameo performance. If Quetelet's place in the history of methodology has been underestimated, Comte's, in my view, has been exaggerated. Nonetheless, he was a dedicated advocate of empiricism, unity of science, and knowledge for the betterment of the world, as he understood it. He influenced other, more important, methodologists. Comte's first publication, in 1819, set the methodological agenda: a plan of scientific work to reorganize society. His massive *Cours de philosophie positive* was published in lesson format in six volumes, nearly one million words, between 1830 and 1842.

Comte's sociology was divided between "static" and "dynamic," ordinary explanatory laws and those explaining changes between epochs respectively. Some form of that distinction, and certainly the terminology, was widely taken up in the discipline. J.S. Mill and Lester Ward are early examples. Underlying all change in the dynamic sphere was Comte's division of all history – in *every* society – into three periods. All people began to formulate their theories or laws with a theological or "fictitious" type of explanation, then to move successively to a metaphysical or "abstract" type, finally to a scientific or "positive" type of law. The *Cours de philosophie positive* followed this order in setting out the history of the acquisition of human knowledge. Comte saw this three-fold division as arising from the nature of the human mind itself. The discovery was "a grand fundamental law" to which all things were subjected by "invariable necessity." Moreover, this law seemed to have been "solidly established" by "rational evidence furnished by knowledge of our own organization" and "historical verification resulting from an attentive examination of the past."[18]

Comte was a major contributor to the understanding – or misunderstanding – of the social sciences as based on the natural sciences and best modelled after them. His own education was in the natural sciences, and he recommended that process of discovery. The *Cours* began with a detailed overview of the state of knowledge in physics, chemistry, and biology before going on, volumes later, to the social. Social phenomena were founded, it was argued, on the "invariable necessities" of physical organization. The social scientist consequently had first to consider biological factors, then historical ones.

Nonetheless Comte did not subscribe to an overbearing determinism.[19] As Marx would later become better known for asserting, people could within limits make their own history. People could at least modify those limits' tendencies or mode of effect, short of changing their basic nature and direction. To modify phenomena, in turn, required knowledge of the natural laws that determined them.[20] This knowledge was necessary for human advancement, which itself could only be introduced gradually.

Comte is also partially responsible for the long-lasting association of sociology and conservative political theory. He was deeply influenced by the horrifying aftermath of the French Revolution. He came to believe that the greatest problems of his time were *moral*, not political. Late in his life he issued an appeal to conservatives.[21] Comte also sought to provide a rallying point for those who had given up on the old faith. His positivism over time became a new religion, complete with a catechism, religious calendar, and saints' days.

Alexis de Tocqueville (1805–59)[22] and his friend Gustave de Beaumont were young, eligible bachelors when they made their historic trip to the United States in 1831, ostensibly to study penitentiaries and especially solitary confinement. Both were aristocrats with introductions to the highest society; Beaumont was a cousin of Lafayette. Both were liberals, or aristocrats who had accepted defeat. Each had reason to get away from the turmoil of France, especially Tocqueville, who had offended family and friends by swearing loyalty to the new Orleanist king. Tocqueville was a junior magistrate, Beaumont a junior prosecutor when they proposed their trip. They asked only for leaves of absence – they would pay their own way – and official standing so as to be able to visit the various prisons. In fact they got better access to American prisons than they had ever got to French. They did their duty on their official project, reading the bulky documents made available to them, and even interviewing sixty-three prisoners, a first in criminological history. Beaumont wrote most of their report, for Tocqueville went into a depression on return to France in 1832.

Tocqueville's celebrated work, *Democracy in America* (1835), conveyed one great message: the desirability and inevitability of democracy. Yet, for all its vigour, influence, and charm it is scarcely social science. Its citation by eminent social scientists from Mill to Harold Laski is because of its liberal, egalitarian philosophy, not its methodology.[23] To be fair, Tocqueville used documents, official and unofficial, as well as intelligent observers. He explained that he had consulted several sources when a point was especially important or doubtful. He had never "knowingly molded facts to ideas, instead of ideas to facts."[24] This is hardly advanced methodology, however, and his most important conclusions grew out of opinions he held before his travels. Before he ever set foot in the U.S. Tocqueville believed that the trend to democracy was universal. Indeed, the real purpose of the trip was to learn about democracy in the country in which it was the most advanced, the better to be able to forestall its ill effects in France.

Tocqueville's understanding of the French Revolution was much like de Staël's, that the people were not ready for democracy; it was his mission to promote the changes in laws, customs, and morals that would make the democratic revolution beneficial. In writing about America Tocqueville always had Europe in mind. His own introduction gave the game away, explaining that *Democracy in America* was "written under the influence of a religious awe" from "that irresistible revolution" advancing everywhere despite obstacles (1:6). Tocqueville maintained that one could "scarcely find a single great event of the last seven hundred years that has not promoted equality of condition" (1:5). It was a "providential fact," universal and lasting, eluding all human interference.

However much Tocqueville was influenced by his own preconceptions, many of his insights have proved to be accurate. He was sensitive to the dangers of democracy. His analysis of the "tyranny of the majority" is still apt. His descriptions of natives and blacks are sensitive and vivid. He understood that racial differences posed a problem quite apart from slavery. "The most formidable of all the ills that threaten the future of the Union arises from the presence of a black population upon its territory" (1:356). He was optimistic about the abolition of slavery, as would be his fellow travellers to the United States (1:381). His discussion of women, on the other hand, was both insulting and incorrect. He even described wives as cheerfully accepting their inequality and lack of freedom, neither of which he saw as violating the Constitution (2:211). There is no hint that the United States was soon to produce the largest and most powerful suffrage movement in the world. But Tocqueville's errors seem not to have been held against him. (In the copy of *Democracy in America* I consulted in the Bibliothèque Nationale in 1989, the pages for the brief chapter on women were uncut!)

Leftists have appreciated Tocqueville's treatment of equality as not only inevitable but good. "A state of equality is perhaps less elevated, but it is more just: and its justice constitutes its greatness and its beauty" (1:333). While many political theorists, notably on the right, have feared equality for possible illiberalism, Tocqueville said precisely the opposite (2:287). He might have been inconsistent in his use of the term "democracy," sometimes meaning a tendency to levelling in conditions, sometimes the vote for all men, but the understanding was always positive. "It appears to me beyond a doubt that, sooner or later, we shall arrive, like the Americans, at an almost complete equality of condition" (1:14).

Like the Bible, *Democracy in America* can be quoted on both sides of many arguments. For all its love of democracy it worries about the "rabble" in towns. It warns of the danger of too great a concentration of wealth and power, "industrial feudalism," yet it also chastises the poor for their vices: "The poor man retains the prejudices of his forefathers without their faith, and their ignorance without their virtue" (1:11). Intellectuals can use Tocqueville to complain of the lack of independence of mind and real freedom of discussion. Geographers, however, seem not to quote Tocqueville's puzzling finding that the Americans have no neighbours, and hence no great wars or financial crises (1:289). The book's last words left the future open rather than determined. "Mankind" was not made entirely independent or free, but the fatal circle drawn around "every man" and around communities is a wide one (2:334).

RESEARCH TECHNIQUES AND
PASSIONATE STATISTICS

How to Observe Morals and Manners (1838) might be "the first book on the methodology of social research."[25] The term "sociology" was not yet in use, but there is no doubt that *Harriet Martineau (1802–76)*[26] had in mind a distinct social science discipline. Martineau earned her living as a journalist, publishing more than fifty books and 1600 articles on an enormous range of issues. Her *Illustrations of Political Economy* (1832) long outsold the Mills' *Principles of Political Economy*. Comte liked her free translation of his *Cours de philosophie positive* so much he had it retranslated into French. She also published pamphlets, history, her autobiography, and numerous novels.

In 1834, when Tocqueville was back in France writing *Democracy in America*, Martineau left on her more extensive trip (two years compared with his nine months) to the U.S. On the ship she wrote the first draft of her methodology, published in 1838 as *How to Observe Morals and Manners*. Her "Essays on the Art of Thinking" (1836) was an attempt to make empirical methodology accessible to all – legislators and ordinary citizens as well as scientific investigators.

In her methodology Martineau stressed that there were two parties to the work of observation: the observed and the observer. The mind of the observer, as the research instrument, was as essential as the material.[27] The observer must not be perplexed or disgusted by what was observed, for "every prejudice ... dims or distorts whatever the eye looks upon" (40). One had not only to overcome prejudice but be sympathetic to the person observed. Without sympathy the most important things would be hidden and symbols would seem absurd. Attention had to be given both to the observation of facts and the establishment of organizing principles for them (14). Good planning was required, including the preparation of questions. The "set of queries" should include "every great class of facts" connected with the condition of the people (232). A journal should be kept for recording and reflecting on the facts. The work of generalization, though, should be deferred until the researcher returned home. A notebook should always be at hand for recording facts and sketches. Martineau's practical advice ended with the caution that "mechanical methods are nothing but in proportion to the power which uses them" (236).

To understand social institutions one should begin by first observing *things* and then commenting on them. Thus for religion one should visit the various temples, noting their location, number, diversity, and theological opinions (63). There was no better place to study the morality of a people than in cemeteries, for "the brief language of the dead will teach ... more than the longest discourses of the living" (105). Gravestone inscriptions indicated whether a people's values were military or commercial. Suicide was an indication of the state of prevalent sentiments, and therefore a key to understanding a society. The comparative ages of the dead, found in burial grounds and civic registers, revealed the state of health and force of various diseases. The health of a community, in turn, was an "almost unfailing" index of its morals (161). "A faithful register of births, marriages, and deaths" was needed as a test of both national morals and welfare. Treatment of the guilty yielded "the principles and views of governments and people upon vice, its causes and remedies." It was "one of the strongest evidences as to the general moral notions of society" (129).

The researcher had to turn to the arts, especially songs, to learn what a society's "fiercest passions" and first lessons of virtue were. Here Martineau argued reciprocal influences. "Popular songs are both the cause and effect of general morals: that they are first formed, and then react" (134). In both respects they were an index of dominant morals. Books showed the spirit of a people while newspapers indicated political will, any restraints of which should be noted. Rural and urban occupations had to be studied. The artisan population was crucial, for it indicated the future; the great ideas of equal rights and popular representation had come from it.

Martineau's assessment of the critical role of manufacturing has stood the test of time. She predicted that Russia would be "despotically governed as long as she has no manufactures." England and the United States had been saved by the extent of their manufacturing from "retrograding" into feudalism (148). Generally speaking Martineau's causal explanations were in the ancient empiricist tradition, beginning with physical characteristics: geography, especially the nature of the soil, affected a society's employment possibilities, which in turn shaped the mental and moral state of its inhabitants. The investigator should observe the country's markets, land tenure system, agriculture, manufacturing, and commerce. The class system, especially whether two-fold or a gradation, was important. "Where there are only two, proprietors and labourers, the Idea of Liberty is deficient or absent" (190). Martineau herself saw the gradations *increasing* a decade before Marx and Engels predicted, incorrectly, the reverse.

Martineau's aim in *Society in America* (1837) was to compare the existing state of U.S. society with the principles on which it was professedly founded, "thus testing Institutions, Morals, and Manners by an indisputable, instead of an arbitrary standard."[28] Both English and American readers, she argued, could then examine the book from the same vantage point. She acknowledged the obligation of researchers to state how their data had been collected in order to permit assessment and replication. Readers could judge for themselves "what my testimony is worth" and were invited to correct "all errors of fact." As to "matters of opinion," she held herself to be "an equal judge" with others. She claimed to have gone to America with as unprejudiced a mind as possible, admitting only a bias to democratic institutions. She emphatically declined the "office of censor," to "put praise and blame as nearly as possible out of the question" (48). Despite these protests of ethical neutrality, however, she found occasions for both praise and blame. Martineau had superb access to people, meeting the president and former president, members of the Cabinet, Supreme Court justices, state legislators, and society high and low. She visited cotton factories, Indian reserves, slave plantations, farms, a Shaker community, universities, prisons, hospitals, and insane asylums. She attended slave auctions, abolition meetings, weddings, rural fairs, and Fourth of July celebrations.

Martineau allocated considerable space to the status of women, drawing the obvious parallels with slavery as a violation of the constitutional principles of equality and consent of the governed. "Equal rights of both halves of the human race" was "the true democratic principle which can never be seriously controverted, and only for a short time evaded" (128). Martineau seemed to expect that slaves would get their freedom before women the vote, but seems not to have realized just how far away – not until 1920 – the latter would be. In spite of the weakness of the abolition movement and the hostility to it, both of which she described well, Martineau was convinced that abolition would succeed. Slavery had become an anomaly, a fundamental contradiction of American democracy and egalitarian values (86). "Its doom is therefore sealed; and its duration now is merely a question of time" (93). Nearly a century later Gunnar Myrdal would make and receive credit for the same argument in *An American Dilemma*. This focus on morals never, however, made Martineau naïve about financial interests. Slavery was bound up with the "worldly interests of the minority" (117). It would take time to awaken the will of the majority, but that would happen.

Martineau was well known, if often insulted by reviewers, in her own day.[29] *Society in America* influenced English opinion on the United States.[30] Her emphasis on values as causal agents made her a precursor of functionalism. The attention she paid to economic variables, especially class considerations, make her more than a functionalist, indeed give her a breadth or multi-dimensionality that the discipline could well have used. Sadly Martineau is now more known for her translation of Comte than for her own work.

With *Adolphe Quetelet (1796–1874)*[31] we begin to see data analyses similar to those of today. It was Quetelet who took up the challenge of Condorcet and de Staël to operationalize variables, which he did with care and imagination. He did not collect new data but got a great deal more than others had out of existing published sources, developing both longitudinal and cross-sectional analyses. He first used what have become known as "the standard demographic variables," controlling for age, sex, region, occupation, and religion in his studies. He helped design the first censuses in Europe. That his own country, Belgium, led in centralized statistical collection is largely due to his efforts. Quetelet both exemplified and was committed to the unity of science; he was an astronomer, a mathematician, and a social scientist. Yet he breaks all the stereotypes of the physical scientist, for his own earliest interests were in the arts. His first statistical work derives from his studies of anatomy for sculpting.

Quetelet was a reformer committed to the use of social knowledge for the betterment of society. The "social physics" of his book titles implies no simplistic determinism or denial of purpose. His "average man" concept similarly signals no tendency to sterile abstraction. Rather it reflects the ideal that all people are citizens and worthy of inclusion in study. He was a democrat and nationalist. I treat him as a significant contributor to the development of mainstream empiricism because of his work on probability theory and the practicalities of statistics collection, a conclusion supported by the reactions of two of his better-known contemporaries. Marx praised *Physique sociale* as "excellent and learned work" and regretted that illness prevented Quetelet from expanding it; Comte condemned it as an abuse of the term he claimed to have coined, and "mere statistics."[32]

After attending the inaugural meeting of the statistics section of the British Association for the Advancement of Science in Cambridge in 1834, Quetelet brought out his first book on social science, *Sur l'homme et le développement de ses facultés ou Essai de physique sociale*. This first edition (1835) was a compilation and expansion of his various statistical analyses. An English version was published in 1842; in it Quetelet defended himself against accusations of fatalism and materialism. His *Letters on the Theory of Probability* followed in 1846, *Système social* in 1848, and a revised, expanded edition of the first book in 1869, with the subtitle promoted to main title: *Physique sociale*.

We would call much of Quetelet's work "demography," but his prime interest and probably his best work was in criminology. Here as elsewhere he made variables go a long way. Age had its effect on crime through the "passions" and "energy" of people at different stages of their life.[33] Thus a simple, objective variable, age, could represent complicated theoretical ideas. The same held for economic data, where Quetelet found that crime rates were high where there were great inequalities of wealth. He accordingly concluded that relative deprivation rather than poverty as such led to crime. Sudden changes in economic conditions had a similar effect, for people accustomed to easier conditions turned to crime more than those who had known nothing but misery.[34] Quetelet examined certain variables while controlling for others. Thus he showed that the effect of climate on crime disappeared when national differences were taken into account. Differences by sex similarly declined with controls for education.

What data actually represented and how they were shaped by the means used to collect them were major questions for Quetelet. He considered how the police and courts influenced crime statistics. There were obvious differences between "known" crimes or "judged" crimes and actually "committed" offences. Yet crime could still be studied with known offences only, for they could be assumed to be a fixed proportion of the real number. His *Letters on Probability* were old-fashioned in style – advice to a reigning duke – but contained advanced statistical theory and its practical application. In them Quetelet warned against the numerous possibilities of error and bias, noting the different directions of bias in data collected by industry and government. He urged careful statistical analysis of all the results of all government initiatives, especially those involving budgetary expenditures. He described the perils of data collection on issues of morality and exclaimed at the extent of errors committed in studying poverty. In short, he showed a sophisticated understanding of the political context of data collection and is an early counter example to the charges of naïvety made by critical school adherents and postmodernists.

Quetelet developed the classic interpretation of the law of large numbers. In literature and art the individual was the focus of study, in social questions the focus was society. "The moral causes that leave their trace on social phenomena are inherent in the nation and not in individuals" (2:321). The laws of society determined through study did not apply to individuals. Tables of mortality, for example, could accurately predict the number of deaths in a year, but not who would die. Individuals had a real, if limited, sphere for action. Members of the social body constantly submitted to necessary causes but, using the energy of their intellectual faculties, in some way mastered these causes to modify their effects and seek to bring themselves to a better state (1:98). Since there was something called "free will," moral facts would be different from physical.[35] Important as free will was for the individual, however, individual particularities neutralized each other. *"Free will obliterates itself and remains without effect when observations are extended over a large number of individuals."*[36]

Quetelet's ambitions for the "average man" concept as a focus for social analysis were not fulfilled. By tracking the average man over time trends could be ascertained; from these trends laws could be formulated and predictions made. In fact theorists did not find the concept helpful and it became another false start in methodology. Marx used the concept in *Capital* to argue the feasibility of measuring inputs of labour for the labour theory of value.

Quetelet preferred the term "hypothesis" to "cause" to indicate that only probable knowledge of causes was possible (2:7). It is important that the "action of causes" was unknown for *both* physical and moral causes. The discovery of causes was the same for physical, social, or moral matters, for all were based on the weight of evidence and the validity of logical arguments. There were no guarantees of truth for any type of causation. Quetelet sought to "rise to an appreciation of the causes" by "the seizure of facts."[37] Quetelet's treatment of the constancy of nature is reminiscent of the early empiricist tradition. "In given circumstances, and under the influence of the same causes, we may reckon upon witnessing the repetition of the same effects." Yet this did not imply any fatalism, for people could intervene to change circumstances. "Laws, education and religion exercise a salutary influence on society, and ... moral causes have their certain effects" (vii). That the causes of ills like crime could themselves be altered indeed gave "new proof" of the wisdom of the Creator: "If the causes were changed, the effects would necessarily be modified. As laws and the principles of religion are influencing causes, I have then not only the hope, but ... the positive conviction that society may be ameliorated and reformed" (vii).

Quetelet's objective was always reformist. When he marvelled at the regularities in and predictability of crime statistics, "the budget of crime," he quickly remarked on the need to reduce recourse to prisons, workhouses, and the scaffold (96). It was possible to improve people, their institutions, habits, the state of their enlightenment, and, in general, anything that influences their manner of being. The "active causes" of the problem had to be discerned to develop the most effective means of change. The ability of people to react to circumstances and to change themselves was one on the noblest of human attributes. Individuals in a social body were subject to the necessity of causes, but also used all the energy of their intellectual faculties to master those causes, modify their effects, and bring themselves to a better state. Quetelet rejected any *a priori* answer to the question of whether moral and intellectual actions were subject to laws. That depended on one's point of view, as experience showed. Close up one would see only rain drops, from a distance the rainbow, and Quetelet was always the student of the rainbow.

Quetelet's influence as a theorist of probability has been questioned,[38] but his key role in the development of the field of statistics is beyond dispute. His criminological work was actually replicated in other countries. Buckle's popular *History of Civilisation* disseminated his ideas to a wide readership. Quetelet took part in the first meeting of the statistics section of the British Association for the Advancement of Science, an organization dominated by natural scientists hostile to social science. There he recommended the creation of a separate statistical association, which was promptly done.[39] The association's journal became a major forum for statistical exchange. Prince Albert became the society's first and loyal patron. At Quetelet's invitation he opened the International Statistical Congress held in London in 1860, at which he urged the use of statistics in public administration. During the congress, incidentally, Quetelet visited his great admirer, Florence Nightingale, herself a major proponent of statistics in public health administration. Nightingale did not attend, but sent her papers and invited major participants to her home for discussions.

Florence Nightingale (1820–1910)[40] had the reforming zeal and superb mind for administration to give her an unusual appreciation for Quetelet's methodology. For her Quetelet was no less than "the founder of the most important science in the whole world," upon which depended every other and each art.[41] On his death she not only wrote an "In Memoriam" praising him but tried to promulgate his ideas. The best means would be to establish a statistical chair or readership at Oxford University on "Social Physics and their practical application."[42] She was prepared to give £2,000 of her own to this end, commissioning Francis Galton to see to the organization. Unfortunately Galton was prepared to use the money on a few essays, and Nightingale withdrew her offer.

Nightingale had a formidable list of potential research topics for the holder of a chair in social physics:

the effects of schooling, secondary, night schools, and other state-funded; how much learning was retained in adulthood?

the results of legal punishments in actually deterring crime; does education decrease crime or only teach how to escape conviction?

the effects of charity and workhouses, including the proportion of children pauperized and de-pauperized by workhouses; how much poverty was intergenerational?

the effect of colonial policy; were the people of India growing richer or poorer? Were they better or worse fed and clothed, their crafts and trades encouraged or ruined under British rule?[43]

Yet the British government uses the statistics in its possession only to "deal damnation" across the floor of the House of Commons.

Nightingale was only thirty-four when, in 1854, she set out for the Crimea to head the nursing services for the British Army. There, apart from meeting all the challenges of war, disease, and poor provisions, she battled incompetent and complacent medical administrators. On her return to England she became an unofficial consultant to the War Office and later for other government departments as well. She became an expert on hospital administration and India as well as transforming the ill-paying and ill-esteemed occupation of nursing to the beginnings of a profession.

While Nightingale actually published little of her considerable writing, she sometimes had papers privately printed for limited circulation. Her *Suggestions for Thought* (1860), if repetitive and poorly organized, sets out her basic philosophy/religion of life. She insisted on dedicating it to the Artizans of England, although both Mill and her friend Benjamin Jowett, Master of Balliol, told her it would interest other people as well.

On her return from the Crimea Nightingale pressed for the establishment of a royal commission to investigate the sanitary state of the British Army. She lobbied for the appointment of appropriate members and provided the commission with her own observations and analysis. She then wrote and privately published her "Contribution to the Sanitary History of the

British Army" (1859), which gives a succinct analysis of the key points and an ingenious depiction of the data.[44] Nightingale's superb visual portrayals of data in pie charts manage to convey both time (the wedges were by month of the war) and to make relevant comparisons – the centre core gave death rates for young males in Manchester, an unhealthy English city, the next circles the death rates for soldiers in the Crimea from wounds and infectious diseases separately. It is clear that, over time, as sanitary conditions were improved, deaths from infectious diseases declined markedly until they actually fell below those of the civilian population.

Harriet Martineau reprinted the diagrams in *England and her Soldiers*, a longer, popular account of this preventive medicine/health promotion approach. Nightingale collaborated behind the scenes on this book, supplying Martineau with the necessary reports and then going over the final text to check for accuracy. Nightingale then offered to buy twenty pounds' worth of copies so that one could be sent to each regiment. The British Army refused permission, however, so she had copies sent instead to local libraries. The Army command feared that the book would make the soldiers "discontented"; that, presumably, was Nightingale's intention.[45]

Nightingale next called for evaluative studies to be undertaken on a routine basis. She deplored the haphazard way social policy was originally determined, and then either altered or retained. "*A government in modifying its laws, especially its financial laws, should collect with care documents to prove ... whether the results obtained have answered their expectation.*"[46] The means of doing this was political science, which should become an exact science (350). Decisions should not be made on the basis of "guesswork," or "what the Germans call intuition" (73). The logical Nightingale considered it strange that millions of pounds should be spent annually without anyone knowing the results. She further warned that good intentions did not always lead to the desired results. The best philanthropist might be doing harm rather than good. "A Note on Pauperism" (1869) pointed out how the Poor Law, designed for an agricultural age, actually increased the pauperism it was intended to relieve. Elsewhere Nightingale called for data to be collected on good happenings – heroism and public virtue – not just crime and death. Echoing Quetelet's "budget of crime" she proposed a "Chancellor of the Exchequer & Budget for Morality."[47]

Nightingale had a mind for practical detail as well as for large questions. Her advice on the 1861 Census included that a column be added on sickness. "In this way we should have a Return of the whole Sick & Diseases in the United Kingdom for one spring day, which would give a good average idea of the Sanitary state of all classes of the population."[48] Her advice was not acted on, although decades later health surveys began to be undertaken. Well aware of class differences in susceptibility to illness, she urged controls for social class in analyzing medical data. Differences in childbirth mortality by institution, for example, might really be due to class differences. Hence death rates should be calculated by class and type of institution.[49]

A letter Nightingale sent to the International Statistical Congress in 1860, which was read by the great reformer Lord Shaftesbury, asked delegates to take to the next meeting statistics on any examples of the diminution of mortality and disease and the savings from sanitary measures. In the letter she gave an example of improved housing's resulting in substantial reductions in mortality. Always the activist, Nightingale called for publication of the data, stressing the savings governments could make by reducing crime, disease, and mortality.

Nightingale's book on mortality in childbirth, *Introductory Notes on Lying-in Institutions* (1871), is a superb example of the evaluative research she advocated. This classic piece of analysis has been ignored in the social science literature, just as her concrete recommendations, which would have saved thousands of women's lives, were ignored by medical authorities. She took on the subject when deaths from puerperal fever rose in a maternity ward she had established for training midwives. Although the rates were no worse than those of many hospitals in Europe she closed the ward. Nightingale then sought to turn "past experience to best account" by extracting the "leading principles" for application.[50] First she had to establish the "real normal death rates" for women in childbirth (1). Then she compared the rates by institution to ascertain if any cause predominated and why. This was no easy task, but Nightingale eventually found data, British and European, from a variety of institutions and home births. The statistics pointed to one truth "namely, that there is a large amount of preventible mortality in midwifery practice, and that, as a general rule, the mortality is far, far greater in lying-in hospitals than among women lying-in at home" (3). She discovered that mortality rates were better for women giving birth in workhouses even than in maternity wards attached to general hospitals, despite the fact that workhouse women were desperately poor and often in bad health. Her conclusions include a series of detailed recommendations following logically from the data.

Nightingale departed from Quetelet on only one fundamental point of methodology, the ability of people to control their own destiny. Here she found Quetelet too pessimistic. By using the laws of society established by induction, or applying his science, people *could* intervene to modify the social state. "God's laws" were simply how God governed, and we could use these same laws when we understood them.[51] Indeed, "the Laws of the Moral & Physical existence of man so act & re-act upon one another that it appears as tho' their express purpose were thus to put power into man's hands" (344). This took care of the problem of free will, which Nightingale viewed as a variable, like intellect.[52]

"Physical monstrosities tend to disappear ... plague, pestilence & famine. Shall not moral monstrosities be also made to disappear when their causes become known?" (108) The causes of the Great Plague of London were now perfectly well known, so that another like it would be impossible. "Shall it not be so with Moral Pestilences?" The same laws that made eclipses predictable also made history predictable. Prone as she was to using biological analogies, though, Nightingale was no advocate of biological explanations of society. She dismissed the scientific foundations of Darwinism with sarcasm: "I deny altogether the 'careful' observation. They have constructed a circle on 2 or 3 points in the circumference & all the points which would not come in to that circumference they have put out of Court" (17). Against the survival of the fittest she pointed out that "the devoted unselfish workers for Humanity do not perpetuate themselves" while "the puny, selfish workers for themselves have large families."[53]

Yet Darwinism was only "a very venial sin" and not "a sin against the Holy Ghost." *That* sin was using the experience of the past "not as a ground for doing something but for doing nothing."[54] "Bewailing our desperate wickedness" would not bring reform but the new Moral World could be grown practically through the discovery of its laws.[55] That Nightingale lost most of her battles with bureaucrats is not the point. The "passionate statistician" was an early voice for rationality in public administration, using the methods of the social sciences.

EMPIRICISM AND WOMEN'S RIGHTS

No one in the English-speaking world had more influence in shaping nineteenth-century empiricism than *John Stuart Mill (1806–73)*.[56] Brought up in the Utilitarianism of his father and Jeremy Bentham, Mill was to alter it significantly. Where James Mill had strayed into abstraction and deduction, John Stuart Mill returned to ordinary inductivist empiricism. With his partnership to *Harriet Taylor (1807–58)*,[57] whom he married in 1851, equality for women became a prime concern. The narrow and deadening calculation of individual pleasure and pain was replaced with insights into all of society and its traditions. Mill was also one of the earliest writers, the first male writer to my knowledge, to comment on the sexism of language. While he used "mankind" and "man" in the conventional way, he did so apologetically. A footnote in *A System of Logic* (1843) explained that the generic "he" was "more than a defect in language," prolonging the "almost universal habit of thinking and speaking of one-half of the human species as the whole."[58] Mill and Taylor Mill took great pains in "On Liberty" to use inclusive language.

The social science of Mill and Taylor Mill was liberal and reformist, as most social science before them had been and would be after them. Their stance was progressive in rejecting reactionary fatalism but sceptical about the benefits of material "progress." The stereotype of materialist methodologists as crassly unaware of anything but material objects here again fails. Another stereotype cracks with Mill's lesser-known ecological concerns, including a denunciation of monoculture and a plea for what we would call wilderness protection. The "saint of rationalism" and heir of Utilitarianism believed that people ought not to live only with their own kind. Finally, the Mill-Taylor collaboration is unique in methodological history. They achieved an unprecedented and remarkably productive working relationship of equals. Mill himself realized that the male sex in general could not tolerate, in his own words, "the idea of living with an equal."[59]

Opinions of the extent, duration, and quality of Harriet Taylor's influence on Mill vary enormously. Some writers say it was largely negative but mercifully negligible; these people believe that Mill's best work was done before the collaboration began and after his wife's death.[60] John Robson holds that Taylor inspired Mill, gave him ideas, and influenced the content of his work but "was not, in any meaningful sense, the 'joint author' of his works."[61] Virtually all critics agree that Harriet Taylor was the socialist of the two, and a few see her as the influence also on the extreme individualism of "On Liberty." Himmelfarb concluded that she gave "impulse and direction" to Mill's choice of subject matter and line of attack, but that the actual crafting was largely his.[62] Mill may have been overly enthusiastic in some of the credit he gave his wife, but since her name never appeared on a title page he had something to make up for. Still, all but the most ardent feminists find much fault in Taylor's work. Even Himmelfarb, who credited Taylor Mill with substantial, and largely positive, influence, concluded that she had a "dogmatic and mediocre" mind.[63] The final volume of the University of Toronto Press's Collected Works of John Stuart Mill gives Taylor Mill qualified "joint author" status for the "On liberty," part of Principles of Political Economy, and many letters to the editor on women's issues.[64]

One way to judge Taylor is to read what she published before her marriage and collaboration. Apart from a few poems, which show talent, there are a number of review articles on such subjects as the French Revolution of 1830, Mirabeau, Hampden, and impressions of the United States. All were published anonymously in 1832 in the Unitarian journal The Monthly Repository.[65] Short pieces, they show vigorous style, firm judgments, and liberal views. Where Mill meandered and qualified, Taylor was witty and brisk. That she was only twenty-five and had had little education makes the accomplishment all that much more remarkable. These articles alone – and her later feminist articles strengthen the case – make it perfectly believable that Harriet Taylor was a significant collaborator with Mill in content and style.

Mill's first methodological work, A System of Logic, was written 1831– 41 and published in 1843. It was the last major work he wrote without

Harriet Taylor's collaboration. The first edition of the jointly written *Principles of Political Economy* followed in 1848. The essay "On Liberty," again very much a joint work, was published in 1859 after Harriet Taylor's death. *Utilitarianism* appeared in 1861, like many Mill works first in a journal, later as a book. *An Examination of Sir William Hamilton's Philosophy*, another technical, methodological work appeared in 1865. Mill produced numerous papers on economics, politics, ethical and social questions, ancient Greek philosophy, French history, and even religion at various stages of his long and productive life. All are now available in an excellent University of Toronto Press critical edition.

Harriet Taylor was clearly the source of Mill's feminism. They early exchanged essays on marriage and divorce which show him to have been sentimental and vague where she was precise and consistently egalitarian.[66] In the 1840s Taylor wrote a paper or pamphlet on women's suffrage that formed the basis of "The Enfranchisement of Women" essay Mill published in 1851. Mill's *Autobiography* called it a "joint production," with his own share being "little more than that of an editor and amanuensis" (91). When Mill wrote the longer essay, "The Subjection of Women," in 1860–1, he used much the same line of argument and again credited his wife with the ideas.[67]

When writing *A System of Logic* Mill was acutely conscious of the minority status of British empiricism.[68] The reaction to Locke and Hume by Reid and the "common sense" school in Britain and by Kant on the Continent had been enormously successful. Mill hoped that "the German or *a priori* view of human knowledge" would diminish in influence but considered that unlikely. While he never claimed originality for his method, he did propose that it would supply what was lacking, "a text book of the opposite doctrine."[69] It was not a new theory but an embodiment and systemization of the best ideas available. During a major rewrite he read Whewell's *Philosophy of the Inductive Sciences*, a full treatment of the subject by an antagonist, which gave him a convenient, recent, idealist model to attack (1:231).

The enemy throughout Mill's methodology was "the intuitive approach," the "fallacy" responsible for two thirds of bad philosophy, an "instrument devised for consecrating all deep-seated prejudices," also known as the German or *a priori* view of human knowledge. A true philosophy might have great or little practical impact, but it was "hardly possible to exaggerate the mischief of a false one." The notion that truths might be known "by intuition or consciousness, independently of observation and experience, is, I am persuaded ... the great intellectual support of false doctrines and bad institutions" (1:233).

Descartes, Spinoza, Leibniz, and the German metaphysical philosophy emanating from them were all severely taken to task. Mill especially disliked the presumption that the natural order had somehow to suit human understanding of it. He gave numerous instances of how this led to error, for example that the planets must move in circular orbits because these were the simplest.[70] In the tradition of Locke, and against Kant, Mill maintained that "our general ideas contain nothing but what has been put into them, either by passive experience, or by our active habits of thought; and the metaphysicians in all ages, who have attempted to construct the laws of the universe by reasoning from our supposed necessities of thought, have always proceeded, and only could proceed, by laboriously finding in their own minds what they themselves had formerly put there" (8:752).

In *A System of Logic* laws of nature are defined as uniformities reduced to their most simple expression. The real cause was the whole of the antecedents, yet the particular condition was treated as the cause, even if its share in the matter might be superficial. Chance was antithetical to law. If accurate knowledge were available at every stage it would be at least abstractly possible to foretell all effects. This was the object of all science. Mill shared the then standard view that prediction would be less exact in the moral than the physical sciences. Induction, however, could never be complete and laws would never fully correspond to real processes. That provisional truths only were possible prevented Mill from outlining a complete sociology. His humility here, concluded Robson, was a direct consequence of his sceptical induction. Human affairs were too complex to claim more.[71]

As had most other empiricists, Mill understood historical explanation to be part of the social sciences and subject to general laws. Uniform laws could be generalized from historical facts; here, as in any other deductive science, "statistics" would provide verification. There was simply no demarcation between historical and other social sciences in Mill's framework. Rather there was a delineation within the historical category for use of the "inverse deductive method" between two different kinds of law. The first was difficult enough: to determine the effect of a given cause such as the repeal of the Corn Laws, the abolition of the monarchy, or the introduction of universal suffrage.[72] The second kind of law shows even more the extent of Mill's ambition: he wished to determine the general circumstances that characterize the state of a society and the simultaneous state of all greater facts or phenomena including knowledge, intellectual and moral culture (both in the community generally and in every class of it), industry, wealth and its distribution, occupations, class divisions and relations, common beliefs on important subjects and the degree of assurance with which they are held, taste, aesthetic development, government, laws, and customs. This list reveals Mill's notions of the predominant causes of social change, quite apart from the number and complexity of influences to be considered in the determination of any scientific law.

Mill kept returning to the free will/determinism issue throughout his life, but his position was clear enough from the start. The doctrine called philosophical necessity simply meant that, given the motives in an individual's mind, the character, disposition, and manner of his or her actions could be unerringly inferred. If we know all the inducements acting upon a person we can foretell conduct with as much certainty as we can predict any physical event. Since Mill conceded that this doctrine could sometimes be degrading to the moral nature, he made sure there was enormous scope for human will. As he explained in his autobiography, "Though our character is formed by circumstances, our own desires can do much to shape those circumstances; and that what is really inspiriting and ennobling in the doctrine of freewill, is the conviction that we have real power over the formation of our own character; that our will, by influencing some of our circumstances, can modify our future habits or capabilities of willing."[73] Causal laws did not mean that human beings were helpless before impersonal forces. A *System* argues that people were shaped by external conditions, but also influenced them. "Human beings, in their turn, mould and shape the circumstances for themselves and for those who come after them."[74] The term "necessity" was often inappropriate, even "pernicious" by implying inevitability and fatalism. But character is formed both by as well as for us by experience. We are able to alter our own character if we wish.

In *A System of Logic* Mill sharply distinguished "mere empirical laws, or generalizations made from observations, from genuine, scientific or causal laws. The really scientific truths ... are not those empirical laws, but the causal laws which explain them" (8:862). It was an error of "many advanced thinkers" to confuse the two kinds of laws, "to imagine that the empirical law collected from a mere comparison of the conditions at different past times, is a real law, *the* law of its changes, not only past but also to come" (8:791). To turn empirical laws into scientific ones meant connecting them "deductively" with the laws of nature from which they resulted. The virtually impossible goal was scientific laws, but often only generalization would be possible. True generalizations could only be achieved in the simpler sciences like astronomy. Observation and theorizing were clearly reciprocal processes; each informed the other. "The conclusions of theory cannot be trusted, unless confirmed by observation," while those of observation could not be "unless affiliated to theory" (8:874). Empirical laws were based on observation in specific circumstances but it was never easy to know how widely applicable those circumstances were. Deduction served as a "sentinel" watching over this process of application.

Scientific laws were difficult to determine for two reasons. Causes had to be estimated that could only be inferred from effects. Worse still was the sheer complexity and changeability of the causes themselves. It was not that theorists predicted *no* change but that they too often assumed that human nature and society would revolve in the same orbit. The causes affecting the moral world combined differently in different ages and societies. Empirical laws held only within "rather narrow" limits, and so were true or false according to the times and circumstances. In a society "the multitude of the causes is so great as to defy our limited powers of calculation" (8:878).

Mill returned repeatedly to this problem of complexity and inter-connectedness in *A System of Logic*. It was difficult enough to predict the movements of planets, for which the operative causes were few. To predict any effect in the social world one had to know *all* its causes and how they interacted. While astronomers had to follow three planets gravitating toward each other, social scientists had to deal with conflicting tendencies in a thousand different directions, promoting a thousand different changes at a given instant. "There is no social phenomenon which is not more or less influenced by every other part ... of the same society, and therefore by every cause which is influencing any other of the contemporaneous social phenomena" (8:899). This fundamentally limits the usefulness of the social sciences. For knowledge of one society to be applied to another, they have to be alike in every circumstance and all their previous history. Otherwise the phenomena will not correspond, so that predictions of effects will be faulty.

Yet Mill always insisted that, though precise prediction was not to be expected in the social world, much that was useful for guidance could be predicted. His arguments here are reminiscent of those of the ancient constructive sceptics. It was not "chimerical" to hope to ascertain general laws on social change for European countries. Individuals had to make decisions with limited information, but were aided by what knowledge they had; the same held for societies. Even if we cannot calculate "the collective result of so many combined elements," beneficial tendencies can be distinguished from injurious ones and so be promoted. This was the aim of practical politics. Knowledge of tendencies without accurate prediction gave us "to a considerable extent" this power (8:898).

Application, or human improvement, was always the goal, although Mill carefully delineated the contributions of scientists and artists. This distinction is clear from Mill's early papers when he was still playing with terminology for the new science, trying out "social economy," "speculative politics," and the "natural history of society."[75] Scientists did not make normative decisions, but their findings enabled artists to avoid futile and foolish proposals. Robson argued that Mill had a systematic philosophy linking scientific findings to application. The improvement of the human lot was the aim "through the Artist's application of the Scientist's findings."[76] Only the artist could apply the normative test, to insure that the rules of conduct devised would not only be practicable but desirable. Alan Ryan has similarly argued the unity and consistency of Mill's thought, using *A System of Logic* as the key. Against frequent, contrary interpretation, Ryan held that Mill's philosophy of science and social science laid the foundation for his Utilitarian ethics.[77]

Mill used terms which idealists often applied in a different sense. The "logic" in the title *A System of Logic* has nothing to do with abstract reasoning but meant rather "the operation of ascertaining truths by means of evidence." Logic always entailed "a process of induction." The book dealt not with how or what to observe but with the estimation of evidence, "what is needful, in order that the fact, supposed to be observed, may safely be received as true."[78] Nor was there any abandoning of induction with Mill's insistence on a role for "deduction" in the formulation of scientific laws. Before the deductions began, rigorous inductive methods had to be used to create the initial generalizations. Verification by experience was indispensable for all the deductive sciences. The ground of confidence for any concrete deductive science was not *a priori* reasoning but the fit between results and actual *a posteriori* observation. Mill is credited with having disposed of the notion that proofs can come from definitions or intuition. Deduction became the application of a previous induction.[79]

Book 6 of *A System of Logic*, "On the Logic of the Moral Sciences," opens with a respectful bow to the physical sciences: "*The backward state of the Moral Sciences can only be remedied by applying to them the methods of Physical Science, duly extended and generalized.*"[80] Yet Mill was never to minimize the difficulties of the physical sciences and often pointed out how inexact they are. There was no simplistic use of physical science models or arguments. Mill has been accused of "psychologism," or relying on individual, psychological explanation as the basis of social explanation. There is some justification for the accusation, for Mill's proposed science of "ethology" played an inordinate role in his scheme of social science. Underlying the ethology, or science of the formation of character, there was also the more conventional science of psychology. Thus the sciences of "individual man," psychology and ethology, form the base of the conceptual structure upon which the science of "man in society," or sociology, was founded. Political science was that part of social science dealing with private, worldly interests. There was a "political ethology" as well, or the science of the formation of national character. Ethology was a derivative science obtained by deducing from the general laws of mind, considering the effect of particularly physical and moral circumstances on the formation of character. Ethology was an exact science but, like the other social sciences, it was hypothetical and dealt with tendencies (8:870).

Mill was critical of Bentham's single-cause system that private, worldly interests were the dominant influence on an individual's goals. Nevertheless he concluded that one among all the many causes of human nature was predominant: the intellect. The state of speculative faculties essentially determined both the moral/political state of the community and its industrial and physical state. History showed that every considerable advance in material civilization had been preceded by an advance in knowledge (8:926).

Here Mill was advancing a major social science law. In its defence he cited a small number of significant examples from European history. Yet he did not use his own method to transform his observations into a "genuine, scientific law" or relate them to ethology, psychology, other scientific law or verify them with further evidence.

A *System of Logic* is a long, difficult book with citations in French, Greek, and Latin. There are painstakingly careful definitions, elaborate classifications, and involved descriptions. As in most pro-empiricist works there is extensive treatment of error, with whole chapters on each of a series of fallacies in reasoning. Mill uses many natural science examples, but there is still more social science than is usual in methodological works. The book ultimately set up standards too rigorous even for its author. In the text Mill conceded that the most effective way to show how to construct the sciences of politics and ethics would be to construct them. He then swore off such an endeavour and never again took up the task. Rather he went on writing, sometimes supporting his reflections with only a few examples, sometimes with considerable evidence. Yet he never distinguished between empirical and genuinely scientific laws in his own work. He never pronounced any generalization to be an empirical law or turned such a generalization into a scientific law by relating it to its causes. He never set up any process for verifying deductions. He never went through the motions of rigorous induction and correction, specifying whether he was using the "Indirect Method of Difference" or the "Method of Concomitant Variations."

Given that so many causes interact and all have to be taken into account in order to arrive at correct predictions, it is not surprising that Mill should have abandoned the effort. Social science could be put to better use in the analysis of tendencies for immediate advice. The *Principles of Political Economy* was accordingly more practical in orientation. With Harriet Taylor as co-author the writing set out the principles that could be used for social intervention/betterment. The work is the major source on the substance of the Mills' social science. Seven editions of the *Principles of Political Economy* appeared in Mill's lifetime, several with major changes reflecting the shift leftward in his political opinion or the growing influence of his more radical co-author. Mill claimed exclusive authorship of only the "abstract and purely scientific" parts of the work. He did most, if not all, the actual writing, and he and Taylor together reworked every line. Mill credited Harriet Taylor with the key methodological insight or "the living principle" of the book, namely the distinction between laws regulating the production of wealth, which "are real laws of nature," and modes of distribution, which "depend on human will."[81] The "common run" of economists, including Mill's own father, confused the two, subsuming economic practices into laws incapable of change by human effort. Mill and Taylor sought to understand causes without treating them as final or inevitable. Existing social arrangements were provisional, "liable to be much altered by the progress of social improvement." Further, in "all that concerned the application of philosophy to the exigencies of human society and progress," Mill claimed to be the pupil of his wife, who was "the more courageous and far-sighted" (1:257).

Political economy could not be treated as a thing itself "but as a fragment of a greater whole; a branch of Social Philosophy, so interlinked with all the other branches." It "never pretended to give advice to mankind with no lights but its own," but people who knew nothing else but political economy, and thus knew it ill, took advice upon themselves (1:243). Max Weber, like empiricists over the ages, would agree on this distinction between fact and value, knowledge and application.

The Mills treated the proper role and limits to government at some length in the *Principles of Political Economy* although "On Liberty" remains the most eloquent exposition of these principles. Yet the two advocated public education, labour laws, public health measures, the protection of young persons and animals, and social assistance as well as the usual curbs on crime and fraud. Apart from prohibitions against certain actions, the state could also compel people to do their duty as citizens, especially in defence. There was also much voluntary action a government could undertake for the public good to aid and stimulate individual exertion and development. Neo-conservatives who would depend on purely voluntary schemes for public charity get no help from the Mills.

The Mills' methodology left open the question of the relative influence of economic or material factors and intellectual or other ideal. Both played a role and both needed to be investigated. "The creed and laws of a people act powerfully upon their economical condition; and this again, by its influence on their mental development and social relations, reacts upon their creed and laws."[82] How a society was conducted was a matter of human institutions, and government helped to determine these institutions. The mode of conduct a society adopts was "as much a subject for scientific enquiry as any of the physical laws of nature" (2:21).

John Stuart Mill's departure from the Utilitarianism of his upbringing can best be seen in his essays. Thomas Macaulay's blistering attack on Mill's father's *Essay on Government* had appeared in 1829. J.S. Mill might have deplored the tone of the attack but he could not disagree with the main thesis, that self interest was not identical with social interest. In an essay on Bentham (1838), Mill complimented him effusively on his contribution to legal analysis, his personal integrity, and his commitment to justice. Yet the essay was otherwise devastating in its condemnation of the basic thrust of Utilitarianism. Bentham had failed to learn from others. His own knowledge of human nature was severely bounded by his limited experience. He had never known prosperity, adversity, passion, or dejection. He denied all spiritual influences and saw no role for conscience. "He committed the mistake of supposing that the *business* part of human affairs was the whole of them."[83] On those aspects, his contribution was great. But he did nothing to help people form character; "that department is a blank in Bentham's system." The pursuit of self-interest did nothing for morals but promoted only "prudence and outward probity" (100).

Mill's essay on Coleridge similarly shows him trying to achieve a balance, to take into account all the relevant aspects of human nature. James Mill and Bentham had erred in stressing individual interest, as had the eighteenth-century encyclopedists. Each had overlooked such fundamental matters as education, loyalty, and nationality. J.S. Mill has been called a Tory for his papers on Bentham and Coleridge, but this conservatism is easily exaggerated. Nowhere is there any sentiment that the past was better, any more than there is a belief in a better future. Mill only veered to Toryism, red Toryism at that, when the competing liberal principle was harsh in its practice. In other words, Mill's humanitarian instinct – the greatest good to the greatest number – was his guiding rule. When socialist measures like producers' co-operatives increasingly seemed viable, he supported them.

Mill found much to criticize in Utilitarianism, but he never attacked the greatest-happiness principle or the process of association by which moral sentiments were said to be acquired. "Questions of ultimate ends are not amenable to direct proof," he affirmed.[84] Rather actions were right in so far as they tended to promote happiness, which meant the absence of pain and the possibility of enjoyment in both quantity and quality. With a long line of empiricists Mill held that there was no "original desire" for virtue, it was instead the result of habitual association of an act with pleasure or protection from pain. Through a process of association actions came to be considered good (or not) in and of themselves, and desired (or not) as such. "Desiring a thing and finding it pleasant, aversion to it and thinking of it as painful" were inseparable, or two modes of naming the same psychological fact (10:237).

Mill is an important example of the empiricist as environmentalist. He saw the preservation of species and their habitat as essential for the well-being of humans as well as a good in itself. There would be little satisfaction in contemplating a world without the spontaneous activity of nature, where every piece of land was brought under cultivation for human food, every "flowery waste or natural pasture ploughed up, all quadrupeds or birds which are not domesticated for man's use exterminated as his rivals for food."[85] Mill pointed to the dangers of "improved agriculture." He advocated what we would call wilderness protection for solitude, meditation, and depth of character. While these were good for the wilderness hiker, society needed the contributions inspired by natural beauty. Nor was it "good for man to be kept perforce at all times in the presence of his species." Mill's green activism included opposing a contest for rare wild flowers that would lead to their destruction if not extinction.[86] Mill was sceptical as to who benefitted from the destruction of nature in the name of progress. It was not society as a whole, but chiefly the middle classes. "It is questionable if all the mechanical inventions yet made have lightened the day's toil of any human being. They have enabled a greater population to live the same life of drudgery and imprisonment, and an increased number of manufacturers and others to make a fortune." "Just institutions" were needed so that the conquests made from the powers of nature by scientific discoveries would "become the common property of the species."[87]

"The Subjection of Women" is a well-crafted and still relevant essay. Along with information concerning the legal, economic, and educational disabilities women suffered, it included new material on the possibility of a distinctive women's cultural contribution. If women lived in a separate country from men and had never read men's writing, "they would have had a literature of their own."[88] Women did not, of course, live in a different country and their literature would need time to emancipate itself from accepted male models and guide itself by its own impulses.

Mill wrote at the same time as Karl Marx but did not know his work, which then had little scholarly following. Mill's understanding of socialism was accordingly pre-Marxist and soon overtaken by the theory and practice of the many new forms of socialism. In other respects, though, a century and a half later Mill and Taylor Mill seem remarkably relevant. Their writing on women's equality can still be used in debates, as is "On Liberty" on civil rights and "private morality." Mill's speeches on Ireland and his writing on colonized blacks are unfortunately not dated. Mill's methodological advice in the broad sense is still useful, despite the fact that not even he could follow its precise instructions. The last major contributor to this history of ideas, Max Weber, exhibits enormous continuities with Mill.

PROBABILITY THEORY AND EVOLUTION

The incorporation of probability theory as a standard component of social science was the work of people whose prime concern was the theory of evolution and its practical application in eugenics. *Francis Galton (1822–1911)*[89] and *Karl Pearson (1857–1936)*[90] turned to probability theory as a means to an end – defence of the theory of evolution. They and others of their school were convinced of the overwhelming importance of nature over nurture as causal factors in society. The research that took them to this conclusion, mainly studies of twins, they believed showed a clear and consistent pattern. Galton and Pearson believed that their results were convincing enough to impose "a new moral duty" as well as provide the "opportunity to further evolution," especially of the human race.[91] Eugenics, the improvement of human stock, not education or social change was the answer to the age-old question of humankind. The conclusion flowed logically enough from the premiss, but the premiss itself would in time be questioned.

That deviations in measurements are today seen as "variations" rather than as "error" is largely an achievement of Galton. Genius was not error, he declared. Rather, such variation was the key to progress in evolution and its application in eugenics. While many earlier methodologists (Condorcet, Laplace, and Quetelet) had a vague notion of correlation, Galton made the breakthrough, at least conceptually, to the creation of a useable tool. Pearson's mathematical ability was required to complete the step, but it was Galton who made the crucial leap of imagination.[92] His development of the theories of regression and correlation reflected a new approach to causation. The aim was to measure the degree to which a factor acknowledged to be not the sole cause of a state or event contributed to the development of some other state or event. The older concept of causation crumbled under the understanding of the universe as a correlated system of variates approaching, but by no means reaching, perfect correlation. It was from Galton's study of inheritance that single numerical quantities were identified to represent the degree of relationship. Galton also pioneered rank ordering techniques, developing such now common measures as the median and quintile.

Karl Pearson subscribed to an astonishing array of causes. He was a socialist (of sorts), a positivist (of an exotic subgroup), an imperialist (with enthusiasm), and a supporter of equal rights to education and occupations for women. Yet he was no social Darwinist – he believed that the unit in the struggle for survival was the group, not the individual. *Laissez-faire* economics weakened the group for that struggle. Contrary to the stereotype it was Pearson's *social* views that took him into natural science and mathematics. Those views, in turn, were acquired while he was pursuing the traditional "humanistic" subjects of German medieval history and literature. He had published on Luther, written a passion play and poetry, and taught socialism to working men before ever crunching a number. His major methodological work, *The Grammar of Science* (1892), was a published version of lectures first given as Gresham lecturer at University College, London.

Pearson's commitment to eugenics was based on the honest belief that nature as a causal factor outweighed nurture at least five-to-one, possibly ten-to-one. "It is essentially the man who makes the environment, and not the environment which makes the man."[93] Pearson did not lack examples to support his assertion, but one might question the hastiness of his conclusions and failure to examine alternatives. Paradoxically, Pearson was instrumental in destroying the chief "nature over nurture" myth in criminology: Lombroso's born criminal. As statistical adviser to Charles Goring's *The English Convict*, Pearson devised the numerous and innovative tests that showed the lack of empirical foundation for the criminal-type thesis. By page 370 of the watershed study the conclusion was unequivocal: "This anthropological monster has no existence in fact."

Apart from his major contribution to the tools of social science, Pearson is known, with Ernst Mach, for advocating an anti-materialist form of positivism. "All science is description and not explanation" would sum it up. The "crude materialism" of the older physicists was rejected for its notion of force as underlying cause. Pearson objected not to the *results* of physics but to the mechanistic language in which they were commonly expressed, the same language as biology and sociology. "Mechanism is not at the bottom of phenomena, but is only the conceptual shorthand by aid of which scientists can briefly describe and resume phenomena."[94] "Cause" as originating or enforcing a particular sequence of perceptions was meaningless. It was valuable as a uniform antecedent if used to mark a stage. Unfortunately "cause" was too often used metaphysically, in a conception of force. "Law," "necessity," "proof," and "certainty" were all concepts found nowhere in the world of perception. "Will" as a first cause explained nothing, but with the advance of knowledge individual acts of will would be seen as secondary causes in a long sequence, including physical factors like climate and disease, and mental factors like education and the passions (109). This anti-materialist conceptualization of positivism was blasted by no less than Vladimir Lenin in *Materialism and Empirio-Criticism* (1908). Lenin argued, among other things, for the old, naturalistic materialism. He called Pearson an "unadulterated idealist." Mach Lenin considered worse, and he found neither any better than Bishop Berkeley.[95]

Whether or not one agrees with Pearson about force and cause there is much good sense in his methodological advice. He was fussy about reserving the term "know" for conceptions, allowing only "believe" for perceptions.[96] The scientist had to strive at "self-elimination" in judgments "to provide an argument which is as true for each individual mind" as one's own (11). The goal of science, "the complete interpretation of the universe," would never be reached, but "the material of science is coextensive with the whole life, physical and mental, of the universe" (18). There is not a smattering of doubt as to the unity of science. The metaphysician, for Pearson, was a poet, but was liable to be dangerous because she or he clothed poetry in the language of reason. Philosophical method did not start with the classification of facts and made its judgments "by some obscure process of internal cogitation" (22).

Pearson had a strong sense of the role of "disciplined imagination" in scientific discovery: "All great scientists have, in a certain sense, been great artists; the man with no imagination may collect facts, but he cannot make great discoveries" (31). It was imagination, after the classification of facts, that yielded the few words that formulated a scientific law from isolated phenomena. Pearson considered Darwin, who worked in the Baconian tradition of induction, a good example.

The qualifications of *Herbert Spencer (1820–1903)*[97] as a sociologist are decidedly shaky. He never did any empirical work, and he travelled and read little. Yet he was extensively read and heeded, especially in the United States. While he did not invent any of the basic sociological terms, he brought into common use such expressions as structure and function. He helped to make "sociology" the accepted term for the subject. He was influential also as an antagonist against whom other sociologists defined themselves. Beatrice Webb, for example, had to go through the valley of the shadow of Spencer before she evolved her own craft and creed.

Spencer published his first book, *Social Statics* (1850), nine years before Darwin's *Origin of Species*. His *Principles of Psychology* appeared in 1855, followed by essays and then volume after volume of his *Synthetic Philosophy* (1862–93), which systematically applied the theory of evolution to every branch of science. While Darwin's theory of evolution was the product of years of observations, Spencer deduced his from broad principles. He used copious and often exotic examples, thus giving the appearance of working inductively. Beatrice Webb considered that he had worked out his theory "by grasping the disjointed theories of his time and welding them into one."[98] She worried about having been his apprentice, or accomplice, in the art of casuistry, finding illustrations in nature for his theories. His "First Principles" had ceased to be hypotheses but had become "a highly developed dogmatic creed" explaining all the processes of nature from the formation of a crystal to party politics in a democratic state (1:44). Spencer also believed that ethics could be discerned from nature, the "ought" from the "is." He even believed that a scientific ought and is could replace conventional religion.

If the Thatcherites had not had Hayek's *The Road to Serfdom* to justify their neo-conservatism, they could have gone back to Spencer's "The Coming Slavery" (1884) and found everything they wanted. Spencer set out to destroy the notion "that all social suffering is removable, and that it is the duty of somebody or other to remove it. Both these beliefs are false."[99] Spencer unqualifiedly asserted that "all socialism involves slavery," warning against everything from the telegraph to publicly financed schools, libraries, and sanitary inspectors (41). Of the many critics who exposed the flaws in this analysis Beatrice Webb is perhaps the best and the briefest. Webb argued that the natural/artificial distinction was nonsense. One could distinguish between a natural and artificial lake easily enough, but *all* social structures, be they market or state, entailed human activity and so were artificial.[100] Lester Ward less charitably pointed out that Spencer had never had to face the competition he so extolled for others; family connections got him his jobs, and legacies later gave him the liberty to write. No survival of the fittest here![101]

Charles Booth (1840–1916)[102] deserves to be known for more than the *quantity* of his work, the massive compilation of facts in *Life and Labour of the People in London* (published in seventeen volumes, 1902–3). True, it is sometimes difficult to discern specific points in his extensive writings, but he did pioneer some of the most-used techniques of social investigation and was fastidious in the use of multiple sources of information and cross-checking between them. He was one of the first researchers to incorporate both participant observation material and census data into a survey structure. He devised the concept of the "poverty line." He also conducted the first comprehensive empirical study on the effects of religion, or putting to empirical test one of the most ancient hypotheses in social life: the relative weight of material and nonmaterial factors as causes. Finally, his work actually had an impact: although Booth was a Tory with a social conscience and no known leanings to socialism, his findings helped to document the need for a welfare state and to take the first steps to it.

Booth took on the research that became *Life and Labour* to win an argument with the socialists.[103] He wanted to disprove their claim that one quarter of the people in the East End lived in extreme poverty. Several years later his first results put the figure at 30 per cent, and further data continued to show a proportion around that level. Booth was genuinely surprised. At first he used overcrowding as the index for poverty, but that did not work. He never did establish a satisfactory criterion, but ultimately relied on the judgment of school visitors to determine who was "poor" or had to "struggle to obtain the necessaries of life," and who was "very poor" or "in chronic want." The massiveness of the task has to be appreciated: a survey of *all* of London, without sampling. In the poor areas every household was rated, in the more prosperous areas every street. Booth later used the 1891 census records to re-examine his own data. He also cross-checked information with the police.

Booth gave his first paper on his research results to the Royal Statistical Society in 1887. The full publication over the next seventeen years included seven volumes on poverty, five on industry/employment, seven on religion, and one volume of conclusions, such as they were. Coloured maps accompanying the text showed degrees of poverty. The books themselves sold well, were much commented on in the press, and were generally favourably reviewed.

Booth collaborated with his wife and an excellent team of co-workers. He enjoyed doing the research. While school visitors collected the data by household, he did participant observation in the East End. He stayed for several weeks in lodgings, content with the porridge and tea, complaining only once of fleas in his bed. He did much of the institutional interviewing himself. For the series on spiritual factors he visited schools, social agencies, settlement houses, churches, and chapels. The "reverent unbeliever" was chagrined to discover that nonmaterial factors were negligible. His observations on the class nature of the churches were astute. Working people saw the churches as a resort for the well-to-do and did not see themselves as "miserable offenders."[104] Other surveys that sought to replicate Booth's findings, such as Rowntree's in York, did not replicate the section on religion.

Ever the opponent of socialism, Booth nonetheless recognized the improvements made by unions at the workplace and by Labour-controlled councils in the wider community. His advocacy of old age pensions was in part a way to preserve the existing, meagre, Poor Law. If many of the old and the sick could be removed from the welfare rolls, further reforms would not be needed.

There was little generalization anywhere in *Life and Labour* and still less moral outrage. He honestly admitted that many people were poor: "Hundreds of thousands of our neighbours in London are ill-fed, ill-clad and ill-housed, and are, from a multitude of causes, ever at the mercy of any misfortune an ill wind may bring" (7:406). Some causal analysis in the industrial sections explained how the ordinary poor were dragged down by the real unfortunate and weak. "Moral shock" at the "wide gulf" between the poor and those with "surplus wealth" was acknowledged. In his closing words Booth still offered "no body of doctrine" but only the "dry bones" of fact. Yet he hoped that someone else would disentangle the issues, reconcile the apparent contradictions, "and make these dry bones live, so that the streets of our Jerusalem may sing with joy."[105] The use of Christian socialist imagery seems odd for so devout a Tory and so reluctant a reformer, but authors may take desperate measures to end a book of so long a series!

THE CRAFT AND CREED OF BEATRICE WEBB

Not the least of Booth's services to the social sciences was that he started his wife's cousin, the then Beatrice Potter, on her career as a researcher. *Beatrice Webb (1858–1943)*,[106] as well as becoming an influential social scientist herself, is also the best source on Booth's methodology, for *Life and Labour* includes almost nothing about method. Miss Potter took extensive notes in her diary and reflected on this first research experience. She then quit the survey to go on to her own work, soon in partnership with Sidney Webb, whom she married. She and her husband produced some twenty volumes of research on social institutions in Britain. With him she worked on founding the London School of Economics and the British Labour

Party. She served as a member of the Royal Commission on the Poor Laws, for which she and Sidney Webb wrote the landmark minority report that moved Britain toward the creation of a welfare state. Beatrice Webb is the subject here, for she was the methodologist of the two.

Beatrice Webb's papers on methodology from the 1880s set out her practices and advice on interviewing, note-taking, organization, and the "mental equipment" required for social research. They are now available as an appendix to *My Apprenticeship* and in *Methods of Social Study* (edited by Sidney Webb). The preface to *Industrial Democracy* (1897), published just two years after Durkheim's *Rules of Sociological Method*, is another excellent source of the Webb method. Beatrice Webb held that questions had to be framed as hypotheses or aids in the collection and classification of facts. One should have in mind "not one hypothesis but many mutually inconsistent hypotheses."[107] Hypotheses could come from anywhere: browsing, free association, even the crankiest pamphlet. At this stage one should let one's imagination play; later it would have to work in harness. Bias "to the greatest possible extent" must be put aside (42). The human mind was "terribly apt to perceive what it looks for ... *A good half of most research work consists in an attempt to prove yourself wrong*" (33-4). The scientist must be eager to see orthodox categories transcended. Webb stressed also the researcher's need for "a sensitive mind and broad human sympathies" along with a wide variety of experience (47-8).

Webb's first foray into participant observation research was partly a quest for her own identity. The Potter family was wealthy, recently upwardly mobile, and out of touch with its textile worker cousins still in Lancashire and Yorkshire. The young Beatrice Potter arranged to visit them anonymously, posing as a "Miss Jones." She later revealed the hoax. The experience she gained in Lancashire led her to question the *laissez-faire* principle by showing the beneficial results of the Factory Acts. The strong social bonds she saw in action in co-operatives, chapel, and community moved her from an individualistic ethic to socialism.

Webb's other experiment in participant observation (and disguise) was also significant for her development as a social investigator. She took lessons in tailoring and got a job as a "plain trouser hand" to find out how the industry functioned. Her results challenged the conventional wisdom on the sweating industries. Her write-up of the material includes observations on the tailoring industry, her analysis of its problems, and her own feelings about it.

Webb was not too proud to report on one colossal research fiasco – a questionnaire on trade unions, the first questionnaire she and her husband designed. It was an impossible 120-question affair (of which 1,000 copies were printed) which required details, documentation, and opinions no trade union official could or would provide. When the questionnaire failed the Webbs obtained the information by interviewing officials, working through documents, and attending relevant events and meetings themselves.

Webb books were famous for thoroughness of material and meticulous verification. The pair's "unit" method for recording data is now done by computer. Their version was to put only one fact, with its source, on each quarto-sized page. This permitted endless sorting and re-assembling by time, place, subject, or whatever. Webb credited Guyot-Daubès' *Art de classer les notes*, as the source on the *fiche* method, another example of cross-channel learning. Unlike so many European methodologists, however, Webb was no partisan of royal commissions as a source of data. She knew that oral evidence given at hearings yielded an "absurdly small" store of facts. Her practical tips to researchers included that the interviewer should never "show off" or argue with the interviewee.

Webb was cautious about what the social researcher could find even as generalization, let alone "laws of nature." It was possible to predict causation only through tendencies – and those few, far between, and tentative (233). We cannot foresee the course of history because "social facts are determined to some extent by others altogether outside the science we have in mind."[108] Change of climate, inventions, and the appearance of great "men" could all radically alter the course of society but could not be foretold. As had the ancient sceptics, however, Webb argued that available knowledge could be used. She herself had seen her own research lead to improvements in society. Yet there was no morality in the nature of things, a conclusion she had reached in rejecting Spencer. One could learn from science how to kill and cure, but not which one to do.[109] Science was and must remain bankrupt with regard to the purpose of life. The question the researcher should ask was, "Will the discovery of the past help the conduct of the present?" (128).

MARX AS AN EMPIRICIST

While mainstream sociology was developing, *Karl Marx (1818–83)*[110] and *Friedrich Engels (1820–95)* were devising their own comprehensive and far more radical social theory complete with its own methodology. Marx was a complex man not easy to place in methodology, not least because much of what he wrote was to sort out his own views. His interest in Engels was sparked by the latter's methodological publications and actual experience with empirical work. Despite his Hegelian past, Marx formulated his methodology in France in the early 1840s. French materialist writers were key and these remained influential for him throughout his life. For some time now Marx has been presented as an anti-empiricist, the Hegelian and Kantian influences on him highlighted, the empirical ones ignored. That both he and Engels lampooned the critical theory of their day is conveniently forgotten. So is the fact that Marx used the emerging terminology of empiricism/positivism with approval. That he himself did much empirical work in economics can hardly be ignored, but that he also attempted a mass social survey is scarcely ever mentioned.

As a university student in Berlin Marx adopted the prevailing Hegelian fashion. He added philosophy to his studies of law and political economy, eventually earning a doctorate for a dissertation comparing Epicurus and Democritus. He learned English, Italian, and French. By graduation he realized that his politics, although then merely liberal and democratic, were too extreme for him to pursue a university career. He settled on journalism instead, but soon found that struggles with the censors curtailed opportunities there. His first publication was actually on censorship. Marx's French period, 1843–5, was crucial for his development as both thinker and activist. He had given up the Hegelianism of his university days but had nothing with which to replace it. By the time he left Paris he was politically a Communist and methodologically a materialist in the French tradition. Proudhon sent him his newly-published *Philosophy of Poverty* for review, to which Marx replied with a scathing book-length attack, *The Poverty of Philosophy* (1847). A century later E.P. Thompson titled his defence of Marx against the French idealists *The Poverty of Theory*.

Marx and Engels met in Paris and began their life-long collaboration. Engels, who had just published *The Condition of the Working Class in England in 1844*, was Marx's senior in economic knowledge and polemics. Marx, the better educated of the two, applied himself to the study of economics and took the lead. Their first work together was in methodology; it established the framework within which they would work. *The Holy Family*, published in 1845, was a biting attack on the young Hegelians, written mainly by Marx against his former soulmates. *The German Ideology* (c. 1846) was a genuine collaboration, a second attack on Hegelians, necessitated by negative response to the first book. Marx was unable to find a publisher for *The German Ideology* and, since it had served to clarify his and Engels' own views, left it in the drawer for "the criticism of the mice." Part of it appeared in the 1880s; it was published in full only in 1932. Papers variously known as the *Paris Manuscripts*, *Economic and Philosophical Manuscripts*, and the *Manuscripts of 1844* record Marx's first work in sociology and economics. Again, this material was not published until 1932, when it provoked a major re-evaluation of "the early Marx." The Paris period came to an abrupt end in January, 1845, when Marx was expelled from France on pressure from Berlin. In 1849, the Marx family and Engels moved to England. The stay was expected to be short for, after 1848, would not the workers soon again rise? In fact, Marx was to remain in England, except for brief visits and health cures, the rest of his life.

In London, at the British Museum, Marx did the years of empirical research that eventually resulted in the critiques of political economy that form the heart of his work. *A Contribution to the Critique of Political Economy* (1859) gives the broad outlines. The massive *Grundrisse*, which was published only in 1939, is an intermediate work. Volume 1 of *Capital*, published in 1867 in German, remains the definitive work of Marxism. (Engels brought out volume 2 in 1885 and volume 3 in 1894 from Marx's notes.[111]) Other works include *The Eighteenth Brumaire of Louis Bonaparte* (1852), the "Critique of the Gotha Program," and *The Civil War in France* (1850). In his last years Marx filled his notebooks with anthropological material that he never published. Engels' *Origin of the Family, Private Property and the State* (1884) draws on this material, but reflects Engels' strong opinions more than Marx's cautious and tentative notes.[112] To earn money Marx became European correspondent for the *New York Tribune*, writing some 300 articles for it, some of which were later published in book form.

Marx described his abandonment of Hegelian philosophy in a letter to his father. "A curtain had fallen, my holy of holies was rent asunder and new gods had to be installed. I left behind the idealism ... and came to seek the idea in the real itself."[113] He did not, of course, leave behind Hegelian idealism all that easily, but Hegelian concepts continued to influence his work and Hegelian expressions find their way even into late work. His doctoral dissertation still had much idealist language in it, although the subject was two Greek materialists, Democritus and Epicurus. Although little primary material was available, the dissertation is nevertheless extremely inaccurate in its portrayal of both men. Marx praised Epicurus for his supposed theory of declination of atoms, which symbolized the freedom and ability of individuals to act, against Democritus' constrained, but scientifically correct, determinism. For later Marxist scholars this enthusiasm for freedom over science gives insights into Marx's development as a thinker and revolutionary. The self-directed atoms were the world's first revolutionaries and their dissident direction no less than revolutionary practice. Marx had originally intended to go on to the Stoic and sceptical schools but never did. Instead his journalism involved him in the political struggles of the day, which in turn inspired more focused social and economic research. His writing from Paris included both reflection on the new subject matter and a coming to terms with the old methodology.

The Holy Family was Marx and Engels' public way of rejecting the Hegelians. It is still a very funny book even if it is guilty of academic overkill. The methodological misdemeanours of Saint Bruno and other members of the holy family are noted in detail, patiently explained, then ridiculed with sarcasm, underlinings, and exclamation marks!! The lampooning begins in the subtitle: A Critique of Critical Critique. The text opens with a spoof on the Gospel of John: "Criticism so loved the mass that it sent its only begotten son, that all who believe in him may not be lost, but may have Critical life."[114] The book accepts empiricism, positive science, French and English materialism, and particular facts. Criticism, absolute criticism, German philosophy, metaphysics, speculation, Truth, mind, abstraction, teleology, and the like are repudiated. Beginning in the foreword Marx and Engels warn of the danger that *"speculative idealism"* might substitute "self-consciousness" or the "spirit" for the *"real individual person"* and might teach, with the evangelist, "that the spirit quickeneth everything and that the flesh profiteth not" (11–12). Critical criticism "separates thinking from the senses, the soul from the body, and itself from the world." At the height of abstraction it considered only its own thoughts. "It separates history from natural science and industry and sees the origin of history not in coarse *material* production on the earth but in vaporous clouds in the heavens" (201).

The young Hegelians were thoroughly consistent in their idealism. Believing that social reform could only be achieved by reform of thought, they declined involvement in any actual social reform movement. Later a number of them became quite reactionary. The heroes in *The Holy Family* were the English and French, the connections among whom were well understood. Bacon and Locke were praised, while Hobbes was too much of a systematizer. The French were said to have civilized British empiricism. Helvétius, who got his empiricism from Locke, influenced Bentham in turn, who influenced Owen. The French communist Cabet similarly had acquired his communism while in exile in England. Teleological thinking in methodology was dismissed with a joke. As plants existed to be eaten by animals, and animals by people, so also did people exist "so that history may exist and history exists so that the *proof of truths* may exist. In that *Critically* trivialized form we have the ... speculative wisdom that people exist and history exists so that *truth* may be brought to *self-consciousness*" (107). But real problems, Marx and Engels insisted, were not understood in isolation.

History, like truth, became a person apart, while human individuals were the mere bearers of abstractions. *"Hegel's* conception of history assumes an *Abstract* or *Absolute Spirit* which develops in such a way that mankind is a mere *mass* bearing it with a varying degree of consciousness or unconsciousness" (115). History did *nothing*, possessed *no* immense wealth, and waged *no* battles. Real living people did that. Critical criticism was reproached also for the separation of natural science and history, Marx arguing instead for unity of science. He derided the Germanic use of the singular, as in *the* spirit, over recognition of individuality and diversity in theory and life (112). The French were better, they had *"social theories*, not *a* social theory" (204).

In *The German Ideology* Marx and Engels jokingly dismissed the young Hegelians as sheep who took themselves for wolves and who combatted "the phrases of this world" but not "the real existing world."[115] Another joke has people drowning because they were "possessed with the idea of gravity" (2). Empirical observation must bring out, without any mystification or speculation, the connection between the social/political structure and production. The social structure and the state were continually evolving out of the life process of real individuals, not as they appeared in someone's imagination, but as they really were materially, active within definite material limits independent of their will. *The German Ideology* has been called "verbose, ill-organised and ponderous," dealing with authors "long dead and justly forgotten," but nonetheless the "most sustained, imaginative and impressive exposition of Marx's theory of history."[116]

The German Ideology unambiguously states Marxist sociology of knowledge. The production of ideas/conceptions/consciousness was directly interwoven with "material activity" and material relations between people. Ideas were produced by real, active people in the course of productive work. While German philosophy descended from heaven to earth, Marx and Engels held that theirs ascended from earth to heaven. "That is to say, we do not set out from what people say, imagine, conceive ... to arrive at people in the flesh. We set out from real, active people, and on the basis of their real life-process we demonstrate the development of the ideological reflexes and echoes of this life-process."[117] They continue: "Morality, religion, metaphysics, all the rest of ideology and their corresponding forms of consciousness, thus no longer retain the semblance of independence. They have no history, no development; but people, developing their material production and their material intercourse, alter, along with their real existence, their thinking and the products of their thinking. Life is not determined by consciousness, but consciousness by life" (14–15). As throughout Marx's life, "positive science" was positive: "where speculation ends – in real life – there real, positive science begins: the representation of the practical activity, of the practical process of development of people" (15).

The German Ideology is a source also on the Marxist vision of a communist society. It is a low-technology society without a rigid division of labour (22). Communism was also described as a process of becoming, like the Kingdom of God in another ideology, "the *real* movement which abolishes the present state of things" (26). Here also is the first Marxist statement about gender relations as class relations, in the "latent slavery" or "first property" of wives and children in the family (21).

The "Theses on Feuerbach" (written 1846, published 1888) is a succinct statement of reflexivity in Marxist methodology. The first thesis criticizes earlier forms of materialism for treating the world as objects instead of as sensed, human activity. The question as to whether human thought can attain objective truth was not theoretical, but practical. Discussion of the reality of thought, isolated from practice, was purely scholastic. The doctrine that had people as products of their circumstances and education forgot that people themselves transformed those circumstances; the educator, too, need to be educated. Thesis II ends with the famous call to action: "The philosophers have only *interpreted* the work in various ways; the point is to *change* it."[118]

In *The Poverty of Philosophy* Marx had to interrupt his criticism of Proudhon's social theory to point out the faults of his Germanic methodology. Proudhon had sought to frighten the French by flinging quasi-Hegelian phrases at them. Marx again explained the English/German difference in methodology in a joke. What is the difference between a Christian and a philosopher? The former believes in only one incarnation, while the latter is never finished with them![119] Another joke has it that "if the Englishman transforms men into hats, the German transforms hats into ideas" (103). Did Marx's status as official ideologist of the Communist world prevent his humour from being recognized? Now that he has lost most of this burden, might his other talents – if not the humour, then the methodology – be recognized?

Marx noted that Proudhon understood that people make cloth, but not that they also make social relations. But social relations were intimately bound up with productive forces. In acquiring new productive forces people change successively the manner of gaining their living and social relations. The hand mill creates feudal society, the steam mill industrial capitalism. The same people who establish these social relations also produce principles, ideas, and categories which conform to them and change with them. That people are not helpless victims of circumstances is even better stated in *The Eighteenth Brumaire of Louis Bonaparte*: "People make their own history, but not just as they please. They do not choose the circumstances for themselves, but have to work upon circumstances as they find them, have to fashion the material handed down by the past."[120]

Marx's denunciation of capitalism for its alienation of labour goes back to his earliest economic writing in Paris. The terms describing it would change over time but the horrifying *fact* of alienation through labour remained. The object labour produced became an alien being confronting the labourer with its own independent power.[121] For the worker this meant "loss of reality," "objectification," "loss" of the object or "slavery to it," "alienation," or "externalization." The life the worker lent to the object then affronted him as a hostile force. "Labour produces works of wonder for the rich, but nakedness for the worker. It produces palaces, but only hovels for the worker; it produces beauty, but cripples the worker ... It produces culture, but also imbecility and cretinism for the worker" (136). Marx's description of alienation directly influenced sociological theory quite apart from its political impact. Ferdinand Tönnies, notably, acknowledged the influence in his distinction between community and society.[122]

The first draft of the communist "confession of faith" was written by Engels in catechism form. Engels himself suggested that more content had to go in than could be managed in a question-and-answer format. He also proposed the title. Marx did the expanded rewrite and the result was both the call-to-arms of 1848 and a clear statement of Marxist theory of class and class struggle without any Hegelian trappings. The language of the *Communist Manifesto* throughout was powerful, from the spectre of communism at the beginning to the losing of the chains at the end. Between came the theory of the dynamic centrality of class struggle: "The history of all hitherto existing society is the history of class struggles. Freeman and slave, patrician and plebian, lord and serf, guildmaster and journeyman, in a word, oppressor and oppressed, stood in constant opposition to one another, carried on an uninterrupted, now hidden, now open fight, a fight that each time ended, either in a revolutionary reconstitution of society at large, or in the common ruin of the struggling classes."[123] Marx, of course, did not discover the existence of classes or class conflict, but he did go further than earlier theorists in arguing the crucial role of class struggle for changes in historical epochs. He also, in a totally untestable manner, held this to be inevitable until the abolition of private property and, in turn, class conflict. Perfectly testable, and eventually proved wrong, were his predictions for the next changes in class composition, consolidation into two, great hostile camps. The *Communist Manifesto* is also the most quotable source on the Marxian theory of the state: "The executive of the modern state is but a committee for managing the common affairs of the whole bourgeoisie" (61).

A Contribution to the Critique of Political Economy constitutes the appearance of the mature Marx and what he then conceived to be the first instalment of a complete treatment of political economy, including law, politics, and a broad range of other social factors. Instead *Capital* came out as a single volume eight years later, and the masses of social and economic data remained in notebooks at his death. The earlier *Contribution* is an excellent source on the central themes of Marxist sociology. The preface recounts how Marx made the transition from the Hegelian "progress of the human mind" to "the material conditions of life," and specifically the decision to seek the "anatomy of civil society" in political economy.[124] The general conclusion he reached in his Paris studies continued to serve as the leading thread:

In the social production which people carry on they enter into definite relations that are indispensable and independent of their will; these relations of production correspond to a definite stage of development of their material powers of production. The sum total of these relations of production constitutes the economic structure of society – the real foundation, on which rise legal and political superstructures and to which correspond definite forms of social consciousness. The mode of production in material life determines the general character of the social, political, and spiritual processes of life. It is not the consciousness of people that determines their existence but, on the contrary, their social existence determines their consciousness. (11–12)

Marx then went on to explain how the forces of production come into conflict with the relations of production, meaning property relations. What had been functional relations of production came to be fetters, which in time instigated revolution. "With the change of the economic foundation the entire immense superstructure is more or less rapidly transformed" (12).

Marx exceeded all the bounds of empiricism by theorizing about what these productive forces could and could not do. No social order could disappear until all its possible productive forces had been developed; new relations of production never appear before the material conditions of their existence have matured in the old society. This, of course, must be taken on faith, for who knows whether any productive forces remain unspent? With unmitigated optimism Marx held that "mankind always takes up only such problems as it can solve." We would "always" find that a problem arose "only when the material conditions necessary for its solution already exist or are at least in the process of formation" (13). To an environmentally conscious world this blind confidence that solutions will be found for all problems seems to be a serious if not the most serious fault of Marxism. This is *not* to say that Marx was exceptional here; rather he was an entirely conventional Victorian in his confidence in technological progress. The chemical industry, apparently, could do no harm with its chemicals, whatever injustices it did as employer.

If *Capital* is not *the* book on which Marx should be judged, it is at least the most thoroughly researched and carefully written and the last he published on political economy. It is the "damned book" to which he devoted so many years of his life, through illness, privation, and organization building. He regarded it as his major scientific contribution, even sending an inscribed copy to fellow scientist Charles Darwin. In the preface he welcomed "every opinion based on scientific criticism" and throughout used terminology and examples from the natural sciences without apology.[125] The physicist observed natural processes where they were least affected by disturbing influences and, wherever possible, conducted experiments under pure conditions. For the same reason Marx used England as the main illustration for his theory. Germany and other countries would follow the same laws and tendencies, which worked themselves out "with iron necessity" (1:90). The ultimate aim of *Capital* was "to reveal the economic law of motion of modern society" (1:92). Knowledge for application was limited in Marx's theory, but he would show what was possible. A nation could and should learn from others. Even though the new society could not leap over or remove the natural phases of development it could "shorten and lessen the birth-pangs."

Capital is fundamentally about capital. Volume 1 considers where it comes from and what it does. How it is distributed *among* capitalists, after extraction from the workers, is the subject of volumes 2 and 3. The first chapter of Volume 1 sets out the basic definitions of commodity and value.

The labour theory of value and surplus value are explained, or how a worker's labour power is transformed into profits and capital. However complicated Marxist theory might become, this basic transformation is conveyed with graphic simplicity. Workers need food, clothing, and shelter for themselves and their families. Yet the labour time required to provide basic subsistence, paid in wages, was less than what could be extracted from them. The difference, surplus value, was the source of profits and the accumulation of capital. Marx rejected both the prevailing accounts of capital – as reward for risk in classical economics and as simple theft in revolutionary literature. The capitalist-worker exchange was perfectly legal, even though it was based on the desperation of the great mass of people who had only their labour power to live on.

Marx was a theorist who believed that what one saw did not necessarily represent what was really happening. His goal was to ascertain underlying dynamics. In the process of inquiry the material had to be appropriated in detail and its different forms of development analyzed to track down their inner connections. Only after this work has been done can the real movement be appropriately presented (1:102). The scientist's goal was to discover the laws of this underlying reality, the real laws of motion that make apples fall and planets spin around their suns. The copious material Marx collected over the decades was digested and rearranged in a deceptively deductive format. Assertions were made and then concrete examples brought in as illustrations. The concept of value itself was at a level of generality that makes it virtually untestable. The value of any particular commodity is not the value of the actual labour that went into its production, but the amount "socially necessary," or the amount required to produce it under average conditions with average workers. Nor can the value of any particular worker's labour be calculated, for production is a social process in which the labour of all involved intermingles. Hegel's ghost can be seen here, where the One is more real than the many and particular.[126] Yet Marx continued to insist on the empiricist orientation of *Capital*. Defending the work shortly before his death, he argued that he had not started with an abstract "concept of value" but the "*commodity*" itself, because it was the simplest form in which the product of labour comes to contemporary society. "I analyse it, and right from the beginning, in the *form in which it appears*."[127]

Marx's high hopes for *Capital* were sadly disappointed. It was at first ignored rather than attacked. An English publisher could not be found until 1883. Ironically the first translation was into Russian, the tsar's censor decided that its strict scientific style made it inaccessible to the masses. Critics have had more than a century to debate the extent to which the propositions of *Capital* have been confirmed. Few would argue today for the labour theory of value, but some hold that its rejection need not imply rejection of Marx's theory of surplus value. Others would concede that most of Marx's specific predictions have been disconfirmed, but still credit him with pointing in the right direction for social and economic factors in theory. His insights and conceptualizations still find favour, for example his finding of commonality in surplus value between such disparate things as rent from land and profits from commodities. Those who acknowledge defeat on specific propositions may yet see the genius of Marx's focus and insights into the *process* of class formation, for example, even if his actual predictions are wrong.

The labour theory of value is most vulnerable, in my view, for its lack of attention to the natural environment. The prophet of materialism was not sufficiently materialistic. Here Marx was more at fault than the classical economists from whom he took the theory, for in *Capital* he held that *all* value derived from labour, denying any contribution from raw materials and the instruments of production. He qualified this position only slightly in "Critique of the Gotha Program," to allow nature a role in the creation of use-values. Any value apparently due to the instruments of production (machines, for example) was really just the sum of the labour that had originally gone into their production. A natural resource was valuable only in so far as people found a use for it. The sea, for example, could be either a barrier or a highway, depending on one's attitude. It is now easier to see, as natural resources are being rapidly depleted, that they are essential and that labour can both enhance and destroy them. While in *Capital* farmers were always creating value, those who now use pesticides, engage in other poor or unsustainable practices, or overfarm can be seen to be diminishing environmental capital. Too much labour in fishing, similarly, far from adding value depletes fish stocks. Clear cutting forests damages a renewable resource, while the depletion of non-renewable resources is even more obvious.

Marx's "historical materialism" might better be called an economic or even sociological interpretation of history. "Historical materialism" was Engels' expression. Neither man believed in Bentham's type of self-interest as the sole motivating factor in social life, and Marx always stressed the *social* nature of his prime causal agents. The mode of production and the social relations of production were *sociological* factors, stressing interaction among the people concerned. Engels' substitution of "material conditions of life" for the "mode of production" changes the emphasis and causes confusion.[128] Marx defined capitalism in sociological terms, as private control over the means of production.

Misunderstanding over the terms "dialectics" and "dialectical materialism" also must be addressed. True, Marx occasionally used the term "dialectics," distinguishing his use from Hegel's. There was never anything mysterious in Marx's use, which simply implied radical change through conflict. He usually avoided the term completely to name the actual causal agents and the nature of the change: mode of production, relations of production, class formation, revolution. The elevation of dialectics to a new science or methodology was Engels' project, never approved by Marx and carried on largely after his death. Engels' *Anti-Dühring* (1878) and the *Dialectics of Nature* (written in 1872–82 and published in 1927) have since become a bit of an embarrassment in Marxism, and scholars have become more attentive to the precise contributions of the two partners. It was Engels, not Marx, who was the author of "a bogus dialectics and a factitious metaphysics."[129]

Late in life Marx made an unsuccessful attempt at practical methodological innovation: the mass survey. The written questionnaire had not yet come into use. John Sinclair and Frédéric LePlay had used investigators to collect their data, for ordinary people were not sufficiently educated to fill in forms themselves. Marx now sent out 25,000 copies of a questionnaire to French workers, using *Revue Socialiste*, trade unions, and sympathetic organizations for distribution. The appeal for participation explained that "socialists of all schools ... wanting social reform, must want an *exact* and *positive* knowledge of the conditions in which the working class works and moves, the class to which the future belongs."[130] Few of these onerous forms were returned, and the July issue of the *Revue* contained a further appeal. Workers, or "our proletarian friends," were told that by participating in the difficult task they would be working directly for their own emancipation.[131] The data represented "the first task which socialist democracy must undertake in preparation for social renewal."[132] Respondents were not asked to answer every question; they were requested to make their answers as comprehensive and detailed as possible. Confidentiality was promised, but names and addresses were requested for contact purposes.

The aim of Marx's questionnaire was not only the collection of information but consciousness raising. With no pretence of neutrality, the introduction to the questionnaire referred to the "odious acts of capitalist exploitation" and the "evils" endured by workers. The one hundred questions included many that would require meticulous household accounts as well as access to company and government records.[133] The first two sections sought descriptive information on the workplace, its occupations, apprentices, health conditions, machinery, hazards, actual accidents, fire precautions, compensation, hours of work, holidays, travel time, breaks, night work, and children's employment. Part 3 covered data presumably directed to testing the labour theory of value. Questions covered wages (the worker's and the family's), living expenses, sample budgets (weekly and annual income and expenditures), wage fluctuations, interruptions of work, and the displacement of workers by machines. Question 76 asked for comparative prices of the article produced or service provided with the price of labour. Had the intensity or duration of work increased or decreased with increased labour productivity? Number 79 asked: "Do you know of any instance of an increase of wages in consequence of the progress of production?" (267) The last section included questions on unions, strikes, co-operatives, friendly associations, profit sharing, employers' associations, and state intervention, including use of the police. Number 92 asked: "Do you know any instances in which the Government has misused the forces of the State, in order to place them at the disposal of employers against their employees?" (268) Similarly, questions 93 and 94 asked: "Do you know any instances in which the Government has intervened to protect the workers against the exactions of the employers and their illegal combinations?" and "Does the Government apply against the employers the existing labour laws?" Finally respondents were asked for the "general physical, intellectual, and moral condition of men and women workers employed in your trade." And, in case anything had been left out, Number 101 called for "General comments" (268).

Evidently few workers sent in their questionnaires despite follow-up pleas. Marx, by then in failing health, abandoned the project without ever analyzing the results. The attempt nonetheless serves to underscore the *continuities* between Marx and the mainstream social sciences.[134]

FRENCH FUNCTIONALISM

If sociology today is preoccupied with such morbid subjects as crime, suicide, and deviant behaviour, *Emile Durkheim (1858–1917)*[135] deserves some of the credit. These were key subjects for him and the functionalism he advanced, for definition at the boundaries was integral to the functioning of the societal whole. Durkheim also helped along the association of sociology with liberalism, anti-clericalism, and atheism. He held the first chair in sociology in France. He was a major source for Talcott Parsons and the American functionalism Parsons popularized. The revival of anomie theory in the United States in the 1950s and 1960s stimulated a new interest in Durkheim. Indeed he is one of the few methodologists in this history still to be read for the substance of his views and not just as a historical figure.

Durkheim completed his doctoral thesis (in Latin) on Montesquieu in 1892. Next he published his major doctoral work, the original and still influential *Division of Labour* (1893). His *Rules of Sociological Method* followed in 1895 and *Suicide* in 1897. Less important for our concerns in methodology, he also published a history of education in France. Durkheim founded, was the first editor of, and wrote many of the articles for *Année Sociologique*. Much of Durkheim's work in methodology can be seen as an attempt to return the subject to course after it had gone in the wrong direction.[136] He held that the biologism of the Italian School and the individualism of the social Darwinists had both to be resisted. Comte was rejected for different reasons – his three-phase approach to all history was unverifiable. Against all of these tendencies Durkheim reasserted the *social* facts in testable form consistent with mainstream empiricism. Against Comte, Spencer, Darwin, and Lombroso, Durkheim turned back to earlier models for the founding of his subject: Montesquieu and Saint-Simon. He then sought, with this solid base in ordinary, causal-explanation sociology, to add a new level of explanation: functionalism. Discernment of the function of a social institution was intended not to replace causal explanation, but to build on it.

Rules of Sociological Method, like Descartes' "Discourse on Method," is a short, fervent work which sets forth a small number of general rules. The rules themselves were said to be provisional, for methods would have to change as science advanced.[137] The conventional fact/value distinction was basic, the use of the social sciences for good. Science does not permit judgments of good or evil but gives us the means to produce either at our will. Application for human betterment is the end of work in the social sciences as anywhere else. The sociologist was to distinguish between health and illness in a society, using objective criteria. Then health could be promoted. There was no abyss between science and art or knowledge and application; both physician and statesman had roles (75). Otherwise stated, the principal object of the social sciences was to extend scientific rationality to human conduct. It was then no less rational to project those relations to the future, in application, for the same relations of cause and effect would hold.

Durkheim maintained that cause and effect could best, if indirectly, be established by experiments. The essence of experiment was to vary phenomena freely so as to offer a broad and rich field for comparison. Montesquieu had done this instinctively in his comparative study of legal institutions. He could be faulted, though, for not adequately distinguishing between the "is" and the "ought."[138] Comte had failed to use the comparative method. He had even made comparison impossible by absorbing all societies into one common type. One had to go back and forth between theory and its application. Ideas, rather, "spring from the heart," which is "the source of our entire life." But feelings have to be governed by reason, meaning the results of careful scientific work (7). Explanations have to be "naturalistic," by which Durkheim simply meant not mystical.

Method was the same as for all the sciences, now it was applied to the distinct subject matter of the social sciences: social facts. Social facts were "things" to be approached from the outside. Sociologists must put themselves in the same state of mind as a physicist or chemist who approached an unexplored domain. "When [the sociologist] penetrates the social world, he must be aware that he is penetrating the unknown; he must feel himself in the presence of facts whose laws are as unsuspected as were those of life before the era of biology; he must be prepared for discoveries which will surprise and disturb him."[139] The sociologist, or other scientist, already has some crude concepts in mind when setting out. One cannot learn much from introspection, for no conception exists in entirety in any one individual. One must turn to external signs, to perception. Not "even the most careful introspection" would suffice (xlii). Data were the "point of departure" of science, and representations of them in one's mind must always be kept distinct from the phenomena themselves (27). Since sensation may be distorted by subjective factors, measurements as objective as possible should be used. The physicist used precise, objective measurements of temperature instead of a vague impression of hot or cold. Similarly, social scientists have to develop objective criteria for their task of distinguishing the normal from the pathological in a society. The sociologist seeks to express the properties of phenomena accurately and *objectively*, not according to some ideal notion.

Durkheim identified himself as a rationalist *and* a positivist, linking the unity of science to both. Although he rejected many of Comte's substantive conclusions, he fully appreciated the positivist cause. The founding of "positive philosophy" was "the most impressive even in the philosophic history of the nineteenth century."[140] Positivism had "enriched human intelligence ... created new horizons" (105). Like Cartesianism, positivism was inspired by the rationalist faith, especially the unity of science. Yet this principle was under attack. For Durkheim positivism represented resistance and a reassertion of the unity of science. All the while he sought to avoid disputes over "metaphysical hypotheses" like free will and determinism. Rather he was eager to get on with the work at hand – applying the principle of causation.

The explanation of social facts for Durkheim had always to be sought in preceding social facts. Social matters could be explained by neither individual nor biological facts, for the whole was greater and different from the sum of the parts.[141] All this was described rather dogmatically in *The Rules of Sociological Method*. Some social scientists might use other factors to decide empirically which variables had more power, but Durkheim was not so open. After determining ordinary cause and effect relations he hoped to establish the function of any given social fact. Durkheim's conservatism has often been exaggerated, but here it is not, for the function was maintenance of social order and cohesion (97). Factors not contributing to the stability of social order wasted energy needed for that purpose.

Durkheim set out his methodological rules simply and with such conviction that explanation might seem easy. In this respect he was Cartesian indeed. Yet where he dealt with the possibilities of success he was as modest as any in the long line of constructive sceptics. In the preface to the second edition of *The Rules* he lamented the lack of sociological knowledge. Little was known of the most fundamental institutions of study: the state, family, property, contract, punishment, and responsibility. The laws governing social facts were often unknown. Yet theorists dogmatized even on complex phenomena, determining their essence, not from facts but their own prior prejudices. Sociologists rarely admitted their ignorance (xlvi).

Durkheim's rejection of Comte was never stronger than in his treatment of social solidarity. For Comte and Spencer the increasing division of labour was a threat to social order, while for Durkheim it prompted a new form of social cohesion in organic solidarity. This theme was the main subject of *The Division of Labour*, and was also well argued in "Deux Lois" (1900). Some common values were needed for a society to hold together. Common values and norms were even *the* means of social solidarity for smaller, simpler societies. This "mechanical solidarity," based on resemblance, was the original means of cohesion for all societies. Then, in accordance with a "law of history," the increasing division of labour led to replacing mechanical with organic solidarity. A more complex division of labour was not only natural and inevitable, it produced its own means of cohesion as individuals became aware of their dependence on society. Thus the division of labour became the great source of social solidarity and the base of the moral order.

Durkheim's development of these two contrasting forms of social cohesion has intrigued social scientists over the years. As a solution to a major theoretical problem it is impressively general and neat, perhaps too much so. Durkheim noted many examples for the replacement of criminal/repressive law by contract/civil law, but counter examples also abound. He cogently argued the normalcy of crime. Criminals themselves might not be normal, but a society without crime was unthinkable, for that would mean a lack of collective sentiments to offend. Durkheim rejected the classical explanations of punishment as a means of deterrence. Rather punishment served for the collective conscience to assert itself, in his language, or for the establishment of limits in American functionalist language. Crime was normal to a society in the same way pain was to illness. It was no occasion for self-congratulation if the crime rate dropped, for this "apparent progress" would be associated with "some social disorder" (72). Crime was a necessary stage in the evolution of a society. Society condemned the great reformers as criminals who offended against prevailing norms. Yet a society could not live without renewing itself periodically. Thus it was normal for a society to have abnormal individuals, just as it was normal for a society to condemn them.

Durkheim's concept of *anomie*, literally normlessness, has attracted a considerable sociological following, but still creates as many problems as it solves. At the societal level *anomie* means that the collective conscience is weak. For the individual it implies divided loyalties or confusion between right and wrong. While the concept appeals – for it allows criminal behaviour to be related to major social upheavals like war and revolution – it remains, in a sense, tautological. Crime is committed because the norms impeding it are weak. Exactly what is explained? The idea of *anomie* also poses problems in the explanation of suicide, where Durkheim rejected the then popular Lombrosian explanation of degeneration. The types of suicide (individualistic, altruistic, anomic) are understandable enough, but applying them in any particular study is problematic. Durkheim's own research was faulted for using indicators on these points incorrectly. Divergence in norms, or any conflict theory of law, is impossible in Durkheim's conceptual framework. Laws reflect the morality of a society by definition. Both law and morality are the product of the society's whole history, varying with the prevailing mentality and social conditions. But this conservative stance simply eliminates, without any empirical testing, any competing theoretical approach.[142]

Durkheim did not discuss his great German contemporary Weber, nor did Weber mention Durkheim. Although Weber's discussion of the relation between the explanation of single and frequently occurring events was far more thorough, his and Durkheim's positions were similar. History done sociologically was sociology to Durkheim. He himself used copious historical examples in his comparative analyses. *Année sociologique* often included reviews of historical works. He held that normally the two disciplines would build on each other, the sociologist using historical data and the historian relating particular events to general trends. There was a place for a separate discipline of history only for the study of events not important enough to fit into a general explanation. Theoretically, knowledge from the past could be applied to the future whenever the circumstances were the same. For Durkheim, however, this would seldom happen. The practical benefits of history were singularly slim because conditions changed too much.

Like other empiricist methodologists in their time, Durkheim distanced himself from the idealist theorists of his.[143] His denunciation of introspection has already been noted. Pragmatism presented a new, fashionable identification of being and knowing to fight. Its leaders were the Americans William James and John Dewey and the French Henri Bergson. Durkheim's lectures on the subject were later (1955) published as a short book, *Pragmatism*. James had led the way in his *Principles of Psychology*, arguing that knowledge would be impossible whenever there were radical differences between subject and object. The gap between thought and reality disappeared in pragmatism by making the prime object neither mind nor thing but "pure experience." Pragmatism was the new monism, identifying existence and knowing, subject and object, fact and value. Truth and value could not be separated but truth was itself judged by expedience or utility.[144]

Durkheim was never a member or public supporter of any political party, but his sympathies were closest to those of the Socialist Party and he was a friend of its leader, Jean Jaurès. Although his methodology contains conservative strains, his idea of the good society was not at all conservative. Rather he was a life-long liberal. Durkheim wrote little on the state and never did the extensive kind of research on it that he did on religion. For him political institutions were simply not that important. He had planned to do his major thesis on individualism and socialism, but was diverted into the division of labour. Later he planned a history of socialism but managed to cover only its ancient and Renaissance roots, ending with a long but uncritical treatment of Saint-Simon. Marxism did not qualify as scientific socialism for Durkheim. The class struggle was not *the* impulse to history and revolution had not produced significant social change. In France many important institutions, such as property, remained much the same after the revolution as before. Marx's doctrine was the result not of fact and observation but of a thirst for justice and pity for the working classes. "The research studies they made were undertaken to establish a doctrine that they previously conceived, rather than the doctrine being a result of research ... Socialism is not a science, a sociology in miniature ... it is a cry of grief, sometimes of anger."[145] Neither was the *laissez-faire* doctrine of Herbert Spencer a scientific theory. Durkheim characterized it as unrestrained competition and the reduction of the state to nothing. It was, he held, a doctrine based on jealousy, love of order, and fear of novelty.

Durkheim saw a certain logic to the central organization of the economy, but insisted that there would always have to be a significant moral component in society, whatever economic reforms were achieved. No economic system could satisfy all demands but people would have to limit their desires in favour of others' needs. Durkheim here considered that the family, state, and church were all inadequate to the task. His alternative source of moral authority – professional organizations, some new version of the old guilds – seems eccentric; perhaps his own department of sociology was unusually amiable.

Elementary Forms of the Religious Life (1912) departs decidedly from all the methodological principles Durkheim had ever followed. The last work in his life, it represents a considerable, although second-hand, effort of comparative research. Its conclusions are strikingly original and totally unverifiable.

Durkheim's "reification" of society met much resistance in France as elsewhere. One of his main critics was *Gabriel Tarde (1843–1904)*, whose own methodological work was based on the individual person. Tarde's three major methodological works, however, do deserve at least brief mention as do his many works on criminology. (Tarde was a provincial magistrate and later director of criminal statistics for France. He also wrote poetry and a novel.) His methodology began with *Lois de l'imitation* (1890), or the search for regularities in normal human interaction. He then went on, in *Opposition universelle* (1897) and *Logique sociale* (1895), to discuss opposition to or competition or conflict with the various forms of adaptation. He then wrote the much shorter *Les lois sociales* (1898), which brought together the main points of his earlier three works. His sources on the dialectic were Aristotle and Hegel, never Marx. However his work was, Tarde insisted on going beyond regularities to conflict and change. His work on crowd behaviour is still cited. In criminology he was a voice for *social* explanation when biological theory was popular. Tarde has only a modest reputation today, although most sociologists' work is closer to his model than Durkheim's. Tarde never had the education of Durkheim or Weber, however, and was unable to relate his work to the broader methodological world. Nor did he have their gifts of expression.

EARLY AMERICAN SOCIOLOGY

American sociology developed extraordinarily rapidly from its beginnings in the 1880s.[146] Moreover, the conflicts and battle lines between conservative and radical were clear from the start. It is perhaps symbolic that the first course in sociology was given by an arch conservative: social Darwinist William Graham Sumner, at Yale University in 1876. Then as now, radicals had more difficulty getting, and keeping, university appointments. Yet they were always a significant part of the profession. Notable among the early radicals were Lester Ward, a civil servant, Thorstein Veblen, who taught at the University of Chicago, and Jane Addams, settlement house innovator and methodologist. Ward's two-volume *Dynamic Sociology* was published in 1883, Veblen's *Theory of the Leisure Class* in 1899, Addams' *Hull-House Maps and Papers* in 1895. Albion Small had an introductory textbook privately printed because of lack of materials for his students. By the turn of the century there would be no lack of choice of texts for the growing number of students. Franklin Giddings' *Principles of Sociology* appeared in 1896, his rather dry text, *Inductive Sociology*, in 1901. Lester Ward's *Outlines of Sociology* was published in 1898, while he began his *Pure Sociology* (1903) on the first day of the twentieth century and dedicated it to that century. *Applied Sociology* was not far behind pure; the book was published in 1906. By the turn of the century also the leaders of the next phase of American sociology were beginning their careers: E.A. Ross, W.I. Thomas, Ernest Burgess, and Robert E. Park. Ross, a leading radical, had begun his classic *Social Control* in 1894, although it was not published until 1901. Ross also became the first American sociologist to be fired for dissident views by an American university, Stanford, in 1900.

Herbert Spencer had a more enthusiastic following in the United States than he ever enjoyed in Britain or on the Continent, but there were both modifiers and enemies of his theory. Many theorists accepted a rudimentary evolutionary framework in order to affirm a substantial component of social/ human choice in evolution and reject the fatalism of Spencer's *laissez-faire* conclusions. John Stuart Mill was also an important source, as were the moderately interventionist German economic historians. It would be wrong, however, to paint a picture of American sociology as only derivative. True, the main founders of the new discipline had studied in Europe, mainly Germany, but this was because they found common problems and relevant approaches there. American sociology was created by Americans seeking to understand their own society and respond to its needs in the light of general laws.

Similar stages in the development of the subject were reached at roughly the same time in Britain, France, Germany, and the United States. Charles Booth had not finished his London survey before Hull House had started its own in Chicago in 1893, beating Rowntree's replication in York by several years. Meanwhile Max Weber was studying the rural poor in East Prussia. The University of Chicago's Department of Sociology was founded in 1892, the first chair in France in 1896, the London School of Economics in 1895. The first issue of the *American Journal of Sociology* appeared in 1895, *Année sociologique* dates from 1898, while Weber and friends took over the *Archiv für Sozialwissenschaft* in 1903. The national sociological associations were founded within a few years of each other: the British in 1903, the American in 1905, and the German in 1908. The Institut International de Sociologie held its first congress in Paris in 1894, with representation from Germany, France, Britain, and Italy. Its papers were duly listed in the new *American Journal of Sociology* to keep American readers informed, a role that journal would play for decades.

It was conventional for the president of Colby College to teach a course in moral philosophy, but when *Albion Small (1854–1926)*[147] took over the office in 1889, he changed the course to sociology. He then went on to the University of Chicago to head the world's first sociology department for over thirty years and to edit the *American Journal of Sociology* for almost as long – at a time when those positions meant real power to hire, fire, admit, and publish. Thus, although he is not known for any original empirical or theoretical work himself, Small helped to shape the new discipline. The shape he gave it was empiricist, for he was an encourager if not a doer. He was also a liberal reformer. His aim was "a morally-relevant and socially-useful academic discipline."[148]

When, in the first issue of the *American Journal of Sociology*, Small announced the new journal's broad intentions, he defined the scope of American sociology for years to come. Marxian explanation was rejected as "utterly out of proportion ... so evidently only partially true" and ignorant both of "existing evolutionary forces" and "the method of action" in human society.[149] Knowledge for application was diffidently expressed, to be more enthusiastically rendered only a few months later in another methodological paper, "Scholarship and Social Agitation." Here Small challenged the claim that neutral, "facts only" scholarship was superior to applied, arguing for the use of science in the realization of one's vision. We could and should move from knowledge of facts to knowledge of forces in order to control those forces. Small wanted American social scientists to "declare their independence of do-nothing traditions" (1:564).

The journal was more eclectic in its early years than academic journals are now. Social policy subjects, including earnest calls for action, were prominent. In the first volume, for example, there were seven articles on Christian sociology and several others on mission work. The social gospel was explained if not proclaimed. So also were the many related causes of peace, unions, women's rights, adequate welfare, and an end to municipal corruption.

William Graham Sumner (1840–1910) was appointed professor of political and social science at Yale in 1872, where he soon introduced the study of sociology with a social Darwinist approach. Sumner's view of social life was Hobbesian in the extreme.[150] The world was a brutal, unreasoning place where progress occurred only through accidents like technological innovation and geographical discovery. The struggle for survival was unremitting. Free societies were possible where resources were plentiful and the struggle for subsistence less savage. Otherwise competition led to slavery. Unlike Darwin, Sumner did not consider progress possible in biological evolution. Given this pessimistic view political action could scarcely provide any remedy. Sumner here was consistent, limiting politics to a stabilizing role. His *Folkways* (1906) influenced the developing discipline of American cultural anthropology.

The sociological mission of *Lester Ward (1841–1913)*[151] was very different. He, too, accepted evolution as the great underlying dynamic of life, but believed it could be controlled by "psychic" factors. Ward was an optimist committed to the use of knowledge for human betterment. A civil servant, he saw a significant role for the state in the application of knowledge to this end. In 1869 Ward set to work on the prospectus of *Dynamic Sociology*, published 1883. With its methodological statement it contains a broad overview of the major areas of the discipline. A series of texts in sociology followed in the next several decades.

Ward's qualifications in natural science were excellent. Yet if he based his sociology on biology, it would be a mistake to consider him a natural scientist applying those theories and methods to the social world. His diary reveals him pursuing the whole gamut of his diverse interests all at the same time: poetry, botany, mineralogy, positivism, spiritualism, classical economics, astronomy, women's suffrage. The social theory he created brought together evolution and intellectual/social factors; no one paradigm dominated any other. The very titles of his major books indicate his convictions. *Pure Sociology* was subtitled *A Treatise on the Origin and Spontaneous Development of Society*. *Applied Sociology* was *Treatise on the Conscious Improvement of Society by Society*. Its preface asserted "the central thought is that of a true science of society, capable, in the measure that it approaches completeness, of being turned to the profit of mankind." Ward further described the book as "a reaction against the philosophy of despair" then dominating even the most enlightened scientific thought. It aimed at remedying the "general paralysis that is creeping over the world" from the *laissez-faire* school.[152]

Although *Jane Addams (1860–1935)*[153] won the Nobel Peace Prize, the honour was insufficient to secure her a safe place in methodological history. At best she is given brief mention among the founders of American sociology; more often she is passed off as "Saint Jane" the social worker. Yet it was Addams and her colleagues at Hull House who pioneered the quantitative methods that would later make the University of Chicago's Department of Sociology famous. *Hull-House Maps and Papers*, published in 1895, has been described as "a scholarly classic ... erased from the annals of sociology."[154] It established the Chicago tradition of studying the city and its inhabitants, making poverty and occupations chief foci of study and mapping the technique. The model for the survey was Charles Booth's survey of London, first results of which had just been published when Addams visited there. The methods themselves were taken up, notably by Burgess and Park in the 1920s and 1930s, and become a standard type of sociological research. Addams is credited with having had a considerable impact on American society. Even those who do not appreciate her intellectual contribution concede that she helped convince Americans of the need and feasibility of welfare-state measures.[155] She established the prototype settlement house in the United States and helped found the profession of social work.

Hull-House Maps and Papers was the first research project of the new settlement house, begun soon after its founding in 1891. There would be no "exhaustive treatises" but only "recorded observations which may possibly be of value, because they are immediate, and the result of long acquaintance."[156] All the writers were residents who contributed both direct experience and data to the project. The data collection itself was co-ordinated with a larger U.S. government survey of slums. The survey's aims were knowledge and application: accurate information for the increasing body of sociology students and improved health and comfort of the people in the neighbourhood. The similarity in "aim and spirit" with the Booth study was noted, but the Hull House group claimed even "greater minuteness," a veritable "photographic reproduction of Chicago's poorest quarters."[157] The data, collected by home visits, were corroborated by other sources as well.

As would countless later researchers, the Hull House team apologized for the "impertinence" of the questions, which would be unpardonable "were it not for the conviction that the public conscience when roused must demand better surroundings for the most inert and long-suffering citizens." It would be idle merely to state symptoms. To ascertain the nature of the disease "and apply, it may be, its cure, is not only scientific but in the highest sense humanitarian" (14). Research results were posted in the building so that local residents could see them. This was sociology to emancipate and empower, not merely to inform.[158] Maps were included in the books as they had been for *Life and Labour of the People in London*. Addams waived the royalties to keep the publisher from excluding maps. The book sold out in a year but was not reprinted.

The survey's analysis went beyond Booth's in its documentation of the need for change. One essay included charts of "defective factory children" and other children, comparing their size and strength. The graphs visibly document the results of deprivation. Addams herself wrote on settlement house philosophy and union organization. The goal was not the rich protecting the poor, as in Carlyle-style Toryism, but political rights for the poor.[159] One of the contributors, Florence Kelley, was a Marxist and translator of Engels' *Condition of the Working Class in England*. As a factory inspector and organizer of the government survey on slums, she wrote the chapter, "The Sweating System." Another paper revealed inefficiency and corruption in the county welfare system and provided an anthropological description of ghetto life. Again reflecting British influences, a chapter on art and labour was based on John Ruskin and William Morris.

Addams and Hull House are an extreme example of the pattern in early American sociology: significant overlap between the academic discipline, the profession of social work, and reform activities motivated by the social gospel, Christian socialism, the single tax, and feminism. However, the radicals were forced out of sociology as the discipline evolved. At Chicago the women faculty who were the social work/social reform advocates were moved from the department of sociology in 1920 to the social work school, leaving an all-male department unsullied by practical concerns.[160] Early, however, both men and women department members did applied research, the difference between them being that the women used quantitative methods, while the men did not.

The early leaders of American sociology were social activists. Many had training in theology and were involved in the social gospel movement. Many fought for workers' education and Chautauqua as well as settlement houses. Sociologists like George Herbert Mead and W.I. Thomas, who are known today wholly for their academic work, were active at the time in the peace movement, workers' rights, and education. The philosopher/educator John Dewey gave his time to a host of such causes, including the board of Hull House. Small, the first head of sociology at Chicago, actively supported Hull House.

UNDERSTANDING MAX WEBER

It is fitting that the last methodologist to be discussed is *Max Weber (1864–1920)*,[161] a proponent of mediation between the growing divisions in approach and one of the most influential founders of sociology. The concern here will be to present the *whole* Max Weber in all the diversity of his work. This approach produces quite a different picture from that in the common treatment of Weber as an opponent of empiricism. Weber's research on religion and bureaucracy are well enough known, so is the theme of his dialogue with Marx. His considerable quantitative work has received much less attention, as has his explicitly pro-empiricist writing, which was slow to be translated. Most of the quantitative work has, to my knowledge, never been translated. All this has been sufficient for Weber to be cited as the exponent of an alternative methodology, *Verstehen* or interpretive sociology, a deliberate rejection of empiricism. Yet the originator of *verstehende Soziologie* has himself been misunderstood, and when all his work is considered he turns out to be very much in the mainstream. His work on great, single events is reminiscent of Thucydides' and, like the early Greek's, related such events to general laws. Weber was acutely sensitive to the deficiencies of the prevailing approaches and sought to overcome their limitations. As Kaspar Naegele observed, Weber struggled "alike against the vague, even irresponsible, claims of the German idealistic and intuitionist tradition of his time and against the too narrow perspective of a classical Marxian analysis."[162] His focus was action, which had to be intentional; his unit of analysis was therefore the person.

Weber was politically involved his entire life. He moved early from the conservative politics of his father to his own, still nationalistic, liberalism.[163] He took part in the negotiations for the Treaty of Versailles and helped found a post-war liberal party. During World War I, too old for the army, he worked as a hospital administrator, gaining practical experience of how bureaucracy functioned which he used in his writing on rationality. His wife, a recognized feminist and scholar in her own right as well as her husband's biographer and editor, was one of the first women elected to a German state legislature.

Weber's first quantitative research arose out of the social concerns in which his mother involved him. He attended the 1890 congress of the Evangelical Social Union, an organization with a social conscience if not a socialist policy. (There was also a not-so-hidden agenda of enticing workers away from the German Social Democratic Party and the influence of Marxism. Weber, though never a socialist, never shared in the denunciation of socialism.) At the 1890 congress he agreed to conduct a study of farm labourers in eastern Prussia for the Verein für Sozialpolitik, a secular organization influenced by the growing social conscience of liberal Protestantism. Many of the people involved in it were academics, the "socialists of the chair." Weber continued to attend the congresses of the Evangelical Social Union, reporting back his findings and taking on further research subjects.

Weber began his methodological work (*Roscher and Knies: The Logical Problem of Historical Economics*) and his first sociology of religion after the severe nervous breakdown which resulted in his having to give up teaching. At that time he and two colleagues also took over the editing of the *Archiv für Sozialwissenschaft und Sozialpolitik*. Articles describing the new board's editorial policy became the occasion for Weber's now famous methodological statements on objectivity and value neutrality. The journal published not only this methodological work but most of *The Protestant Ethic and the Spirit of Capitalism*. (The *Archiv*, judged the best social science journal of Germany, if not the world, in its day was closed down by the Nazis in 1933.) In 1904 the Webers travelled to the United States, where Max Weber gave a paper at a congress held at the World's Fair in St Louis and rounded out the *Protestant Ethic* research. The couple visited factories and slaughterhouses to see capitalism at its purest and attended sect meetings to see Protestantism at its extreme. At the outbreak of the Russian Revolution of 1905 Weber learned Russian to follow events and comment on them in newspaper articles.

Weber was much involved in the 1910 founding of the German Sociological Association and the organization of its first convention. Later he left it over the issue of objectivity. He edited an encyclopedia of social science. Weber's last teaching, as successor to Brentano at Munich, was a triumph. He filled the university's largest lecture hall; politicians, civil servants, and professors as well as students attended. His last full course took him back to the Protestant ethic theme, now in a broader context and with more materialistic results. Published posthumously as *General Economic History* (1923), the course subtitle was more descriptive and provocative: "Positive Criticism of the Materialist Interpretation of History." When he died suddenly of pneumonia at age fifty-six, Weber left behind much unfinished work. Marianne Weber edited the first part of *Economy and Society* (1925). A German collected works, in thirty-two volumes, began to be published in 1984.

Weber's first quantitative research was commissioned by the Verein für Sozialpolitik, an organization in which both Weber and his brother Alfred were active for many years.[164] The Verein's object was practical social reform, specifically the research to guide it. Max Weber was much involved in the debates and actual planning of research, including projects for which he acted as methodological advisor. From the beginning he argued for a sharp distinction between fact and value and between the Verein's social goals and its purely scientific work in collecting and disseminating relevant facts. The research on agricultural workers broke new ground methodologically by asking pastors as well as employers for information and by including intellectual and moral concerns as well as economic ones. Discussion of the political implications of the findings shows Weber's nationalism: He believed in the threat to the state from the influx of non-German workers and the need to keep the area populated by Germans.

In 1907 Weber undertook a study of industrial workers which directly questioned the workers themselves. Careful statistical analysis of the data was followed by analysis of data collected by other researchers on 8,000 industrial workers (miners, steel and textile workers) in eight locations. The study included both attitudinal and factual material. Workers' roles were examined, and family, political, religious, and cultural aspects considered along with economic ones. Weber's concern for empirical research lasted throughout his life. He was "explicitly interested in quantitative techniques, and steadily gaining methodological competence and awareness."[165] Weber found the experience of immersing himself in data stimulating. His 1918 "Science as a Vocation" lecture, discussed below, included the advice not to transfer tedious computational tasks to assistants. "No sociologist should think himself too good even in his old age to make tens of thousands of trivial computations."[166]

This quantitative work cannot be dismissed as youthful excess after which Weber saw the light. His lengthy analysis of industrial workers appeared in 1908–10, *after* his major methodological papers and *The Protestant Ethic and the Spirit of Capitalism*, indeed in the same journal, the *Archiv für Sozialwissenschaft und Sozialpolitik*. A major quantitative analysis of agrarian workers appears in the *same* volume as Weber's essay on objectivity in the social sciences, the first volume for which he was co-editor. The four-part series on industrial work, totalling 170 pages, refers to possible interdisciplinary efforts with experimental psychology, physiology, and psychopathology. "The Psychophysics of Industrial Work" is laced with tables, percentages, controls, and references to such indices as "performance curves."

Weber subscribed to *all* the defining characteristics of empiricism: the search for general laws, causal explanation, unity of the natural and social sciences, nominalism in definitions, probability in results, the hypothetical nature of generalizations, and ethical neutrality. Much of his own research was applied and he even considered quantitative results better than unquantified ones. But he did eloquently highlight what was unique in the social sciences: human meaning, variously termed "interpretive sociology" or "*Verstehen*," German for understanding. This notion was built right into Weber's definition of sociology as "a science which attempts the interpretive understanding of social action in order thereby to arrive at a causal explanation of its course and effects."[167] For Weber explanation and interpretation were always *complementary*.[168] Since it is an article of faith for many sociologists that Weber rejected causal explanation, I will take care here to set out exactly what he did and did not claim as *Verstehen*.

Understanding was a part of Weber's approach both in the search for general explanations and in the establishment of causal sequences for single events. The focus in both cases was "action," which always pertained to an individual. Only *persons* could have conscious motives, therefore only persons could have subjective understanding. States, corporations, and other collectivities were involved in action through their individual members and could influence action by allotting some normative authority to persons. Weber rejected all notions of "collective personality" or collective consciousness à la Durkheim. In order to determine the understanding of a collective one had to take the average or an approximation of the meanings held by the component members.[169] Below the level of the individual there could be no "understanding." Cell behaviour could be studied, functional relations observed, and generalizations drawn, but cells were not capable of understanding.

There were two kinds of understanding: simple observation and the explanation of motive. Observation included anger on someone's face or the direct "rational understanding" of ideas like $2 \times 2 = 4$; explanatory understanding required ascertaining the motives of the individual actor or actors involved. Conscious motives might, however, conceal the "real, driving force." Thus verification of subjective interpretation by the concrete course of events, as for all hypotheses, was indispensable (97). Unfortunately, such verification could only be achieved accurately in special cases like psychological experiments. Otherwise "imaginary experiments" had to be conducted, thinking through the chain of events to arrive at a probable causal judgment. Subjective interpretation, so crucial to Weber's methodology, was always hypothetical and probable. There is no notion of certain intuition anywhere in his work.

Action was "social" for Weber in so far as the actor took into account the behaviour of others and was oriented by it (88). An act could be positive, a failure to act, or passive acquiescence. Nevertheless, nonsocial action was not excluded. Hereditary or biological factors could be introduced into sociological analysis. Nutrition and aging were examples of physical factors already being used. Phenomena not capable of understanding were not necessarily less important but had to be treated differently. They were conditions or stimuli, furthering or hindering action. Weber, it seems, would not exclude any sort of variable on *a priori* grounds. Whether or not any such factor survived scrutiny was the point of empirical investigation. His insistence on subjective meaning was related rather to the *choice* of the subject of investigation – some subjects are more worthy of investigation than others – and the interpretation of results. What we choose to study must be humanly or culturally meaningful, and the results must be so interpreted.

Interpretive understanding, as distinguished from external observation, was obtained at a price. It was more "hypothetical and fragmentary" in its results than mere external observation (104). Functional analysis posed other problems. It might be convenient for practical illustration or for "provisional orientation," but its concepts could be reified and so were dangerous. Weber did not consistently relate understanding to causal explanation. In many places he stressed the role of subjective judgment in the choice of the subject of study, including that subject's causal factors. The number and types of causes influencing any possible event or person was always infinite, stretching from the past into eternity. There was nothing inherent in the things themselves to set apart any particular factors. The choice of any one presupposed a value orientation. In other places Weber reversed the means and ends. "The knowledge of causal *laws* is not the *end* of an investigation, but only a *means*."[170] In yet other places he simply put the two together: the sciences of human conduct seek to "understand" this conduct and by means of this understanding to "explain" it "interpretatively."[171] We seek to understand the cultural significance of individual events and the causes of their being the way they are "and not otherwise."[172] This subjective interpretation is created, not inherent in the data. We cannot learn the meaning of the world from empirical analysis but must create it. There is absolutely no "objective" science of culture or of social phenomena. Human beings confer meaning on culture. All knowledge of cultural reality reflects a particular point of view. "All evaluative ideas are 'subjective'" (83).

Far from rejecting general causal explanation Weber advocated its integration into particular studies. Since Herodotus histories of important events have often tacitly assumed underlying general explanations. Weber took the step of showing how this could be done in the framework of general explanation. Weber was influenced by Rickert's distinction between the cultural and natural sciences as ideographic and nomothetic respectively. He then both modified this treatment and went beyond it. Far from stressing the points of difference between the natural and social sciences, Weber repeatedly underlined the similarities, as will be seen in the discussion of the unity of science.

Understanding, for Weber, became a heuristic device for the formulation of hypotheses. Yet confirmation depended on testing. No rejector of empiricism, Weber strove to show how history could be included in the search for general laws and empirical verification. The object was to study single, significant events in a way consistent with the principles of scientific method. What was only roughly understood and implicit in Thucydides, Weber now made concise and explicit. The "science of sociology" sought to formulate concepts and "generalized uniformities," while history was oriented to "the causal analysis and explanation of individual actions, structures, and personalities possessing cultural significance."[173] The relations were causal in both cases. Much of the material underlying sociological concepts was the same as that in the actions dealt with by historians. Weber's own historical studies, notably those on capitalism and bureaucracy, were full of causal explanations.

"A correct causal interpretation of a concrete course of events" requires correct apprehension of the overt action, its motives, and a meaningful relation between them. No matter how high the degree of uniformity and how precise the probability, if meaning is lacking the result would be but "an incomprehensible statistical probability" (99). Yet even the most perfect grasp of meaning lacks causal significance if there is no proof that the action in question normally takes that course. Clearly Weber had no intention of substituting interpretation for normal causal explanation; his aim was always to link them.

After the selection of the subject of study and possible causal factors on the basis of cultural significance, the method of comparison came into play. Here Weber was entirely consistent with the method Mill set out in Book 6 of *System of Logic*. Indeed it has been suggested that Weber owed more to Mill than he acknowledged.[174] The process required considering what other causal sequence would have occurred if the factor in question (person, event) had not been present. What if the Greeks had lost to the Persians at Marathon? Would a distinctive Greek society and culture have emerged? Weber showed that other societies defeated by the Persians were changed by their new rulers. He concluded that Greece would have been, too. The Greek victory at Marathon thus became a "causally adequate" explanation, although not necessarily the only one, for the development of a distinctive Greek culture.[175] This method permitted the determination of what was "objectively possible" and an assessment of its probability from high to low, or from "adequate causation" to mere "accidental" causes. For all Weber's emphasis on singularities his use of the comparative method clearly assumes a commonness of human nature underlying changes in circumstances similar to those in Thucydides and the Hippocratics.

Weber saw dangers in generalizing from historical laws, especially in predicting the future. Knowledge was always only partial. The attempt to arrive at a wholly deductive science on the observation of regularities and creation of concepts was suspect.[176] Concepts so attained might seem clear cut but could entail an overly hasty anticipation of the future. The concepts themselves would have to be changed over time. Concepts were incorrectly assumed to reproduce objective reality in the analyst's imagination, but concepts were means, not ends. They should not be confused with reality any more than should an ideal type.

Weber's use of ideal types was entirely in line with earlier empiricists like Montesquieu. It entailed no more departure from the principles of empiricism than his usage of *Verstehen*. The ideal type was a heuristic device. Not itself a hypothesis, it aided in the construction of hypotheses by providing clarity of focus. Nor was the ideal type a description of reality but an analytical construct, a "utopia," which was "not to be found empirically anywhere in reality" (90). It was deliberately one sided, stressing a particular point of view and synthesizing many diffuse phenomena arranged according to that one-sided point of view. Some commentators have stressed the bridging role of the ideal type, linking together individualistic interpretation and general explanation. I maintain that history need not be incapable of relation to general explanation. Yet the researcher could stop short of an extreme positivism whose generality obliterates distinctive features.

Weber's views on the influence of ideas in history are well known if controversial. His treatment of ideas in methodology by contrast has received scant attention. He conceded an element of serendipity then: "Ideas occur to us when they please, not when it pleases us." Often they come when we do not expect them, during a walk, perhaps. "Yet ideas would certainly not come to mind had we not brooded at our desks and searched for answers with passionate devotion." Ideas were no substitute for work, nor work for ideas. "Both enthusiasm and work, and above all both of them *jointly*, can entice an idea."[177] Yet if ideas normally come with hard work, sometimes the dilettante has better insights and comes up with better hypotheses.

For Weber the fact/value distinction was fundamental, a principle he argued vigorously and at length from early in his methodological writings and speeches to the end of his life. In addition to the strictures on the researcher there was a particular duty for teachers, "privileged hirelings of the state," not to become "petty prophets" (153). Teachers had all the opportunities of other citizens to work for their causes. In a political meeting it was "one's damned duty to take a stand" (145); in the classroom it was one's duty not to. "The prophet and the demagogue do not belong on the academic platform" (146). It was all too convenient to demonstrate one's courage in taking a stand where the audience and possible opponents were condemned to silence. Weber did not always follow his own advice, but he was forceful in giving it. He recognized also that some students want to be told what to believe. Such people crave "a leader and not a teacher" (149).

Failure to respect the fact/value distinction leads to bad results scientifically. Whenever a scientist introduces a personal value judgment, full understanding of the facts ceases. The teacher's duty is to state the facts and consequences so that students can weigh and judge them in terms of their own values. Teachers should provide knowledge and scientific experience and not imprint their own views on students. Teachers and scientific investigators should keep "unconditionally separate" the establishment of empirical facts from their evaluations of them as satisfactory or unsatisfactory, an "intrinsically simple demand."[178]

Consistent with the empiricist tradition Weber declared himself emphatically opposed to the view that science can produce an ethics about "what *should* happen" (13). Questions of ends are "entirely matters of choice," and the social sciences cannot save the individual from making that choice (19). Weber mused about who would dare to scientifically refute the ethics of the Sermon on the Mount. "In our opinion, it can never be the task of an empirical science to provide binding norms and ideals from which directives for practical activity can be derived."[179] Rather, the "acting, willing person" must weigh and choose among values according to his or her own conscience and personal world view. Science will make one realize the consequences of any action or inaction, but the act of choice remains one's own responsibility. Science helps individuals to make those choices by clarifying what is possible: what one *can* do not what one *should* do. Nonetheless, there are good reasons for examining value judgments even if they cannot be proved right or wrong. Discussion helps to elaborate and explicate ultimate values. The implications that follow from one's choice can be determined. Empirical analysis slotted into this kind of discussion yet served to provide solutions to the means, not the ends.

Weber had an explanation for the frequent blurring of the "is" and "ought" in earlier writing. What should be a clear logical distinction was hampered by theories connecting them, especially in the natural-law identification of the "normatively right" with the "immutably existent" (51). More recently the theory of evolution promulgated a similar identification, now between the "normatively right" and the "inevitably emergent" (52).

Weber's commitment to the unity of science is evident from his opening definition of sociology as a "science" in *The Theory of Social and Economic Organization*. Weber called himself and his colleagues "scientists." His great lecture on methodology, with its passionate pleading for the separation of fact and value, was entitled "Science as a Vocation." The process was cumulative for all the sciences. A work of art might be forever, but scientists have to expect their work to be outdated in ten, twenty, or fifty years. "We cannot work without hoping that others will advance further than we have."[180]

The fact/value distinction held for both the natural and the cultural sciences. No science gives answers to values, which have to be decided by individuals on the basis of other criteria: "Natural science gives us an answer to the question of what we must do if we wish to master life technically. It leaves quite aside ... whether we should and do wish to master life technically and whether it ultimately makes sense to do so" (144). Similarly: "The historical and cultural sciences ... teach us how to understand and interpret political, artistic, literary and social phenomena in terms of their origins. But they give us no answer to the question, whether the existence of these cultural phenomena have been and are *worth while*" (145). Yet, as well as serving practical ends, scientific method helps people to answer these questions of value. This method helps people see the consequences of various alternative courses of action. Not only does it give people the means to chosen ends, it helps them account to themselves for the *"ultimate meaning"* of their own conduct (152). To the disillusioned students of war-weary Germany, Weber argued that clarification as to which god you served was no trifling matter.

The one significant area where Weber postulated differences between the natural and social sciences was on the desirability of general laws. For the natural sciences, where understanding was not at issue, the more general the law the better. For the social sciences, however, the more general the law the less specific and hence the less meaningful the content. "In the cultural sciences, the knowledge of the universal or general is never valuable in itself." Still, Weber made clear that this downplaying of generalization for the social sciences was not because they were any "less governed by laws."[181] Values are not wholly irrelevant in the natural sciences but, just as much as in the social sciences, guide the choice of research problems and possible causes. The possible causal factors are infinite for both types of science. For both the selection as to what to research reflects the researcher's interests and judgments of practical utility or other values.

The notion that Weber's use of *Geisteswissenschaften*, literally the sciences of the mind, implies a rejection of social science or empiricism is based on a misunderstanding. Weber used that term for all the social sciences together, as well as using what are now the standards terms of social sciences and sociology. The term *Geisteswissenschaften* itself came into use in a translation of Mill's *System of Logic*. It was simply the German expression devised for the old-fashioned "moral sciences," a term that itself fell into disuse as social scientists, including Mill and Weber, took up the new vocabulary. Etymology should not be taken too far, but perhaps it could be noted that "culture" itself has a similar derivation as "physics" and "nature," all with roots in the verb for growing.

Weber is still typically seen as the remote scholar whose work was at a rarefied level on esoteric subjects without any practical application. That the reality is quite different has already been shown by his numerous early studies of workers, including protracted discussion of such applied matters as "performance curves." Later in life he pursued other practical subjects as well, notably political parties and the press. The title of the journal Weber edited included social policy with social science. The editors promised they would continue coverage of the "labour question," with articles from all political persuasions. They would guard against confusion between science and politics in all discussions of social policy (62).

Weber viewed the links between theory and practice as both legitimate and natural. Virtually all the social sciences had begun as practical activities, "technique" in his terminology. Economics was concerned with increasing wealth, politics with power. Even now, with a clearer distinction between theory and practice, the two were necessarily intertwined. Values, or utility in some form, guided the very choice of what to study and what causal factors to examine. Finally, the results of empirical study led to application, which meant the "reformulations of causal propositions."[182]

The Protestant Ethic and the Spirit of Capitalism (1904–5), Weber's most famous work, is still read and debated. The object of this, his first attempt to reply to Marx's economic conception of history, was to relate modern, rational capitalism, whose defining characteristic was the permanent, rational enterprise, with the rise of the "Protestant ethic," especially the inner-worldly asceticism of Calvinism. Capitalism in the form of profit seeking had always existed, Weber acknowledged, with brigands, crusaders, merchants, and traders. But it was only with the rise of Protestantism that business enterprises geared to profit and using rational accounting procedures emerged. The book opened with a factual statement on the preponderance of successful capitalists in Protestant countries and regions, compared with Catholic, data which have since been disputed. Weber argued that there had to have been a *psychological* change for these changes in business practices to have developed. This he found in the concept of the "calling." While the term had earlier had an exclusively religious connotation, people being called out of the world, with Calvinism a this-worldly understanding emerged. The calling sanctified ordinary secular work. Success in business could serve as a sign of election or salvation in the doctrine of predestination.

The bulk of *The Protestant Ethic and the Spirit of Capitalism* described this transformation, including copious quotes from Puritan leaders. At no time did Weber argue a one-way influence. "It is ... not my aim to substitute for a one-sided materialistic an equally one-sided spiritualistic causal interpretation of culture and history. Each is equally possible but each, if it does not serve as the preparation, but as the conclusion of an investigation, accomplishes little in the interest of historical truth." It was necessary to investigate how the Protestant ethic was influenced in its turn by "the totality of social conditions, especially economic."[183] Yet Weber did not, then or later, go onto a systematic examination of these competing causal influences. This was the crux of Tawney's critique of Weber in *Religion and the Rise of Capitalism*, that it was not possible to assign any relative weights without looking at both directions of the influence. "While Puritanism helped to mould the social order, it was, in turn, moulded by it."[184] Ironically, Weber, the proponent of the religious factor, was himself not a believer while Tawney, his opponent, was.

Instead of pursuing these reverse influences Weber extended his studies in other ways. He looked back in time and out to a great diversity of societies, notably those in which capitalism did not develop at all. Instead of only one subject of study (capitalism) and one causal factor (the Protestant ethic) there were many causes: economic, political, and social, and in modern times their complicated interplay. Quite a different Weber emerges in these late books, beginning with *Agrarian Sociology* (1909). This work, an expansion of pre-*Protestant Ethic* research, takes the causal links back to ancient Egypt, Mesopotamia, Greece, and Rome. As it had for Democritus, the ancient historians, and up through Montesquieu, geography now took a significant causal role for Weber (83–4; 97–8). Notably, in *Agrarian Sociology*, as in *General Economic History*, Weber argued that river systems and sea connections affected transportation costs and, as a consequence, trading opportunities and general economic development.[185]

In a later edition of *The Protestant Ethic and the Spirit of Capitalism*, Weber again excused himself from pursuing the reverse direction of the causal chain. His friend Ernest Troeltsch had dealt with much of it in his *The Social Teaching of the Christian Churches* (1911). As a theologian Troeltsch was better able to handle the material, a rare *non sequitur* for Weber. Yet Troeltsch's hefty two-volume work did nothing to answer the pertinent question. He discussed the Weberian thesis with great respect and concluded that the "utmost reserve" was required on the issue of the calling's effect upon the whole of civilization. The facts were known only in part, and the "perpetually fluctuating power and range of influence" made very difficult "any certain interpretation of the facts."[186] Weber continued to hold that the influence of economic development on the fate of religious ideas was very important. Again he promised further work "to show how ... the process of mutual adaptation of the two took place." Yet he repeated his original conclusions without doing that next stage of work. "Religious ideas ... cannot be deduced from economic circumstances. They are in themselves, that is beyond doubt, the most powerful plastic elements of national character, and contain a law of development and a compelling force entirely their own."[187] Of the nonreligious factors, Weber now asserted that political factors were more important than economic or social ones.[188]

In *The Sociology of Religion* (1922) Weber turned to major civilizations, China and India, where modern capitalism did not develop at all. In his last work on the subject, a course of lectures published as *General Economic History*, Weber did not abandon the Protestant ethic thesis but incorporated it into a wide-sweeping analysis of the interplay of social, political, and economic factors. Geography again had a crucial causal influence, but "In the last resort the factor which produced capitalism is the rational permanent enterprise, rational accounting, rational technology and rational law, but again not these alone. Necessary complementary factors were the rational spirit, the rationalization of the conduct of life in general, and a rationalistic economic ethic."[189] This rational spirit, with its origins in ancient Judaism, had its greatest force in the Puritan concept of the calling. Admission to communion in Protestant ascetic communities was based on one's ethical fitness – conduct in this world – and identified with business honour. "Such a powerful, consciously refined organization for the production of capitalistic individuals has never existed in any other church or religion, and in comparison with it what the Renaissance did for capitalism shrinks into insignificance" (368). This is not the careful, systematic weighing of influences Weber promised, but it is an implicit one, and his judgment was still that the religious factor was the weightiest.

Weber not only dealt causally with significant single events in the past, he used causal laws to predict significant events. He has been faulted for not having any understanding of the coming forces of fascism, but he did make a number of other astonishingly accurate if thoroughly gloomy predictions. For Germany itself he predicted the demise of both the Kaiser and the proletariat. An opponent of the harsh terms of the Versailles peace treaty, he predicted that the peace would be discredited, not the war.[190] Weber was always extremely pessimistic as to its direction. He could anticipate no good end to the civil war in his own country: "Not the summer's bloom lies ahead of us, but rather a polar night of icy darkness and hardness, no matter which group may triumph externally now" (128). Weber's general predictions on the possibilities of centrally planned economies were equally unhappy and accurate.

Weber's methodology did not change over his lifetime. He made the same arguments at the Verein für Sozialpolitik in the 1890s, in his methodological essays of 1903–4, and in his famous lectures at the end of his life. Substantively his work changed, both in the subjects of study and the causal variables examined. His work on bureaucracy is still used in the sociology of organization, his conceptualization of legitimation of power in political science. For some commentators his treatment of rational organization constitutes no less than a new framework of analysis capable of absorbing fundamental elements of Marx. Thus Marx's alienation of workers in capitalism becomes a special case of the process of rationalization of society in Weber. For this he has been called "the most subtle critic of Marx."[191] Whether he deserves to be called the world's finest sociologist is still debated. He was certainly a dedicated scholar in the empiricist tradition and the best modern exponent of one of its branches, the explanation of single important events in the context of general laws. In this he was a fit successor to Thucydides.

The last chapter will look briefly at developments in the twentieth century before we take a last overview of the critique of methodology, both for the nineteenth century and earlier.

7 Revisiting the Critiques of Methodology

Before revisiting the critique of empiricism in the social sciences that prompted this study we will briefly tour developments in methodology in the mid to late twentieth century. I have argued from the outset that the foundations of social science methodology are ancient indeed. Nineteenth-century theorists built on them, and although this book ends with Weber, the sheer scale of work in recent decades deserves mention. Prodigious work has been done in both the empiricist and idealist traditions, and increasing specialization by academic discipline now complicates matters. Idealism has been characterized by a rejection of unity in method; the cultural or social sciences are seen as essentially different from the natural sciences and as requiring quite different research methods. The main developments in idealism have been phenomenology (notably Husserl), some structuralism/semiology (although not Lévi-Strauss), existentialism/engagement (Sartre), critical social theory (Horkheimer, Adorno, Marcuse, and Habermas), "interpretive" sociology (usually referring to Weber but understanding him as anti-empirical), and ethnomethodology (especially Schutz and Garfinkel).

Marxism split early in the century as acrimoniously into methodological factions (empiricist and idealist) as into political ones (revolutionary and evolutionary). This had an enormous impact on development in both methodological traditions. Marxist empiricists fought both Marxist idealists and bourgeois empiricists. Others interested in methodology sought various kinds of *rapprochement*. Sartre, for example, railed against empiricism and "hyper-empiricism," yet credited sociology with enough truthfulness to be an effective arm against capitalism.[1] Lenin attacked the first wave of idealized Marxisms with *Materialism and Empirio-Criticism* (1908). The idealizing trend was only to become stronger. Methodologists turned increasingly to idealist interpretations which were immune to disconfirmation by events as concrete predictions failed. Lukacs, Gramsci, and Althusser led the movement, which remains strong on the Continent.[2] An empiricist Marxism was developed in Soviet Russia, most notably by Bukharin, who was killed in the 1930s purges and only recently rehabilitated.[3] An Austro-Marxist movement continued the empiricist tradition in the West for some time.[4] Bukharin and the Austro-Marxists, though, were no more sceptical than the idealist Marxists.

Nor was Mao, whose methodological works reveal elements of both the idealist and empiricist roots in both Marx and ancient Chinese philosophy. The empiricists stressed external reality; if a theory is wrong that will become clear in practice. Yet Mao referred in places to "essences" and the possibility of intuitive knowledge, when sufficient perceptual awareness had been accumulated. His focus on movement/change/dialectic is reminiscent of the young Marx, and he opposed "metaphysical mechanical materialism." Similarly he rejected the empiricist primacy of external conditions; significant qualitative change was caused by internal contradictions.[5]

An impressive body of research based on empiricist Marxist principles is accumulating, and a methodological literature is growing.[6] British historian E.P. Thompson and sociologist T.B. Bottomore have been influential in both theory and practice. The American sociologist, C. Wright Mills, characteristically with a softer Marxism, also contributed substantially. Socialist Jean Ziegler's *Retournez les fusils!* defends empirical social science with examples of its use in the struggle against imperialism in Africa. Ziegler considered sociology necessarily subversive; whatever the intention of the sociologist the act of exposing social reality, "de-masking," is in conflict with the strategies of the dominant society. Sociology gives a voice to the peoples of silence.

Roy Medvedev's criticism of the repression of the social and natural sciences in the then Soviet Union sounds like a seventeenth-century plea for empiricism instead of Aristotle. All the sciences, he maintained, had fallen behind in the abandonment of empiricism for truth per the "canonized classics of Stalin."[7] Because of historical materialism concrete sociological investigations were halted in favour of expounding general theoretical schemes. Philosophers, instead of analyzing the data of science, rehearsed examples chosen to fit their own predetermined stereotypes. Thus philosophy was turned into scholasticism (503).

The Frankfurt School's critical theory is probably the most inconsistent attack on empiricism ever.[8] At times its proponents opposed all quantitative research and all research for purposes of application. This was "domination," the according of pre-eminence of "facts" to "Reason." Yet Adorno,

Frenkel-Brunswick, et al. did quantified research, notably for *The Authoritarian Personality* (1950). This massive project of survey research/scale development also was directed at application: education for more democratic, less anti-semitic attitudes.

As did idealist methodologists, critical theorists claimed to go beyond empiricism to the "objective essence of appearances," and who are we to say whether or not they succeeded? These theorists insisted on the study of totalities, or total society, an impossible task at which they succeed no better than anyone else. The reference to totalities comes honestly enough from the theory, which was grounded on Marxism. Critical theorists rejected, however, nearly every other principle of Marxist methodology. The one consistent theme in critical theory was its opposition to natural science, of which Marx and Engels just as consistently and enthusiastically approved. Empirical work, at best, could serve to illustrate a point otherwise decided on, not to support or disconfirm a theory. Marcuse's *One-Dimensional Man* argued that it was impossible for modern "man" to apprehend the truth, to distinguish true from false needs. Only critical theorists could see "behind the curtain" of advertising, propaganda, and repressive social structures.[9] Marcuse claimed the ability not only to distinguish truth from falsehood but to apprehend relevant social structures, ascertain the determining factors of social life, and project the limits and alternatives available to modern society! Horkheimer was content similarly to dismiss empiricism as false or inadequate. For him, "a great many metaphysicians contain a more profound insight into reality than can be found in the special sciences."[10] In the end, critical theory is an assertion that a certain group of people possess privileged intuitive access to the truth. It is now social structure, not personal sin, that prevents the rest of us from seeing it. A re-incarnated Marx and Engels could have as much fun with "the holy family" of the Frankfurt school as with their own critical theorists in *Critique of Critical Critique*.

There have been developments at both extremes of mainstream, non-Marxist empiricism, from global systems approaches to psychological reductionism or behaviourism. Practical advice on how to do research has gone ahead with a vengeance. There is now a vast literature on social survey design, sampling techniques, statistical tests, content analysis, the use of secondary data, scaling, and so forth. The quantitative treatment of historical data has advanced enormously, so that one is less pressed than Thucydides and Polybius to research contemporary societies.

THE EVILS OF EMPIRICISM REVISITED

The Nineteenth Century

It has become clear that in the nineteenth century as earlier the description of social science empiricists as blind or slavish followers of natural science models just does not hold. Not one empiricist fits the stereotype. Frédéric LePlay, a mining engineer and marginal methodologist, is the only one to come close. Herbert Spencer also had an engineering background, but he never actually did any empirical work in sociology himself. Comte's early training was in natural science but he resisted the application of statistics to sociology. Methodologists like Saint-Simon, Mill, Taylor Mill, Martineau, Tocqueville, Webb, Addams, Durkheim, and Weber simply had little acquaintance with the natural sciences. Quetelet was an eminent statistician with credits for mathematical discovery as well as for the practical work of organizing centralized data collection. Yet his first love was art – he studied sculpture before astronomy, and like the ancient methodologists maintained an interest in both the natural and social sciences throughout his life.

Nightingale strongly advocated the mathematical basis of the social sciences, but her education had been largely in Greek philosophy and literature. She learned some statistics, with difficulty and late in life, to address such practical questions as reducing mortality in childbirth. Karl Pearson certainly was firm in his insistence on a rigorous mathematical foundation to the social sciences. Yet far from applying the methods of natural to social sciences, he began his scholarly career in medieval literature. His social science interests arose from social concerns which led him in turn to applied mathematics and finally to eugenics. Although Galton had studied medicine he never practised it. He published travel books before he took up statistics in the cause of eugenics. Marx did no work in the natural sciences but came to methodology with a classical education and passionate social concerns. He developed an interest in the natural sciences later in life, keenly following developments in biology, especially theory of evolution.

The work of many writers in the nineteenth century and earlier refutes the contention that the social sciences exclude treatment of the particular and concrete, especially history. Max Weber obviously heads the list, but Tocqueville, Comte, Martineau, Marx, Engels, Pearson, Webb, and Addams were other notable writers of history. Mill wrote copiously on particular problems in the manner of contemporary history. So did Nightingale and Booth. Even Durkheim, a strong advocate of general explanation, wrote a history of education and included much historical material in *Année Sociologique*, while earler empiricists had made no strict demarcation between the quest for generality and elucidation of the particular.

The pattern of interest in both the arts and the social sciences continues. Quetelet trained in sculpture and produced a libretto and a play; he taught mathematics only to earn a living. Harriet Taylor published poetry before collaborating with Mill on methodology. Tarde wrote poetry and a novel, Pearson a passion play. Martineau published novels and poetry. Marx, who loved classical literature, was another youthful poet. Beatrice Webb's autobiography revealed literary talent otherwise submerged in the work she published jointly with Sidney.

Thoroughly contrary to the charge of inherent conservative bias in empiricism, the vast majority of contributors to empirical methodology were critics of their society, seeking reform on a vast range of issues. Webb and Pearson were socialists, Marx a Communist; Durkheim and the Mills were liberals with (slight) socialist leanings. A brief list of particular causes includes rights for women (the Mills, Martineau, Addams), mass education (Quetelet, the Mills), the abolition of slavery (Martineau, Tocqueville), anti-semitism (Durkheim), a rational public service (Nightingale, Addams, Webb), workers' rights (the Mills, Webb, Addams). Even Weber, who is marginal as a reformer, was deeply committed to democratic institutions. Booth, who remained a Tory, supported the old-age pension and medicare for the needy. The two exceptions are Sumner (a social Darwinist) and Spencer. The great conservatives of the era, like Hegel, were idealists in philosophy, not empiricists.

Although by the nineteenth century prison and execution were not the threat they had been, the association between spending time behind bars and a preference for empiricism continued. J.S. Mill apparently spent a few days behind bars for distributing literature on birth control. Quetelet visited his friends in prison but managed to stay free himself. Marx never went to jail but had an impressive police record and had to leave three countries in haste.

The association of empiricism with religious dissidence also continued, but orthodox believers had become the exception. Saint-Simon's earliest act of rebellion was to refuse first communion. He, Comte, Spencer, and Durkheim sought secular substitutes to religion. Other methodologists – Marx, the Mills, Pearson, Booth, Martineau – were outright atheists or agnostics; Weber was "religiously unmusical." Orthodox religious believers were rare exceptions: Tocqueville, Nightingale, Addams. Webb, with an agnostic husband, struggled on as a closet believer. By now, however, lack of belief was no social or professional handicap. Indeed, Webb complained of the social pressure toward unbelief.

An understanding of empiricism as a methodology that could be used by ordinary people to improve their lives emerged in the nineteenth century, continuing the association between empiricism and democratic choice. Martineau popularized political economy and explained how to use empiricism in everyday life. Addams and her Hull-House colleagues posted their results so that residents could draw their own conclusions. Quetelet wrote a simplified version of his statistics to make it more accessible, and cheap "workingmen's editions" of the words of various writers (e.g., J.S. Mill) were produced.

Back to the Origins

From the earliest origins of the social sciences the empiricists were prone to support the less powerful portions of their societies, usually the bourgeoisie or a wider citizenry against the aristocracy/monarchy. In ancient times the defenders of slavery were the idealists – Plato circumspectly,

Aristotle and Augustine explicitly – while the first questioning of slavery came from the sophists. The first identifiable contribution to empiricism was the work of the law reformer Solon. In the Puritan period empiricists like Winstanley supported the mass of the population against any aristocracy, as had Thomas More earlier. The empiricist-reform connection continued with Locke, Astell, Voltaire, Beccaria, Hutcheson, Helvétius, Millar, Holbach, Diderot, Condorcet, Priestley, Godwin, Sinclair, Saint-Simon, the Mills, Quetelet, Nightingale, Pearson, Addams, and Durkheim, not to speak of the revolutionary Marx. Meanwhile, idealists from Spinoza to Kant taught resignation and respect for authority. The Cambridge Platonists were no more radical than Plato or Cambridge. Methodologists of both schools flattered royalty, in the case of the empiricists often for opportunistic motives: research grants, or the hope thereof.

The prospect of dungeon or death, if it did not concentrate the mind wonderfully, seems to have made it aware of objective realities. The history of empiricism is replete with unlikely jail birds. Several were never convicted of any crime, some were prisoners of war, and many were prisoners of religious rather than state authorities. The idealists who suffered this fate tend to be anomalies. Socrates, for instance, was imprisoned (and drank hemlock) at age sixty-nine, long after his dialogues were well known. The natural law theorists, Grotius and Pufendorf, are also exceptions; they were prisoners of war. In ancient times Thucydides, Polybius, and Eusebius were jailed, in medieval Europe Roger Bacon, William of Ockham, and Nicolas of Autrecourt probably spent time in prison. By the Reformation Machiavelli, Montaigne, and probably Bodin, can be added to the list. Montchrétien was killed in Huguenot revolts. Baxter and Harrington were imprisoned as Puritans, Francis Bacon for corruption. Most of the Encyclopedists moved fast enough to escape the police; Voltaire, Diderot, and Condorcet did not. Germaine de Staël spent years in exile and organized escapes for others. Mme Roland was executed. Buffon died the year before the Revolution but his son was killed in the Terror. Châtelet's son was also a victim of the Terror. Joseph Priestley had to leave the country as a result of mob violence in which his house, laboratory, and library were burned. Idealists other than Socrates tended to stay on the right side of the law. It is difficult to imagine the suave courtier Leibniz, the clerical Malebranche, the proper Kant, the Cambridge Platonists, Bishop Berkeley, or Hegel in leg irons.

The religious dissidence of the nineteenth century continued an old tradition. In a society with many gods, Xenophanes was the first known deviant monotheist in Greece. The sceptic Anaxagoras and other materialists were known atheists. Empedocles tried to start a new religion; Epicurus had a subversive theology. Augustine's scathing denunciation of scepticism was to protect the faith. For centuries piety depended on an idealist commitment to certain knowledge, with only a brief exception during the Renaissance. This was true for both Catholics and Protestants; Martin Luther was one of the firmest "asserters" ever. It was only with Erasmus, Castellion, the Puritans, and the English divines that a new form of piety gradually emerged which was consistent with a more sceptical methodology. Probability and doubt even became virtues, for the wonders of God's creation were too great to be easily captured by mere mortal intelligence. John Wesley and Joseph Priestley in the eighteenth century echoed this theme from a more devout age.

If Adam Smith was seen smiling at divine service many of the eighteenth-century methodologists, Diderot, Condorcet, Hume, Helvétius, Holbach, LaMéttrie, and Bentham among them, were outright agnostics or atheists. Voltaire always claimed to be a Christian, but the Catholic Church did not agree with him. De Staël was a Protestant in Catholic France. The British women empiricists showed decided traces of feminist theology. Idealists like Bishop Berkeley and the Scottish "common sense" school were more likely to be conventionally religious. Yet Francis Hutcheson was a Church of Scotland clergyman. At the century's end Church of Scotland clergy aided in the collection of the world's first large survey.

THE FEMINIST CRITIQUE REVISITED

However negative many contemporary feminists may be toward empiricism, the women methodologists who emerged in this study were almost all empiricists. Hildegard of Bingen was a twelfth-century Platonist and Anne of Conway was a seventeenth-century idealist. The Electress Sophia supported Leibniz's idealist methodology. Châtelet collaborated with Voltaire on Newton and wrote on Leibniz. Otherwise the women methodologists were unambiguous empiricists: Martineau, Taylor Mill, Webb, and Addams joined Astell, Hays, Macaulay, Wollstonecraft, Roland, and de Staël from the earlier period. Against the contention that empiricist methodology supports male domination, feminists over the centuries *chose* empiricism as their methodology. As did other social reformers, advocates of education, legal rights, and the vote for women found in empiricism the wherewithal to fight. Women from Astell in the late seventeenth century, through Wortley Montagu, Macaulay, Hays, Roland, Nightingale, Taylor Mill, Martineau, and Addams used empirical evidence in their arguments for social change and helped to develop empiricist methodology as they did so. The male supporters of women's rights similarly were empiricists: Saint-Simon and Mill joining the ranks of Thomas More, Hutcheson, Millar, Holbach, Helvétius, and Condorcet.

THE ENVIRONMENTALIST CRITIQUE

It is no coincidence that the environmentalist and feminist critiques of empiricism overlap. There has been an association between methodologists' views on non-human nature and women since the emergence of idealism in the fifth century B.C. Since Plato and Aristotle women have been identified with matter/biology/inferiority, while men have been identified with spirit/intellect/superiority. The sharp differentiation between people and animals (the exaggeration of differences in skills, use of machines, language, and social life) is associated with a sharp differentiation between men and women. The theorists who viewed humans and animals on some kind of a continuum were empiricists. Except the physiocrats, all those who believed in day-and-night differences between humans and other animals were idealists.

Through most of history most people, of whatever methodological persuasion, have taken the survival of the environment for granted. The Puritans raised such issues as animal rights and human responsibility, but the issue has never had the urgency it does now. Problems of deforestation, soil exhaustion, and air pollution were identified by at least the seventeenth century. Macaulay and Bentham in the eighteenth century were pioneers in the ethical debate, questioning anthropocentrism and arguing for some recognition of animals' rights. John Stuart Mill argued the need for wilderness areas and species diversity. The few social scientists who contributed to a better understanding of the environment happen to have been empiricists; the proponents of the most harmful position environmentally were idealists. Descartes did not promulgate the thesis that animals could not feel, hence could be treated as anyone wished. His most idealist reviser, Malebranche, did. Malebranche's source, in turn, was another idealist, Augustine, although to reach his conclusions Malebranche had to repudiate what Augustine had actually said and speculate from Augustine's premises.

Alchemy and astrology were popular methodological frameworks for many centuries in western Europe, and many environmentalists now approve of their holistic, organic conceptualization of the world/universe. Yet this holistic approach carried with it just as much inclination to domination/exploitation as ever occurred in the mechanical philosophy. Both alchemy and astrology should be seen simply as alternative approaches to the same end, the advancement of human goals. The same holds for Plotinus' neo-Platonism. The world may have been seen as one living body, but humans were no more prepared to defer to the needs of their fellow members of that body than the more mechanically oriented empiricists. With vitalism and neo-Platonism there was also a hierarchy of value, usually with non-material entities (souls or gods) on top, humans next (thanks to their non-material qualities), and purely material creatures like animals beneath them. Contrary to the stereotype, the materialist, mechanical empiricists *raised* the status of animal creation by stressing sensation and the greatest happiness of the greatest number. Few advocates of environmental ethics appeared in this chronicle, but those who did came from the empiricist tradition.

This is not the place to address the really difficult issues of why we have been so destructive of nature and what we should think and do differently now that we realize the desperate plight of the planet. But naming the wrong culprit, empiricism, is no solution; indeed to do so wastes time and energy and distracts attention from the real problems of interests, values, attitudes, and images. Nor is this the place to argue for an alternative vision, but only to caution against false solutions in vitalism, pantheism, or nostalgia for a simpler past.

LAST WORDS

As the end of this book approaches I am deeply conscious of the need for a more sceptical spirit in research. The United States persists in its research for star wars, an awesome project predicated on a confidence in prediction and application. Beyond the fact that it advances a technological solution for human conflict, it assumes that error-free technological solution is possible. Yet even the most optimistic advocates of the system estimate only 95 per cent success. Nor, even with the end of the cold war and the disappearance of the "evil empire," has the program been cancelled. With the prospect of sudden death for millions followed by nuclear winter and slow death for the rest, we could wish that military planners were imbued with a greater sense of scepticism. A humbler methodological understanding becomes ever more inviting.

Although the democratic movements in the former Soviet Union lessen the prospect of nuclear war, we have no reason to relax. If the bomb does not get us the reactors, their radioactive wastes, global warming, the ozone hole, acid rain, deforestation, soil erosion, or toxic wastes in our drinking water just might. In the Two-Thirds World poverty means starvation for millions, while debt payments transfer funds from poor to rich nations. In the affluent cities of the industrial world poverty means food banks for the needy, while governments impose ever more of the tax burden onto the poor. The problems of today, in short, are *both* physical and social, and both the natural and the social sciences are needed for their solution. Boyle's criterion for success in natural science – to grow a better garden – seems ever more relevant. But so is the need for social and economic justice, a better social as well as natural garden. Both require political will, moral fibre, and knowledge.

Young people especially have to find a methodology for their own lives. We and they rightly reject the overly confident empiricism that was part of an earlier intellectual environment. But we must also reject the return to invoked authorities and the escapism of idealism, ancient or contemporary. For those of us in reform movements – social democrats, feminists, environmentalists, or whatever – the issue of methodology is critical if rarely addressed as such. The reformers of today, as before, must believe that knowledge for application to practical problems is possible, if always only at the level of probability and not certitude. Advocates of social and ecological justice require a methodology of hope but not of blind confidence. The development of an adequate methodology, respectful of the environment and conscious of human limitations, is an essential part of any movement for reform. The centuries of examples related here point to an honourable tradition capable of adaptation and use. The scepticism and caution so desperately needed today have been a fundamental part of that empiricist tradition from the earliest origins of the social sciences.

Notes

CHAPTER ONE

1 Marshall, *Praise of Sociology*.
2 Pawson, *Measure*, 2.
3 On the feminist critique of objectivity and scientific methodology see Harding, *Science Question*; Miles and Finn, *Feminism*; Millett, *Sexual Politics*; Vickers, *Taking Sex Into Account*; Millman and Kanter, *Another Voice*; Keller, *Reflections*. Multiple references within a note appear in order of their importance in relation to *The Early Origins of the Social Sciences*. The most highly recommended work is listed first, others appear in descending order.
4 Merchant, *Death of Nature*, and White, "Historical Roots," although White blames the biblical command to subdue nature more than positivism.
5 Berman, *Re-enchantment*, 189.
6 Schumacher, *Small is Beautiful*, 72.
7 Gouldner, *For Sociology*, 398.
8 Collins, *Conflict Sociology*, 27.
9 Alexander, *Theoretical Logic*, 1:9.
10 Grant, "Tyranny and Wisdom," *Technology*, 81.
11 Touraine, *Production*, 521.
12 Gurvitch, *Dialectique*, 185.
13 Bramson, *Political Context*, vi.
14 Willer and Willer, *Systematic Empiricism*, 1.
15 Habermas, *Logic*, 16.
16 In Harries-Jones, *Making Knowledge*, 221.
17 Flax, *Thinking Fragments*, 8.

18 Mazlish, *New Science*, 46.

19 Grant, "Tyranny and Wisdom," *Technology*, 81.

20 The following are good examples from several different societies over several decades: Blalock and Blalock, *Methodology*; Bottomore, *Sociology*; Galtung, *Papers on Methodology*; Goode and Hatt, *Methods*; Greer, *Logic of Social Inquiry*; Kaplan, *Conduct*; Homans, *Nature of Social Science*; Lynd, *Knowledge for What?*; Mills, *Sociological Imagination*; Myrdal, *Objectivity*; Riley, *Sociological Research*; Sjoberg and Nett, *Methodology*; Williamson, *Research craft*; Matalon, *Décrire*.

21 Etzioni, "Nonconventional Use," in Lazarsfeld, *Uses of Sociology*, 832.

22 "Science as a Vocation," in Weber, *From Max Weber*, 148.

23 Durkheim, *Règles*, ix.

24 Marx and Engels, *German Ideology*, 13.

25 Baker, *Condorcet*, Appendix B.

CHAPTER TWO

1 Quoted in Freeman, *Ancilla* 93.

2 Quoted in Freeman, *Ancilla*, 22.

3 Thucydides, *Peloponnesian Wars*, 1:15.

4 Lucretius, *De Rerum Natura*, 238.

5 Major sources used here are Winspear, *Genesis*; Popper, *Open Society*, vol. 1; Thomson, *Studies in Ancient Greek Society*, vol. 1; Freeman, *Pre-Socratic Philosophers*; Guthrie, *History of Greek Philosophy*; Farrington, *Science in Antiquity*; Robin, *Greek Thought*; Collingwood, *Idea of Nature*; Finley, *Ancient Economy*.

6 On Solon's life and work see Freeman, *Work and life*; Woodhouse, *Solon the Liberator*; Ehrenberg, *From Solon*; Vlastos, "Solonian Justice."

7 The author, short title, and page reference are given in the notes the first time a work is cited. Page numbers for subsequent references to the same work are given in parentheses in the text.

8 Freeman, *Work and Life*, 207.

9 Freeman, *Pre-Socratic Philosophers* and *Ancilla*; Nahm, *Selections*; Farrington, *Science and Politics*; Nizan, *Matérialistes*; Guthrie, *In the Beginning*; DeSantillano, *Origins*; Bailey, *Greek Atomists*; Havelock, *Preface*; Burnet, *Early Greek Philosophy*; Heidel, "Antecedents."

10 See Winspear and Silverberg, *Who was Socrates?*, and Kahn, *Anaximander*.

11 DeSantillano, *Origins*, 35.

12 Winspear and Silverberg, *Socrates*, 17.

13 DeSantillano, *Origins*, 39.

14 Kahn, *Anaximander*, 220.

15 Farrington, *Head and Hand*, 8.

16 In addition to the general sources cited above see Gershenson and Greenberg, *Anaxagoras*, and Schofield, *Essay*.

17 Popper, *Open Society*, 1:12.

18 Freeman, *Ancilla*, 30.

19 Lambridis, *Empedocles*; O'Brien, *Empedocles' Cosmic Cycle*.

20 Freeman, *Ancilla*, 64.

21 Chief sources on Democritus are Guthrie, *History*, vol. 3; Cole, *Democritus*; Cleve, *Giants*, vol. 2.

22 Freeman, *Ancilla*, 104.

23 Marx, *Difference between the Democritean and Epicurean Philosophy of Nature*. See also Markovits, *Marx dans le jardin d'Epicure*, and Mehring, "Thèse de Karl Marx."

24 Cleve, *Giants*, 2:438.

25 Freeman, *Ancilla*, 93.

26 Havelock, *Liberal Temper*, and Cole, *Democritus*.

27 Freeman, *Ancilla*, 114.

28 Freeman, *Pre-Socratic Philosophers*, 294.

29 Main sources on Epicurus are DeWitt, *Epicurus*; Farrington, *Faith of Epicurus*; Bailey, *Epicurus. The Extant Remains*, and *Greek Atomists*; Asmis, *Epicurus' Scientific Method*; Festugière, *Epicurus*.

30 Nichols, *Epicurean*, 20.

31 DeWitt, *Epicurus*, 95.

32 Bailey, *Epicurus*, 131.

33 DeWitt, *Epicurus*, 34.

34 Winspear, *Lucretius*; Hadzsits, *Lucretius and his Influence*.

35 Lucretius, *De Rerum Natura*, 9.

36 Farrington, *Science and Politics*, 191.

37 Main sources on the Pythagoreans and Eleatics are: Lee, introduction, *Zeno of Elea*; Raven, *Pythagoreans*; Cherniss, "Characteristics" in Furley and Allen, *Studies in Presocratic Philosophy*; Verdenius, *Parmenides*; Mourelatos, *Route of Parmenides*.

38 Von Fritz, *Pythagorean Politics*; Minar, *Early Pythagorean*.

39 Onians, *Origins*, 61.

40 Freeman, *Ancilla*, 42.

41 Mourelatos, *Route*, xi.

42 Cleve, *Giants*, 2:523.

43 Heidel, *Hippocratic Medicine*, and "Antecedents."

44 Hippocrates, *Medical Works*, 107.

45 Heidel, *Hippocratic*, 23.

46 Hippocrates, *Medical Works*, 12–13.

47 Beginning with Grote, *History of Greece*. See also Kerford, *Sophistic Movement*; Havelock, *Liberal*; Untersteiner, *Sophists*; Guthrie, *History*, vol. 3.

48 Guthrie, *Sophists*, 10.
49 Popper, *Open Society*, 1:185.
50 Plato, *The Sophist*, 146.
51 Freeman, *Ancilla*, 147.
52 Winspear, *Genesis*, 146.
53 Freeman, *Ancilla*, 125; I have substituted "human" for "man" as a better translation of "anthropos."
54 Plato, *Protagorus*, 14.
55 See M. Grant, *Ancient Historians*; Hunter, *Past and Process*; Waters, *Herodotus*; Lateiner, *Historical Method*.
56 L. Pearson, *Early Ionian*; Usher, *Historians*; Starr, *Awakening*; Austin, *Greek Historians*.
57 Hunter, *Thucydides. the Artful Reporter*; Adcock, *Thucydides*; Rawlings, *Structure*; Westlake, *Individuals in Thucydides*; Connor, *Thucydides*; Hornblower, *Thucydides*; Romilly, *Thucydides*; Cochrane, *Thucydides*; Jowett's introduction to Thucydides, *Peloponnesian Wars*.
58 Thucydides, *Peloponnesian Wars*, 1:1.
59 *General History of Polybius*, 1:4.
60 Grant, *Ancient Historians*, 149.
61 Collingwood, *Idea of History*, 35.
62 *General History of Polybius*, 2:366.
63 On Tacitus' life and work see Syme, *Tacitus*; Mendell, *Tacitus*; Martin, *Tacitus*.
64 Tacitus, "Germany," *Works*, 7:68.
65 Portrayals range from the saint and martyr, as in Zeller, *Socrates*, to the enemy of democracy: Stone, *Trial of Socrates*; Crossman, *Plato To-Day*; and Winspear and Silverberg, *Who was Socrates?* More moderate accounts appear in Guthrie, *History*, vol. 3, and *Socrates*; Gulley, *Philosophy of Socrates*; Taylor, *Socrates*; Vlastos, *Philosophy of Socrates*; Turlington, *Socrates*; O'Brien, *Socratic Paradoxes*.
66 Crossman, *Plato Today*, 59.
67 Popper, *Open Society*, 1:185.
68 Socrates, "Phaedo," *Dialogues*, 2:204.
69 Guthrie, *Socrates*, 108.
70 On Plato's methodology see Melling, *Understanding Plato*; Burnet, *Platonism*; Cornford, *Plato's Theory*; Field, *Plato* and *Philosophy of Plato*; Ryle, *Plato's Progress*; Gouldner, *Enter Plato*; Cherniss, *Riddle of the Early Academy*.
71 Taylor, *Platonism and its Influence*, 3, and see his *Plato*.
72 Jowett, "Introduction," in Plato, *Republic*, xvii.
73 Popper, *Open Society*, 1:35.
74 Winspear, *Genesis*, 170. I tend here to the negative view. On the tactics used in Plato's opposition to democracy see also Wood and Wood, *Class Ideology*.

75 Innis, *Bias*, 44.

76 Plato, *Republic*, 170.

77 Plato, *Dialogues*, 3:715–16.

78 Plato, *Republic*, 229.

79 Winspear, *Genesis*, 137.

80 Ryle, *Plato's Progress*, 16.

81 Lovejoy, *Great Chain of Being*, 35.

82 On Aristotle's life and work see Evans, *Aristotle*; Grayeff, *Aristotle*; Anscombe, "Aristotle"; Grene, *Portrait*; Woodbridge, *Aristotle's Vision*; Allan, *Philosophy of Aristotle*; Ross, *Aristotle*; Mansion, *Aristote*; Day and Chambers, *Aristotle's History*; Mulgan, *Aristotle's Political Theory*.

83 Aristotle, *Physics*, 8.

84 Aristotle, *Politics*, 5.

85 Aristotle, *De Anima*, book 3, chap. 8.

86 Aristotle, *Metaphysics*, 5.

87 Aristotle, *Physics*, 8.

88 Aristotle, *Politics*, 2.

89 Aristotle, *Metaphysics*, 3.

90 Aristotle, *Posterior Analytics*, xiv.

91 Aristotle, *De Anima*, 69.

92 Aristotle, *Ethics*, 129.

93 Main sources on scepticism are Popkin, *High Road*; Patrick, *Greek Sceptics* and *Sextus Empiricus*; Stough, *Greek Scepticism*; Annas and Barnes, *Modes of Scepticism*; Zeller, *Stoics, Epicureans and Sceptics*.

94 Popper, *Conjectures*, 149.

95 Freeman, *Ancilla*, 24.

96 Patrick, *Greek Sceptics*, 57.

97 Sextus Empiricus, *Outlines of Pyrrhonism*, 1:19.

98 Sextus, *Outlines of Pyrrhonism*, 1:xxxvi.

99 Cicero, *Academica Prior*, 2:595.

100 See Rackham, "Introduction," in Cicero, *De Natura Deorum*; Hunt, *Humanism of Cicero*; and Henry, *Relation*.

101 Rackham, "Introduction," *De Natura*, xii.

102 Cicero, *Academica*, 475.

103 Stough, *Greek Scepticism*, 106.

104 On the methodology see Rist, *Stoic Philosophy*; Alain, *Théorie*; Reesor, *Political Theory*; Brun, *Stoïcisme*; Virieux-Reymond, *Logique*; Spanneut, *Permanence*.

105 Sambursky, *Physics*, 49–65.

106 Needham, *Shorter Science*, 291.

107 Farrington, *Head and Hand*, 66.

108 Collingwood, *Idea of History*, 51.

109 *History of the Church*, 22.

110 The main sources used here are Rist, *Plotinus*; Armstrong, *Plotinus* and *Architecture*; Nash, *Light*; Wallis, *Neo-Platonism*; Merlan, *From Platonism*; Whittaker, *Neo-Platonists*.

111 Rist, *Plotinus*, 16.

112 Plotinus, *Six Enneads*, 118.

113 Rist, *Plotinus*, 81.

114 Kirwan, "Augustine against the Sceptics," in Burnyeat, *Skeptical Tradition*.

115 Augustine, *Against the Academics*, 137.

116 Augustine, "Trinity," *Works*, 7:285.

117 Augustine, "Teacher," *Earlier Writing*, 95.

118 Augustine, "Trinity," *Works*, 7:406.

119 Augustine, *City of God*, 2:256.

120 Augustine, "Trinity," *Works*, 7:256.

121 Discussed in *City of God*, and see Deane, *Political and Social Ideas*.

CHAPTER THREE

1 Bacon, *Novum Organum*, *Philosophical Works*, 264.

2 Glanvill, *Scepsis Scientifica*, 144.

3 Boyle, *Christian Virtuoso*, *Works*, 5:13.

4 Baxter, *Knowledge and Love Compared*, 35–6.

5 Locke, *Conduct of the Understanding*, *Educational Writings*, 248.

6 Locke, *Conduct of the Understanding*, *Educational Writings*, 248.

7 Locke, *Essay concerning Human Understanding*, 2:457.

8 Astell, *Serious Proposal*, 94.

9 Schmitt, "Unstudied Translation," and *Cicero Scepticus*.

10 Montaigne, "Cruelty," *Essays*, 2:94.

11 General references to the period are Jones, *Ancients and Moderns*; James, *Social Problems*; Trevor-Roper, *Religion*; Wilson, *England's Apprenticeship*; Brailsford, *Levellers*; Robertson, *Religious Foundations*; C. Hill, *Intellectual Origins* and *World Turned Upside Down*; Thomas, *Religion*; White, *History of the Warfare*; Popkin, *History of Scepticism*; Greenleaf, *Order*; Woolhouse, *Empiricists*; Koyré, *Astronomical Revolution*; Willey, *Seventeenth Century*; Webster, *Great Instauration*; Wiley, *Subtle Knot*; Clark, *Science and Social Welfare*; Haller, *Rise*; Westergaard, *Contributions*; Jacob, *Newtonians*.

12 DeSantillano, *Crime of Galileo*. With new data from the Vatican archives, Redondi argues, in *Galileo Heretic*, that Galileo was more of a threat because his nominalism and atomism undermined Church teaching on the eucharist.

13 E. Grant, *Physical Sciences*, 87.

14 See especially Farrington, *Philosophy of Francis Bacon* and *Francis Bacon, Philosopher of Industrial Science*; Anderson, *Philosophy of Francis Bacon* and *Francis Bacon. His Career*; Briggs, *Francis Bacon*; Rossi, *Francis Bacon*; Quinton, *Francis Bacon*; Whitney, *Francis Bacon and Modernity*;

Broad, *Philosophy of Bacon*; Luxembourg, *Francis Bacon and Denis Diderot*.

15 Merton's "Puritanism, Pietism and Science" applies here. More recent scholarship, however, challenges this interpretation. Hunter's *Science and Society* points to the diversity of political and religious views held by leading scientists, especially those in the Royal Society. See also Webster, *Great Instauration*, for a challenge to the theory of a Puritan impulse to science.

16 Farrington, *Philosophy of Bacon*, 40–2.

17 Bacon, "Masculine Birth of Time," in Farrington, *Philosophy of Bacon*, 62.

18 Bacon, *Advancement, Philosophical Works*, 79.

19 Bacon, *Novum Organum, Philosophical Works*, 259.

20 Rossi, *Francis Bacon*, 11.

21 Brathwaite, *Survey of History*, 136, 156.

22 On Hobbes' life and work see Macpherson, *Possessive Individualism* and introduction to *Leviathan*; Mintz, *Hunting*; Reik, *Golden Lands*; Oakeshott, *Hobbes*; Watkins, *Hobbes's System*; Spragens, *Politics of Motion*; Warrender, *Political Philosophy*; Hood, *Divine Politics*; Stephen, *Hobbes*; Goldsmith, *Hobbes's Science*.

23 Hobbes, *Leviathan, English Works*, 3:1.

24 Hobbes, "Short Tract," *Elements of Law*, 205.

25 Hobbes, *Leviathan, English Works*, 3:4.

26 Hobbes, *Elements of Law*, 20.

27 Reik, *Golden Lands*, 66–72.

28 Strauss, *Political Philosophy*, xii.

29 Mintz, *Hunting*, 26.

30 Main sources are Haldane, *Descartes*; Beck, *Method*; Gaukroger, *Cartesian Logic*; Popkin, *History*; Balz, *Descartes and the Modern Mind*; Maritain, *Dream*; Gibson, *Philosophy of Descartes*; N.K. Smith, *New Studies*; Caton, *Origins of Subjectivity*; LeRoy, *Descartes*.

31 Astell, *Enquiry after Wit*, 98.

32 Descartes had already worked out his methodology in detail in the *Rules for the Direction of the Mind* eight years earlier, but it was not published until fifty years after his death.

33 Descartes, "Discourse," *Philosophical Works*, 1:81.

34 Gassendi was replying to the next version of Descartes' methodology, *Méditations*, 2:27.

35 This is argued further in the *Méditations*, 2:177.

36 Sartre, *Descartes*, 42.

37 Descartes, *Principles, Philosophical Works*, 1:231–9.

38 Needham, *Shorter Science*, 291.

39 In Descartes, *Lettres sur la morale*, 11.

40 See Rosenfield, *From Beast-Machine*, for a review of Descartes' actual statements pro and con. Thomas, *Man and the Natural World*, 35, states that

Descartes never said that animals were incapable of sensation. Boas, *Happy Beast*, stresses the *ambiguity* of Descartes' position.

41 Descartes, *Rules, Philosophical Works*, 1:1.

42 Descartes, *Principles, Philosophical Works*, 1:240.

43 By Popkin, notably, *History of Scepticism*, "Father Mersenne's War Against Pyrrhonism" and preface to Van Leeuwen, *Problem of Certainty*. See also Lenoble, *Mersenne*.

44 Mersenne, *Vérité des sciences*, 194.

45 On Gassendi's life and work see Rochot, "Le philosophe"; Brett, *Philosophy of Gassendi*; Spink, *French Free-Thought*; Bloch, *Philosophie de Gassendi*; Pintard, *Libertinage érudit*.

46 Gassendi, *Dissertations*, 246.

47 Gassendi, *Abrégé*, 3:371.

48 Gassendi, *Recherches métaphysiques*, 210.

49 Gassendi, *Dissertations*, 504.

50 Coirault, "Gassendi et non Locke créateur de la doctrine sensualiste moderne sur la génération des idées," in *Actes du Congrès tricentenaire*, 72.

51 On Montchrétien's life and work see Duval, *Mémoire*, and Dessaix, *Montchrétien*.

52 On Malebranche's life and work see *Oeuvres Complètes*, vol. 20; Rodis-Lewis, *Nicolas Malebranche*; Jolley, *Light*; McCracken, *Malebranche*; Connell, *Vision in God*; Robinet, *Malebranche*.

53 Malebranche, *Recherche de la vérité, Oeuvres complètes*, 1:9.

54 Rodis-Lewis, *Malebranche*, 325.

55 Locke, "An Examination of P. Malebranche's Opinion," *Works*, 9:213. For another critique of the period see Arnauld, *Oeuvres philosophiques*.

56 Malebranche, *Recherche de la vérité, Oeuvres complètes*, 1:437.

57 Arnauld and Nicole, *Logique du Port-Royal*, xxx.

58 On Bayle's life and work see Labrousse, *Pierre Bayle*; Niderst, *Pierre Bayle*; Dibon, *Pierre Bayle*.

59 Labrousse, *Bayle*, 97.

60 Bayle, *Système de philosophie*, 6 (my translation).

61 Bayle, *Dictionnaire*, 101.

62 On Spinoza's life and work see Scruton, *Spinoza*; Friedmann, *Liebniz et Spinoza*; Elwes, introduction, Spinoza, *Chief Works*, vol. 1; McKeon, *Philosophy of Spinoza*; Wolfson, *Philosophy of Spinoza*; Roth, *Spinoza, Descartes and Maimonides*; K. Pearson, "Maimonides and Spinoza." The first volume of a new collected works in English has been published.

63 Spinoza used the term "perception" to include intuition or the direct apprehension of essences, as well as sensation.

64 Spinoza, "Improvement of the Understanding," *Chief Works*, 1:11.

65 Spinoza, *Ethics, Chief Works*, 2:114.

66 Spinoza, "Improvement of Understanding," *Chief Works*, 2:12.

67 Spinoza, *Theologic-Political Treatise*, *Chief Works*, 1:259.

68 Spinoza, *Ethics*, *Chief Works*, 2:91.

69 On Leibniz's life and work see Loemker, introduction to Leibniz, *Philosophical Papers and Letters* and *Struggle*; Russell, *Philosophy of Leibniz*; McRae, *Leibniz*; Beck, *Early German Philosophy*; Broad, *Leibniz*.

70 Russell, *Philosophy of Leibniz*, 1.

71 Politella, *Platonism*.

72 Leibniz's *Discourse on Metaphysics*, written in 1686, was not published until the nineteenth century. His "Elements of Natural Science," written 1682–4, shows the influence of Bacon and Boyle in a short-lived materialism. His first published methodology was a short article, "Meditations on Knowledge, Truth and Ideas," 1684. His *Monadology*, largely metaphysical, also contains some methodology. Finally there is the *Leibniz-Clarke Correspondence*, published after Leibniz's death by his correspondent.

73 Leibniz, *Nouveaux essais*, 2:60.

74 Beck, *Early German Philosophy*, 210.

75 Leibniz, "On the Elements of Natural Science," *Philosophical Papers*, 283.

76 Leibniz, *Nouveaux essais*, 1:32 (my translation).

77 Leibniz, "Letter to Herman Conring," *Philosophical Papers*, 188.

78 Mills, "On Intellectual Craftsmanship," *Sociological Imagination*, 221.

79 Loemker, introduction to Leibniz, *Philosophical Papers*, 44.

80 On Grotius' life and work see Knight, *Life and Works*; Tuck, *Natural rights*; Vreeland, *Hugo Grotius*.

81 Kelsen, *Justice*, 137.

82 Grotius, *Rights of War and Peace*, xxxi.

83 Grotius, *Freedom of the Seas*, 1.

84 Pufendorf, *Law of Nature*, 2.

85 Krieger, *Politics of Discretion*, 104.

86 Conring (1606–82) is acknowledged as the first German statistician, credited with massive compilations of national level data. Since his framework was Aristotelian and he wrote in Latin he did not become a model for later empirical work. His work has not been translated, but see Lazarsfeld, "Notes on the History of Quantification."

87 Hill, "Religion of Gerrard Winstanley"; Frank, *Levellers*; Petegorsky, *Left-Wing Democracy*; Sabine, introduction, *Works of Winstanley*; Lutaud, *Winstanley*; Brockway, *First Socialists*; Sharp, *Political Ideas*.

88 Winstanley, *New Law*, *Works*, 185.

89 Macpherson, "Harrington's 'Opportunity State'"; Pocock, introduction, *Political Works of James Harrington*; Tawney, "Harrington's Interpretation."

90 Harrington, *Oceana*, *Political Works*, 180.

91 Baxter, *Treatise*, 1.

92 Chillingworth, *Religion of Protestants*, 140–4.

93 Wilkins, *Principles and Duties*, 2.

94 On Glanvill's life and work see Popkin, *History of Scepticism* and Van Leeuwen, *Problem of Certainty.*

95 Glanvill, *Scepsis Scientifica*, 51.

96 Glanvill, "Scepticism and Certainty," *Essays*, 39.

97 Boyle, "Sceptical Chemist," *Works*, 1:459. On his science see M. Boas, *Robert Boyle.*

98 Boyle, "Reconcilableness of Reason and Religion," *Works*, 4:173–4.

99 Boyle, "The Excellency of Theology," *Works*, 4:28.

100 Boyle, "Christian Virtuoso," *Works*, 5:513.

101 Evelyn, *Silva*, 11.

102 Graunt, "Observations upon the Bills of Mortality," in Petty, *Economic Writings*, 317.

103 E. Strauss, *Sir William Petty* and "Life," in *Economic Writings of Sir William Petty.*

104 Petty, *Political Anatomy, Economic Writings*, 1:129.

105 See especially "Verbum Sapienti," in Petty, *Economic Writings*, 1:108–10.

106 Halley, "Estimate of the Degrees of Mortality," *Philosophical Transactions*, 3:483.

107 Macpherson, "Sir William Temple;" Clark, introduction to Temple, *Observations.*

108 Temple, "Essay upon the Original," *Works*, 1:29.

109 Temple, *Observations*, 93.

110 Temple, "Essay upon the Original," *Works*, 1:53.

111 Macpherson, "Sir William Temple," 40.

112 On Newton's life and work see North, *Isaac Newton*; Westfall, *Never at Rest*; Manuel, *Religion of Isaac Newton* and *Isaac Newton Historian*; Cohen, *Introduction to Newton's "Principia"*; Butts and Davis, *Methodological Heritage.*

113 Kuhn, "Newton's Optical Papers," in *Isaac Newton's Papers*, 27.

114 Newton, "Queries," *Opticks*, 399–402.

115 Newton, *Mathematical Principles*, 398.

116 Newton, *Correspondence*, 1:144.

117 Newton, "Queries," *Opticks*, 405.

118 Keynes, "Newton the Man," 27.

119 On Locke's life and work see Bourne, *Life of John Locke*; Aaron, *John Locke*; Parry, *John Locke*; Cranston, *John Locke*; Woolhouse, *Locke*; Yolton, *John Locke and the Way of Ideas* and *Locke and the Compass*; Lough, *Locke's Travels*; Dewhurst, *John Locke, Physician*; Harrison and Laslett, *Library of John Locke*; Mandelbaum, *Philosophy.*

120 On Locke's sources see Wood, "Baconian Character of Locke's Essay" and *Politics of Locke's Philosophy*; Gibson, *Locke's Theory*; Ware, "Influence of Descartes."

121 Locke, *Essay*, 1:26.

122 Locke, *Essay*, 2:270–1.

123 Locke, *Two Treatises*, 462–4.
124 As to how *illiberal* he was see Macpherson, "Social Bearing." See also Andrew, *Shylock's Rights*.
125 Russell, *History of Western Philosophy*, 613.
126 On Astell's life see Perry, *Celebrated*; F. Smith, *Mary Astell*; Spender, *Women of Ideas*; Hays, *Female Biography*; B. Hill, introduction to *First English Feminist*.
127 For example, Marx and Engels' *Holy Family* on German critical theory or Boyle's *Christian Virtuoso* on scientific method.
128 Astell, *Serious Proposal*, 19.
129 Astell, *Enquiry after Wit*, 18.
130 Astell, *Serious Proposal*, 81.
131 Astell, *Reflections*, 7.
132 Drake, *Essay in defence*, 7–8.
133 Henry More, *Philosophical Writings*, 116.
134 Ray, *Wisdom of God*, preface and 367.

CHAPTER FOUR

1 Diderot, "Pensées philosophiques," *Oeuvres*, 1:140.
2 Voltaire, *Lettres philosophiques*, 58.
3 Voltaire, dedication, *Elémens de la philosophie de Newton*.
4 Condorcet, "Discours sur les Sciences Mathématiques," *Oeuvres*, 1:454.
5 De Staël, *Circonstances actuelles*, 32.
6 On the eighteenth-century background, see Lindsay, *Old Regime*; Lough, *Introduction*; Brumfitt, *French Enlightenment*; Rothkrugg, *Opposition*; Lefebvre, *Révolution française*.
7 On Montesquieu's life and work see Shackleton, *Montesquieu*; Shklar, *Montesquieu*; Desgraves, *Montesquieu*; Stark, *Montesquieu*; Dodds, *Récits de voyages*; Carrithers, introduction to Montesquieu, *Spirit of Laws*.
8 De Staël, "Littérature," *Oeuvres complètes*, 1871 ed., 285.
9 Montesquieu, *L'Esprit des lois*, *Oeuvres Complètes*, 1:1 (my translation).
10 On Voltaire's life, see Aldridge, *Voltaire*; Ayer, *Voltaire*; Pomeau, *Voltaire en son temps*; Wade, *Voltaire and Madame du Châtelet*; Torrey, *Spirit of Voltaire*; Libby, *Attitude of Voltaire*; Besterman, *Voltaire Essays*; Ballantyne, *Voltaire's Visit*.
11 On Châtelet's life see Wade, *Voltaire and Mme du Châtelet*; Vaillot, *Avec Mme du Châtelet* in Pomeau, *Voltaire*, vol. 3; Ehrman, *Mme du Chatelet*; Besterman, *Voltaire Essays*; Maurel, *Marquise du Châtelet*; Badinter, *Emilie, Emilie*.
12 Voltaire, "Candide, ou l'Optimisme," *Contes et romans*, 221.
13 Voltaire, letter 12, *Lettres Philosophiques*; the translations to follow are mine.
14 Châtelet, *Institutions de Physique*, 9 (my translation).

15 Published in Wade, *Studies on Voltaire*, 131–87.

16 Voltaire, *Essai sur les moeurs*, 27.

17 Brumfitt, *Voltaire Historian*, and introduction, *Philosophie de l'histoire*.

18 Gay, *Voltaire's Politics*; Maestro, *Voltaire and Beccaria*.

19 Voltaire, *Dictionnaire philosophique*, 175.

20 On Beccaria's life see Maestro, *Cesare Beccaria*.

21 Venturi, *Utopia*, 103.

22 Beccaria, *On Crimes and Punishments*, 13.

23 Beccaria, *Discourse on Public Economy*, 1.

24 On Diderot's life and work see Wilson, *Diderot: The Testing Years*; Crocker, *Embattled Philosopher*; Vartanian, *Diderot and Descartes*; Luppol, *Diderot*; Venturi, *Jeunesse*; Cru, *Diderot as Disciple*.

25 Morley, *Diderot and the Encyclopedists*, 2:121; Tourneux, *Diderot et Catherine II*.

26 Lough, *The Encyclopédie*; Proust, *Diderot et l'Encyclopédie*; Darnton, *Business of Enlightenment*.

27 Wilson, *Diderot*, 241.

28 Diderot, "L'Interprétation," *Oeuvres complètes*, 9:43.

29 Oestreicher, *Pensée politique*, 49.

30 Diderot, "Autorité politique," *Encyclopédie*, *Oeuvres complètes*, 5:537.

31 Diderot, "Voyages," *Oeuvres complètes*, 12: 577–647.

32 Luppol, *Diderot*, 10.

33 Vartanian, "Introduction," La Méttrie, *L'homme machine*.

34 La Méttrie, *L'homme machine*, 156.

35 Rosenfield, *From Beast-Machine*, 180.

36 On Helvétius' life see Smith, *Helvétius*; Horowitz, *Claude Helvétius*, Cumming, *Helvetius*.

37 Helvétius, *De l'esprit*, *Oeuvres*, 2:364 (my translation).

38 Helvétius, *De l'homme*, *Oeuvres*, vol. 7, conclusion.

39 On Holbach's life see Naville, *Paul Thiry d'Holbach* and Wickwar, *Baron d'Holbach*.

40 Wickwar, *Baron*, 87.

41 Holbach, *Système de la nature*, 1:3 (my translations).

42 Holbach, *Ethocratie*, 208.

43 Holbach, *Politique naturelle*, 39 (my translation).

44 Holbach, *Système de la nature*, 1:171.

45 Holbach, *Politique naturelle*, 107.

46 On Condillac's life and work see Knight, *Geometric Spirit*; Lefèvre, *Condillac*; McRae, *Problem of Unity*.

47 Condillac, *Essai sur l'origine*, *Oeuvres philosophiques*, 1:15.

48 Condillac, *Traité des systèmes*, *Oeuvres philosophiques*, 1:217 (my translation).

49 Condillac, *Cour d'études*, *Oeuvres*, vol. 1. Later Condillac moved closer to the idealists.

50 Condillac, "Traité des animaux," *Oeuvres philosophiques*, 1:347.

51 Condillac, *Traité des systèmes*, *Oeuvres philosophiques*, 1:124.

52 On Buffon's life see Rivière, *Buffon*; Hanks, *Buffon*.

53 Buffon, *Histoire naturelle*, *Oeuvres philosophiques*, 1:31.

54 Buffon, "Discours prononcé," *Oeuvres philosophiques*, 1:501 (my translation).

55 On the physiocrat school see Meek, *Economics*; Fox-Genovese, *Origins of Physiocracy*; Higgs, *Physiocrats*; Grandamy, *Physiocratie*.

56 On Quesnay's life and work see Schelle, *Le docteur Quesnay*.

57 Fox-Genovese, *Origins*, 304.

58 Quesnay, *Tableau économique*, i.

59 Quesnay, "Analyse du tableau," *Oeuvres économiques*, 308.

60 Quesnay, *Tableau*, viii.

61 Quesnay, "Mémoires de l'Académie," *Oeuvres*, 724 (my translation).

62 On Turgot's life see Stephens, *Life and Writings of Turgot*; Dakin, *Turgot*; Manuel, *Prophets of Paris*.

63 Dakin, *Turgot*, 268.

64 Turgot, "Lettre à Condorcet," *Oeuvres*, 3:670.

65 On Vico's life and work see Flint, *Vico*; Berlin, *Vico and Herder*; Grimaldi, *Universal Humanity*; Pompa, *Vico*; Tagliacozzo, *Vico – Past and Present*, and *Giambattista Vico*.

66 Vico, *New Science*, 96.

67 On Rousseau's life see Grimsley, *Philosophy of Rousseau*; J. McDonald, *Rousseau*.

68 For a range of interpretations of Rousseau's vision see Gay, introduction to Cassirer, *Question of Jean-Jacques Rousseau*. Concerning consistency see Cassirer, *Question*; Starobinski, *Jean-Jacques Rousseau*.

69 Rousseau, *Discours sur les sciences et les arts*, *Oeuvres complètes*, 3:14.

70 Rousseau *Discours sur l'origine et les fondemens de l'inégalité*, *Oeuvres complètes*, 3:125.

71 On Rousseau's political philosophy see: Horowitz and Horowitz, *Everywhere*; Horowitz, *Rousseau, Nature and History*; Masters, *Political Philosophy*; McDonald, *Rousseau*; Starobinski, introduction to "2ᵉ Discours," *Oeuvres*, vol. 3.

72 De Staël, *Circonstances actuelles*, 280.

73 Rousseau, "Discours sur l'inégalité," *Oeuvres complètes*, 3:158. Yet Rousseau continued to refer to women as "ruling" men, by manipulation, although women were legally subordinate to their husbands in French law. See Shklar, *Men and Citizens*.

74 Rousseau, *Contrat social*, *Oeuvres complètes*, 3:361 (my translation).

75 Rousseau, *Emile*, *Oeuvres complètes*, 4:568 (my translation).

76 On Condorcet's life and work see Baker, *Condorcet*; Badinter and Badinter, *Condorcet*; Rosenfield, *Condorcet Studies I*; Arago, "Biographie," in Condorcet, *Oeuvres*, vol. 1.

77 Schapiro, *Condorcet*, 271.

78 Condorcet, *Vie de Monsieur Turgot*, 222 (my translation).

79 Published posthumously as *Elémens du calcul des probabilités*. See especially the second letter.

80 On his social arithmetic see Baker, *Condorcet* and Pearson, *History of Statistics*.

81 Condorcet, *Elémens du calcul*, 174–5 (my translation).

82 Manuel, *Prophets*, 299.

83 Condorcet, "Lettres d'un bourgeois," *Oeuvres*, vol. 9.

84 Condorcet, "Admission des femmes au droit de la cité," *Oeuvres*, vol. 10.

85 Condorcet, "Fragment sur l'Atlantide," *Oeuvres*, 6:633.

86 Condorcet, "Lettres d'un bourgeois," *Oeuvres*, 9:4 (my translation).

87 Condorcet, *Esquisse*, 84. See Frazer, "Condorcet."

88 Condorcet, *Esquisse*, 253 (my translation).

89 See also her "Huit lettres sur la sympathie."

90 Baker. *Condorcet*, Appendix B.

91 Condorcet, *Rapport et projet* and "Report on the General Organization of Public Instruction."

92 Lagrange, "Essai d'arithmétique politique," in Lavoisier, *Mélanges*, 608–14.

93 Laplace, *Essai philosophique*, 47.

94 On Mme Roland's life see May, *Madame Roland* and *De Jean-Jacques Rousseau à Madame Roland*; Willcocks, *Madame Roland*.

95 Roland, "De la liberté," *Oeuvres*, 2:170 (my translation).

96 [M-J?] Roland, "Lettre de M. Roland," 43 (my translation).

97 On Mme de Staël's life and work see Balayé, *Madame de Staël*; Diesbach, *Madame de Staël*; Blennerhasset, *Madame de Staël*; Larg, *Madame de Staël*; Herold, *Mistress to an Age*; Goldsmith, *Madame de Staël*; Forsberg and Nixon, *Madame de Staël and Freedom*; Escarpit, *L'Angleterre*; Gwynne, *Madame de Staël*; Munteaud, *Idées politiques*.

98 De Staël, *Unpublished Correspondence of Madame de Staël and the Duke of Wellington*.

99 De Staël, "Appel aux Souverains," and "Préface pour la traduction," *Oeuvres Complètes*, 1821 ed., vol. 17.

100 De Staël, *Influence des Passions*, *Oeuvres complètes*, 1871 ed., 108 (my translation).

101 De Staël, *Littérature*, *Oeuvres complètes*, 1871 ed., 199 (my translation).

102 De Staël, "A quels signes," *Oeuvres complètes*, 1821 ed., 17:318.

103 Herold, *Mistress*, 208.

104 De Staël, *Circonstances*, 5 (my translations).

105 De Staël, "Reflections on Suicide," *Oeuvres complètes*, 1871 ed. 189.
106 Herold, *Mistress*, 208.

CHAPTER FIVE

1 Macaulay, *Letters on Education*, 237.
2 Wollstonecraft, *French Revolution*, 235.
3 Ferguson, *Principles of Moral and Political Science*, 1:91.
4 Smith, *Theory of Moral Sentiments*, 165.
5 For general background on the eighteenth century see Mathias, *First Industrial Nation*; Jacob, *Radical*; Willey, *Eighteenth Century*; Stephen, *History*; Ashton, *Economic History*; Lane, *Industrial Revolution*; Plumb, *England*; Camic, *Experience and Enlightenment*.
6 On Hutcheson's life and work see Scott, *Francis Hutcheson*; Blackstone, *Francis Hutcheson*; Jensen, *Motivation* and Taylor, *Francis Hutcheson*; Bryson, *Man and Society*.
7 Hutcheson, "Letter," *Collected Works*, 7:12.
8 Hutcheson, *System of Moral Philosophy*, 1:1.
9 On Hume's life see Mossner, *Life*; Greig, *David Hume*.
10 On Hume's scepticism, see Popkin, "David Hume: His Pyrrhonism" and "David Hume and the Pyrrhonian Controversy;" Strawson, *Secret Connexion*; Wright, *Sceptical realism*. On his methodology generally see N.K. Smith, *Philosophy of David Hume*; Letwin, *Pursuit*; Church, *Hume's Theory*; MacNab, *David Hume*; Noxon, *Hume's Philosophical Development*; Forbes, *Hume's Philosophical Politics*; Capaldi, *David Hume*; Norton, *David Hume*.
11 Hume, *Inquiry, Philosophical Works*, 4:39.
12 Hume, "Treatise," *Philosophical Works*, 1:260.
13 Hume, *Inquiry, Philosophical Works*, 4:55–6.
14 Hume, "Abstract," 16.
15 Hume, *Inquiry, Philosophical Works*, 4:118–22.
16 Hume, *Essays, Literary, Moral and Political*, 284.
17 Hume, "Advertisement," *Philosophical Works*, vol. 4.
18 Hume, *Treatise, Philosophical Works*, 1:284.
19 Russell, *History of Western Philosophy*, 672.
20 On Smith's life see Raphael, *Adam Smith*; Campbell and Skinner, *Adam Smith*; Scott, *Adam Smith*; Pike, *Adam Smith*.
21 On Smith's methodology see Campbell, *Adam Smith's Science*; Reisman, *Adam Smith's Sociological Economics*; Winch, *Adam Smith's Politics*; Foley, *Social Physics*; Brown, *Adam Smith's Economics*; Macfie, *Individual*; Mossner, "Adam Smith;" Thomson, "Adam Smith's Philosophy;" Haakonssen, *Science of a Legislator*.
22 A. Smith, *Theory of Moral Sentiments*, 166.

23 On the relation between Smith's economic and ethical views see Morrow, *Ethical and Economic Theories* and Teichgraeber, *"Free Trade" and Moral Philosophy*.

24 A. Smith, *Wealth*, 13.

25 A. Smith, *Wealth*, 30. See also Hutcheson, *System of Moral Philosophy*, 2:53.

26 A. Smith, *Wealth*, 314.

27 A. Smith, "History of Astronomy," *Early Writings*, 45.

28 Foley, *Social Physics*, 30.

29 On Millar see Lehmann, *John Millar*; Macfie, "John Millar," in *Individual*.

30 In Lehmann, *John Millar*, 175.

31 On Priestley's life see Crowther, "Joseph Priestley;" Hiebert, *Joseph Priestley*; Gibbs, *Joseph Priestley*.

32 Priestley, *Hartley's Theory of the Human Mind*.

33 Priestley, "Examination of Dr. Reid's Inquiry into the Human Mind," *Theological and Miscellaneous Works*, 3:7.

34 Willey, *Eighteenth Century*, 136.

35 On Godwin's life and work see Grylls, *William Godwin*; Woodcock, *William Godwin*; Marshall, *William Godwin*; Monroe, *Godwin's Moral Philosophy*; Brailsford, *Shelley, Godwin and their Circle*.

36 Godwin, *Enquiry concerning Political Justice*, 1:375.

37 On Bentham's life and work see Mack, *Jeremy Bentham*; Harrison, *Bentham*; Lyons, *In the Interest*; Boralevi, *Bentham and the Oppressed*; Dinwiddy, *Bentham*; Halévy, *Growth of Philosophic Radicalism*.

38 Bentham, *Introduction to the Principles of Morals*, *Works*, 1:25.

39 On Wesley's life and methodology see Edwards, *John Wesley*; Faulkner, *Wesley as Sociologist*; MacArthur, *Economic Ethics*; Fitchett, *Wesley and his Century*.

40 Wesley, *Compendium*, 1:iii.

41 Wesley, "Thoughts on the Present Scarcity of Provisions," *Works*, 11:53–9.

42 On Reid see Grave, *Scottish Philosophy*; Reid's chief publications were *Inquiry into the Human Mind*, 1764, and *Essays on the Intellectual Powers of Man*, 1785, both in his *Philosophical Works*.

43 Reid, *Inquiry*, *Philosophical Works*, 1:196.

44 Reid, *Essays*, *Philosophical Works*, 1:335.

45 Reid, *Inquiry*, *Philosophical Works*, 1:194.

46 On Ferguson's life and work see Kettler, *Social and Political Thought*.

47 Ferguson, *Principles of Moral and Political Science*, 1:160.

48 On Berkeley's life and work see Winkler, *Berkeley*; Grayling, *Berkeley*; Brook, *Berkeley's Philosophy*; Luce, *Life of George Berkeley* and *Berkeley and Malebranche*; Warnock, *Berkeley*; Wisdom, *Unconscious Origins*; Armstrong, *Berkeley's Philosophical Writings*; Cassirer, *Rousseau, Kant, Goethe*; Johnston, *Development*.

49 See Berkeley, "Querist" and "Essay towards Preventing the Ruin," *Works*, vol. 6.

50 Berkeley, "Discourse to Magistrates," *Works*, vol. 6.

51 Related in his *Commonplace Book*, known as *Philosophical Commentaries*.

52 Berkeley, "Principles of Human Knowledge," *Works*, 2:52.

53 Berkeley, *Dialogues*, *Works*, 2:249.

54 Berkeley, "Principles," *Works*, 2:53.

55 Popkin, "New Realism of Bishop Berkeley," 3.

56 Berkeley, *Dialogues*, *Works*, 2:168.

57 Berkeley *Philosophical Commentaries*, 199.

58 On Kant's life and work see Scruton, *Kant*; Lindsay, *Kant*; Rescher, *Kant's Theory*; Velkley, *Freedom*; Strawson, *Bounds of Sense*; Williams, *Unity of Kant's Critique*; N.K. Smith, *Commentary to Kant's "Critique"*; Wilm, *Immanuel Kant*; Körner, *Kant*; Prichard, *Kant's Theory*; Goldmann, *Immanuel Kant*; Cassirer, *Rousseau, Kant, Goethe*.

59 Books completing the canon are *Fundamental Principles of the Metaphysics of Morals*, 1785; *Critique of Practical Reason*, 1788; *Critique of Judgement*, 1790.

60 Kant, *Critique of Pure Reason*, xiii.

61 Kant, *Prolegomena*, 9.

62 Kant, *Critique*, xvi-xvii.

63 Kant, *Prolegomena*, 71.

64 Kant, *Critique*, xv.

65 Kant, *Prolegomena*, 82.

66 Despland, *Kant On History*, 46.

67 See *Kant's Political Writings*.

68 Kant, "Idea for a Universal History," *Political Writings*, 43.

69 *Kant's Critique of Teleological Judgement*, 94.

70 Kant, "Idea for a Universal History," *Political Writings*, 42.

71 Goldmann, *Immanuel Kant*, 35.

72 On Wortley Montagu's life see Halsband, *Life of Lady Wortley Montagu*; Spender, *Women of Ideas*.

73 Wortley Montagu, *Complete Letters* 1:xiv.

74 Halsband, "New Light"; Dixon, "Mary and Caroline."

75 Sophia, *Woman not Inferior*, 13.

76 On Macaulay's life and work see Spender, *Women of Ideas*, and the introduction to Macaulay, *Letters on Education*.

77 Macaulay, *Letters on Education*, 23.

78 Macaulay, *History of England from James I*, 1:vii.

79 Macaulay, *History of England from the Revolution*, 182.

80 Macaulay, *Loose Remarks*, 9.

81 Macaulay, *Observations*, 17.

82 On Wollstonecraft's life and work see Nixon, *Mary Wollstonecraft*; Sunstein, *Different Face*; Wardle, *Mary Wollstonecraft*; Flexner, *Mary Wollstonecraft*; Tomalin, *Life and Death*.

83 Virginia Woolf, *Second Common Reader*, 17.

84 Wollstonecraft, *Vindication of the Rights of Men*, 23.
85 Wollstonecraft, *Vindication of the Rights of Woman*, 247.
86 Wollstonecraft, *French Revolution*, 32.
87 Wollstonecraft, *Vindication of the Rights of Woman*, 299.
88 Wollstonecraft, *French Revolution*, 522.
89 Wollstonecraft, *Vindication of the Rights of Woman*, 18.
90 On Hays' life and work see Spender, *Women of Ideas* and Luria, "Introduction," in Hays, *Memoirs of Emma Courtney*.
91 Hays, *Female Biography*, 1:vi.
92 Hays, "Thoughts on Civil Liberty," *Letters and Essays*, 12.
93 Hays, "Letter on Materialism," *Letters and Essays*, 180.
94 Hays, "Essay on Civil Liberty," *Letters and Essays*, 12.
95 Malthus, *Essay*, 2.
96 See Süssmilch, *Die Göttliche Ordnung*, for the contrast.
97 Sinclair, *Statistical Account*, 1:26.
98 Eden, *State of the Poor*, preface.

CHAPTER SIX

1 J.S. Mill, *Logic, Collected Works*, 8:894.
2 J.S. Mill and H.T. Mill, "On Liberty," in J.S. Mill, *Collected Works*, 18:238.
3 B. Webb and S. Webb, *Industrial Democracy*, xvii.
4 Marx and Engels, *German Ideology*, 115.
5 Marx and Engels, *German Ideology*, 99.
6 On the early development of statistics see: MacKenzie, *Statistics in Britain*; Stigler, *History of Statistics*; Abrams, *Origins of British Sociology*; Porter, *Rise of Statistical Thinking*; Cullen, *Statistical Movement*; Wrigley, *Nineteenth-century*; Raison, *Founding Fathers*; Turner, *Search for a Methodology*; Collini, *Liberalism*; Oberschall, *Establishment*.
7 Cook, *Regenerators*.
8 Ames, *City below the Hill*.
9 LePlay, *Ouvriers Européens*, 11.
10 On Saint-Simon's life and work see: Manuel, *New World of Henri Saint-Simon*; Saint-Simon, "Histoire de ma vie," in *Lettres aux jurés*; LeRoy, *La vie véritable*; Hubbard, *Saint-Simon*; Gurvitch, *Fondateurs*, and introduction to *Physiologie sociale*.
11 Saint-Simon, *Mémoire sur la science de l'homme, Oeuvres*, 11:160.
12 Saint-Simon, *Introduction aux travaux*, 54.
13 Saint-Simon, "Physiologie sociale," *Oeuvres*, 10:176 (my translation).
14 See Gurvitch, "Introduction," and Manuel, *New World*.
15 Saint-Simon, *Mémoire, Oeuvres*, 11:177.
16 Marx and Engels, *German Ideology*, 15.

17 On Comte's life and work see Thompson, *Auguste Comte*; Aron, *Main Currents*, vol. 1; Sokoloff, *"Mad" Philosopher*; Lepenies, *Between Literature and Science*; Evans-Pritchard, "Sociology of Comte."

18 Comte, *Cours*, 1:21.

19 See McDonald, *Sociology of Law and Order*, 263–4.

20 Comte, *Cours*, vol. 2, lesson 48.

21 Comte, *Appel aux Conservateurs*.

22 On Tocqueville's life and work see Pierson, *Tocqueville*; Aron, *Main Currents*, vol. 1; Schleifer, *Making of Tocqueville's Democracy*.

23 In the Mill, *Collected Works*, vol. 18 and foreword to Tocqueville, *Democracy in America*, respectively.

24 Tocqueville, *Democracy in America*, 1:15.

25 Lipset, "Introduction," Martineau, *Society in America*, 7.

26 On Martineau's life see her own *Autobiography* and Wheatley, *Life and Work*; Webb, *Harriet Martineau*; Pichanick, *Harriet Martineau*; David, *Intellectual Women*; Nevill, *Harriet Martineau*.

27 Martineau, *How to Observe*, ll.

28 Martineau, *Society in America*, 48.

29 Spender, *Women of Ideas*, 133.

30 Lipset, "Introduction," Martineau, *Society in America*, 10.

31 On Quetelet's life and work see Lazarsfeld, "Notes"; Mailly, *Essai sur la vie*; Stigler, *History of Statistics*; Diamond, introduction to Quetelet, *Treatise on Man*; Lottin, *Quetelet*; Porter, *Rise*; Cullen, *Statistical Movement*.

32 *New York Tribune* reprinted in Marx, *Selected Writings*, 234, and Comte, *Cours de philosophie positive*, 2:15.

33 Quetelet, *Recherches sur le penchant au crime*, 57.

34 Quetelet, *Physique sociale*, 2:315.

35 Quetelet, "Sur la statistique morale," 37.

36 Quetelet, *Physique sociale*, 2:320 (my translation).

37 Quetelet, *Treatise on Man*, viii.

38 MacKenzie, *Statistics*, 8. See Schoen, "Prince Albert," on Quetelet's influence on British government statistics and Turner, *Search*, on his influence generally in Britain and the United States.

39 Mouat, "History of the Statistical Society."

40 The most relevant biographies on Nightingale are: Cook, *Life*; Woodham-Smith, *Florence Nightingale*; Strachey, *Eminent Victorians*; Bishop and Goldie, *Bio-Bibliography*.

41 Florence Nightingale Papers, British Library, No. 45,482, Feb. 1874.

42 Pearson, *Life*, 2:416.

43 Pearson, *Life*, 2:417.

44 Guerry used bar graphs and shaded maps in *Essai sur la statistique morale* (1833) to present crime and other social data, but Nightingale's analysis is much more sophisticated.

45 Nightingale, Letter to Harriet Martineau, 21 August 1859, Nightingale Papers, British Library, Add. Mss. no. 45, 788.

46 Diamond and Stone, "Nightingale on Quetelet," 184.

47 Nightingale, Papers, no. 45,842, f. 53.

48 Nightingale, Papers, no. 43,398, f. 175.

49 Nightingale, Papers, no. 43,400, f. 268.

50 Nightingale, *Introductory Notes on Lying-in Institutions*, x.

51 Diamond and Stone, "Nightingale," 347.

52 Nightingale, Papers, no. 45,842, f. 56.

53 Nightingale, Papers, no. 45,843, f. 305.

54 Nightingale, Papers, no. 45,842, f. 17.

55 Diamond and Stone, "Nightingale," 333.

56 On Mill's life and work see Packe, *Life*; Britton, *John Stuart Mill*; Thomas, *Mill*; Mazlish, *James and John Stuart Mill*; Borchard, *John Stuart Mill*.

57 On Harriet Taylor's life and work see Spender, *Women of Ideas*, and Rossi, introduction to *Essays on Sex Equality*.

58 J.S. Mill, *System of Logic*, *Collected Works*, 8:837.

59 J.S. Mill, "Subjection of Women," in Rossi, *Essays*, 181.

60 Hayek, *John Stuart Mill and Harriet Taylor*; Pappe, *John Stuart Mill*; Lepenies, *Between Literature and Science*.

61 Robson, *Improvement*, 68.

62 Himmelfarb, *On Liberty and Liberalism*, 238. For a more positive view see Rossi, *Essays*.

63 Himmelfarb, "Introduction," *Essays on Politics and Culture*, xix.

64 Jean O'Grady, introduction to J.S. Mill, *Collected Works*, 33: viii–x.

65 Titles and page numbers of Taylor Mill's early essays are listed in Mineka, *Dissidence*.

66 Rossi, *Essays*, 41.

67 J.S. Mill, *Autobiography*, *Collected Works*, 1:265.

68 Main sources on Mill's methodology are Ryan, *Philosophy*; Mueller, *John Stuart Mill*; Anshutz, *Philosophy of John Stuart Mill*; Fletcher, *John Stuart Mill*; Robson, *Improvement*.

69 J.S. Mill, *Autobiography*, *Collected Works*, 1:233.

70 J.S. Mill, *System of Logic*, *Collected Works*, 8:755–6.

71 Robson, *Improvement*, 161.

72 J.S. Mill, *System of Logic*, *Collected Works*, 8:911.

73 J.S. Mill, *Autobiography*, *Collected Works*, 1:177.

74 J.S. Mill, *System of Logic*, *Collected Works*, 8:913.

75 J.S. Mill, "On the Definition of Political Economy," *Collected Works*, 4:320.

76 Robson, *Improvement*, 160.

77 Ryan, *Philosophy*, x.

78 J.S. Mill, *System of Logic*, *Collected Works*, 8:641.

79 Stephen, *English Utilitarians*, 3:150.

80 J.S. Mill, *System of Logic, Collected Works*, 8:833.

81 J.S. Mill, *Autobiography, Collected Works*, 1:255.

82 J.S. Mill, *Principles of Political Economy, Collected Works*, 2:3.

83 J.S. Mill, "Bentham," in *Essays on Politics and Culture*, 102.

84 J.S. Mill, "Utilitarianism," *Collected Works*, 10:207.

85 J.S. Mill, *Principles of Political Economy, Collected Works*, 3:756.

86 Anna J. Mill, "John Stuart Mill, Conservationist," 2–3.

87 J.S. Mill, *Principle of Political Economy, Collected Works*, 3:756–7.

88 J.S. Mill, "Subjection of Women," in Rossi, *Essays on Sex Equality*, 207.

89 On Galton's life see Pearson, *Life*; Galton, *Memories*; Stigler, *History of Statistics*.

90 On Pearson's life see MacKenzie, *Statistics*, and Stigler, *History*.

91 Galton, *Inquiries*, 220.

92 Stiglir, *History*, 266.

93 Pearson, "Nature and Nurture," 27.

94 Pearson, *Grammar of Science*, 5.

95 Lenin, *Materialism, Collected Works*, 14:224.

96 Pearson, *Grammar of Science*, 130.

97 On Spencer's life and work see Peel, *Herbert Spencer*; Wiltshire, *Social and Political Thought*; Rumney, *Herbert Spencer's Sociology*.

98 B. Webb, *My Apprenticeship*, 1:45.

99 Spencer, "The Coming Slavery," *Man versus the State*, 23.

100 B. Webb, *My Apprenticeship*, 2:388–9.

101 Ward, *Glimpses of the Cosmos*, 6:105–8.

102 On Booth's life and work see Simey and Simey, *Charles Booth* and Mary Booth, *Charles Booth*.

103 Beatrice Webb's *My Apprenticeship* is still the best source on how the survey was organized.

104 Booth, *Life and Labour, Religious Influences*, 7:426.

105 Booth, *Life and Labour*, Final Volume, 216.

106 On Webb's life and work see her *My Apprenticeship, Our Partnership*, and *Diary of Beatrice Webb*; Nord, *Apprenticeship of Beatrice Webb*; Letwin, *Pursuit of Certainty*; Tawney, "Beatrice Webb"; Cole, *The Webbs*; Radice, *Beatrice & Sidney Webb*; Seymour-Jones, *Beatrice Webb*.

107 S. Webb, *Methods of Social Study*, 61.

108 B. Webb, "Methods of Investigation," 350.

109 S. Webb, *Methods of Study*, 256.

110 Still the best general biography of Marx is Mehring, *Karl Marx*. See also Berlin, *Karl Marx*; Blumenberg, *Karl Marx*; Payne, *Unknown Karl Marx*; Carver, *Marx & Engels*; McLellan, *Marx before Marxism*.

111 Kautsky brought out four more volumes from these notes as *Theories of Surplus Value*, 1905–10.

112 Marx's views are now available in *Ethnological Notebooks*.

113 Marx, *Early Texts*, 7.

114 Marx and Engels, *Holy Family*, 17. I have substituted "person" for "man" in quotations where the original German was *Mensch*.

115 Marx and Engels, *German Ideology*, 6.

116 Berlin, "Historical Materialism," in Bottomore, *Interpretations*, 93.

117 Marx and Engels, *German Ideology*, 14.

118 Marx, *Selected Writings*, 84.

119 Marx, *Poverty of Philosophy*, 105.

120 Marx, *Eighteenth Brumaire*, 23.

121 Marx, *Early Texts*, 135.

122 Tönnies wrote both *Community and Society* and a biography of Marx.

123 Marx and Engels, *Communist Manifesto*, 58.

124 Marx, *Contribution*, 10.

125 Marx, *Capital*, 1:93.

126 See Cole's introduction to *Capital*, xxviii.

127 Carver, *Karl Marx: Texts*, 198.

128 Carver, *Marx & Engels*, 108.

129 Carver, *Marx & Engels*, 152. See also Bottomore, *Interpretations*; Ball and Farr, *After Marx*; Little, *Scientific Marx*; Schumpeter, *Capitalism, Socialism*.

130 *Revue socialiste*, 20 April 1880:193. No investigator's name appears on the form or covering article, but expert opinion has the work to be Marx's, and certainly the style is his. For an English translation of the questions and discussion of the survey, see Weiss, "Karl Marx's 'Enquête ouvrière,'" in Bottomore, *Interpretations of Marx*, 258–68.

131 *Revue socialiste*, 5 July 1880: 416.

132 *Revue socialiste*, 20 April 1880: 193.

133 Weiss, "Karl Marx's 'Enquête ouvrière,'" in Bottomore, *Interpretations of Marx*, 263.

134 The questionnaire is a major counter example to the contention that Marx was a different kind of scholar, above and beyond the mundane world of surveys. That it is still ignored in discussions of Marx suggests wilful blindness rather than mere ignorance. Weiss published the questionnaire and its history in German in 1936. The Bottomore and Rubel translation into English appeared first in 1956, and in subsequent editions of *Karl Marx: Selected Writings*; Bottomore then included the full translation of Weiss's original article in *Interpretations of Marx* in 1988.

135 On Durkheim's life and work see Lukes, *Emile Durkheim*; Nisbet, *Emile Durkheim*; LaCapra, *Emile Durkheim*; Fenton, *Durkheim and Modern Sociology*; Mestrovic, *Emile Durkheim*; Filloux, *Durkheim*; Pearce, *Radical Durkheim*, Alpert, *Emile Durkheim and his Sociology*; Aron, *Main Currents*, vol. 2.

136 See Turner, *Search*, 107 for discussion of the "interregnum" between Mill and Durkheim.

137 Durkheim, *Rules*, xlii.

138 Durkheim, *Montesquieu and Rousseau*, 16.

139 Durkheim, *Rules*, xlv.

140 Durkheim, *Socialism*, 104.

141 Durkheim, *Rules*, 110.

142 I argue this further in *Sociology of Law and Order*.

143 See his preface to Hamelin, *Système de Descartes*.

144 Durkheim, *Pragmatism and Sociology*, 43.

145 Durkheim, *Socialism*, 7.

146 On early American sociology see Bernard and Bernard, *Origins*; Barnes and Becker, *Social Thought*, vol. 2; Kurtz, *Evaluating Chicago Sociology*; Smith, *Chicago School*; Matthews, *Robert E. Park*; Lewis and Smith, *American Sociology*; Weinberg, *Edward Alsworth Ross*; Hofstadter, *Social Darwinism*.

147 On Small's life and work see Dibble, *Legacy*; Christakes, *Albion W. Small*.

148 D. Smith, *Chicago School*, ix.

149 Small, *American Journal of Sociology*, 1(1):11.

150 See Sumner, *Social Darwinism*.

151 On Ward's life and work see Chugerman, *Lester F. Ward* and Commager, *Lester Ward*.

152 Ward, *Applied Sociology*, iii.

153 On Addams' life and work see Deegan, *Jane Addams*; Lasch, *Social Thought*; Addams, *Twenty Years at Hull-House*.

154 Deegan, *Jane Addams*, 55.

155 Levine, *Jane Addams and the Liberal Tradition*, x.

156 Addams, prefatory note, *Hull-House Maps and Papers*.

157 Holbrook, "Map Notes & Comments," in Addams, *Hull-House Maps and Papers*, 13.

158 Deegan, *Jane Addams*, 254.

159 Addams, *Hull-House Maps and Papers*, 197.

160 Deegan, *Jane Addams*, 309.

161 Marianne Weber's *Max Weber: a Biography* stressed his mother's values and influence. Other biographies give greater prominence to the father's *Realpolitik*. See Käsler, *Max Weber*; Parkin, *Max Weber*; MacRae, *Max Weber*; Collins, *Max Weber. A Skeleton Key*.

162 Naegele, "Some Observations," in Parsons, *Theories of Society*, 1:22.

163 On Weber's political career see: Mommsen, *Max Weber and German Politics*; Dronberger, *Political Thought*; Mayer, *Max Weber and German Politics*.

164 See especially Lazarsfeld and Oberschall, "Max Weber and Empirical Social Research," and Bendix, *Max Weber*.

165 Lazarsfeld and Oberschall, "Max Weber," 194.

166 Weber, "Science as a Vocation," *From Max Weber*, 135.

167 Weber, *Theory of Social and Economic Organization*, 88.

168 See especially Käsler, *Max Weber* on this point. On the methodology see Alexander, *Theoretical Logic*, vol. 3; Collins, *Weberian Sociological Theory*; Sica, *Weber*; Hennis, *Max Weber*; Hughes, *Consciousness*; Aron, *German*

Sociology; Tribe, *Reading Weber*; Burger, *Max Weber's Theory*; Runciman, *Critique*; Freund, *Sociology of Max Weber*; Hamilton, *Critical Assessments*.

169 Weber, *Theory of Social and Economic Organization*, 96.

170 Weber, "Objectivity in Social Science," *Methodology of the Social Sciences*, 79.

171 Weber, "The Meaning of Ethical Neutrality," *Methodology of the Social Sciences*, 40.

172 Weber, "Objectivity," *Methodology of the Social Sciences*, 72.

173 Weber, *Theory of Social and Economic Organization*, 109.

174 Runciman, *Critique*, 1.

175 Weber, *Theory of Social and Economic Organization*, 98–9.

176 Weber, "Objectivity," *Methodology*, 106.

177 Weber, "Science as a Vocation," *From Max Weber*, 136.

178 Weber, "The Meaning of Ethical Neutrality," *Methodology*, 11.

179 Weber, "Objectivity," *Methodology*, 52.

180 Weber, "Science as a Vocation," *From Max Weber*, 138.

181 Weber, "Objectivity," *Methodology*, 80.

182 Weber, "Ethical Neutrality," *Methodology*, 37.

183 Weber, *Protestant Ethic*, 183.

184 Tawney, foreword to Weber, *Protestant Ethic*, 11.

185 Weber, *Agrarian Sociology*, 354.

186 Troeltsch, *Social Teaching*, 2:816.

187 Footnote 84, Weber, *Protestant Ethic*, 277–8.

188 Swanson's empirical refutation of the Weberian thesis, *Religion and Regime*, found political factors to be key.

189 Weber, *General Economic History*, 354.

190 Weber, "Politics as a Vocation," *From Max Weber*, 120.

191 Hughes, *Consciousness*, 317. For other Weber-Marx comparisons see Löwith, *Max Weber and Karl Marx*; Antonio and Glassman, *Weber-Marx Dialogue*; Weiss, *Weber and the Marxist World*; Alexander, *Theoretical Logic*, vol. 3.

CHAPTER SEVEN

1 Sartre, *Critique de la Raison Dialectique*, 50.

2 See especially Lukacs, *History and Class Consciousness*.

3 Bukharin, *Historical Materialism. A System of Sociology*.

4 Bottomore and Goode, *Austro-Marxism*.

5 Mao Tse-tung, *Four Essays in Philosophy*.

6 Neurath, *Empiricism and Sociology*; Mills, *The Marxists*; Bottomore, *Marxist Sociology*; Vaillancourt, *When Marxists Do Research*.

7 Medvedev, *Let History Judge*, 499.

8 See especially Horkheimer, *Critical Theory*; Marcuse, *One-Dimensional Man*; Habermas, *On the Logic of the Social Sciences*; Adorno, "Scientific

Experiences." On the school see: Tar, *Frankfurt School*; Jay, *Dialectical Imagination*; Slater, *Origin*; Bottomore, *Frankfurt School*; Rose, *Melancholy Science*; Connerton, *Tragedy of enlightenment*.

9 Marcuse, *One-Dimensional Man*, 185.

10 Horkheimer, *Critical Theory*, 185.

Bibliography

Note: Where there are multiple references for an author, those references are listed in descending order of their importance for the purposes of research for this book.

Aaron, Richard I. *John Locke*. Oxford: Clarendon, 1971 [1937].

Abrams, Philip. *The Origins of British Sociology*. Chicago: University of Chicago Press, 1968.

Actes du Congrès tricentenaire de Pierre Gassendi. Paris: Presses universitaires de France, 1955.

Adcock, F.E. *Thucydides and his History*. Cambridge: Cambridge University Press, 1963.

Addams, Jane, ed. *Hull-House Maps and Papers*. Reprint. New York: Arno, 1970 [1895].

– *Twenty Years at Hull House*. New York: Macmillan, 1910.

Adorno, Theodor, E. Frenkel-Brunswick, et al., eds. *The Authoritarian Personality*. New York: Harper, 1950.

– "Scientific Experiences of a European Scholar in America." In *The Intellectual Migration*, ed. D. Heming and B. Bailyn. Cambridge, MA: Harvard University Press, 1969.

Alain. *La théorie de la connaisance des stoïciens*. Paris: Presses universitaires de France, 1964 [1891].

Aldridge, A. Owen. *Voltaire and the Century of Light*. Princeton, NJ: Princeton University Press, 1975.

Alexander, Jeffrey C. *Theoretical Logic in Sociology*. 4 vols. Berkeley: University of California Press, 1982.

Allan, D.J. *The Philosophy of Aristotle*. London: Oxford University Press, 1963 [1952].

Alpert, Harry. *Emile Durkheim and his Sociology*. New York: Columbia University Press, 1939.

Ames, Herbert Brown. *The City below the Hill*. Toronto: University of Toronto Press, 1972 [1897].

Anderson, F.H. *The Philosophy of Francis Bacon*. Chicago: University of Chicago Press, 1948.

– *Francis Bacon. His Career and Thought*. Los Angeles: University of Southern California Press, 1962.

Andrew, Edward. *Shylock's Rights*. Toronto: University of Toronto Press, 1988.

Annas, Julia, and Jonathan Barnes. *The Modes of Scepticism*. New York: Cambridge University Press, 1985.

Anscombe, G.E.M. "Aristotle." In G.E.M. Anscombe and P.T. Geach, *Three Philosophers*. Ithaca: Cornell University Press, 1961.

Anshutz, R.P. *The Philosophy of John Stuart Mill*. Oxford: Clarendon, 1953.

Antonio, Robert J., and Ronald M. Glassman, eds. *A Weber-Marx Dialogue*. Lawrence: University of Kansas Press, 1985.

Aristotle. *De Anima*. Trans. D.W. Hamlyn. Oxford: Clarendon, 1968.

– *Metaphysics*. Trans. Richard Hope. Ann Arbor: University of Michigan Press, 1968.

– *Physics*. Trans H.G. Apostle. Bloomington: Indiana University Press, 1969.

– *The Politics of Aristotle*. Trans. Ernest Barker. Oxford: Clarendon, 1961 [1946].

– *Posterior Analytics*. Trans. Jonathan Barnes. Oxford: Clarendon, 1975.

– *Aristotle's Ethics*. London: Faber & Faber, 1972.

– *Historia Animalium*. 3 vols. Trans. A.L. Peck. London: Heinemann, 1965.

Armstrong, A.H. *Plotinus*. London: Allen & Unwin, 1953.

– *The Architecture of the Intelligible Universe in the Philosophy of Plotinus*. Cambridge: Cambridge University Press, 1940.

Armstrong, David M. *Berkeley's Philosophical Writings*. New York: Collier, 1965.

Arnauld, Antoine. *Oeuvres philosophiques*. Paris: Charpentier, 1843.

– and Pierre Nicole. *Logique du Port-Royal*. Paris: Hachette, 1861 [1662].

Aron, Raymond. *Main Currents in Sociological Thought*. 2 vols. Trans. Richard Howard and Helen Weaver. London: Weidenfeld & Nicolson, 1967.

– *German Sociology*. Trans. Mary Bottomore and Thomas Bottomore. Free Press of Glencoe, 1964.

Ashcraft, Richard. *Locke's Two Treatises of Government*. London: Allen & Unwin, 1987.

Ashton, T.S. *An Economic History of England*. London: Methuen, 1955.

Asmis, Elizabeth. *Epicurus's Scientific Method*. Ithaca: Cornell University Press, 1984.

Astell, Mary. *A Serious Proposal to the Ladies for the advancement of their true and greatest interest*. London: J.R., 1701 [1694].

– *Some Reflections upon Marriage*. London: Parker, 1730 [1700].

– *An Enquiry after Wit*. London: Bateman, 1723 [1709].

– *The Plain Dealer*, 1724 (4):239–48.

Augustine of Hippo. *Against the Academics*. Trans. J.J. O'Meara. Westminster, Maryland: Newman, 1951.

– *Augustine: Earlier Writing*. Trans. and Ed. J.H.S. Burleigh. London: SCM Press, 1953.

– *The City of God*. 2 vols. Trans. John Healey. London: Dent, 1945.

– *The Works of Aurelius Augustine*. Trans. A.W. Haddan. Ed. M. Dods. Edinburgh: Clark, 1873.

Austin, Norman, ed. *The Greek Historians*. New York: Van Nostrand, 1969.

Ayer, A.J. *Voltaire*. London: Weidenfeld & Nicolson, 1986.

Bacon, Francis. *Philosophical Works*. Reprint of Ellis and Spedding ed., 1905. Freeport, NY: Books for Learning, 1976.

Badinter, Elisabeth. *Emilie, Emilie: l'ambition féminine au XVIIIe siècle*. Paris: Flammarion, 1983.

– and Robert Badinter. *Condorcet*. Paris: Fayard, 1988.

Bailey, Cyril. *Epicurus. The Extant Remains*. Oxford: Clarendon, 1926.

– *The Greek Atomists and Epicurus*. Oxford: Clarendon, 1928.

Baker, Keith Michael. *Condorcet: From Natural Philosophy to Social Mathematics*. Chicago: University of Chicago Press, 1975.

Balayé, Simone. *Madame de Staël. Lumière et liberté*. Paris: Klincksieck, 1979.

Ball, Terence and James Farr, eds. *After Marx*. Cambridge: Cambridge University Press, 1984.

Ballantyne, Archibald. *Voltaire's Visit to England*. Geneva: Slatkine Reprints, 1970 [1893].

Balz, Albert G.A. *Descartes and the Modern Mind*. New Haven: Yale University Press, 1952.

Barnes, Harry Elmer, and Howard Becker. *Social Thought from Lore to Science*. 2 vols. Boston: Heath, 1938.

Baxter, Richard. *A Treatise of Knowledge and Love Compared*. 2 vols. London: Parkhurst, 1689.

Bayle, Pierre. *Système de philosophie*. Berlin: Pitra, 1785.

– *Dictionnaire historique et critique*. Paris: Desoer, 1820 [1696].

Beattie, James. *An Essay on the Nature and Immutability of Truth*. rev. ed. Hildesheim: Georg Olms, 1975 [1770].

Beccaria, Cesare. *On Crimes and Punishments*. Trans. Henry Paolucci. New York: Bobbs-Merrill, 1963 [1764].

– *A Discourse on Public Economy and Commerce*. Trans. S. Douglas. New York: Franklin Re-prints, 1970 [1769].

Beck, L.J. *The Method of Descartes*. Oxford: Clarendon, 1964 [1952].

Beck, Lewis White. *Early German Philosophy*. Cambridge, MA: Belknap, 1969.

Bendix, Reinhard. *Max Weber. An Intellectual Portrait*. Garden City, NY: Anchor, 1962 [1960].

Bentham, Jeremy. *The Works of Jeremy Bentham*. 11 vols. Re-print of 1838 ed. Ed. John Bowring. New York: Russell & Russell, 1962.

Berkeley, George. *The Works of George Berkeley*. 9 vols. Ed. A.A. Luce and T.E. Jessop. London: Thomas Nelson, 1949.

– *Philosophical Commentaries*. Ed. A.A. Luce. London: Thomas Nelson, 1944.

Berlin, Isaiah. *Karl Marx*. New York: Oxford University Press, 1959.

– *Vico and Herder*. London: Hogarth, 1976.

Berman, Morris. *The Re-enchantment of the World*. Ithaca: Cornell University Press, 1981.

Bernard, L.L., and Jessie Bernard. *Origins of American Sociology*. New York: Crowell, 1943.

Besterman, Theodore. *Voltaire Essays*. London: Oxford University Press, 1962.

Bishop, W.J., and Sue Goldie, eds. *A Bio-Bibliography of Florence Nightingale*. London: Dawson, 1962.

Blackstone, William T. *Francis Hutcheson and Contemporary Ethical Theory*. Athens: University of Georgia Press, 1965.

Blalock, Hubert M., Jr., and Ann B. Blalock, eds. *Methodology in Social Research*. New York: McGraw-Hill, 1968.

Blennerhasset, Lady. *Madame de Staël*. 3 vols. London: Chapman & Hall, 1889.

Bloch, Olivier René. *La philosophie de Gassendi*. La Hague: Nijhoff, 1971.

Blumenberg, Werner. *Karl Marx*. Trans. Douglas Scott. London: NLB, 1972 [1962].

Blundeville, Thomas. *True Order of Writing and Reading Histories*. London: Willyam, 1979 [1574].

Boas, George. *The Happy Beast*. Baltimore: Johns Hopkins University Press, 1933.

Boas, Marie. *Robert Boyle and Seventeenth-Century Chemistry*. Cambridge: Cambridge University Press, 1958.

Bodin, Jean. *Method for the Easy Comprehension of History*. Trans. Beatrice Reynolds. New York: Norton, 1969.

Booth, Charles, ed. 17 vols. 3d. series. *Life and Labour of the People in London*. London: Macmillan, 1902–3.

Booth, Mary. *Charles Booth. A Memoir*. London: Macmillan, 1918.

Boralevi, Lea Campos. *Bentham and the Oppressed*. Berlin: DeGruyter, 1984.

Borchard, Ruth. *John Stuart Mill*. London: Watts, 1957.

Bottomore, T.B. *Sociology*. London: Unwin, 1962.

– ed. *Interpretations of Marx*. Oxford: Blackwell, 1988.

– *Marxist Sociology*. London: Macmillan, 1975.

– *The Frankfurt School*. Chichester: Ellis Horwood, 1984.

– and Patrick Goode, eds. *Austro-Marxism*. Oxford: Clarendon, 1978.

Bourne, H.R. Fox. *The Life of John Locke*. 2 vols. New York: Harper, 1876.

Boyle, Robert. *The Works*. 6 vols. London: Nivington, 1772.

Brailsford, H.N. *The Levellers and the English Revolution*. London: Cresset, 1961.

– *Shelley, Godwin and their Circle*. London: Williams & Norgate, 1919.

Bramson, Leon. *The Political Context of Sociology*. Princeton, NJ: Princeton University Press, 1961.

Brathwaite, Richard. *A Survey of History*. London: Okes, 1638.

Brett, G.S. *The Philosophy of Gassendi*. London: Macmillan, 1908.

Briggs, John C. *Francis Bacon and the Rhetoric of Nature*. Cambridge, MA: Harvard University Press, 1989.

Britton, Karl. *John Stuart Mill*. Harmondsworth: Penguin, 1953.

Broad, C.D. *The Philosophy of Francis Bacon*. Cambridge: Cambridge University Press, 1926.

– *Leibniz*. Cambridge: Cambridge University Press, 1975.

Brockway, Fenner. *Britain's First Socialists*. London: Quartet, 1980.

Brook, Richard J. *Berkeley's Philosophy of Science*. The Hague: Nijhoff, 1973.

Brown, Maurice. *Adam Smith's Economics*. London: Croom Helm, 1988.

Brumfitt, J.H. *Voltaire Historian*. Oxford: Oxford University Press, 1958.

– *The French Enlightenment*. London: Macmillan, 1972.

– ed. *La philosophie de l'histoire*. In *Studies on Voltaire and the Eighteenth Century*, vol. 28 (1963).

Brun, Jean. *Le stoïcisme*. Paris: Presses universitaires de France, 1969.

Bryson, Gladys. *Man and Society: The Scottish Inquiry of the Eighteenth Century*. Reprint. New York: Kelley, 1968 [1945].

Buffon, Georges Louis Leclerc de. *Oeuvres philosophiques*. Paris: Presses universitaires de France, 1954.

Bukharin, Nikolai. *Historical Materialism. A System of Sociology*. New York: Russell & Russell, 1965.

Burger, Thomas. *Max Weber's Theory of Concept Formation*. Rev. ed. Durham: Duke University Press, 1986 [1976].

Burnet, John. *Early Greek Philosophy*. London: Black, 1930 [1892].

– *Platonism*. Berkeley: University of California Press, 1928.

Burnyeat, Myles, ed. *The Skeptical Tradition*. Berkeley: University of California, 1983.

Butts, Robert E., and John W. Davis, eds. *The Methodological Heritage of Newton*. Toronto: University of Toronto Press, 1970.

Camic, Charles. *Experience and Enlightenment*. Chicago: University of Chicago Press, 1983.

Campbell, R.H., and A.S. Skinner. *Adam Smith*. London: Croom Helm, 1982.

Campbell, T.D. *Adam Smith's Science of Morals*. London: Allen & Unwin, 1971.

Capaldi, Nicholas. *David Hume*. Boston: Twayne, 1975.

Carrithers, D.W. "Introduction." In C.S. de Montesquieu, *The Spirit of Laws*. Berkeley: University of California, 1977.

Carver, Terrell. *Marx & Engels*. Brighton: Wheatsheaf, 1983.

Cassirer, Ernst. *The Question of Jean-Jacques Rousseau*. Trans. Peter Gay. New York: Columbia University Press, 1954 [1932].

– *Rousseau, Kant, Goethe*. rev. ed. Trans. J. Gutmann. Princeton: Princeton University Press, 1970 [1945].

Castellion, Sébastien. *De l'art de douter*. Trans. C. Baudoin. Geneva: Jeheber, 1953 [1553].

Caton, Hiram. *The Origins of Subjectivity*. New Haven: Yale University Press, 1973.

Chadwick, N. Kershaw. *Poetry and Prophecy*. Cambridge: Cambridge University Press, 1942.

Châtelet, Emilie du. *Institutions de physique*. Paris: Prault, 1740.

Cherniss, Harold. *The Riddle of the Early Academy*. New York: Russell & Russell, 1962 [1945].

Chillingworth, William. *The Religion of Protestants*. Reprint. Oxford: Lichfield, 1972 [1638].

Christakes, George. *Albion W. Small*. Boston: Twayne, 1978.

Chugerman, Samuel. *Lester F. Ward: The American Aristotle*. New York: Octagon, 1965.

Church, Ralph W. *Hume's Theory of the Understanding*. Reprint. London: Allen & Unwin, 1968 [1935].

Cicero. *De Natura Deorum/Academica*. Trans. H. Rackham. Cambridge, MA: Harvard University Press, 1951.

Clark, George. *Science and Social Welfare in the Age of Newton*. Oxford: Clarendon, 1970 [1937].

Cleve, Felix M. *The Giants of Pre-Sophistic Greek Philosophy*. 2 vols. The Hague: Nijhoff, 1965.

Cochrane, Charles Norris. *Thucydides and the Science of History*. London: Oxford University Press, 1929.

Cohen, I. Bernard. *Introduction to Newton's "Principia."* Cambridge, MA: Harvard University Press, 1971.

Cole, G.D.H. "Introduction." In Karl Marx, *Capital*. London: Dent, 1929.

Cole, Margaret, ed. *The Webbs and their Work*. London: Muller, 1949.

Cole, Thomas. *Democritus and the Sources of Greek Anthropology*. American Philological Association Monographs, no. 25. American Philological Association, 1967.

Collingwood, R.G. *The Idea of Nature*. Oxford: Clarendon, 1949 [1934].

– *The Idea of History*, London: Oxford University Press, 1961 [1946].

Collini, Stefan. *Liberalism and Sociology*. Cambridge: Cambridge University Press, 1979.

Collins, Randall. *Max Weber: A Skeleton Key*. Beverley Hills: Sage, 1986.

– *Weberian Sociological Theory*. Cambridge: Cambridge University Press, 1986.

– *Conflict Sociology*. New York: Academic, 1975.

Commager, Henry Steele, ed. *Lester Ward and the Welfare State*. Indianapolis: Bobbs-Merrill, 1967.

Comte, Auguste. *Cours de philosophie positive*. 2 vols. Paris: Hermann, 1975 [1830–42].

– *Appel aux conservateurs*. Paris: Dalmont, 1855.

Condillac, Etienne Bonnot de. *Oeuvres philosophiques*. Paris: Presses universitaires de France, 1947.

Condorcet, Jean Antoine Nicolas Caritat de. *Oeuvres*. 12 vols. Ed. O'Connor and Arago. Paris: Didot, 1847.

– *Esquisse d'un tableau historique*. Paris: Editions sociales, 1966 [1794].

– *Elémens du calcul des probabilités*. Paris: Royez, 1805.

– *Vie de Monsieur Turgot*. Geneva: Slatkine, 1976 [1786].

– "Report on the General Organization of Public Instruction." In *French Liberalism and Education in the Eighteenth Century*, ed. F. de la Fontainerie. New York: McGraw-Hill, 1932 [1792].

– *Rapport et projet de décret sur l'organisation générale de l'instruction publique*. Paris: Imprimerie Nationale, 1792.

Condorcet, Sophie Grouchy de, trans. *Théorie des sentimens moraux* and "Huit lettres sur la sympathie." 2 vols. 1798.

Connell, Desmond. *The Vision in God*. Louvain: Nauwelaerts, 1967.

Connerton, Paul. *The Tragedy of Enlightenment*. Cambridge: Cambridge University Press, 1980.

Connor, W. Robert. *Thucydides*. Princeton, NJ: Princeton University Press, 1984.

Cook, Edward. *The Life of Florence Nightingale*. 2 vols. London: Macmillan, 1913.

Cook, Ramsay. *The Regenerators*. Toronto: University of Toronto Press, 1985.

Cornford, F. M. *Plato's Theory of Knowledge*. London: Kegan Paul, 1935.

Cranston, Maurice. *John Locke*. London: Longmans, 1961.

Crocker, Lester G. *The Embattled Philosopher*. London: Spearman, 1955.

Crossman, R.H.S. *Plato To-Day*. rev. ed. London: Allen & Unwin, 1959 [1937].

Crowther, J.G. "Joseph Priestley." In *Scientists of the Industrial Revolution*, ed. J.G. Crowther. London: Cresset, 1962.

Cru, R. Loyalty. *Diderot as a Disciple of English Thought*. New York: Columbia University Press, 1913.

Cullen, M.J. *The Statistical Movement in Early Victorian Britain*. New York: Harvester, 1975.

Cumming, Ian. *Helvetius*. London: Routledge & Kegan Paul, 1955.

Dakin, Douglas. *Turgot and the Ancien Régime in France*. New York: Octagon, 1965 [1937].

Darnton, Robert. *The Business of Enlightenment*. Cambridge, MA: Belknap, 1979.

Darwin, Charles. *The Origin of Species*. 6th ed. London: John Murray, 1902 [1859].

David, Deirdre. *Intellectual Women and Victorian Patriarchy*. London: Macmillan, 1987.

Day, James, and Mortimer Chambers. *Aristotle's History of Athenian Democracy*. Amsterdam: Hakkert, 1967.

Deane, Herbert A. *The Political and Social Ideas of St Augustine*. New York: Columbia University Press, 1963.

Deegan, Mary Jo. *Jane Addams and the Men of the Chicago School*. New Brunswick, NJ: Transaction, 1988.

DeSantillano, Georgio. *The Origins of Scientific Thought*. Chicago: University of Chicago Press, 1961.

– *The Crime of Galileo*. Chicago: University of Chicago Press, 1955.

Descartes, René. *The Philosophical Works of Descartes*. 2 vols. Trans. Elizabeth L. Haldane and G.R.T. Ross. Cambridge: Cambridge University Press, 1973.

– *Lettres sur la morale*. Ed. Jacques Chevalier. Paris: Boivin, 1935.

Desgraves, Louis. *Montesquieu*. Paris: Mazarine, 1986.

Despland, Michel. *Kant on History and Religion*. Montreal: McGill-Queen's University Press, 1973.

Dessaix, Paul. *Montchrétien et l'économie nationale*. New York: Franklin, 1970 [1901].

Dewhurst, Kenneth. *John Locke, Physician and Philosopher*. London: Wellcome Historical Medical Library, 1963.

DeWitt, Norman Wentworth. *Epicurus and his Philosophy*. Minneapolis: University of Minnesota Press, 1954.

Diamond, Marion, and Mervyn Stone. "Nightingale on Quetelet." *Journal of the Royal Statistical Society* (series A) 144 (1981): Pt 1, 66–79; Pt 2, 176–213; Pt. 3, 332–51.

Dibble, Vernon K. *The Legacy of Albion Small*. Chicago: University of Chicago Press, 1975.

Dibon, Paul, ed. *Pierre Bayle*. Paris: Vrin, 1959.

Diderot, Denis. *Oeuvres complètes*. 33 vols. Paris: Hermann, 1975–.

Diesbach, Ghislain de. *Madame de Staël*. Paris: Perrin, 1983.

Dinwiddy, John. *Bentham*. Oxford: Oxford University Press, 1989.

Dixon, C. W. *Mary and Caroline and the Lay Contribution to Preventive Medicine*. Duneden, New Zealand: University of Otago Press, 1961.

Dodds, Muriel. *Les récits de voyages de Montesquieu*. Paris: Champion, 1929.

[Drake, Judith?] *An Essay in defence of the Female Sex*. Reprint of 2nd ed. New York: Source, 1970 [1696].

Dronberger, Ilse. *The Political Thought of Max Weber*. New York: Appleton-Century-Crofts, 1971.

Durkheim, Emile. *Montesquieu and Rousseau*. Ann Arbor: University of Michigan Press, 1960 [1892].

– *The Rules of Sociological Method*. Trans. Sarah A. Solway and John H. Mueller. New York: Free Press, 1938 [1895].

– *Les règles de la méthode sociologique*. 10th ed. Paris: Presses Universitaires de France, 1947.

– *On the Division of Labor in Society*. Trans. George Simpson. New York: Macmillan, 1933 [1893].

– *Suicide*. New York: Free Press, 1965 [1897].

– *Socialism and Saint-Simon*. Trans. Charlotte Sattler. Yellow Springs, OH: Antioch, 1958.

– *The Elementary Forms of the Religious Life*. Trans. J.W. Swain. London: Allen & Unwin, 1964 [1912].

– *Pragmatism and Sociology*. Trans. J.C. Whitehouse Cambridge: Cambridge University Press, 1983 [1955]

– "Preface." In O. Hamelin, *Le système de Descartes*. Paris: Alcan, 1911.

Duval, Jules. *Mémoire sur Antoine de Montchrétien*. Geneva: Slatkine, 1971 [1868].

Eden, Frederic Norton. *The State of the Poor*. 3 vols. Facsimile of 1797 ed. London: Frank Cass, 1966.

Edwards, Maldwyn. *John Wesley and the Eighteenth Century*. London: Epworth, 1985 [1933].

Ehrenberg, Victor. *From Solon to Socrates*. London: Methuen, 1973 [1967].

Ehrman, Esther. *Mme du Châtelet*. Leamington Spa: Berg, 1986.

Engels, Friedrich. *The Condition of the Working Class in England*. Trans. W.O. Henderson and W.H. Chaloner. Oxford: Blackwell, 1971 [1845].

Escarpit, Robert. *L'Angleterre dans l'oeuvre de Madame de Staël*. Paris: Didier, 1954.

Eusebius. *The History of the Church from Christ to Constantine*. Trans. G.A. Williamson. Harmondsworth: Penguin, 1965.

Evans, J.D.G. *Aristotle*. Sussex: Harvester, 1987.

Evans-Pritchard, E.E. *The Sociology of Comte*. Manchester: Manchester University Press, 1970.

Evelyn, John. *Silva: or, a Discourse of Forest-Trees*. 1662.

– *Fumifugium*. Reprint. London: Godbid, 1772 [1661].

Farrington, Benjamin. *The Faith of Epicurus*. London: Weidenfeld & Nicolson, 1967.

– *Science and Politics in the Ancient World*. London: Allen & Unwin, 1939.

– *Head and Hand in Ancient Greece*. London: Watts, 1947.

– *Science in Antiquity*. London: Butterworth, 1936.

– *The Philosophy of Francis Bacon*. Liverpool: Liverpool University Press, 1964.

– *Francis Bacon. Philosopher of Industrial Science*. London: Lawrence & Wishart, 1951 [1949].

Faulkner, John Alfred. *Wesley as Sociologist, Theologian, Churchman*. New York: Methodist Book Concerns, 1918.

Fenton, Steve. *Durkheim and Modern Sociology*. Cambridge: Cambridge University Press, 1984.

Ferguson, Adam. *Principles of Moral and Political Science*. 2 vols. Reprint. Hildesheim: Georg Olms, 1975 [1792].

– *Institutes of Moral Philosophy*. rev. ed. Basel: Decker, 1800 [1769].

Festugière, A.J. *Epicurus and his Gods*. Trans. C.W. Chilton. Oxford: Blackwell, 1955 [1946].

Field, G.C. *Plato and his Contemporaries*. London: Methuen, 1967 [1930].

- *The Philosophy of Plato*. 2d ed. London: Oxford University Press, 1969 [1949].

Filloux, Jean-Claude. *Durkheim et le socialisme*. Geneva: Droz, 1977.

Finley, M.I. *The Ancient Economy*. London: Hogarth, 1985 [1973].

Fitchett, W.H. *Wesley and his Century*. London: Smith, Elder, 1906.

Flax, Jane. *Thinking Fragments*. Berkeley: University of California Press, 1990.

Fletcher, Ronald, ed. *John Stuart Mill: A Logical Critique of Sociology*. London: Michael Joseph, 1971.

Flexner, Eleanor. *Mary Wollstonecraft*. New York: Coward, McCann and Geoghegan, 1972.

Flint, Robert. *Vico*. Edinburgh: Blackwood, 1884.

Foley, Vernard. *The Social Physics of Adam Smith*. West Lafayette, IN: Purdue University Press, 1976.

Forbes, Duncan. *Hume's Philosophical Politics*. Cambridge: Cambridge University Press, 1975.

Forsberg, Roberta J., and H.C. Nixon. *Madame de Staël and Freedom Today*. London: Vision, 1963.

Fox-Genovese, Elizabeth. *The Origins of Physiocracy*. Ithaca: Cornell University Press, 1976.

Frank, Joseph. *The Levellers*. New York: Russell & Russell, 1969 [1955].

Frazer, James George. *Condorcet on the Progress of the Human Mind*. Oxford: Clarendon, 1933.

Freeman, Kathleen. *The Pre-Socratic Philosophers*. Oxford: Blackwell, 1946.

- *Ancilla to the Pre-Socratic Philosophers*. Oxford: Blackwell, 1948.

- *The Work and Life of Solon*. Cardiff: University of Wales, 1926.

Freund, Julien. *The Sociology of Max Weber*. Trans. Mary Ilford. London: Allen Lane, 1968 [1966].

Friedmann, Georges. *Leibniz et Spinoza*. Paris: Gallimard, 1962.

Furley, David J., and R.E. Allen, eds. *Studies in Presocratic Philosophy*. London: Routledge & Kegan Paul, 1970.

Galton, Francis. *Inquiries into Human Faculty and its Development*. 2d ed. London: Dent, 1907 [1883].

- *Memories of My Life*. London: Methuen, 1908.

Galtung, Johan. *Papers on Methodology*. Copenhagen: Ejlers, 1979.

Gassendi, Pierre. *Abrégé de la philosophie de Gassendi*. 7 vols. 2d ed. Ed. F. Bernier. Lyon: Anisson, 1684.

- *Dissertations en forme de paradoxes contre les Aristotéliciens*. Trans. B. Rochot. Paris: Vrin, 1959 [1624].

Gaukroger, Stephen. *Cartesian Logic*. Oxford: Clarendon, 1989.

Gay, Peter. *Voltaire's Politics*. Princeton, NJ: Princeton University Press, 1959.

Gershenson, Daniel E., and Daniel A. Greenberg. *Anaxagoras and the Birth of Physics*. New York: Blaisdell, 1964.

Gibbs, F.W. *Joseph Priestley*. London: Nelson, 1965.

Gibson, A. Boyce. *The Philosophy of Descartes*. New York: Russell & Russell, 1967 [1932].

Gibson, James. *Locke's Theory of Knowledge and its Historical Relations*. Cambridge: Cambridge University Press, 1917.

Giddings, Franklin Henry. *Principles of Sociology*. New York: Macmillan, 1899 [1896].

– *Inductive Sociology*. New York: Macmillan, 1901.

Glanvill, Joseph. *Scepsis Scientifica* or *The Vanity of Dogmatizing*. London: Everdon, 1665.

– *Plus Ultra*. London: Collins, 1668.

– *Essays on Several Important Subjects in Philosophy and Religion*. London: Baker, 1676.

Godwin, William. *Enquiry concerning Political Justice*. 3 vols. Ed. F.E.L. Priestley. Toronto: University of Toronto Press, 1946 [1790].

Goldmann, Lucien. *Immanuel Kant*. Trans. Robert Black. London: NLB, 1971.

Goldsmith, M.M. *Hobbes's Science of Politics*. New York: Columbia University Press, 1966.

Goldsmith, Margaret. *Madame de Staël*. London: Longmans, Green, 1938.

Goode, William J., and Paul K. Hatt. *Methods in Social Research*. New York: McGraw-Hill, 1952.

Goring, Charles. *The English Convict*. London: His Majesty's Stationery Office, 1913.

Gouldner, Alvin W. *For Sociology*. New York: Basic, 1973.

– *Enter Plato*. London: Routledge & Kegan Paul, 1965.

Grandamy, René. *La physiocratie*. Paris: Mouton, 1973.

Granger, Gilles-Gaston. *La mathématique sociale du Marquis de Condorcet*. Paris: Presses universitaires de France, 1956.

Grant, Edward. *Physical Science in the Middle Ages*. New York: Wiley, 1971.

Grant, George. *Technology and Empire*. Toronto: Anansi, 1969.

Grant, Michael. *The Ancient Historians*. London: Weidenfeld & Nicolson, 1970.

Grave, S.A. *The Scottish Philosophy of Common Sense*. Oxford: Clarendon, 1960.

Grayeff, Felix. *Aristotle and his School*. London: Duckworth, 1974.

Grayling, A.C. *Berkeley*. London: Duckworth, 1986.

– *The Ancien Régime*. Edinburgh: University Press, 1958.

Greenleaf, W.H. *Order, Empiricism and Politics*. London: Oxford University Press, 1964.

Greer, Scott. *The Logic of Social Inquiry*. Chicago: Aldine, 1969.

Greig, J.Y.T. *David Hume*. London: Cape, 1931.

Grene, Marjorie. *A Portrait of Aristotle*. London: Faber & Faber, 1963.

Grimaldi, Alfonsina Albini. *The Universal Humanity of Giambattista Vico*. New York: Vanni, 1958.

Grimsley, Ronald. *The Philosophy of Rousseau*. London: Oxford University Press, 1973.

Grote, George. *History of Greece.* 12 vols. London: Murray, 1869–1907 [1846–56].

Grotius, Hugo. *On the Rights of War and Peace.* Trans. W. Whewell. Cambridge: Cambridge University Press, 1853.

– *The Freedom of the Seas.* Trans. R.V. Deman Magoffin. New York: Oxford University Press, 1916 [1608].

– *De Rebus Belgicis: or, The Annals and History of the Low-Country-Warrs.* Trans. T. Manley. London: Twyford, 1665.

– "On the Origins of the Native Races of America."

Grube, G.M.A. *Plato's Thought.* Boston: Beacon, 1958.

Grylls, Rosalie Glynn. *William Godwin and his World.* London: Odhams, 1958.

Guerry, A.M. *Essai sur la statistique morale.* Paris: Crochard, 1833.

Guicciardini, Francesco. *The History of Italy.* Trans. Sidney Alexander. New York: Macmillan, 1969 [1561].

Gulley, Norman. *The Philosophy of Socrates.* London: Macmillan, 1968.

Gurvitch, Georges. *Dialectique et sociologie.* Paris: Flammarion, 1962.

– *Les fondateurs français de la sociologie contemporaine.* Paris: Centre de documentation universitaire, 1955.

– "Introduction." In Henri de Saint-Simon, *La physiologie sociale.* Paris: Presses universitaires de France, 1965.

Guthrie, W.K.C. *Socrates.* Cambridge: Cambridge University Press, 1971.

– *A History of Greek Philosophy.* 6 vols. Cambridge: Cambridge University Press, 1962–80.

– *In the Beginning.* London: Methuen, 1957.

Guyot-Daubès. *L'art de classer les notes.* Paris: Bibliothèque d'éducation attrayante, 1891.

Gwynne, G.E. *Madame de Staël et la révolution française.* Paris: Nizet, 1969.

Haakonssen, Knud. *The Science of a Legislator.* Cambridge: Cambridge University Press, 1981.

Habermas, Jürgen. *On the Logic of the Social Sciences.* Trans. S.W. Nicholsen and J.A. Stark. Cambridge: Polity Press, 1988 [1967].

Hadzsits, George Depue. *Lucretius and his Influence.* New York: Longmans, Green, 1935.

Haldane, Elizabeth S. *Descartes.* New York: American Scholar, 1966 [1905].

Halévy, Elie. *The Growth of Philosophic Radicalism.* Trans. Mary Morris. London: Faber & Faber, 1934 [1928].

Haller, William. *The Rise of Puritanism.* New York: Cornell University Press, 1938.

Halley, Edmund. "An Estimate of the Degrees of Mortality of Mankind." *Philosophical Transactions*, abridged series, 17, no. 3: (1809):483–95.

– "Some further Considerations on the Breslau Bills of Mortality." *Philosophical Transactions*, abridged series 17, no. 3 (1809):510–11.

Halsband, Robert. *The Life of Lady Mary Wortley Montagu.* Oxford: Clarendon, 1956.

– "New Light on Lady Mary Wortley Montagu's Contribution to Inoculation." *Journal of the History of Medicine and Allied Sciences* 8 (1953):391–405.

Hamilton, Peter. *Max Weber: Critical Assessments*. 4 vols. London: Routledge & Kegan Paul, 1991.

Hanks, Lesley. *Buffon avant l'"histoire naturelle."* Paris: Presses universitaires de France, 1966.

Harding, Sandra. *The Science Question in Feminism*. Ithaca: Cornell University Press, 1986.

Harries-Jones, Peter, ed. *Making Knowledge Count*. Montreal: McGill-Queen's University Press, 1991.

Harrington, James. *The Political Works of James Harrington*. Ed. J.G.A. Pocock. Cambridge: Cambridge University Press, 1977.

Harrison, John, and Peter Laslett. *The Library of John Locke*. Oxford: Oxford University Press, 1965.

Harrison, Ross. *Bentham*. London: Routledge & Kegan Paul, 1983.

Havelock, Eric A. *The Liberal Temper in Greek Politics*. London: Cape, 1957.

– *Preface to Plato*. Oxford: Blackwell, 1963.

Hayek, F.A. *John Stuart Mill and Harriet Taylor*. London: Routledge & Kegan Paul, 1957.

Hays, Mary. *Female Biography*. 6 vols. London: Phillips, 1803.

– *Letters and Essays, Moral and Misc*. London: Knott, 1793.

– *Memoirs of Emma Courtney*. New York: Garland, 1974.

– *Appeal to the Men of Great Britain in Behalf of Women*. Reprint. New York: Garland, 1974 [1798].

Heidel, William Arthur. *Hippocratic Medicine*. New York: Columbia University Press, 1941.

– "Antecedents of Greek Corpuscular Theories." *Harvard Studies in Classical Philosophy*. 22 (1911):111–72.

Helvétius, Claude. *Oeuvres complètes*. 7 vols. Paris: Deux Ponts, 1784.

Hennis, Wilhelm. *Max Weber*. Trans. Keith Tribe. London: Allen & Unwin, 1988.

Henry, Margaret Y. *The Relation of Dogmatism and Scepticism in Cicero*. New York: Humphrey, 1925.

Herodotus. *The History of Herodotus*. 4 vols. Trans. George Rawlinson. New York: Appleton, 1861.

Herold, J. Christopher. *Mistress to an Age. A Life of Madame de Staël*. London: Hamilton, 1959.

Hiebert, Edwin N., et al. eds. *Joseph Priestley, Scientist Theologian and Metaphysician*. Lewisburg, NJ: Bucknell University Press, 1971.

Higgs, Henry. *The Physiocrats*. New York: Langland, 1952.

Hill, Bridget, ed. *The First English Feminist*. Aldershot: Gower, 1986.

Hill, Christopher. "The Religion of Gerrard Winstanley," *Past and Present*, supplement no. 5, 1978.

- *Intellectual Origins of the English Revolution*. Oxford: Clarendon, 1965.
- *The World Turned Upside Down*. London: Temple-Smith, 1972.
Himmelfarb, Gertrude. *On Liberty and Liberalism*. New York: Knopf, 1974.
- ed. *Essays on Politics and Culture*. Garden City, NY: Anchor, 1963.
Hippocrates. *The Medical Works of Hippocrates*. Trans. John Chadwick and W.N. Mann. Oxford: Blackwell, 1950.
Hobbes, Thomas. *English Works*. 10 vols. Ed. William Molesworth, London: Bohn, 1839.
- *The Elements of Law*. Ed. Ferdinand Tönnies. London: Cass, 1969 [1650].
Hofstadter, Richard. *Social Darwinism in American Thought*. Philadelphia: University of Pennsylvania Press, 1945.
Holbach, Paul Thiry d'. *Système de la nature*. 2 vols. Paris: Ledoux, 1821 [1771].
- *Système social*. London, 1773.
- *Ethocratie*. Reprint. Amsterdam: Rey, 1967 [1776].
- *La politique naturelle*. London, 1773.
Homans, George C. *The Nature of Social Science*. New York: Harcourt, Brace, 1967 [1965].
Hood, F.C. *The Divine Politics of Thomas Hobbes*. Oxford: Clarendon, 1964.
Horkheimer, Max. *Critical Theory*. Trans. M.J. O'Connell. New York: Herder & Herder, 1972.
Hornblower, Simon. *Thucydides*. Baltimore: Johns Hopkins University Press, 1987.
Horowitz, Asher. *Rousseau, Nature, and History*. Toronto: University of Toronto Press, 1987.
- and Gad Horowitz. *"Everywhere They Were in Chains"*. Toronto: Nelson, 1988.
Horowitz, Irving Louis. *Claude Helvétius: Philosopher of Democracy and Enlightenment*. New York: Paine-Whitman, 1954.
Hubbard, M.G. *Saint-Simon*. Paris: Guillaumin, 1857.
Hughes, H. Stuart. *Consciousness and Society*. New York: Knopf, 1958.
Hume, David. *The Philosophical Works of David Hume*. 4 vols. Boston: Little, Brown, 1864.
- *An Abstract of a Treatise of Human Nature*. Ed. J.M. Keynes. Hamden, CT: Archon, 1965 [1740].
- *The History of England*. 4 vols. Philadelphia: Library Edition, 1828 [1754–62].
- *Essays, Literary, Moral, and Political*. London: Ward, Lock & Taylor, 1870.
Hunt, H.A.K. *The Humanism of Cicero*. Melbourne: Melbourne University Press, 1954.
Hunter, Michael. *Science and Society in Restoration England*. Cambridge: Cambridge University Press, 1981.
Hunter, Virginia J. *Thucydides: The Artful Reporter*. Toronto: Hakkert, 1973.
- *Past and Process in Herodotus and Thucydides*. Princeton, NJ: Princeton University Press, 1982.
Hutcheson, Francis. *A System of Moral Philosophy*. 2 vols. Reprint of 1755 ed. Hildesheim: Georg Olms, 1969. [1733–37].

– *Collected Works.* 7 vols. Reprint. Hildesheim: Olms, 1971.

Ibn Khaldun. *The Muqaddimah.* 3 vols. Trans. Franz Rosenthal. London: Routledge & Kegan Paul, 1958.

Innis, Harold A. *The Bias of Communication.* Toronto: University of Toronto Press, 1964 [1951].

Jacob, Margaret C. *The Newtonians and the English Revolution.* Ithaca, NY: Cornell University Press, 1976.

– *The Radical Enlightenment.* London: Allen & Unwin, 1981.

James, Margaret. *Social Problems and Policy during the Puritan Revolution.* London: Routledge, 1930.

Jay, Martin. *The Dialectical Imagination.* Boston: Little, Brown, 1973.

Jensen, Henning. *Motivation and the Moral Sense in Francis Hutcheson's Ethical Theory.* The Hague: Nijhoff, 1971.

Johnston, G.A. *The Development of Berkeley's Philosophy.* New York: Russell & Russell, 1965.

Jolley, Nicholas. *The Light of the Soul.* Oxford: Clarendon, 1990.

Jones, R.F. *Ancients and Moderns.* St Louis: Washington University Press, 1962 [1961].

Kahn, Charles H. *Anaximander and the Origins of Greek Cosmology.* New York: Columbia University Press, 1960.

Kant, Immanuel. *Critique of Pure Reason.* rev. ed. Trans. J.M.D. Meiklejohn. New York: Colonial Press, 1900 [1781].

– *Kant's Critique of Teleological Judgement.* Trans. J.C. Meredith. Oxford: Clarendon, 1928.

– *Prolegomena to any Future Metaphysics that will be able to Present Itself as a Science.* Trans. P.G. Lucas. Manchester: Manchester University Press, 1953 [1783].

– *Kant's Political Writings.* Trans. H.B. Nisbet. Cambridge: University Press, 1970.

– *Anthropology from a Pragmatic Point of View.* Trans. Mary Gregor. The Hague: Nijhoff, 1974 [1797].

Kaplan, Abraham. *The Conduct of Inquiry.* San Francisco: Chandler, 1964.

Käsler, Dirk. *Max Weber.* Trans. Philippa Hurd. Chicago: University of Chicago Press, 1988 [1979].

Keller, Evelyn Fox. *Reflections on Gender and Science.* New Haven: Yale University Press, 1985.

Kelsen, Hans. *What is Justice?* Berkeley: University of California Press, 1971 [1951].

Kerferd, G.B. *The Sophistic Movement.* Cambridge: Cambridge University Press, 1981.

Kettler, David. *The Social and Political Thought of Adam Ferguson.* Cleveland: Ohio State University Press, 1965.

Keynes, J.M. "Newton, the Man." In Royal Society, *Newton Tercentenary Celebrations.* Cambridge: Cambridge University Press, 1947.

Kline, George R., ed. *Spinoza in Soviet Philosophy*. London: Routledge & Kegan Paul, 1952.

Knight, Isabel. *The Geometric Spirit*. New Haven: Yale University Press, 1968.

Knight, W.S.M. *The Life and Works of Hugo Grotius*. London: Sweet and Maxwell, 1925.

Körner, S. *Kant*. Harmondsworth: Penguin, 1955.

Koyré, Alexander. *The Astronomical Revolution*. Trans. R.E.W. Maddison. Paris: Hermann, 1973 [1961].

Krieger, Leonard. *The Politics of Discretion*. Chicago: University of Chicago Press, 1965.

Kropotkin, Peter. *Mutual Aid*. London: Heinemann, 1915 [1902].

Kurtz, Lester R. *Evaluating Chicago Sociology*. University of Chicago Press, 1984.

Labrousse, Elisabeth. *Pierre Bayle*. 2 vols. Trans. Denys Potts. Oxford: Oxford University Press, 1983 [1963].

La Capra, Dominick. *Emile Durkheim*. Ithaca, NY: Cornell University Press, 1972.

Lambridis, Helle. *Empedocles*. University of Alabama Press, 1976.

La Méttrie, Julien Offray de. *Oeuvres philosophiques*. 3 vols. Paris: Tutot, 1796.

– *La Méttrie's l'Homme machine*. Ed. Aram Vartanian. Princeton: Princeton University Press, 1960 [1747].

Lane, Peter. *The Industrial Revolution*. London: Weidenfeld & Nicolson, 1978.

Laplace, Pierre-Simon. *Essai philosophique sur les probabilités*. Paris: Courcier, 1814.

Larg, David Glass. *Madame de Staël*. Paris: Champion, 1924.

Lasch, Christopher, ed. *The Social Thought of Jane Addams*. Indianopolis: Bobbs-Merrill, 1965.

Lateiner, Donald. *The Historical Method of Herodotus*. Toronto: University of Toronto Press, 1989.

Lavoisier, Antoine-Laurent. *Mélanges d'économie politique*. Paris: Guillaumin, 1847.

Lazarsfeld, Paul F. "Notes on the History of Quantification." *Isis* 52 (1961):277–333.

– and Anthony R. Oberschall. "Max Weber and Empirical Social Research." *American Sociological Review*. 30, no. 2 (1965):185–99.

– et al., eds. *The Uses of Sociology*. New York: Basic, 1967.

Lefebvre, Georges. *La Révolution Française*. Paris: Presses Universitaires de France, 1963.

Lefèvre, Roger. *Condillac*. Editions Seghers, 1966.

Lehmann, William C. *John Millar of Glasgow*. Cambridge: University Press, 1960.

Leibniz, Gottfried Wilhelm. *Nouveaux essais sur l'entendement humain*. 2 vols. Darmstadt: Wissenschaftliche Buchgesellschaft, 1959.

– *Philosophical Papers and Letters*. Trans. L.E. Loemker. Dordrecht: Reidel, 1969.

– *The Leibniz-Clarke Correspondence*. Ed. H.G. Alexander. Manchester: Manchester University Press, 1956.

Lenin, Vladimir I. *Materialism and Empirio-Criticism. Collected Works*, vol. 14. Trans. A. Fineberg. London: Lawrence & Wishart, 1947.

Lenoble, Robert. *Mersenne ou la naissance du mécanisme*. Paris: Vrin, 1943.

Lepenies, Wolf. *Between Literature and Science*. Trans. R.J. Hollingdale. Cambridge: Cambridge University Press, 1988.

Le Play, Frédéric. *Les ouvriers européens*. Paris: Imprimerie Impériale, 1855.

Le Roy, Maxime, et al., eds. *Descartes*. Paris: Rieder, 1929.

– *La vie véritable du Comte Henri de Saint-Simon*. Paris: Grasset, 1925.

Letwin, Shirley Robin. *The Pursuit of Certainty*. Cambridge: Cambridge University Press, 1965.

Levine, Daniel. *Jane Addams and the Liberal Tradition*. Madison: State Historical Society of Wisconsin, 1971.

Lewis, J. David, and Richard L. Smith. *American Sociology and Pragmatism*. Chicago: University of Chicago Press, 1980.

Libby, Margaret S. *The Attitude of Voltaire to Magic and the Sciences*. New York: Columbia University Press, 1935.

Lindsay, A.D. *Kant*. London: Oxford University Press, 1934.

Lindsay, J.O., ed. *The Old Regime*. Cambridge: Cambridge University Press, 1957.

Little, Daniel. *The Scientific Marx*. Minneapolis: University of Minnesota Press, 1986.

Locke, John. *An Essay concerning Human Understanding*. 2 vols. Ed. A.C. Fraser. New York: Dover, 1959 [1690].

– *Two Treatises of Government*. Ed. Peter Laslett. Cambridge: Cambridge University Press, 1960 [1690].

– *The Educational Writings of John Locke*. Ed. J.W. Adamson. Cambridge: Cambridge University Press, 1922.

– *Works*. 10 vols. 10th ed. London: Johnson, 1801.

Loemker, Leroy L. *Struggle for Synthesis*. Cambridge, MA: Harvard University Press, 1972.

Lottin, Joseph. *Quetelet. Statisticien et sociologue*. Louvain: Institut supérieur de philosophie, 1912.

Lough, John. *Locke's Travels in France*. Cambridge: University Press, 1953.

– *An Introduction to Eighteenth Century France*. London: Longmans, 1960.

– *The Encyclopedie*. London: Longmans, 1971.

Lovejoy, Arthur O. *The Great Chain of Being*. Cambridge, MA: Harvard University Press, 1936.

Löwith, Karl. *Max Weber & Karl Marx*. Trans. Hans Fantel. London: Allen & Unwin, 1982 [1932].

Luce, A.A. *Berkeley and Malebranche*. Oxford: Clarendon, 1967 [1934].

– *The Life of George Berkeley Bishop of Cloyne*. London: Thomas Nelson, 1949.

Lucretius. *De Rerum Natura*. Trans. Alban Dewes Winspear. New York: Russell-Harbor, 1956.

Lukacs, Georgy. *History and Class Consciousness*. London: Merlin, 1971 [1923].

Lukes, Steven. *Emile Durkheim*. London: Allen Lane, 1973.

Luppol, I.K. *Diderot*. 2d ed. Trans. V. Feldman and U. Feldman. Paris: Editions sociales internationales, 1936 [1924].

Lutaud, Olivier. *Winstanley, socialisme et christianisme sous Cromwell*. Paris: Didier, 1976.

Luxembourg, Lilo K. *Francis Bacon and Denis Diderot*. Copenhagen: Munksgaard, 1967.

Lynd, Robert S. *Knowledge for What?* Princeton; NJ: Princeton University Press, 1945 [1939].

Lyons, David. *In the Interest of the Governed*. Oxford: Clarendon, 1973.

MacArthur, Kathleen Walker. *The Economic Ethics of John Wesley*. New York: Abingdon, 1936.

Macaulay, Catharine. *Letters on Education*. New York: Garland, 1974 [1790].

– *The History of England from the Accession of James I to that of the Brunswick Line*. 8 vols. London: Nourse, 1763–83.

– *The History of England from the Revolution to the Present Time*. London: Cruttwell, 1778.

– *Loose Remarks on Hobbes's Philosophical Rudiments*. London: Davies, 1767.

– *Observations on the Reflections of the Rt Hon Edmund Burke on the Revolution in France*. London: Dilly, 1790.

McCracken, Charles J. *Malebranche and British Philosophy*. Oxford: Clarendon, 1983.

McDonald, Joan. *Rousseau and the French Revolution*. London: Athlone, 1965.

McDonald, Lynn. *The Sociology of Law and Order*. Toronto: Methuen, 1979 [1976].

Macfie, A.L. *The Individual in Society*. London: Allen & Unwin, 1967.

MacIntyre, Alasdair. *After Virtue*. University of Notre Dame Press, 1984 [1981].

Mack, Mary P. *Jeremy Bentham*. London: Heinemann, 1962.

MacKenzie, Donald A. *Statistics in Britain*. Edinburgh: Edinburgh University Press, 1981.

McKeon, Richard. *The Philosphy of Spinoza*. New York: Longmans, Green, 1928.

McLellan, David. *The Thought of Karl Marx*. London: Macmillan, 1971.

– *Marx before Marxism*. London: Macmillan, 1970.

MacNab, W.G.C. *David Hume*. Oxford: Blackwell, 1966 [1951].

Macpherson, C.B. *The Political Theory of Possessive Individualism*. Oxford: Clarendon, 1962.

– "Harrington's 'Opportunity State.'" *Past and Present*, 1960:45–70.

– "Sir William Temple, Political Scientist?" *Canadian Journal of Economics and Political Science*. 9 (1943):39–54.

– "Introduction." In T. Hubbes, *Leviathan*, 9–63. Harmondsworth: Penguin, 1968.

– "The Social Bearing of Locke's Political Theory." *Western Political Quarterly*, 1954:1–22.

MacRae, Donald G. *Max Weber*. New York: Viking, 1974.

McRae, Robert. *The Problem of the Unity of the Sciences.* Toronto: University of Toronto Press, 1961.

– *Leibniz: Perception, Apperception, and Thought.* Toronto: University of Toronto Press, 1976.

Maestro, Marcello T. *Cesare Beccaria and the Origins of Penal Reform.* Philadelphia: Temple University Press, 1973.

– *Voltaire and Beccaria.* New York: Columbia University Press, 1942.

Mailly, Edouard. *Essai sur la vie et les ouvrages de L.A.J. Quetelet.* Brussels: Académie Royale, 1875.

Malebranche, Nicolas. *Oeuvres complètes.* 20 vols. Paris: Vrin, 1962.

Malthus, Thomas Robert. rev. ed. *An Essay on the Principles of Population.* London: Ward, Cook, 1890 [1798].

Mandelbaum, Maurice. *Philosophy Science and Sense Perception.* Baltimore: John Hopkins University Press, 1964.

Mansion, Suzanne, ed. *Aristote et les problèmes de méthode.* Louvain: Publications Universitaires, 1961.

Manuel, Frank E. *Isaac Newton, Historian.* Cambridge: Belknap, 1963.

– *The Religion of Isaac Newton.* Oxford: Clarendon, 1974.

– *The Prophets of Paris.* Cambridge, MA: Harvard University Press, 1962.

– *The New World of Henri Saint-Simon.* Cambridge, MA: Harvard University Press, 1956.

Mao Tse-tung. *Four Essays in Philosophy.* Peking: Foreign Languages Press, 1966.

Marcuse, Herbert. *One-Dimensional Man.* Boston: Beacon, 1964.

Maritain, Jacques. *The Dream of Descartes.* Trans. Mabelle Anderson. Port Washington: Kennikat Press, 1969 [1944].

Markovits, Francine. *Marx dans le jardin d'Epicure.* Paris: Minuit, 1974.

Marshall, Gordon. *In Praise of Sociology.* London: Unwin, Hyman, 1990.

Marshall, Peter H. *William Godwin.* New Haven: Yale University Press, 1984.

Martin, Ronald. *Tacitus.* London: Batsford, 1981.

Martineau, Harriet. *How to Observe Morals and Manners.* London: Knight, 1838.

– *Society in America.* Ed. S.M. Lipset. Garden City, NY: Anchor, 1962 [1837].

– *Illustrations of Political Economy.* 9 vols. London: Charles Fox, 1834 [1832].

– "Essays on the Art of Thinking." *Miscellanies.* 2 vols. Boston: Hilliard, Gray, 1836.

– ed. and trans. *The Positive Philosophy of Auguste Comte.* 2 vols. London: Kegan, Paul, 1895.

– *Autobiography.* 3 vols. London: Smith, Elder, 1877.

Marx, Karl. *Capital.* Trans. Ben Fowkes. Harmondsworth: Penguin/New Left Review, 1977 [1867].

– *A Contribution to the Critique of Political Economy.* Trans. N.I. Stone. Chicago: Kerr, 1904 [1859].

– *Grundrisse.* Trans. Martin Nicolaus. London: Allen Lane, 1973.

– *The Eighteenth Brumaire of Louis Bonaparte*. Trans. Eden Paul and Cedar Paul. New York: International, 1926 [1852].
– *The Poverty of Philosophy*. New York: International, 1963 [1847].
– *Critique of the Gotha Program*. Moscow: Foreign Languages Publishing House, 1947 [1875].
– *The Difference Between Democritean and Epicurean Philosophy of Nature*. In *Activity in Marx's Philosophy*, ed. Norman D. Livergood. The Hague: Nijhoff, 1967.
– *Selected Writings in Sociology and Social Philosophy*. Eds. T.B. Bottomore and M. Rubel. Harmondsworth: Penguin, 1961.
– *Early Texts*. Trans. David McLellan. Oxford: Blackwell, 1971.
– *Karl Marx. Texts on Method*. Ed. Terrell Carver. Oxford: Blackwell, 1975.
– *The Ethnological Notebooks of Karl Marx*. Ed. Lawrence Kracler. Assen: Van Gorcum, 1972.
– and Friedrich Engels. *The German Ideology*. London: Lawrence & Wishart, 1938.
– and Friedrich Engels. *The Holy Family*.Trans. R. Dixon. Moscow: Foreign Languages Publishing House, 1956 [1845].
– and Friedrich Engels. *The Communist Manifesto*. Trans. Samuel Moore. New York: Washington Square Press, 1964 [1848].
Masters, Roger D. *The Political Philosophy of Rousseau*. Princeton, NJ: Princeton University Press, 1968.
Matalon, Benjamin. *Décrire, expliquer, prévoir*. Paris: Colin, 1988.
Mathias, Peter. *The First Industrial Nation*. London: Methuen, 1969.
Matthews, Fred H. *Robert E. Park and the Chicago School*. Montreal: McGill-Queen's University Press, 1977.
Maurel, André. *La Marquise du Châtelet*. Paris: Hachette, 1930.
May, Gita. *De Jean-Jacques Rousseau à Madame Roland*. Geneva: Droz, 1914.
– *Madame Roland and the Age of Revolution*. New York: Columbia University Press, 1970.
Mayer, J.P. *Max Weber and German Politics*. London: Faber & Faber, 1956 [1944].
Mazlish, Bruce. *James and John Stuart Mill*. New York: Basic Books, 1975.
– *A New Science*. New York: Oxford, 1989.
Medvedev. Roy A. *Let History Judge*. Trans. Colleen Taylor. New York: Vintage, 1973 [1971].
Meek, Ronald L. *The Economics of Physiocracy*. Cambridge, MA: Harvard University Press, 1962.
Mehring, Franz. *Karl Marx*. Trans. Edward Fitzgerald. Ann Arbor: University of Michigan Press, 1962 [1918].
– "La thèse de Karl Marx sur Démocrite et Epicure." *La nouvelle critique*, 61 (1955):17–29.
Melling, David J. *Understanding Plato*. Oxford: Oxford University Press, 1987.
Mendell, Clarence W. *Tacitus*. New Haven: Yale University Press, 1957.

Merchant, Carolyn. *The Death of Nature*. San Francisco: Harper & Row, 1980.

Merlan, Philip. *From Platonism to Neoplatonism*. 2d ed. rev. The Hague: Nijhoff, 1960 [1953].

Mersenne, Marin. *La vérité des sciences*. Paris: Toussainct du Bray, 1625.

Merton, Robert K. "Puritanism, Pietism and Science." In *Social Theory and Social Structure*. New York: Free Press, 1968 [1936].

Mestrovic, Stjepan G. *Emile Durkheim and the Reformation of Sociology*. Totowa, NJ: Rowman & Littlefield, 1982.

Miles, Angela R., and Geraldine Finn, eds. *Feminism in Canada*. Montreal: Black Rose, 1982.

Mill, Anna J. "John Stuart Mill, Conservationist." *The Mill News Letter* 10, no. 1 (1975):2–3.

Mill, John Stuart. *Collected Works of John Stuart Mill*. 33 vols. Toronto: University of Toronto Press, 1981–91.

Millett, Kate. *Sexual Politics*. Garden City, NY: Doubleday, 1970 [1969].

Millman, Marcia, and Rosabeth Moss Kanter, eds. *Another Voice*. Garden City, NY: Anchor, 1975.

Mills, C. Wright. *The Sociological Imagination*. New York: Oxford University Press, 1959.

– *The Marxists*. Harmondsworth: Penguin, 1973 [1962].

Minar, Edwin L. *Early Pythagorean Politics*. Baltimore: Waverly, 1942.

Mineka, Francis E. *The Dissidence of Dissent*. Chapel Hill: University of North Carolina Press, 1944.

Mintz, Samuel I. *The Hunting of Leviathan*. Cambridge: Cambridge University Press, 1962.

Mommsen, Wolfgang J. *Max Weber and German Politics*. Trans. Michael S. Steinberg. Chicago: University of Chicago Press, 1984 [1959].

Monroe, D.H. *Godwin's Moral Philosophy*. London: Oxford University Press, 1953.

Montaigne, Michel de. *The Essays of Michel de Montaigne*. Trans. Jacob Zeitlin. New York: Knopf, 1935.

Montchrétien, Antoyne de. *Traité de l'économie politique*. Paris: Plon, 1889 [1615].

Montesquieu, Charles Secondat de. *Oeuvres complètes*. Ed. André Masson. Paris: Nagel, 1950.

More, Henry. *Philosophical Writings of Henry More*. Ed. Isabel MacKinnon. New York: Oxford University Press, 1925.

More, Thomas. *Utopia*. Trans. R.M. Adams. New York: Norton, 1975 [1516].

Morley, John. *Diderot and the Encyclopedists*. 2 vols. London: Chapman & Hall, 1878.

Morrow, Glenn R. *The Ethical and Economic Theories of Adam Smith*. Reprint. New York: Kelley, 1969 [1923].

Mossner, Ernest Campbell. "Adam Smith: The Biographical Approach." University of Glasgow lecture, 1969.

– *The Life of David Hume*. London: Nelson, 1954.

Mouat, Frederic J., "History of the Statistical Society of London." *Journal of the Statistical Society*, Jubilee Volume (1885):14–71.

Mourelatos, Alexander P.D. *The Route of Parmenides*. New Haven: Yale University Press, 1970.

Mueller, Iris Wessel. *John Stuart Mill and French Thought*. Urbana: University of Illinois Press, 1956.

Mulgan, R.G. *Aristotle's Political Theory*. Oxford: Clarendon, 1977.

Munteaud, B. *Les idées politiques de Staël et la Constitution de l'an III*. Paris: Belles Lettres, 1931.

Myrdal, Gunnar. *Objectivity in Social Research*. New York: Pantheon, 1969.

– *An American Dilemma*. New York: McGraw-Hill, 1964 [1944].

Naegele, Kaspar. "Some Observations on the Scope of Sociological Analysis." In *Theories of Society*, vol. 1, ed. Talcott Parsons, et al., 3–29. New York: Free Press of Glencoe, 1961.

Nahm, Milton, G., ed. 4th ed. *Selections from Early Greek Philosophy*. New York: Appleton-Century, 1964 [1934].

Nash, Ronald H. *The Light of the Mind: St Augustine's Theory of Knowledge*. University of Kentucky Press, 1963.

Naville, Pierre. *Paul Thiry d'Holbach*. Paris: Gallimard, 1943.

Needham, Joseph. *The Shorter Science and Civilization in China*. Cambridge: Cambridge University Press, 1978.

Neurath, Otto. *Empiricism and Sociology*. Trans. Paul Foulks and Marie Neurath. Boston: Reidel, 1973.

Nevill, John Cranstoun. *Harriet Martineau*. London: Muller, 1943.

Newton, Isaac. *Mathematical Principles of Natural Philosophy*. Trans. A. Motte. Cambridge: Cambridge University Press, 1934.

– *Opticks*. New York: Dover, 1952 [1704].

– *The Correspondence of Isaac Newton*. 7 vols. Ed. A. Rupert and Laura Tilling. Cambridge: Cambridge University Press, 1975.

– *Isaac Newton's Papers and Letters on Natural Philosophy*. Ed. I. Bernard Cohen. Cambridge: Cambridge University Press, 1958.

– *Principes mathématiques de la philosophie naturelle*. 2 vols. Trans. Emilie du Châtelet. Paris: Desaint & Saillant, 1759.

Nichols, James. H. *Epicurean Political Philosophy*. Ithaca, NY: Cornell University Press, 1976 [1972].

Niderst, Alain. *Pierre Bayle*. Paris: Editions Sociales, 1971.

Nightingale, Florence. *Introductory Notes on Lying-in Institutions*. London: Longmans, Green, 1871.

– *A Contribution to the Sanitary History of the British Army during the late war with Russia*. London: Parker, 1859.

– *Notes on Matters affecting the Health, Efficiency and Hospital Administration of the British Army*. London: Harrison & Sons, 1858.

– Papers. British Library Manuscripts, London.

– Papers. Wellcome Institute of the History of Medicine, London.

– *Suggestions for Thought to Searchers after Religious Truth.* 3 vols. London: Eyre & Spottiswoode, 1860.

– "A Note on Pauperism." *Fraser's Magazine.* 79, March (1869):281–90.

– Letter to the International Statistical Congress. London, 1860.

Nisbet, Robert A., ed. *Emile Durkheim.* Westport, CT: Greenwood, 1965.

Nixon, Edna. *Mary Wollstonecraft.* London: Dent, 1971.

Nizan, Paul. *Les matérialistes de l'Antiquité.* Paris: Maspero, 1965 [1938].

Nord, Deborah Epstein. *The Apprenticeship of Beatrice Webb.* London: Macmillan, 1985.

North, J.D. *Isaac Newton.* London: Oxford University Press, 1967.

Norton, David Fate. "From Moral Sense to Common Sense." Ph.D. diss., University of California, San Diego, 1966.

– *David Hume.* Indianapolis: Bobbs-Merrill 1983.

Noxon, James. *Hume's Philosophical Development.* Oxford: Clarendon, 1973.

Oakeshott, Michael. *Hobbes on Civil Association.* Oxford: Blackwell, 1975 [1937].

Oberschall, Anthony, ed. *The Establishment of Empirical Sociology.* New York: Harper & Row, 1972.

O'Brien, D. *Empedocles' Cosmic Cycle.* Cambridge: Cambridge University Press, 1969.

O'Brien, Michael J. *The Socratic Paradoxes and the Greek Mind.* Chapel Hill: University of North Carolina Press, 1967.

Oestreicher, Jean. *La pensée politique et économique de Diderot.* Vincennes: Rosay, 1936.

Onians, Richard B. *The Origins of European Thought.* Cambridge: Cambridge University Press, 1951.

Packe, Michael St John. *The Life of John Stuart Mill.* London: Secker and Warburg, 1954.

Pappe, H.O. *John Stuart Mill and the Harriet Taylor Myth.* Melbourne: Melbourne University Press, 1960.

Parkin, Frank. *Max Weber.* London: Tavistock, 1982.

Parry, Geraint. *John Locke.* London: Allen & Unwin, 1978.

Patrick, Mary M. *Sextus Empiricus and Greek Scepticism.* Cambridge: Deighton Bell, 1899.

– *The Greek Sceptics.* New York: Columbia University Press, 1929.

Pawson, Ray. *A Measure for Measures.* London: Routledge, 1989.

Payne, Robert, ed. *The Unknown Karl Marx.* London: University of London Press, 1972.

Pearce, Frank. *The Radical Durkheim.* London: Unwin Hyman, 1989.

Pearson, A.G., ed. *The Fragments of Zeno and Cleanthes.* London: Clay, 1891.

Pearson, Karl. *The Grammar of Science.* rev. ed. London: Dent, 1937 [1892].

– "Nature and Nurture." London: Dulau, 1910.

– ed. *The Life, Letters and Labours of Francis Galton*. 3 vols. Cambridge: Cambridge University Press, 1924.

– "Maimonides and Spinoza." In *The Ethic of Free Thought*, ed. Karl Pearson, 137–55. London: Unwin, 1888.

– *The History of Statistics in the 17th and 18th Centuries*. Ed. E.S. Pearson. London: Griffin, 1978.

Pearson, Lionel. *Early Ionian Historians*. Oxford: Clarendon, 1939.

Peel, J.D.Y. *Herbert Spencer*. London: Heinemann, 1971.

Perry, Ruth. *The Celebrated Mary Astell*. Chicago: University of Chicago Press, 1986.

Petegorsky, David W. *Left-Wing Democracy in the English Civil War*. London: Gollancz, 1940.

Petty, William. *The Economic Writings of Sir William Petty*. 2 vols. Reprint. New York: Kelley, 1983.

Pichanick, Valerie Kossew. *Harriet Martineau*. Ann Arbor: University of Michigan Press, 1980.

Pierson, George Wilson. *Tocqueville in America*. Garden City, NY: Anchor, 1959.

Pike, E. Royston. *Adam Smith*. London: Weidenfeld & Nicolson, 1965.

Pintard, René. *Le libertinage érudit*. Paris: Boivin, 1943.

Plato. *The Dialogues of Plato*. 3d ed. Trans. B. Jowett. Oxford: Oxford University Press, 1892.

– *The Republic of Plato*. rev. ed. Trans. B. Jowett. London: Colonial Press, 1901.

– *Protagorus*. Trans. C.C.W. Taylor. Oxford: Clarendon, 1976.

– *The Sophist and the Statesman*. Trans. A.E. Taylor. London: Thomas Nelson, 1961.

Plekhanov, Georges. *Essais sur l'histoire du matérialisme*. Paris: Editions sociales, 1957 [1896].

Plotinus. *The Six Enneads*. 2d ed. Trans. Stephen MacKenna and B.S. Page. London: Faber & Faber, 1952.

Plumb, J.H. *England in the Eighteenth Century*. Harmondsworth: Penguin, 1950.

Politella, Joseph. *Platonism, Aristotelianism, and Cabalism in the Philosophy of Leibniz*. Ph. D. diss., University of Pennsylvania, 1938.

Polybius. *The General History of Polybius*. 2 vols. Trans. James Hampton. London: Oxford University Press, 1823.

Pomeau, René. *Voltaire en son temps*. 5 vols. Oxford: Voltaire Foundation, 1985–.

Pompa, Leon. *Vico*. Cambridge: Cambridge University Press, 1975.

Popkin, Richard H. *The History of Scepticism from Erasmus to Descartes*. rev. ed. Assen: Van Gorcum, 1964 [1960].

– *The High Road to Pyrrhonism*. San Diego, CA: Austin Hill, 1980.

– "Father Mersenne's War Against Pyrrhonism." *The Modern Schoolman*. 34, no. 1 (1959):61–78.

– "The New Realism of Bishop Berkeley." In *George Berkeley*, R.H. Papkin. Berkeley: University of California Press, 1957:1–19.

– "David Hume: His Pyrrhonism and His Critique of Pyrrhonism." *Philosophical Quarterly.* 1 (1951):385–407.

– "David Hume and the Pyrrhonian Controversy." *Review of Metaphysics.* 6 (1952):64–81.

Popper, K.R. *The Open Society and its Enemies.* 4th ed. London: Routledge & Kegan Paul, 1962 [1945].

– *Conjectures and Refutations.* London: Routledge & Kegan Paul, 1963.

Porter, Theodore M. *The Rise of Statistical Thinking.* Princeton: Princeton University Press, 1986.

Prichard, H.A. *Kant's Theory of Knowledge.* Oxford: Clarendon, 1909.

Priestley, Joseph. *The Theological and Miscellaneous Works of Josephy Priestley.* 25 vols. Reprint. New York: Kraus, 1972.

– *Hartley's Theory of the Human Mind.* London: J. Johnson, 1790.

Proust, Jacques. *Diderot et l'Encyclopédie.* Paris: Colin, 1967 [1961].

Pufendorf, Samuel. *The Law of Nature and Nations.* Trans. Basil Kennet. London: Bonwicke, 1749.

Quesnay, François. *Oeuvres économiques et philosophiques.* Reprint. Ed. Auguste Onken. Aalen: Scientia, 1965 [1888].

– *Quesnay's Tableau économique.* London: Macmillan, 1972 [1758].

Quetelet, Lambert Adolphe Jacques. *Sur l'homme et le développement de ses facultés.* Paris, 1835.

– *Physique sociale.* 2d ed. 2 vols. Brussels: Muquardt, 1869.

– *A Treatise on Man.* Scholars' Facsimile. Trans. R. Knox. Edinburgh, 1969 [1842].

– "Sur la statistique morale." *Mémoires de l'Académie royale,* vol. 21. Brussels: Académie royale, 1848.

– *Recherches sur le penchant au crime aux différens âges.* Brussels: Académie royale, 1831.

– *Lettres sur la théorie des probabilités.* Brussels: Hayez, 1846.

– *Du système social.* Paris: Guillaumin, 1848.

Quinton, Anthony. *Francis Bacon.* Oxford: Oxford University Press, 1980.

Radice, Lisanne, *Beatrice and Sidney Webb.* London: Macmillan, 1984.

Raison, Timothy, ed. *The Founding Fathers of Social Science.* rev. ed. London: Scolar, 1979 [1969].

Raphael, D.D. *Adam Smith.* Oxford: Oxford University Press, 1985.

Raven, J.E. *Pythagoreans and Eleatics.* Cambridge: Cambridge University Press, 1948.

Rawlings, Hunter R. *The Structure of Thucydides' History.* Princeton, NJ: Princeton University Press, 1981.

Ray, John. *The Wisdom of God Manifested in the Works of Creation.* New York: Arno, 1979 [1691].

Redondi, Pietro. *Galileo Heretic.* Trans. Raymond Rosenthal. Princeton, NJ: Princeton University Press, 1987 [1983].

Reesor, Margaret E. *The Political Theory of the Old and Middle Stoa*. New York: Augustin, 1951.

Reid, Thomas. *Philosophical Works*. 2 vols. Reprint. Edinburgh, 1895.

Reik, Miriam M. *The Golden Lands of Thomas Hobbes*. Detroit: Wayne State University Press, 1977.

Reisman, D.A. *Adam Smith's Sociological Economics*. London: Croom Helm, 1976.

Rescher, Nicholas. *Kant's Theory of Knowledge and Reality*. Washington, D.C.: University Press of America, 1983.

Riley, Matilda White. *Sociological Research*. 2 vols. New York: Harcourt, Brace, 1963.

Rist, J.M. *Plotinus: The Road to Reality*. Cambridge: Cambridge University Press, 1967.

– *Stoic Philosophy*. Cambridge: Cambridge University Press, 1969.

Rivière, R. Dujarric de la. *Buffon*. Paris: Peyronnet, 1971.

Robertson, D.B. *The Religious Foundations of Leveller Democracy*. New York: King's Crown, 1951.

Robin, Léon. *Greek Thought and the Origins of the Scientific Spirit*. Trans. M.R. Dobie. London: Kegan Paul, 1967 [1928].

Robinet, André, ed. *Malebranche de l'Académie des sciences*. Paris: Vrin, 1970.

Robson, John. *The Improvement of Mankind*. Toronto: University of Toronto Press, 1968.

Rochot, Bernard. *Les travaux de Gassendi sur Epicure et sur l'atomisme*. Paris: Vrin, 1944.

– "Le Philosophe." In *Pierre Gassendi*. Paris: Michel, 1955.

Rodis-Lewis, Geneviève. *Nicolas Malebranche*. Paris: Presses Universitaires de France, 1963.

Roland, Marie-Jeanne Phlipon. *Oeuvres*. 2 vols. Paris: Bidault, an VIII.

– *The Works*. Ed. L.A. Champagneux. London: J. Johnson, 1800.

– "Lettre de M. Roland." In *Histoire parlementaire de la révolution française*, ed. P.-J.-B. Buchez and P.C. Roux, 15:39–45. Paris: Paulin, 1835.

Romilly, Jacqueline de. *Thucydides and Athenian Imperialism*. Trans. Philip Thody. Oxford: Blackwell, 1963 [1947].

Rose, Gillian. *The Melancholy Science*. London: Macmillan, 1978.

Rosenfield, Leonora Cohen. *From Beast-Machine to Man-Machine*. New York: Oxford University Press, 1941.

– ed. *Condorcet Studies I*. Atlantic Highlands, NJ: Humanities Press, 1984.

Ross, David. *Aristotle*. London: Methuen, 1964 [1923].

Ross, Edward Alsworth. *Social Control*. Reprint. New York: Johnson, 1970 [1901].

Rossi, Alice S., ed. *Essays on Sex Equality*. Chicago: University of Chicago Press, 1970.

Rossi, Paolo. *Francis Bacon, From Magic to Science*. Trans. Sacha Rabinovitch. London: Routledge & Kegan Paul, 1968 [1957].

Roth, Leon. *Spinoza, Descartes and Maimonides*. Oxford: Clarendon, 1924.

Rothkrug, Lionel. *Opposition to Louis XIV*. Princeton: Princeton University Press, 1965.

Rousseau, Jean-Jacques. *Oeuvres complètes*. 4 vols. Ed. B. Gagnebin. Paris: Bibliothèque de la Pléiade, 1959–69.

Rumney, Jay. *Herbert Spencer's Sociology*. New York: Atherton, 1965 [1937].

Runciman, W.G. *A Critique of Max Weber's Philosophy of Social Science*. Cambridge: Cambridge University Press, 1972.

Russell, Bertrand. *A History of Western Philosophy*. New York: Simon & Schuster, 1945.

– *Philosophy of Leibniz*. 2d ed. London: Allen & Unwin, 1951 [1900].

Ryan, Alan. *The Philosophy of John Stuart Mill*. 2d ed. London: Macmillan, 1987 [1970].

Ryle, Gilbert. *Plato's Progress*. Cambridge: Cambridge University Press, 1966.

Saint-Simon, Henri de. *Oeuvres*. 10 vols. Ed. A. Enfantin. Paris, 1875.

– *Introduction aux travaux scientifiques du dix-neuvième siècle*. Paris: Scherff, 1807.

– *Lettres de Henri Saint-Simon à Messieurs les Jurés*. Paris: Corréard & Pélicier, 1820.

– *Appel aux conservateurs*. Paris: Dalmont, 1855.

Sambursky, Samuel. *Physics of the Stoics*. London: Routledge & Kegan Paul, 1959.

Sartre, Jean-Paul. *Descartes*. Paris: Trois Collines, 1946.

– *Critique de la raison dialectique*. Paris: Gallimard, 1960.

Schapiro, J. Selwyn. *Condorcet and the Rise of Liberalism*. New York: Harcourt, Brace, 1934.

Schelle, Gustave. *Le docteur Quesnay*. Paris: Alcan, 1907.

Schleifer, James T. *The Making of Tocqueville's Democracy in America*. Chapel Hill: University of North Carolina Press, 1980.

Schmitt, Charles B. "An Unstudied Fifteenth-Century Latin Translation of Sextus Empiricus by Giovanni Larenzi." In *Cultural Aspects of the Italian Renaissance*, ed. Cecil H. Clough. Manchester: Manchester University Press, 1976.

– *Cicero Scepticus*. The Hague: Nijhoff, 1972.

Schoen, Harriet H. "Prince Albert and the Application of Statistics to Problems of Government." *Osiris* 1938:276–318.

Schofield, Malcolm. *An Essay on Anaxagoras*. Cambridge: Cambridge University Press, 1980.

Schumacher, E.F. *Small is Beautiful*. London: Sphere, 1974 [1973].

Schumpeter, J.A. *Capitalism, Socialism, and Democracy*. New York: Harper & Row, 1942.

Scott, W.R. *Adam Smith as Student and Professor*. Glasgow: Jackson, 1937.

– *Francis Hutcheson*. Cambridge: Cambridge University Press, 1900.

Scruton, Roger. *Kant*. Oxford: Oxford University Press, 1982.

– *Spinoza*. Oxford: Oxford University Press, 1986.

Sextus Empiricus. *Outlines of Pyrrhonism*. Trans. R.G. Bury. Cambridge, MA: Harvard University Press, 1955.

Seymour-Jones, Carole. *Beatrice Webb*. London: Allison & Busby, 1992.

Shackleton, Robert. *Montesquieu*. Oxford: Oxford University Press, 1961.

Sharp, Andrew. *Political Ideas of the English Civil Wars*. London: Longmans, 1983.

Shklar, Judith. *Montesquieu*. New York: Oxford University Press, 1987.

– *Men and Citizens*. Cambridge: Cambridge University Press, 1969.

Sica, Alan. *Weber, Irrationality, and Social Order*. Berkeley: University of California Press, 1988.

Simey, T.S., and M.B. Simey. *Charles Booth. Social Scientist*. London: Oxford University Press, 1960.

Sinclair, John. *The Statistical Account of Scotland*. 21 vols. Reprint. 1976 [1791–99].

Sjoberg, Gideon, and Roger Nett. *A Methodology for Social Research*. New York: Harper & Row, 1968.

Skinner, Andrew S., and Thomas Wilson, eds. *Essays on Adam Smith*. Oxford: Clarendon, 1975.

Slater, Phil. *Origin and Significance of the Frankfurt School*. London: Routledge & Kegan Paul, 1977.

Small, Albion W. "The Era of Sociology." *American Journal of Sociology*. 1, no. 5 (1895):1–15.

– "Scholarship and Social Agitation." *American Journal of Sociology*. 1 (1896):564–82.

Smith, Adam. *The Theory of Moral Sentiments*. Ed. D.D. Raphael and A. Macfie. Oxford: Clarendon, 1976 [1759].

– *An Inquiry into the Nature and Causes of the Wealth of Nations*. 5th ed. Ed. Edwin Cannan. New York: Modern Library, 1937 [1776].

– *The Early Writings of Adam Smith*. Ed. J. Ralph Lindgren. New York: Kelley, 1967.

Smith, D.W. *Helvétius: A Study in Persecution*. Oxford: Clarendon, 1965.

Smith, Dennis. *The Chicago School*. London: Macmillan, 1988.

Smith, Florence, M. *Mary Astell*. New York: AMS, 1966 [1916].

Smith, Norman Kemp. *New Studies in the Philosophy of Descartes*. New York: Russell & Russell, 1963.

– *The Philosophy of David Hume*. London: Macmillan, 1941.

– *A Commentary to Kant's "Critique of Pure Reason."* rev. ed. London: Macmillan, 1930 [1918].

Sokoloff, Boris. *The "Mad" Philosopher Auguste Comte*. Westport, CT: Greenwood, 1961.

Sophia. *Woman not Inferior to Man*. Reprint. London: Hawkins, 1970 [1739].

Spanneut, Michel. *Permanence du stoïcisme*. Gembloux: Duculot, 1973.

Spencer, Herbert. *Social Statics*. New York: Appleton, 1888 [1850].

– *The Principles of Sociology.* 3 vols. London: Williams & Norgate, 1893 [1874–77].

– *The Man versus the State.* Caldwell, ID: Caxton, 1960 [1884].

Spender, Dale. *Women of Ideas.* London: Routledge & Kegan Paul, 1982.

Spink, J.S. *French Free Thought from Gassendi to Voltaire.* London: Athlone, 1960.

Spinoza, Benedict. *Chief Works.* 2 vols. Trans. R.H.M. Elwes. London: Bell, 1883–4.

Spragens, Thomas A., Jr. *The Politics of Motion.* London: Croom Helm, 1973.

Staël, Germaine Necker de. *Oeuvres complètes.* Paris: Treuttel & Würtz, 1821.

– *Oeuvres complètes.* Paris: Firmin Didot, 1871.

– *Considérations sur les principaux événemens de la Révolution française.* 3 vols. London: Baldwin, Craddock, 1818 [1816].

– *Des circonstances actuelles.* Ed. Lucia Omacini. Geneva: Droz, 1979.

– *De l'Allemagne.* 3 vols. Paris: Hachette, 1958 [1813].

– *Lettres sur les ouvrages et le caractère de J.-J. Rousseau.* Reprint. Geneva: Slatkine, 1979 [1788].

– *The Unpublished Correspondence of Madame de Staël and the Duke of Wellington.* London: Cassell, 1965.

– "Unpublished Correspondence of Mme. de Staël with Thomas Jefferson." Ed. and Trans. Marie G. Kimball. *North American Review.* 208, no. 752 (1918):63–71.

Stark, Werner. *Montesquieu.* Toronto: University of Toronto Press, 1961.

Starobinski, Jean. *Jean-Jacques Rousseau.* Paris: Plon, 1957.

Starr, Chester G. *The Awakening of the Greek Historical Spirit.* New York: Knopf, 1968.

Strauss, Emil. *Sir William Petty.* London: Bodley Head, 1954.

Stephen, Leslie. *Hobbes.* London: Macmillan, 1904.

– *History of English Thought in the Eighteenth Century.* 2 vols. London: Smith, Elder, 1876.

– *The English Utilitarians.* 3 vols. London: Duckworth, 1900.

Stephens, W. Walker. *The Life and Writings of Turgot.* New York: Franklin, 1971.

Stigler, Stephen M. *The History of Statistics.* Cambridge, MA: Belknap Press, 1986.

Stone, I.F. *The Trial of Socrates.* Boston: Little, Brown, 1988.

Stough, Charlotte L. *Greek Scepticism.* Berkeley: University of California Press, 1969.

Strachey, Lytton. *Eminent Victorians.* London: Folio Society, 1967 [1918].

Strauss, Emil. *Sir William Petty. Portrait of a Genius.* London: Bodley Head, 1954.

Strauss, Leo. *The Political Philosophy of Hobbes.* Trans. Elsa M. Sinclair. Chicago: University of Chicago Press, 1952 [1936].

Strawson, Galen. *The Secret Connexion.* Oxford: Clarendon, 1989.

Strawson, P.F. *The Bounds of Sense.* London: Methuen, 1966.

Sumner, William Graham. *Folkways.* Boston: Ginn, 1906.

– *Social Darwinism*. Englewood Cliffs, NJ: Prentice-Hall, 1963.

Sunstein, Emily W. *A Different Face*. New York: Harper & Row, 1975.

Süssmilch, Johann Peter. *Die Göttliche Ordnung*. 2 vols. Berlin: Realschule, 1765 [1741].

Swanson, Guy E. *Religion and Regime*. Ann Arbor: University of Michigan Press, 1967.

Syme, Ronald. *Tacitus*. 2 vols. Oxford: Clarendon, 1958.

Tacitus, Cornelius. *The Works of Cornelius Tacitus*. rev. ed. vol. 7. London: Stockdale, 1805.

Tagliacozzo, Giorgio. *Vico–Past and Present*. Atlantic Highlands, NJ: Humanities, 1981.

– ed. *Giambattista Vico*. Baltimore: Johns Hopkins University Press, 1969.

Tar, Zoltan. *The Frankfurt School*. New York: John Wiley, 1977.

Tarde, Gabriel. *Les lois sociales*. Paris: Alcan, 1898.

Tawney, R.H. *Religion and the Rise of Capitalism*. London: Murray, 1926 [1922].

– "Beatrice Webb." *Proceedings of the British Academy*. vol. 29.

– "Harrington's Interpretation of his Age." *Proceedings of the British Academy*, vol. 27, 1941.

Taylor, A.E. *Plato*. New York: Dial, 1927.

– *Platonism and its Influence*. New York: Longmans, Green, 1927 [1924].

– *Socrates*. New York: Appleton, 1933.

Taylor, W.L. *Francis Hutcheson and David Hume as Predecessors of Adam Smith*. Durham, NC: Duke University Press, 1965.

Teichgraeber, Richard T. *"Free Trade" and Moral Philosophy*. Durham: Duke University Press, 1986.

Temple, William. *The Works of Sir William Temple*. 4 vols. London: Clarke, 1757.

– *Observations upon the United Provinces of the Netherlands*. Ed. George Clark. Oxford: Clarendon, 1972 [1673].

Thomas, Keith. *Religion and the Decline of Magic*. London: Weidenfeld & Nicolson, 1971.

– *Man and the Natural World*. London: Allen Lane, 1983 [1979].

Thomas, William. *Mill*. Oxford: Oxford University Press, 1985.

Thompson, E.P. *The Poverty of Theory*. London: Methuen, 1978.

Thompson, Kenneth. *Auguste Comte: The Foundations of Sociology*. London: Nelson, 1976.

Thomson, George. *Studies in Ancient Greek Society*. 2 vols. London: Lawrence & Wishart, 1972 and 1978 [1949 and 1955].

Thomson, Herbert F. "Adam Smith's Philosophy of Science." *Quarterly Journal of Economics*. 76, May (1965):212–33.

Thucydides. *The Peloponnesian Wars*. 2 vols. Trans. B. Jowett. Oxford: Clarendon, 1881.

Tocqueville, Alexis de. *Democracy in America*. 2 vols. Trans. Henry Reeve. New York: Knopf, 1945 [1835].

Tomalin, Claire. *The Life and Death of Mary Wollstonecraft*. New York: Mentor, 1974.

Tönnies, Ferdinand. *Karl Marx*. Trans. C.P. Loomis and I. Paulus. East Lansing: Michigan State University Press, 1974.

Torrey, Norman L. *The Spirit of Voltaire*. New York: Columbia University Press, 1938.

Touraine, Alain. *Production de la société*. Paris: Seuil, 1973.

Tourneux, Maurice, ed. *Diderot et Catherine II*. Paris: Calmann, 1899.

Trevor-Roper, H.R. *Religion, the Reformation and Social Change*. London: Macmillan, 1967.

Tribe, Keith, ed. *Reading Weber*. London: Routledge, 1989.

Troeltsch, Ernest. *The Social Teaching of the Christian Churches*. 2 vols. Trans. Olive Wyon. New York: Barnes & Noble, 1956 [1911].

Tuck, Richard. *Natural Rights Theories*. Cambridge: Cambridge University Press, 1979.

Turgot, Anne Robert Jacques. *Oeuvres de Turgot*. 5 vols. Ed. Gustave Schelle. Paris: Alcan, 1913.

Turlington, Bayley. *Socrates*. New York: Watts, 1969.

Turner, Stephen P. *The Search for a Methodology of Social Science*. Dordrecht: Reidel, 1986.

Untersteiner, Mario. *The Sophists*. Trans. Kathleen Freeman. New York: Philosophical Library, 1954 [1946].

Usher, Stephen. *The Historians of Greece and Rome*. New York: Taplinger, 1970.

Vaillancourt, Pauline Marie. *When Marxists Do Research*. New York: Greenwood, 1986.

Van Leeuwen, Henry G. *The Problem of Certainty in English Thought*. The Hague: Nijhoff, 1963.

Vartanian, Aram. *Diderot and Descartes*. Princeton: Princeton University Press, 1953.

Veblen, Thorstein. *Theory of the Leisure Class*. New York: Macmillan, 1908 [1890].

Velkley, Richard L *Freedom and the End of Reason*. Chicago: University of Chicago Press, 1989.

Venturi, Franco. *Utopia and Reform in the Enlightenment*. Cambridge: Cambridge University Press, 1971.

– *Jeunesse de Diderot*. Trans. Juliette Bertrand. Paris: Skira, 1939.

Verdenius, W.J. *Parmenides*. Groningen: Wolters, 1942.

Vickers, Jill McCalla, ed. *Taking Sex Into Account*. Ottawa: Carleton University Press, 1984.

Vico, Giambattista. *The New Science of Giambattista Vico*. Trans. T.G. Bergin and M.H. Fisch. Ithaca, NY: Cornell University Press, 1968 [1744].

Virieux-Reymond, Antoinette. *La logique et l'épistémologie des stoïciens*. Chambéry: Editions Lire, 1950.

Vlastos, Gregory. "Solonian Justice." *Classical Philology*. 41, April (1946):65–83.

– ed. *The Philosophy of Socrates*. Garden City, NY: Anchor 1971.

Voltaire, François-Marie Arouet. *Oeuvres complètes*. Moland, 1877–85.

– *Elémens de la philosophie de Newton*. London, 1741.

– *Lettres philosophiques ou lettres anglaises*. Paris: Garnier, 1962 [1733].

– *Dictionnaire philosophique*. 2 vols. Paris: Garnier, 1963 [1739].

– *Contes et romans*. Paris: Boutin, 1967.

– *Essai sur les moeurs*. 2 vols. Paris: Garnier, 1963.

Von Fritz, Kurt. *Pythagorean Politics in Southern Italy*. New York: Columbia University Press, 1940.

Vreeland, Hamilton. *Hugo Grotius*. New York: Oxford University Press, 1917.

Wade, Ira O. *Voltaire and Madame du Châtelet*. Princeton: Princeton University Press, 1941.

– *Studies on Voltaire. With some Unpublished Papers of Mme du Châtelet*. Princeton: Princeton University Press, 1947.

Waldinger, Renée. *Voltaire and Reform*. Geneva: Droz, 1959.

Wallis, R.T. *Neo-Platonism*. London: Duckworth, 1972.

Ward, Lester F. *Pure Sociology*. 2d ed. New York: Macmillan, 1907 [1903].

– *Applied Sociology*. Boston: Ginn, 1906.

– *Dynamic Sociology*. 2 vols. New York: Appleton, 1883.

– *Glimpses of the Cosmos*. 6 vols. New York: Putnam, 1913.

Wardle, Ralph M. *Mary Wollstonecraft*. Lawrence: University of Kansas Press, 1951.

Ware, Charlotte S. "The Influence of Descartes on John Locke–a Bibliographical Study," *Revue internationale de philosophie*. 4 (1950):210–30.

Warnock, G.J. *Berkeley*. Oxford: Blackwell, 1969.

Warrender, Howard. *The Political Philosophy of Hobbes*. Oxford: Clarendon, 1957.

Waters, K.H. *Herodotus, the Historian*. London: Croom Helm, 1985.

Watkins, J.W.N. *Hobbes's System of Ideas*. London: Hutchinson University Library, 1965.

Webb, Beatrice. *My Apprenticeship*. 2 vols. London: Pelican, 1938 [1926].

– *The Diary of Beatrice Webb*. 4 vols. Ed. Norman MacKenzie and Jeanne MacKenzie. London: Virago & LSE, 1982–5.

– *Our Partnership*. Ed. Barbara Drake and Margaret Cole. New York: Longmans, 1948.

– *Methods of Investigation*. London: Sociological Society, 1906.

– and Sidney Webb. *Industrial Democracy*. London: Longmans, Green, 1902 [1897].

– and Sidney Webb. *Methods of Social Study*. Cambridge: LSE/Cambridge University Press, 1975 [1932].

Webb, R.K. *Harriet Martineau*. London: Heinemann, 1960.

Weber, Marianne. *Max Weber: A Biography*. Trans. Harry Zohn. New York: Wiley, 1975 [1926].

Weber, Max. *The Methodology of the Social Sciences*. Trans. E.A. Shils and H.A. Finch. New York: Free Press, 1949.

– *The Protestant Ethic and the Spirit of Capitalism.* Trans. Talcott Parsons. New York: Scribner, 1958 [1904–6].
– *From Max Weber: Essays in Sociology.* Trans. H.H. Gerth and C. Wright Mills. London: Kegan Paul, 1947.
– *General Economic History.* Re-print of 1927 ed. Trans. Frank H. Knight. Glencoe, IL: Free Press, 1950 [1923].
– *The Theory of Social and Economic Organization.* Trans. A.M. Henderson and Talcott Parsons. New York: Free Press of Glencoe, 1964.
– *The Sociology of Religion.* Trans. Ephraim Fischoff. Boston: Beacon, 1963 [1922].
– *Roscher and Knies: The Logical Problems of Historical Economics.* Trans. Guy Oakes. New York: Free Press, 1975 [1903–6].
– *The Agrarian Sociology of Ancient Civilization.* Trans. R.I. Frank. London: NLB, 1976 [1909].
– "Zur Psychophysik der industriellen Arbeit." *Archiv für Sozialwissenschaft und Sozialpolitik.* Pt 1, 27 (1908):730–70; Pt 2, 28 (1909):219–77; Pt 3, 29 (1909): 513–42; Pt 4, 30 (1910):455–513.
Webster, Charles. *The Great Instauration.* New York: Holmes & Meier, 1975.
Weinberg, Julius. *Edward Alsworth Ross and the Sociology of Progressivism.* Madison, WI: State Historical Society, 1977.
Weiss, Johannes. *Weber and the Marxist World.* Trans. Eliz. King Utz and Michael J. King. London: Routledge & Kegan Paul, 1986 [1981].
Wesley, John. *The Works of the Rev. John Wesley.* 14 vols. London: John Mason, 1830.
– *A Compendium of Natural Philosophy.* 3 vols. London: Tegg, 1836.
Westergaard, Harald. *Contributions to the History of Statistics.* New York: Agathon, 1968 [1932].
Westfall, Richard S. *Never at Rest.* Cambridge: Cambridge University Press, 1980.
Westlake, H.D. *Individuals in Thucydides.* Cambridge: Cambridge University Press, 1968.
Wheatley, Vera. *The Life and Work of Harriet Martineau.* London: Secker & Warburg, 1957.
White, Andrew Dickson. *A History of the Warfare of Science with Theology in Christendom.* 2 vols. New York: Appleton, 1910.
White, Lynn Jr. "The Historical Roots of Our Ecologic Crisis." In *The Environment Handbook*, ed. Garrott de Bell, 12–26. New York: Ballantine, 1970.
Whitney, Charles. *Francis Bacon and Modernity.* New Haven: Yale University Press, 1986.
Whittaker, Thomas. *The Neo-Platonists.* 2d ed. Cambridge: Cambridge University Press, 1928 [1901].
Wickwar, W.H. *Baron d'Holbach.* Reprint. New York: Kelley, 1968 [1935].
Wiley, Margaret. *The Subtle Knot.* London: Allen & Unwin, 1952.
Wilkins, John. *Of the Principles and Duties of Natural Religion.* London: Bonwick, 1715 [1675].

Willcocks, Mary Patricia. *Madame Roland*. Trans. Joseph Thérol. Paris: Hachette.

Willer, David, and Judith Willer. *Systematic Empiricism*. Englewood Cliffs, NJ: Prentice-Hall, 1973.

Willey, Basil. *The Eighteenth-Century Background*. London: Chatto & Windus, 1953 [1940].

– *The Seventeenth-Century Background*. Garden City, NY: Doubleday, 1953.

Williams, T.C. *The Unity of Kant's Critique of Pure Reason*. Lewiston: Mellen, 1987.

Williamson, John B., et al., eds. *The Research Craft*. Boston: Little, Brown, 1982 [1977].

Wilm, E.C., ed. *Immanuel Kant*. New Haven: Yale University Press, 1925.

Wilson, Arthur M. *Diderot: The Testing Years*. New York: Oxford University Press, 1957.

Wilson, Charles. *England's Apprenticeship*. London: Longmans, Green, 1965.

Wiltshire, David. *The Social and Political Thought of Herbert Spencer*. Oxford: Oxford University Press, 1978.

Winch, Donald. *Adam Smith's Politics*. Cambridge: Cambridge University Press, 1976.

Winkler, Kenneth P. *Berkeley*. Oxford: Clarendon, 1989.

Winspear, Alban Dewes. *The Genesis of Plato's Thought*. 2d ed. New York: Russell, 1956 [1940].

– *Lucretius and Scientific Thought*. Montreal: Harvest House, 1963.

– and Tom Silverberg. *Who was Socrates?* 2d ed. New York: Russell & Russell, 1960 [1939].

Winstanley, Gerrard. *The Works of Gerrard Winstanley*. Ed. George Sabine. Ithaca: Cornell University Press, 1941.

Wisdom, John Oulton. *The Unconscious Origin of Berkeley's Philosophy*. London: Hogarth, 1953.

Wolff, Kurt H., ed. *Emile Durkheim*. Columbus: Ohio State University Press, 1960.

Wolfson, Harry A. *The Philosophy of Spinoza*. Cambridge, MA: Harvard University Press, 1948 [1934].

Wollstonecraft, Mary. *A Vindication of the Rights of Men*. Reprint. Gainesville, FL: Scholars', 1960 [1790].

– *A Critical Edition of Mary Wollstonecraft's Vindication of the Rights of Woman*. Ed. Ulrich H. Hardt. Troy, NY: Whiston, 1982 [1792].

– *An Historical and Moral View of the Origin and Progress of the French Revolution*. Reprint of 1795 ed. London: J. Johnson, [1794].

Wood, Ellen Meiksins, and Neal Wood. *Class Ideology and Ancient Political Theory*. Oxford: Blackwell, 1978.

Wood, Neal. "The Baconian Character of Locke's Essay" *Studies in History and Philosophy of Science* 41 (1975):43–84.

– *The Politics of Locke's Philosophy*. Berkeley: University of California Press, 1983.

Woodbridge, Frederick J. E. *Aristotle's Vision of Nature*. New York: Columbia University Press, 1965.

Woodcock, George. *William Godwin*. London: Porcupine, 1946.

Woodham-Smith, Cecil. *Florence Nightingale*. London: Constable, 1950.

Woodhouse, W.J. *Solon the Liberator*. London: Oxford University Press, 1938.

Woolf, Virginia. *The Second Common Reader*. New York: Harcourt, Brace, 1932.

Woolhouse, R.S. *Locke*. Brighton: Harvester, 1983.

– *The Empiricists*. Oxford University Press, 1988.

Wortley Montagu, Mary. *The Complete Letters of the Lady Mary Wortley Montagu*. 3 vols. Ed. Robert Halsband. Oxford: Clarendon, 1965–7.

– *The Nonsense of Common-Sense*. Ed. Robert Halsband. Evanston, IL: Northwestern University Press, 1947.

Wright, John P. *The Sceptical Realism of David Hume*. Manchester: Manchester University Press, 1983.

Wrigley, E.A., ed. *Nineteenth-century Society*. Cambridge: Cambridge University Press, 1972.

Yolton, John W. *John Locke and the Way of Ideas*. Oxford: Oxford University Press, 1956.

– *Locke and the Compass of Human Understanding*. Cambridge: University Press, 1970.

Zeller, Eduard. *The Stoics, Epicureans and Sceptics*. Trans. O.J. Reichel. London: Longmans, Green, 1892 [1880].

– *Socrates and the Socratic Schools*. Trans. O.J. Reichel. New York: Russell & Russell, 1962 [1885].

Zeno of Elea. *Zeno of Elea. A Text with Translation*. Trans. H.D.P. Lee. Cambridge: Cambridge University Press, 1936.

Ziegler, Jean. *Retournez les fusils!* Paris: Seuil, 1980.

Index